T0330035

Fictions of State

Also by Patrick Brantlinger—

Bread and Circuses:
  Theories of Mass Culture as Social Decay

Rule of Darkness:
  British Literature and Imperialism, 1830–1914

Fictions of State

CULTURE AND CREDIT IN BRITAIN, 1694–1994

Patrick Brantlinger

Cornell University Press | *Ithaca and London*

First published 1996 by Cornell University Press.

Library of Congress Cataloging-in-Publication Data

Brantlinger, Patrick, 1941–
    Fictions of state : culture and credit in Britain, 1694–1994 /
Patrick Brantlinger.
        p.   cm.
    Includes bibliographical references (p.   ) and index.
    ISBN 0-8014-3190-5 (alk. paper). — ISBN 0-8014-8287-9 (alk.
paper)
    1. English fiction—History and criticism.   2. Economics in
literature.   3. Literature and state—Great Britain.   4. Great
Britain—Economic conditions.   5. Popular culture—Great Britain.
6. Credit—Great Britain.   7. Debt in literature.   I. Title.
PR830.E37B73   1996
823.009'355—dc20   95-43125

To Ellen

CONTENTS

Illustrations ix

Acknowledgments xi

1 Debt, Fetishism, and Empire: A Postmodern Preamble 1

2 The Assets of Lilliput (1694–1763) 48

3 Upon Daedalian Wings (1750–1832) 88

4 Banking on Novels (1800–1914) 136

5 Consuming Modernisms, Phallic Mothers
(1900–1945) 185

6 Postindustrial, Postcolonial, Postmodern:
"Anarchy in the U.K." (1945–1994) 235

Works Cited 265

Index 283

Illustrations

FIGURE 1. Prime Minister William Pitt "ravishing" the "Old Lady
of Threadneedle Street" (James Gillray, 1797)   56

FIGURE 2. William Hogarth's "The South Sea Scheme" (1721)   61

FIGURE 3. Prime Minister Pitt and other ministers bilking John
Bull with French invasion scares (James Gillray, 1796) 119

FIGURE 4. Prime Minister Pitt consuming gold and issuing
paper money (James Gillray, 1797)   120

FIGURE 5. John Bull taking paper money instead of gold
(James Gillray, 1797)   121

FIGURE 6. The Daedalian "Sinking Fund" to lower the
national debt: "But is it going down or up?"
(James Gillray, 1802)   122

Acknowledgments

"A WORLD without debts! The stars will be thrown off course. Everything will be in disarray," says Panurge in Rabelais's *Gargantua and Pantagruel.* The academic world is certainly indebted to debt, and I have more IOUs to friends, students, and colleagues than I can possibly repay. By inviting me to participate in a conference on debt at the Dickens Project, Regenia Gagnier got me started (others at that conference to whom I am grateful in various ways include Murray Baumgarten, Diane Elam, Lydia Fillingham, Catherine Gallagher, and John Jordan). I am grateful also to David Simpson, Margaret Ferguson, and their colleagues at the University of Colorado for comments on another early version of this book. In 1992, I had the good fortune to be a faculty presenter at a National Endowment for the Humanities Summer Institute at the Yale Center for British Art, where again I offered early pieces of this book (thanks to Linda Peterson, Duncan Robinson, and others at that institute, including Harriet Adams, Martin Danahay, Phillip Smith, and Anthony Wohl).

Among my colleagues at Indiana, I owe a lot to Jim Naremore and Bob Arnove for many conversations and ideas, especially when we team-taught together. Both Jim and I participated in the Multidisciplinary Faculty Seminar on Cultural Studies sponsored by our Dean of Faculties Office (for which I thank our former dean, Anya Royce, and also the other participants: Chris Anderson, Richard Bauman, Casey Blake, Donna Eder, Kathryn Flannery, Barbara Klinger, Christine Ogan, and Beverly Stoeltje). Other friends and colleagues who have helped include Jim Adams, Michelle Moody Adams, Purnima Bose, Mary and Bill Burgan, Bill Cagle, Linda Charnes, Eva Cherniavsky, John Eakin, Jonathan Elmer, Mary Favret, Don Gray, Sheila Lindenbaum, Chris and Pam Lohmann, Andrew Miller, Richard Nash, Joan Pong Linton, Tony Shipps, Johanna Smith, Janet Sorensen, Lee Sterrenburg, Steve Watt, Perry Willett, Nick Williams, Cary Wolfe, and Paul Zietlow.

As always, I have also learned much from the graduate students with whom I have had the privilege to work, including Joe Bizup, Russ

Coon, Salah El-Moncef, John Glendening, Brian Goldberg, Scott Harter, Pranav Jani, Jean Kowaleski, Bill Little, Eileen Morgan, Cynthia Patton, Tom Prasch, Suk-Koo Rhee, Rob Richardson, Elizabeth Rosdeitcher, Cannon Schmitt, John Shanahan, Gary Willingham-McLain, and Mohammed Zayani. Matthew Rowlinson provided a helpful reading, and Janet Mais, some excellent editing; thanks also, as usual, to Bernhard Kendler for being so supportive. Parts of this book appeared in earlier versions in *Victorian Literature and Culture* and *Victorian Studies*; thanks to their editors for permission to revise and reprint. And Ellen Brantlinger has been my constant partner, friend, colleague, and creditor. I am probably forgetting to thank a few dozen others . . . thus accumulating more debts.

PATRICK BRANTLINGER

Bloomington, Indiana

1

Debt, Fetishism, and Empire: A Postmodern Preamble

> As Light vanishes into Darkness; [Credit] comes with Surprize,
> and goes without Notice. . . . while it dwells in a Nation, it dou-
> bles their Strength, they can fit out Fleets without Money, have
> Money without Funds, and Funds without Deficiencies. What has
> this invisible Phantom done for this Nation, and what miserable
> Doings were there here before without her?
>
> —Daniel Defoe, *Review* (14 June 1709)

> In the long and involved history of political economy there is one
> word that stands out beyond all others as a triumph of imposture.
> That word is Credit.
>
> —Freeman Tilden, *A World in Debt* (1936)

> Actual history occurs, so to speak, on credit.
>
> —Slavoj Žižek, *The Sublime Object of Ideology* (1989)

1

FOR BRITAIN but also for other western nation-states from the Renaissance forward, modern history certainly "occurs . . . on credit," and in
the postmodern era the bills are falling due. Key to this era (beginning
in 1945) has been the collapse, decline, or relative weakening of at
least some modern nation-states. The post-1989 triumphal rhetoric of
liberals and conservatives in the United States, Britain, Germany, and
elsewhere suggests that it is only previously socialist nation-states that
have weakened or collapsed, but Russia, Czechoslovakia, and Yugoslavia
continue fragmenting even though they have supposedly grown capitalistic. Canadian unity is threatened by Quebecois separatism; both
Sikh and Muslim separatists are waging war against India; Mexico is
struggling to contain the Zapatista rebellion in Chiapas; Turkey and
Iraq are both battling Kurdish guerrillas; Palestinians continue to resist

1

Israel; and on and on. The United States is no exception, moreover: wracked by ethnic, racial, class, gender, and religious conflict, for the first time in a century it is experiencing a relative decline in its leading position as an economic and industrial world power.[1]

For Britain, the first modern nation-state to emerge from the cocoon of the Middle Ages and the leading imperialist and industrial power in the world for more than a century, the decline has been even more dramatic. Since World War I, Britain has lost its empire and also its leading role in industrial and economic affairs. It is also wracked by ethnic, racial, class, and regional conflicts, exacerbated, if not directly caused, by its imperial and economic decline. "There is no doubt that the old British state is going down," wrote Tom Nairn in 1977 in *The Break-Up of Britain*; "so far at least, it has been a slow foundering rather than the *Titanic*-type disaster so often predicted" (13); but so was the decline and fall of the Roman Empire "a slow foundering."

Nairn points out that that imperial and economic decline has engendered a resurgence of neonationalisms—Irish, Scottish, Welsh—striving to disunite the supposedly United Kingdom. The growth of East and West Indian immigrant populations, meanwhile, has spurred the reactionary racism of Enoch Powell and National Front fascism. Together, the new nationalisms and the fascism and racism that helped make Margaret Thatcher's return to "Victorian values" seem almost moderate have partially overshadowed class conflict, despite episodes like the miners' strike of 1984/85. According to Paul Gilroy, "Racism plays an active role, articulating political, cultural and economic elements into a complex and contradictory unity. It ensures . . . that for contemporary Britain 'race is the modality in which class is lived' [in the words of Stuart Hall], the medium in which it is appropriated and 'fought through'" (Gilroy 30).

Gilroy emphasizes "the contemporary association of British racism and British nationalism" (26), but racism and nationalism have been

1. The end of the post–World War II era of U.S. economic growth and prosperity was clearly marked by the oil crisis of 1973, followed by a global economic downturn that is not over. As Alain Lipietz wrote about the 1980s, "A huge number of 'collective servants', such as parking-lot attendants, golf-course caddies, or fast-food employees, throw into sharp relief the image of the U.S. as the 'Brazil of the 1980s'. Undergoing third-worldization, the American economy—including its industry—has undoubtedly enjoyed a boom, but on the basis of credit that is becoming more and more expensive" ("Debt Problem" 40–41). High unemployment, the "deskilling" of the labor force, the continually widening gap between rich and poor, the transnational flight of productive resources, and other economic woes continue in the 1990s, despite the supposed renewal of "growth" starting in 1993.

inseparable since the formation of the modern English, then from 1707, British, nation-state. War and empire are the furnaces in which these symbiotic ideologies have been forged. The economic baseline of capitalism's state formation was not a clear-cut mode of production of the sort that orthodox Marxists tend to identify with industrialization. Marx himself was careful to stress that the successful consolidation of modern nation-states was purchased both through the "primitive accumulation" of imperialist plunder and through the regulation of governmental financing by means of the funding of massive national debts. All modern nation-states including Britain have been founded and funded on the economic basis of national debt and "public credit." Modern currencies and monetary institutions (the Bank of England, for instance, established in 1694 to fund the British national debt) are forms of debt misrecognized (i.e., fetishized through public credit) as wealth. According to Freeman Tilden, "If you were to credit the mere arithmetic of any modern government's finance minister, you might believe that there was actually a sum of money, free from claim, lying in the national strong-box. The truth is that every modern state is penniless, and worse" (229).

John Brewer, Eric Hobsbawm, Paul Kennedy, and Charles Tilly are among the historians who have argued that nationalism and nation-state unification both cause and are caused by wars and imperial expansion, which in turn have exponentially multiplied national debts. The development of modern monetary and credit systems has been a direct response to warfare on a global scale (Rasler and Thompson 115). Wars coupled with mounting fiscal difficulties at home have repeatedly produced crises of public credit, even as those crises have been partially resolved through more nationalism, more patriotic, warmongering fervor (including jingoism, or the political fetishization of empire), with war's obvious corollary of the often racist demonizing of enemies, those *other* peoples of the world who just happen to be other.[2]

When Carlton J. Hayes published *Nationalism: A Religion* in 1960, he was echoing an old tradition of analysis which has treated nationalism as a secular form of idolatry or fetishism—a critical tradition that, in

2. Paul Kennedy, after noting the skyrocketing of the U.S. national debt into the trillions of dollars under the supposedly fiscally conservative Reagan and Bush regimes (527), stresses the "conundrum" that being a "Great Power—by definition, a state capable of holding its own against any other nation—demands a flourishing economic base." But this in turn demands war against rival nation-states, which "runs the risk of eroding the national economic base" (539). As Kennedy indicates throughout his book, and as Jack Snyder demonstrates quite clearly in *Myths of Empire,* this "risk" is often far greater than just the erosion of a national economy.

the British context, begins with the Enlightenment. Often, however, such criticism attacks only the manifest excesses of chauvinism, xenophobia, and jingoism while failing to grapple with the easy, everyday, or unconscious operation of nationality as a powerful factor in individual identity formation. Ironically, many of the great works in the canons of national literatures are antinationalistic and iconoclastic at least superficially (consider Charles Dickens's satire on Podsnappery in *Our Mutual Friend*, for instance, despite the quite strident chauvinism and racism he displayed in many other contexts). But even when overtly antinationalistic, such canonical works are, from the standpoint of traditional literary and cultural history, revered as *national* treasures, part of the cultural wealth of particular nation-states (the literary masterpiece as national fetish). For this very reason, the great works of modern, national literatures—perhaps especially the novels—are highly symptomatic forms of evidence about the modern pseudoreligions of racism, nationalism, and imperialism and also about past and present struggles against these ideologies. The irony is compounded because the novel, as the most characteristic modern literary genre, is also, along with newspapers and other forms of mass communication, one of the factors in the development of the "imagined communities" of modern nation-states and their empires (Benedict Anderson 25–36). Throughout this book, therefore, I pay close attention to novels (though also to other discursive forms and disciplines, especially economics) as sites where both the growing hegemony of and the critical resistance to nationalism, national identity formation, and imperialism are inscribed.

Drawing on Marxist, psychoanalytic, and poststructuralist theories of fetishism, I examine most closely those counterdiscourses (from Augustan satire as in *Gulliver's Travels* to postmodern satire as in Martin Amis's *Money: A Suicide Note*) that recognize the misrecognition at work under the aegis of public credit and national identity formation. As Slavoj Žižek points out, however, misrecognition does not necessarily entail false consciousness; it entails instead the behavior of "practical solipsists," who, no matter what they believe, behave as, for instance, Americans, Turks, Thais, or Brazilians. National identity formation is partly the result of the externalization of ideology—its embeddedness in social structures as much as in individual psyches. But the behavior of the "practical solipsist" is also that of the fetishist, whose typical form of disavowal says, in effect, "I know very well that such-and-such is not the case, but all the same" (*Sublime Object* 20–21).[3] *I know very well that*

---

3. Žižek is here echoing Octave Mannoni on the basic formulation of disavowal, or *Verleugnung*, involved in all fetishistic behavior: "Je sais bien que . . . mais quand même"

my identity as an Algerian (a Swede, . . . or a Peruvian) is a matter of ideology,
but all the same. . .

Accounts of fetishism evolve from Enlightenment descriptions of
West African idolatry (Eurocentric stereotypes that, however, were almost immediately applied to European practices such as imperial aggrandizement, slavery, and stock market "gambling") into the postmodern currency of theories that treat "commodity fetishism" as the
dominant, all-pervasive ideological formation of "late capitalism." In
Postmodernism, or The Cultural Logic of Late Capitalism, Fredric Jameson
argues that "modernism was still minimally and tendentially the critique of the commodity and the effort to make it transcend itself,"
whereas "postmodernism is the consumption of sheer commodification
as a process." This means, Jameson continues, that the "'life-style' of
the superstate therefore stands in relationship to Marx's 'fetishism' of
commodities as the most advanced monotheisms to primitive animisms
or the most rudimentary idol worship." But in the postmodern regime
of total commodification and commodity fetishism, the "superstate" is
slipping. Jameson uses the phrase "late capitalism" partly to refer to the
emergence of transnational corporations (with little or no allegiance to
the economic well-being of particular nation-states), to "the new international division of labor, [and to] a vertiginous new dynamic in international banking and the stock exchanges (including the enormous
Second and Third World debt)" (x).[4]

A wide array of intellectuals—from such celebrant/mourners of the
postmodern as Jameson or Jean Baudrillard through Madison Avenue
advertising agents—understand fetishism in both a Freudian and an at
least quasi-Marxist way. Powerful versions of cultural modernism attempted to combine Marxist with psychoanalytic categories, including

---

(Mannoni 9–33). As perhaps the most sophisticated current theoretician of national
identity formation (sophisticated precisely because he makes critical use of both Marxist-
Hegelian and Lacanian psychoanalytic categories), Žižek crops up often throughout this
book.

4. Echoing Ernest Mandel's *Late Capitalism*, Jameson writes that "late" "rarely means
anything so silly as the ultimate senescence, breakdown, and death of the system [of
capitalism] as such. . . . What 'late' generally conveys is rather the sense that something
has changed . . . that we have gone through a transformation of the life world which is
somehow decisive but incomparable with the older convulsions of modernization and
industrialization" (*Postmodernism* xxi). Maybe. But insofar as "late capitalism" means the
unrelenting continuation of modernization and industrialization, perhaps all Jameson is
really talking about is just more of the same, with the chief economic and political
difference being that transnational capitalism is rapidly outgrowing its old nation-state
cocoons or, better, defensive shells. On the corrosive effects of transnational corporatism
on nation states, see Brecher, Childs, and Cutler 4–5; Kennedy 536–540; Sklair 70–86
and passim.

both commodity and sexual fetishisms. Under the sign of the post-modern, the two fetishisms seem finally to have merged. As Žižek explains, "In Marxism a fetish conceals the positive network of social relations, whereas in Freud a fetish conceals the lack ('castration') around which the symbolic network is articulated" (*Sublime Object* 49). But this difference does not negate the fact that Marx's commodity and Freud's sexual fetishisms coincide or fuse all the time in people's fantasy lives. Further, as Žižek contends, a major, indeed hallowed, site of this fusion today lies in the average citizen's narcissistic self-reflection in the grand mirror of the nation-state.

What Michael Taussig, David Wells, and others have called "state fetishism" is not merely the misrecognition through reification of what is socially and politically constituted for something natural, God-given, and seemingly eternal (Taussig, *Nervous System* 111–140; Wells 127–164). Also at issue is the construction of that powerful aspect of individual subjectivity involved in national identity. Here Louis Althusser's theory of the "interpellation" of "the subject" by the "Ideological State Apparatuses" is clearly applicable. Further, the mechanisms of racist stereotyping in imperialist discourse are at work in the construction of positive national and imperial identities (Bhabha, *Location* 66–84). These positive self-images also operate as stereotypes, marked by a fetishism that endows the subject with a portion of the phallic power attributed to the nation-state. The point is not that nations and national identities are *merely* phantasmal or *merely* the products of an ideology that can be easily demystified as false consciousness. Every historian and theorist of nations and nationalisms since Hegel or even Hobbes has emphasized that these are *the* major political realities that, over the last four or five centuries, humanity has constructed and which now confront humanity as at once major achievements of solidarity and major obstacles to the achievement of international or post-national peace, justice, and ecological sanity.

During the eighteenth century, when, as Linda Colley stresses, both "Great Britain" and "the British Empire" were emergent from the almost continuous wars against France, Spain, and the American colonists, the counterdiscourses that attacked public credit as a form of idolatry or fetishism and the national debt as "alchemical" tended to be politically reactionary or "residual" rather than "emergent."[5] These were the voices especially of Bolingbroke and his circle of Tory intellec-

---

5. For "residual" versus "emergent" and "dominant" cultural formations, see Raymond Williams, "Base and Superstructure," 40–42.

tuals (Swift and Pope among them), defending aristocratic values and landed property against Whiggism and the new "money'd interest." The development of an adequate, somewhat stabilizing or at least stable theorization of national debt and public credit came only after the bursting of the South Sea Bubble in 1721, and really only after midcentury, in the work of David Hume, Adam Smith, Henry Thornton, and others.

Early "political economy" was both paralleled and attacked by Romantic writers from Blake to Shelley, with two very different versions of public credit rubbing elbows during the so-called Bank restriction, or paper money, era (1797–1821). Although most of the Romantics were hostile not just to orthodox economics but also to defenses of public credit, Coleridge was a powerfully idiosyncratic exception, whose speculations about money, debt, and the nature of value come closer to Henry Thornton's in *Paper Credit* than to anything in Blake, Wordsworth, or Shelley. British global hegemony was strengthened both through the Industrial Revolution and through the defeat of Napoleon; during the nineteenth-century Pax Britannica, industrializing, imperializing Britain was so prosperous and powerful that voices of skepticism or outright dissent seemed distinctly minor and apparently crackpot (e.g., the utopian socialists from Robert Owen to William Morris). But the Victorian novel simultaneously registers both the substantiality of British power and prosperity and its insubstantiality, its basis only in "credit" and "debt," in part by metaphorizing its own lack of reality (its fictionality) as no different from that of money (always a form of debt).

During the era of high modernism, the identification of a supposedly transcendent realm of high culture as genuine value or wealth (largely in opposition to commodified mass culture) helped John Maynard Keynes, for one, to overcome skepticism about national indebtedness and the constructed or imagined (mere "credit," mere "fetishism") nature of the nation-state, of its currency, and of national identity formation. But some modernist writers—Joseph Conrad in *Nostromo* and Virginia Woolf in *Three Guineas* and *Mrs. Dalloway* are key examples—already approximate that critical recognition of what is fetishistic about the very construction of national identity which has become the common coin, so to speak, of postmodernist British culture during and since the Thatcher era. Examples abound: Tom Nairn's treatise *Enchanted Glass*, Amis's novel *Money*, Caryl Churchill's play *Serious Money*, and Derek Jarman's film *The Last of England*, to mention a few.

Relating this broad, cultural-historical trajectory (emergence, dominance, decline) to current Marxist, poststructuralist, and postmodernist theories about the dismantling of the European empires after World War II, about the international debt crisis, and about the uneven weakening of all postmodern, western nation-states, I conclude on a pessimistic note in regard to the future of "Great Britain" but, also, with an open question about what new, postnational forms of global cooperation and community will be necessary to move beyond the debt-fetishism-empire structures that have dominated both western and nonwestern history since the Renaissance.

2

IN POSTSTRUCTURALIST theories of culture and discourse, debt, fetishism, and empire are often almost synonymous with representation. The antithesis of representation is presence, and therefore it is always a lack, a debt of sorts. Representation may also be inescapably fetishistic—at least in the hyperreality of late capitalism, where commodity fetishism reigns supreme; and perhaps throughout history, because as Freud declares, "A certain degree of . . . fetishism is . . . regularly found in the normal [self], especially during those stages of wooing when the normal sexual aim seems inaccessible." Freud then quotes *Faust*: "'Get me a handkerchief from her bosom—a garter of my love'" (*Basic Writings* 567). Finally, representation may be inherently imperialistic, because it seems always to involve an attempt to "master" some aspect of the external world. From this perspective, all forms of representation appear to be intrinsically irrational and violent, based on a will to power that is simultaneously infantilizing and imperializing.

Thus in relation to lack or debt, Michel Foucault writes of "the void to which and from which we speak" (*Language* 53), and Žižek declares, "Today it is a commonplace that the Lacanian subject is divided, crossed-out, identical to a lack in a signifying chain" (*Sublime Object* 122). Fetishism on the Freudian model itself arises from the "unveiling of a lack," a "symbolic drama" that, according to Christian Metz, is reduplicated in cinematic representation (70). But it is possible to go even farther, as does Valie Export, who asserts that, in the inescapable context of "phallocratic culture," "the structure of [all] representation is a structure of fetishism" (19). Like Metz's "imaginary signifier" of the cinema, all fetishes—and if one accepts the identification, all signifiers—assert a reality or presence that they lack. In *For a Critique of the Political Economy of the Sign*, Baudrillard initially rejects Marx's theory of "commodity fetishism" by arguing that that theory itself "fetishizes" its apparent opposite, the transcendent, rational subject. But there is no such subject, Baudrillard contends, only the "code" or the "system" of signs that produces the illusions of reason and the subject. These seemingly substantial, positive phenomena are mere lacks in chains of signifiers (or better, mere chains of lacks). Instead of a "fetishism of the signified," Baudrillard claims, there is only a "fetishism of the signifier," which is "the passion for the code" (92)—another way of saying that all representation is fetishistic. This inevitable fetishism of representation is, moreover, imperialistic: "The more the system is systematized, the more the fetishist fascination is reinforced; and . . . it is always invading new territories" (92).[6]

What has led to this "postmodern condition," to use Jean-François Lyotard's phrase, in which all forms of representation are identified with debt, fetishism, and empire, or with absence, ideology, and violence? Variants of these terms coalesce in postmodernist critiques of Enlightenment reason, though these critiques are not the cause of that coalescence. Postmodernism can be defined in relation to some other *post* words, including postindustrial and postcolonial, as involving increasing skepticism both about progress through technology (the ecology movement is one obvious symptom) and about Eurocentrism, or the belief that specifically Western "civilization" is and ought to be dominant over other cultures and societies (Amin, *Eurocentrism*; Young 19). Furthermore, the postmodern condition corresponds to a global political and economic situation characterized by the hegemony of late capitalism, but this hegemony is no longer entirely American and Eurocentric; it is instead increasingly transnational or, perhaps, postnational. Ironically, the state apparatuses that capitalism sponsored, so to speak, and that protected capitalism as it evolved, are now being undermined by capitalist globalization. The contemporary capitalist "world system" is not anchored in any single nation-state or even combination of states, and it may in fact be less a "system" than, to borrow the title

6. Jacques Derrida also identifies representation with debt, fetishism, and empire. He connects both lack and imperialism by arguing that writing or representation "always already" involves violence and domination. Derrida criticizes both Lévi-Strauss and Rousseau for imagining an escape from this violence into some primitive, innocent preliteracy (*Grammatology* 101–140). Just as there is "nothing outside the text" (158), and therefore no outside to writing, and therefore no outside to *mis*representation, so there is no outside to some version of violent domination and of its supplementary shadow, absence or lack. "There is no ethics without the presence *of the other* but also, and consequently, without absence, dissimulation, detour, differance, writing. The arche-writing is the origin of morality as of immorality. The nonethical opening of ethics. A violent opening" (139–140).

of one of Samir Amin's books on global politics, an "empire of chaos." When Lyotard writes of the "defaillancy" of modernity ("Universal History" 317), part of what he means is the general weakening of the claims of nation-states to be all-providing, omnicompetent organizations, able to deal with (or, depending on one's perspective, to interfere with) all aspects of their economies and of their citizens' lives, including their very identities.

Like subjects or citizens, modern cultures have grown up with national identities, which is one reason why current debates about "multiculturalism" are so contentious. As nation-states weaken, neonationalisms and neoconservative versions of "protectionism" grow (Sklair 70–75). From Herder and Hegel forward, much standard political rhetoric has suggested or assumed that nation-states express themselves in unique or idiosyncratic cultural forms that they are then held in some sense to control or possess.[7] Insofar as systems of representation—cultures—are dependent on or bound up with the fate of nations, the postmodern "defaillancy" of nation-states has perhaps necessarily evoked theoretical discourses that identify all forms of representation with debt, fetishism, and empire. Nation-states produce a variety of more or less official narratives, or forms of national representation, to create and sustain their legitimation. Above all, they produce nationalist histories about their origins and teleological progress toward "freedom" or toward utopian fulfillment. Nation-states also produce (though usually with fewer official strings attached than they attach to historical narratives) literatures and art forms that are understood as belonging to them—such cultural property as "the Russian ballet," "the English novel," and "French impressionist painting."

Nation-states are themselves, as Timothy Brennan claims, "imaginary constructs that depend for their existence on an apparatus of cultural fictions in which imaginative literature plays a decisive role. And the rise of European nationalism coincides especially with one form of literature—the novel" (49). Echoing the poststructuralist (more specifically, Foucauldian) idea that nation-states and their empires are "discursive formations," Brennan and the other contributors to Homi Bhabha's anthology *Nation and Narration* all attempt versions of the deconstruction of those discursive formations as fetishistic, as imperialistic, and as based on absence or lack (they are "imaginary constructs"). An assertion such as Brennan's is, however, bound to be disturbing to

7. I have in mind, of course, Johann Gottfried Herder's *Thoughts on the Philosophy of Mankind* (1784–91) and G. W. F. Hegel's *Philosophy of History* (1822–31).

more traditional (non-poststructuralist) scholars and historians, and especially to those who think of nation-states as "real" rather than "imaginary." Indeed, they undoubtedly have been the most "real" factors or agents or units in modern world history, at least in the West, for the past four centuries. As Hegel put it, in world history, "the *Individuals* we have to do with are *Peoples*," or nations, and the "Totalities that are States" (*History* 14).

Despite the massive historical "reality" of nations and states, it was not Foucault or Derrida but David Hume who first observed that all governments rest on nothing more substantial than "opinion" ("First Principles"). Unfortunately for those historians who would like to believe they are working with materials solider than discursive formations, nation-states are—as Bhabha, Brennan, and their co-contributors contend—in some fundamental sense no more or less than fictional constructions. Hume's "opinion" is, no doubt, too vague and general to cover all aspects of what unifies nation-states; in another of his essays, he analyzed an additional category that plays a major role in this book, the partly economic category of "public credit." A survey of recent work on nationalism and imperialism shows that, no matter what the perspective or methodology, analysts of all stripes are agreed in understanding these phenomena as ideologies, hence as versions of belief or imagination. Whether they emanate from something "real" called the nation-state, or rather are what give rise to nation-states and their empires in the first place, is however a matter of controversy.

The historian Tony Judt cautions against those theorists who treat nationalism as "a collective hallucination": "In this perspective, nationalism, and nations, are inventions, whether of rulers or intellectuals. They are images of an identity that does not 'really' exist, even though the belief that it does so has significant material consequences" (45). Among works that take this view, Judt cites Benedict Anderson's *Imagined Communities: Reflections on the Origin and Spread of Nationalism*. Especially through his treatment of novels as contributing to the "invention" of modern nation-states, Anderson has influenced an array of writers (including those in *Nation and Narration*) who treat national identification and unification as a "form of cultural elaboration" (Bhabha, *Nation* 3), or in other words as a sort of fiction of state not much different from novels. But granted that Anderson emphasizes and perhaps overemphasizes (as did Marshall McLuhan in *The Gutenberg Galaxy* and elsewhere) the forms of discourse—novels, newspapers, museums, maps, and statistics—that contribute to the illusion of a uniform public or "socioscape" existing in "homogeneous, empty time" and space (Anderson 22–32), and hence to the modern "imagining" of nationalities, Judt's caveat seems contradictory. *Every* contemporary commentator on nationalism including Judt recognizes that it is an ideology (though not necessarily in the sense of false consciousness or "collective hallucination") and therefore that it "does not 'really' exist" even though it obviously has "significant material consequences." Judt stresses that "in any attempt to clarify the concept of nation, two features stand out": language and religion (46). But although it is perhaps plausible to think of belonging to a language community as non- or pre-ideological, religions are the classic instances of ideologies from the Enlightenment forward. Religions no more "'really' exist" than do nationalisms, even though no one denies that they have real consequences (Benedict Anderson writes of "the reality of such apparitions" [14]).[8]

But, though unhappy with analysts such as Anderson, who, he believes, exaggerate the fictiveness of nationalism, Judt acknowledges that "many of the most 'ancient' traditions, dates, and ceremonies associated with expressions of national identification in Europe are inventions of the last century" (45). What is true of Europe is equally true or truer of other parts of the world—North and South America, Africa, Australasia, much of Asia—where modern nation-states did not exist before 1776. Both the recentness and the fictiveness of national and imperial identities in the British context were main themes of Eric Hobsbawm and Terence Ranger's influential anthology, *The Invention of Tradition* (published in 1983, the same year as the first edition of *Imagined Communities*). Without benefit of either poststructuralism or postcolonialism, the collection demonstrated not just that national and imperial identities were imaginary constructions but that the exercise of power was inseparable from its symbolic expression. (In contrast to his negative assessment of Anderson's book, Judt calls the essays in *The Invention of Tradition* "excellent.")

Hobsbawm pursues these themes in his own 1990 book, *Nations and Nationalism since 1780: Programme, Myth, Reality*, in which he endorses Anderson's "useful phrase, an 'imagined community,'" which, he spec-

---

8. The idea of language as pre-ideological is untenable. From Lacanian and poststructuralist perspectives, language is the Symbolic Order that speaks us—that inscribes and authorizes our very identities. From a Marxist perspective, language is the battleground of conflicting "ideologemes." "Each word . . . is a little arena for the clash and criss-crossing of differently oriented social accents. A word in the mouth of a particular individual person is a product of the living interaction of social forces. . . . The psyche and ideology dialectically interpenetrate in the unitary and objective process of social intercourse" (Vološinov 41).

ulates, "no doubt . . . can be made to fill the emotional void left by the retreat or disintegration, or the unavailability of *real* human communities and networks" (46). But here Hobsbawm may be expressing the same epistemological confusion that marks Judt's caveat against theorists of nationalism such as Anderson: whatever a "real" community might once have been (and perhaps Hobsbawm has in mind some such contrast as Ferdinand Tönnies's between *Gemeinschaft* and *Gesellschaft*), it would just as surely have consisted of discursive, symbolic, or ideological forms of bonding as the modern nation-state—the community as "cultural elaboration." Still, Hobsbawm's survey stresses the connections between nationalisms and economic and political modernization in Europe over the last two or three centuries, and concludes with the hopeful thought that (despite much evidence to the contrary, which he acknowledges) the erosion of nation-states will lead to an erosion of nationalisms (182), opening the way, presumably, for some genuine new world order or "real" global community beyond war and beyond the other ravages of capitalism and imperialism.

The fictiveness and symbolism of British nationalism and imperialism have been stressed in a number of books in the eighties and nineties. These are themes in Raphael Samuel's History Workshop anthology *Patriotism: The Making and Unmaking of British National Identity*. Samuel writes, "The idea of nation, though a potent one, belongs to the imaginary rather than the real" (1:16). They are also themes in several of the volumes under the general editorship of John MacKenzie, including his own *Propaganda and Empire: The Manipulation of British Public Opinion, 1880–1960*. Certainly the late-Victorian and early-modern British Empire, MacKenzie demonstrates, depended as much on advertising and other forms of ideological tom-tom beating as any more "real" or less illusory factors.[9] Similarly, Edward Said's *Culture and Imperialism* and Thomas Richards's *The Imperial Archive: Knowledge*

9. From about 1870 on, writes MacKenzie, "advertising, bric-a-brac, and packaging all exploited royalty and imperialism, taking symbols of colonial adventures into every home" (5). The aggressive "new imperialism" of the fin-de-siècle was coterminus with and (though it is difficult to say how) influenced by the new consumerist orientation associated with the second Industrial Revolution. In *The Psychology of Jingoism* and his classic *Imperialism*, John Hobson identified advertising, along with sensationalistic mass journalism, as one of the main fomenters of the rabid protofascism that helped trigger the Boer War (see Chapter 5). Unlike the novel, however, commercial mass advertising was not a factor in the initial "invention" of modern nation-states and empires. Advertising entered the picture belatedly, with decolonization just over the horizon. Like late-Victorian jingoism in general, the political themes of early mass advertising seem therefore reactionary, compensatory: "Empire [was] portrayed as a means of arresting national decline" (MacKenzie 10).

and the Fantasy of Empire both treat imperialism as a "form of cultural elaboration." Said's book replays Raymond Williams's *Culture and Society, 1780–1950* by self-consciously attempting to fill a major gap in Williams's work: Williams had little to say about the British imperial experience. Said adapts Williams's generously open-ended, albeit ambiguous, conception of culture to his own analysis of numerous texts, both canonical and noncanonical, and both British and otherwise (*Aida*, for instance), showing the wide variety of resonances and complexities that the imperial experience has introduced into British and other modern cultures, including postcolonial ones. Said's use of Williams's idea of "cultural formations" is not much different from his use of Foucault's "discursive formations" in his earlier magnum opus *Orientalism*: one effect in both cases is that he does not worry much about causality, because Williams's "culture" like Foucault's "discourse" is in some sense both cause and effect, or (perhaps more fairly) it is a term that, for the postmodern genealogist, does not demand a causal explanation.

In *The Imperial Archive*, Richards emphasizes the fictive or, better, phantasmal basis of empire building. "An empire is partly a fiction" (1): though "partly" gives Richards an escape from the (merely?) fictive, presumably in the direction of Judt's "significant material consequences," Richards mainly analyzes novels (*Kim, Lost Horizon, Dracula, Tono-Bungay, Riddle of the Sands,* and *Gravity's Rainbow* among others). But he also demonstrates how novelistic discourse reflects and reinforces scientific discourse, and especially how the late-Victorian fantasy of attaining universal knowledge defined the "imperial archive" that was in complex ways both the outcome of Britain's imperial past and the inspiration for the present defense and future expansion of the empire.[10] Forever chasing "a lost horizon of comprehensive knowledge," scientific discourse collaborated with literature in linking that impossibly encyclopedic knowledge to "national security" (39, 5). In the early twentieth century, the imperialistic dream of universal knowledge grew crazily insupportable and dangerous, in part because of "entropy" or the "epistemological levelling process" (112) that reduces the attempts of nation-states to control information to the paranoia and espionage of modern and now postmodern war machines.

The overarching discursive formation or, perhaps, supreme fiction, Richards suggests, has had all sorts of massively real social and political

10. The sciences Richards discusses are economics, ethnography, morphology (both pre- and post-Darwin), and thermodynamics (Maxwell's demon and the concept of entropy).

consequences (war, for instance). The "imperial archive" thus takes on some of the qualities of general cause or primum mobile, like Althusser's conception of ideology. Richard's term *paranoia*, moreover, is certainly the correct diagnosis for the modern, war-making, empire-building "security state." The day-to-day political decision making that has led to wars and imperial land grabs can in general be characterized as variations on a realpolitik that looks manifestly rational but that, finding rivals and enemies everywhere beyond the borders of the nation-state, engaged in the same activities on behalf of their nation-states, always places "national security" at the head of its agenda. In *Myths of Empire: Domestic Politics and International Ambition*, Jack Snyder has analyzed the motivations of the political leaders of five modern nation-states that plunged into "overly aggressive foreign policies" (1)—policies that, though they may have produced imperial aggrandizement and national security for awhile, sooner or later became "counterproductive" from the standpoint of the very "political realism" that generated them. Central to the imperialistic decision making of all of these nation-states has been the idea that "security requires expansion," which is in turn based on "hydra-headed justifications for aggressive policies" (3), for instance, the thesis that territorial expansion increases power or the thesis that, in international affairs, offense is the best defense. These rationalizations may well be correct in the short run, but they also draw the nation-states that accept them into escalating conflicts with rivals, including the rival nationalisms that they seem invariably to inspire.

Britain, however, managed to avoid the catastrophes that befell Germany and Japan; in his chapter on "social imperialism" in the Victorian era, Snyder asks why that was the case. Were Palmerston and Britain's other leaders *better* "realists" than the leaders of Germany and Japan? In general, Snyder thinks, they were more cautious, more concerned with the economic costs and benefits of imperial expansion, and obviously also more experienced in colonial defense and governance. Palmerston thus emerges as, in "realist" terms, a better (i.e., more successful) "realist" than his later counterparts in both Wilhelmine and Nazi Germany. Although Snyder's own "realist" (empiricist political science) approach does not lend itself to theorizing about the fictive underpinnings or superstructures of modern nation-states and their empires, he nevertheless calls the realpolitik of the politicians whom he surveys "mythical." If their "myths" about national security worked out in the short run, then they were less "mythical," perhaps, than they invariably proved to be in the long run. Snyder does not speculate about either the epistemological or the psychological nature of these "myths." But perhaps the rationalizations for war and expansion espoused by Palmerston, Disraeli, Joseph Chamberlain, and others can be understood as the *parole* to the *langue* of Richards's "imperial archive," constituting the most consequential of the specific, micropolitical units of discourse that have been uttered, so to speak, by the macropolitical discursive formations or "cultural elaborations" known as modern nation-states and their empires.

Ernst Gellner asserted that "nationalism is not the awakening of nations to self-consciousness: it *invents* nations where they do not exist" (169). Anderson quotes him in *Imagined Communities* (6), and Hobsbawm also says that "with Gellner I would stress the element of artefact, invention and social engineering which enters into the making of nations"; and he proceeds to declare that "nationalism comes before nations" (*Nations* 10). Perhaps these are extreme versions of the insistence on the fictiveness of national identities: rather than nation-states giving rise to national identities, certain collectivities based on geographic proximity, language, religion, and/or customs give rise to nationalisms that in turn give rise to modern nation-states. But they also amount to a thesis that Judt accepts, because the book he praises most highly, Liah Greenfeld's *Nationalism: Five Roads to Modernity*, argues that "the basic framework of modern politics—the world divided into nations—is simply a realization of nationalist imagination; it is created by nationalism" (488). Whereas most historians including Hobsbawm and Anderson have seen nationalism as an ideological epiphenomenon of capitalist, industrial modernization, Greenfeld contends that modernity is the effect of nationalism. The inference follows that nationalism is the most "real" causal factor in modern history: instead of class conflict (for instance), nationalism is the engine that drives modernity. But this inference hardly makes nationalism any less fictive or ideological. Indeed, Greenfeld starts with the assertion that "the only foundation of nationalism as such, the only condition, that is, without which no nationalism is possible, is an idea" (3).

According to Greenfeld, this "idea of the nation" arose first "in sixteenth-century England, which was the first nation in the world (and the only one, with the possible exception of Holland, for about two hundred years)." She adds that "the individualistic civic nationalism which developed there was inherited by its colonies in America, and later became characteristic of the United States" (14). England emerged first as a modern nation-state, Greenfeld contends, because of the nation-centeredness of its Reformation. Protestantism then collaborated with commerce, war, and overseas expansion to give England, along with Holland, a competitive edge in the business of empire building during and after the seventeenth century. Although the Spanish, Portuguese, and French monarchies had centralized regimes in the 1500s, they did not have the proto-nationalist glue that officially supported religious militancy provided in England.

Besides (once again) the fictiveness of nationalism, a further irony of Greenfeld's argument is that "individualistic civic nationalism"—the kind most closely bound up both with Protestantism and with democratic liberalism (10)—was diffused from England via colonization and empire building. European imperialism over the last four centuries has everywhere inspired nationalisms, independence movements, and the rush to modernize, though not always with any impetus toward democracy. From this perspective, nationalisms may seem not so much liberating as, to borrow from Partha Chatterjee's subtitle for *Nationalist Thought and the Colonial World*, "derivative discourses." Chatterjee stresses the connection between the nationalist impulse to modernize and European Enlightenment thought, or "the bourgeois-rationalist conception of knowledge" (11). Nationalism tends to be essentialist, centralizing, and ruthlessly bent on economic "modernization" to the destruction of local patterns, customs, beliefs, and identities. As a "derivative discourse," nationalism in the Indian or African context turns out to be imperialism by other means, less post- than neocolonial. Therefore, Chatterjee concludes, "the critique of nationalist discourse must find . . . the ideological means to connect the popular strength of [local] struggles with the consciousness of a new universality, to subvert the ideological sway of a state which falsely claims to speak on behalf of the nation and to challenge the presumed sovereignty of a science which puts itself at the service of capital" (170). If imperialism has sown the seeds of its own undoing in nationalisms around the globe, those nationalisms have not escaped the maelstrom of modernization—that is, westernization—as they are drawn into the world system of transnational capitalism. Nor (though India with its diverse populations and its legal and parliamentary system is a partial exception, more like the United States than like, say, Iran) have nationalisms proved to be intrinsically democratic.

Meanwhile, to return to Britain and (according to Greenfeld's account) the origins of the ideology of nationalism and hence of modernity, it was out of the sixteenth-century process of becoming distinctively English that a subsequent national or, rather, supranational identity emerged: from England to Great Britain, and from Englishness to Britishness. The strains and cracks evident in this later "invention" or "cultural elaboration" of national identity are largely the results of the contradiction between democracy and civic individualism (liberalism) on the one hand and imperialism on the other—a contradiction that runs straight through eighteenth- and nineteenth-century culture down to the Thatcher-Major era. This is so because to forge British, as opposed to merely English, national identity, the differences (and age-old hostilities) between the English and the Irish, the Welsh, and the Scots had to be overlooked, mystified, or at least partly resolved.

The invention of this modern British togetherness is the theme of Linda Colley's *Britons: Forging the Nation, 1707–1837.* "Great Britain" was, Colley demonstrates, "an invention forged above all by war" (5). And it was forged in the first instance by war close to home, including the imperial subjugation of both Ireland and Scotland. "As a would-be nation, rather than a name, Great Britain was invented in 1707 when the Parliament of Westminster passed the Act of Union linking Scotland to England and Wales. From now on, this document proclaimed, there would be 'one united kingdom by the name of Great Britain'" (11). The end date in Colley's title, moreover, implies that, by the start of Queen Victoria's reign, the thoroughly modern and modernizing, industrializing, and imperializing nation-state of Great Britain had been "forged." For Victorian culture in general, this sense of completion—of being, so to speak, on top of the world—seemed incontestable, as sound and creditable as the Bank of England itself. But like Hobsbawm and Ranger's *Invention of Tradition* with its emphasis on recent symbolism and ritual, Colley's cultural history stresses both the recentness and the fragility of the invention called, from 1707, "Great Britain." She suggests that this fragile unity was ultimately doomed by the very energies (nationalist, ethnic, regional, and particularist) it sought to corral: "As an invented nation heavily dependent for its *raison d'être* on a broadly Protestant culture, on the threat and tonic of recurrent war, particularly war with France, and on the triumphs, profits and Otherness represented by a massive overseas empire, Britain is bound now to be under immense pressure" (6).

Colley here strikes a note similar to that of numerous contemporary books on the decline and fall of the British Empire, of Great Britain as a faltering industrial and economic power, and even of England as a once-special place or of the English as a once-special race who used to be destined (once upon a time, so the story goes) to rule a quarter of the globe. Within the "socioscape" of Great Britain, in constant friction with the civic-individualistic nationalism that was at first English, are those neonationalisms—Welsh, Scottish, Irish, and more recently East and West Indian—whose contemporary dissonance, Nairn declares in *The Break-up of Britain,* is symptomatic of the decline of "Great Britain" as a once great industrial, imperial superpower. A Marxist champion of Scottish nationalism, Nairn is actively seeking ways of aligning Welsh, Scottish, and Irish neonationalisms with class struggle, though he acknowledges that these two forces making for the "break-up" are often pulling against each other. But Nairn is also only stating the obvious about Britain's relative industrial, economic decline since the 1880s and loss of imperial power and glory since the end of World War I.

Whether one national identity is more fictive, more artificial or in some sense less "real," than another is obviously debatable. But English national identity is older and seems bound to outlast the latecomer, British supranational identity. The latter has been dependent on dominion over other, non-English nationalities, both within the circumference of what were once blithely called "the British Isles" and around the world, through possession of an empire on which, as Macaulay, Tennyson, and other Victorians liked to think, the sun would never set. In much nineteenth-century British literature and culture, the only things that seemed more "real" and certain to endure forever than the glorious British Empire itself were the virtues of the mainly *English* heroes—adventurers, soldiers, and rulers—who had constructed that empire. These were distinctly *English* virtues, moreover—definitely not Irish, and only occasionally, grudgingly Scottish:

> In English mythology the uniqueness [of English history] is ascribed to a mixture of magic and "long experience." In fact, it should be ascribed to Empire. In a sense quite distinct from the habitual icons of imperialism—militarism, uniformed sadism, cults of violence, etc.—this was . . . the most profoundly and unalterably imperialist of societies. Of all the great states, the British was the most . . . conditioned by prolonged external depredations, and the most dependent on fortunate external relations. From the time of its Indian conquests to that of its cringing dependence on the United States, its power was the internal translation of these fortunes. (Nairn, *Break-up* 69)

And imperialism, Nairn also contends, both as a politicoeconomic practice and as an ideology (a supplement to or extension of nationalism), was what has made it possible for the conservative "patriciate" to continue to fatten their private bank accounts as industrialism declined, while also dodging the bullets of socialism and, since Thatcher's first election in 1979, Labourism.

The dual ideologies of nationalism and imperialism have been major forces in the shaping of British culture and society over several centuries. If the Thatcherites and National Front demagogues have their way, the sun will still never set on these ideologies, even if it has already set on Britain's actual industrial and imperial hegemony. These are the fictions whose reality effects, at least, realist historians such as Tony Judt privilege in their constructions of causal explanations. But as Greenfeld, echoing Max Weber, declares, "Social reality is intrinsically cultural; it is necessarily a symbolic reality, created by the subjective meanings and perceptions of social actors" (18). As does the concept of "cultural elaboration" in Bhabha's *Nation and Narration* or of "cultural formation" in Said's *Culture and Imperialism*, Greenfeld's use of the adjective "cultural" here allows for an escape from the questionable binary division that Judt invokes in his review: the "real" on one side; the merely "fictive" or "invented" on the other. But to put it mildly, the invented fictions of nationalism and imperialism have had, through the course of modern and now postmodern history, very "significant material consequences."

Nation-states are invented through a process of fetishistic misrecognition whereby debt, absence, and powerlessness are transubstantiated, mainly through class exploitation at home and war abroad, into their opposites—into wealth, a plenitude of laws and institutions, and power, including power in the form of imperial aggrandizement. In economic terms, public credit underwrites this plenitude and power. Nationalism and imperialism are the corresponding political ideologies that endow nation-states and their empires with the symbolic legitimation to interpellate their subjects or to establish hegemony. In this sense, fetishism mediates between debt and empire, because it names the otherwise mystified and mystifying process whereby the one is transformed into the other. I also invoke the term *hegemony* here, because the process of inventing nation-states and their empires is at least partly a consensual one in Antonio Gramsci's terms. This process is always more or less open to various challenges (revolutions, most obviously), while at the same time, through much of modern and now postmodern history, it has seemed to reflect unproblematic common sense. Nationalism, or what Gramsci calls the "popular-national" belief in the coherence and legitimacy of the "people-nation," is a creature of "common sense, which is the 'philosophy of non-philosophers,' or in other words the conception of the world which is uncritically absorbed by the various social and cultural environments in which the moral individuality of the average man is developed" (Gramsci 419–421). And the dominant mode of common sense is the fetishization of what is historically, socially produced by people themselves, including nation-states and their empires, as permanent, God-given fixtures of nature and the universe.

From the Enlightenment forward, much British literary and social-critical discourse has struggled to demystify commonsense emotional and intellectual investments in the nation-state and its imperial extensions. It is in these moments of cultural struggle that the interconnections among debt, fetishism, and empire are most clearly revealed, as seen, for instance, in Conrad's *Heart of Darkness*. Marlow claims that the only thing that could "redeem" imperialism is "an idea at the back of it," but he immediately undermines this "idea" by aligning it with fetishism and "sacrifice": "The conquest of the earth, which mostly means the taking it away from those who have a different complexion or slightly flatter noses than ourselves, is not a pretty thing when you look into it too much. What redeems it is the idea only. An idea at the back of it; not a sentimental pretence but an idea; and an unselfish belief in the idea—something you can set up, and bow down before, and offer a sacrifice to" (7). Conrad's fetishistic "idea" is precisely what forms "the only foundation of nationalism" as well as of imperialism, "the only condition . . . without which no nationalism is possible" (Greenfeld 3).

3

INSOFAR AS poststructuralist and postmodernist theories claim that representation in general is based on or identical with forms of debt, fetishism, or empire, they point inexorably to the question of nationalism and nation-states. A genealogy of such claims would show that national debts emerge as key factors in the economic base, or mode of production, underlying the superstructures of modern, western cultures. That base, however, is in the form of a financial abyss rather than of a positive, material economic force in the orthodox Marxist sense. National debts are the *mise en abîme* from which modern, western systems of representation spring, like shadows radiating from the black hole of the modern nation-state, tangents of that state and its imperial satellites. Not only did the Enlightenment discover the disciplines that contradict the liberties it enshrined, as Foucault contends in *Discipline and Punish* (222); its culture was rooted in the discovery of public credit as an instrument of state power. Public credit in turn was a primary promoter of the commercializing aristocracy and bourgeoisie, of preindustrial and early industrial capitalism, and of the nation building, nationalisms, and imperialisms that characterize modern, western history from the late seventeenth century forward.

The emergence of Great Britain, France, the United States, and all modern nation-states was quite literally paid for through the invention and massive application or exploitation of "public credit," a phrase that, in one of its frequent uses, is only a euphemism for public debt. The warring nation-states of Europe, energized by expansion abroad and industrialization at home, were able to carry on their war making, imperializing, and industrializing only on the basis of pervasive, new fiscal arrangements. The modern financial revolution included the establishment of national banks (even when those national banks remained private corporations, like the Bank of England until its nationalization in 1946); the use of bills of exchange and bank notes as symbols for metallic moneys (and eventually, as in revolutionary America and France, the substitution of paper money for convertible currencies); the rise of stock markets; and the proliferation of credit mechanisms including, above all, the funding of national debts. Temporally, these new instruments of national debt and middle-class commerce were all future oriented; spatially or geographically, they were directed toward war and expansion beyond the nation-state's borders. These are the main economic aspects of what, specifically in regard to the Netherlands, Britain, and France, has been called the "financial revolution" of the early modern era (Dickson).

There is, perhaps, nothing newsworthy about the history of national debts, or about the significance of public credit to the formation and long-term prosperity of modern nation-states under capitalism. But, as Marx recognized, the capitalist mode of production is based on public credit, or on the modern money form. Public credit is at once tied to state legitimacy, and hence to national debts, and to the political category of public opinion as an aspect of the democratic public spheres emergent during the Enlightenment. Money and its corollary public credit (or public debt), which is all that legitimates money to begin with, are thus even more fundamental to the fictional or ideological creation and maintenance of the imagined communities of modern nation-states than are more explicitly nationalistic cultural forms including both literary canons and competing political ideologies.

With the waning of religious authority, the concept of culture gradually emerged as a locus of higher value supposedly transcending the strictly material realm of necessity and self-interest, that is, the economic realm, where money is the measure of value. But, as Raymond Williams maintained, culture in its romantic, Arnoldian or liberal humanist guise is at best only a set of wishful, loosely connected ideals that, "while appearing to resemble an absolute . . . has in fact no absolute ground" (*Culture and Society* 127). Culture could hardly function as an alternative to the economic or the commercial when it, too, was relentlessly undergoing commodification, as was obviously the case with the novel. Also, starting with the Enlightenment, various forms of materialism—Positivism, Marxism, Darwinism, Zolaism, but especially bourgeois economics—treated culture as the illusory or ideological product of material, especially economic, forces. As Balzac and many other nineteenth-century novelists suggested in countless works of fiction, the ultimate standard of value in modern society was not religion, or even a nation's culture, but money. This idea, however, had already been expressed by Defoe and other eighteenth-century novelists; the universal, leveling power of money is a theme apparently intrinsic to, perhaps even definitive of, the novel form itself (see Chapter 4).

Money itself, however, is cultural. Even money based on a metallic standard is not "material" as are gold, silver, or for that matter paper. As both Marx and the bourgeois economists recognized, money may be the universal commodity form or "general equivalent" for all other commodities, but it is not a thing in itself (a *Ding-an-sich*). Whether made of metal or convertible into silver or gold, money is a symbol of value, itself insubstantial. But the more objective or reified money becomes, the more subjective value becomes. Money is thus even more mystified and mystifying than other commodities because even more governed by the mystification Marx called "commodity fetishism." In a sense, money *is* that mystification: as Theodor Adorno says, "the dance of the money veils" disguises rather than expresses the true value of things (*Minima Moralia* 155). "It is . . . precisely this finished form of the world of commodities—the money form," writes Marx, "which conceals the social character of . . . labour" (*Capital* 1:168). With the waning of religion, as Georg Simmel also recognized, money as the universal representative and solvent of all values ironically itself takes on some of the functions of religious symbolism and ritual. Paralleling modern secularization including the development of economic and scientific materialism, Simmel pointed out, was the gradual *dematerialization* of money:

> The broad cultural ramifications of the nature and significance of money are to be seen in the movements that lead money towards its pure concept and away from its attachment to particular substances [gold, silver]—even though it never attains the goal that determines its course of development. Thus, money is involved in the general development which in every domain of life and in every sense strives to dissolve substance into free-floating processes. (168)

Although Simmel thought that money would never completely dematerialize (i.e., would never be cut loose from some metallic or other material standard), like Marx he recognized "the growing spiritualization of money" (198) as central to the experience of modernity.

Although it would obviously be hyperbolic to claim that money takes the place of religion in modern and now postmodern national cultures, money is nevertheless one of the supreme fictions—perhaps the supreme counterfeit—on which the legitimacy (or illegitimacy) of those cultures is based. In his recent study of counterfeit money and its fictions, Jacques Derrida contends that all money is in some sense counterfeit, because based only on "credit" or "faith," whereas through credit "counterfeit money can become true capital" (*Given Time* 124). For Derrida, moreover, credit (and counterfeiting) in monetary or economic terms is in some sense identical to "credit in literature"—the story of culture is ultimately also "the story of money" (129). In *Money, Language, and Thought*, Mark Shell similarly writes, "Credit, or belief, involves the very ground of aesthetic experience, and the same medium that seems to confer belief in fiduciary money (bank notes) and in scriptural money (created by the process of bookkeeping) also seems to confer it in literature" (7). For both Derrida and Shell, the medium in question is writing—hence, literacy and literature, but also such texts as bank notes and stocks and bonds.

John Locke and many subsequent philosopher-economists[11] have insisted that any legitimate currency either has to be metal or has to be directly convertible into metal (coins or bullion). But capitalism has led unevenly yet relentlessly through the abandonment of silver and gold standards to the postmodern, global situation in which wealth is no longer measured by or dependent on any single, convertible, national currency (the pound, the dollar, the yen, which in turn are no longer officially convertible into gold or silver). Wealth, like corporations, is increasingly transnational and also vertiginously complex, electronic, and hypothetical. Jeremiads about or celebrations of the decline and fall of nation states are paralleled by Jeremiads like Joel Kurtzman's *The Death of Money: How the Electronic Economy Has Destabilized the World's Markets and Created Financial Chaos* (for other examples, see Davidson; Delamaide; George; Hogan and Pearce; MacEwan; Malkin; Payer). Writing of the emergence, since about 1970, of what he calls "xenomoney" (i.e., money that, like "Eurodollars," is no longer

11. Until, perhaps, David Ricardo, the roles of philosopher and economist were difficult or perhaps impossible to keep apart; as an aspect of the postmodern condition, they may be becoming so again. Besides Derrida, consider the examples of Baudrillard, Lyotard, and Jean-Joseph Goux among others.

validated or underwritten by the supposed solvency of a specific nation-state), Brian Rotman points out that those who are "convinced that it is not 'real' money but a dangerously unstable kind of pseudo-money" believe that it "will either be drowned in the debt weight of its past or burned up in vertiginous and anarchic volatility derived from its future" (96). But in contrast to the postmodern monetary doomsayers, ultraconservative Nobel Prize economist F. A. Hayek has called for the "denationalisation of money" precisely because "the government monopoly of the issue and control of money" is "the source and root of all monetary evil" (23). (Whether Hayek recognizes that "money is the root of all evil" is another question.) Public credit and national debt have been part of a generalized system of state oppression and robbery, according to Hayek, who defines history itself, an "all too monotonous and depressing . . . story," as "largely inflation engineered by government" (33).[12]

At least it is evident that, since the era of the international gold standard between 1867 and World War I, money has *transubstantiated* (as well as "inflated," though there must be an originary, stable base value, if not an essentialist gold standard, for "inflation" to be a clearly definable category). Money is today more insubstantial ("liquid," "volatile," "nonconvertible," etc.) than ever, and therefore it also seems to be more religious or, rather, more mystified, more counterfeit, than it was when Marx and Simmel wrote and apparently far more so than when John Locke wrote his essays on money and the recoinage controversy of the 1690s. As Freeman Tilden declared in 1936 in the midst of the Great Depression, in the history of money, "power over wealth" has gradually been "projected farther and farther from the source: symbols take the place of tokens, as tokens had taken the place of money, and as money had taken the place of commodities. Even symbols seem to be giving way to a sort of black magic that only the diabolists understand" (19).[13] Basic to the gradual transubstantiation of money has been the increasing reliance on credit at all levels of economic activity,

12. In *A World in Debt*, Freeman Tilden had said much the same in retelling the story of Dionysius of Syracuse, who eliminated his governmental debt when he recalled all of the coins of his creditors and doubled (inflated) their value by overstamping them, thus "putting himself handsomely in pocket." Tilden continues: "At least the half of all economic history is concerned with the tragi-comedy of governments getting into debt by extravagance and trying to get out by fraud" (137).

13. More recent commentators say much the same; according to Alain Lipietz, "even in international relations, there no longer seems to be any final exchange of the monetary symbol for the money commodity, gold. Capitalism has passed into the era of credit money in which 'real money' is no longer a 'true' commodity" (Lipietz, *Enchanted World* 78).

from transactions between private individuals to those between governments. And as Simmel declares, credit contains "an element of . . .
supratheoretical belief": credit is a "social-psychological quasi-religious
faith" (179).

What is involved in the "quasi-religious faith" of credit is not just the
worship of money, however, but the worship of the economy itself, or
more specifically of the supposedly ever expansive "growth" or "progress" of the economy. In *Money and Magic*, his interpretation of *Faust* as
a critique of modern economic, industrial, and imperial expansiveness,
Hans Binswanger contends that the economy's generation of "surplus
value," immediately commodifiable or assuming the form of money,
seems nothing short of miraculous to its worshipers: "This act of creation by the economy exerts a huge fascination, the fascination of the
infinitely augmentable, that is, of eternal progress. Thus the economy
gains the transcendental character (i.e., surpassing all limits) which
man formerly sought in religion. It is not belief in a hereafter, but
economic activity in the here and now, that opens up modern man's
perspective on eternity" (37). But, as Goethe understood, economic
and imperial expansion have limits; in ecological terms in particular,
the postmodern world is reaching or exceeding them. Further, the economic history of the modern and now postmodern capitalist world system is rooted in patterns of national debt, war, and empire that have
evolved from the Enlightenment forward into today's global debt crisis.
The British national debt was a concern for Adam Smith, though at the
end of *The Wealth of Nations* he thought he had found the solution
through taxing Ireland, India, and the other colonies to pay that debt.
This has been the pattern of western imperialism, whether the imperial power in question is Britain, Holland, Spain, France, Germany, Japan, Italy, Russia, or the United States: national debts mushrooming
largely because of the costs of imperial rivalries and wars; imperialized
territories, and also the poor at home, exploited and taxed to service
those debts, if not completely to repay them.

In his study of international debt, economic instability, and "U.S.
imperial decline," Arthur MacEwan declares:

> A massive expansion of international banking activity in the 1970s, tak-
> ing place out of the public eye, laid the foundation for the [global] debt
> buildup. Then, at the beginning of the 1980s—in the summer of 1982,
> to be precise [when Mexico defaulted on its enormous debt]—the third
> world debt crisis became a public event. By the end of the 1980s, while
> third world debt difficulties were alive as ever, the huge growth of the
> U.S. foreign debt had also come into the spotlight. (14)

"Alive as ever?" MacEwan's phrasing implies an alternative narrative whereby "the third world debt crisis" is not new but arose much earlier than the 1980s. Indeed, perhaps "debt" or "debt crisis" is the very condition of modernity, or of national identity, or just of identity, as when Žižek declares that "the Lacanian subject is . . . identical to a lack" (*Sublime Object* 122), or when Gilles Deleuze and Félix Guattari declare that "debt is the unit of alliance, and alliance is representation itself" (*Anti-Oedipus* 185).[14] "Alive as ever" might further mean that the "third world" has "ever" existed as colonies to something called the "first world" and that colonies are so impoverished from the beginning that their colonized, debtor status is self-explanatory: to be a colony is to be perpetually in hock to some colonizing power or other. This is not MacEwan's meaning, but since Adam Smith the belief that there is something inevitable about the debtor/creditor relationship between colonies and colonizers has been powerful.

MacEwan contends that the effects of national and international indebtedness are not calculable. On the contrary, he says, "There is no way to determine in advance when a debt burden will become unsustainable." But that there is a limit to how much debt a nation or the world can sustain neither MacEwan nor most commentators, present or past, question. Partly because this limit is simultaneously believed in and indeterminable, it is an economic equivalent of what Lyotard, Jameson, and others identify as "the postmodern sublime." In *The Condition of Postmodernity*, David Harvey writes: "Awash in liquidity, and perturbed by an indebtedness that has spiraled out of control since 1973, the world's financial system has . . . eluded any collective control on the part of even the most powerful advanced capitalist states. . . . The debt of third world countries [has] likewise mushroomed out of control" (163). One result of the mushrooming of global debt has been a weakening of "the nation-state . . . as an autonomous power" (194) — MacEwan's "U.S. imperial decline," for instance, but also Tom Nairn's "break-up of Britain." Nor is there anything to put in its place except the vertiginous financial networks and processes that are the primary superstructural effects of the invisible economic infrastructure of ever

14. Deleuze and Guattari reject Lacan's identification of desire—and hence, of the subject—with lack or need. Desire is instead the continual production of the world by "desiring machines" of all sorts. But they nevertheless make "debt" the primum mobile of primitive "exchangist" societies, and trace the history of social formations through "the regime of debts" until they arrive at capitalism and the universalization of money: "In a word, money—the circulation of money—*is the means for rendering the debt infinite*" (*Anti-Oedipus* 197), of course with the official blessing of the state.

accelerating debt. And the debt itself is in some sense nonpresent or even nonexistent because it is a matter of, as it were, *negative* faith.

That this now global situation has sublime, quasi-theological, or at least mystified and mystifying, qualities follows. Evident in W. P. Hogan and Ivor Pearce's title, *The Incredible Eurodollar: Or Why the World's Money System is Collapsing*, are both the negativity and the sublime incomprehensibility of today's "market in international debt": "We do not know what will be the manner of its collapse; or whether indeed it will truly 'collapse', or simply wither away" (2). About all that seems certain, to Hogan and Pearce as to many other analysts, is that, at least for the short run, "insolvency is booming" (Henwood 360). According to Harvey, "The structure of this global financial system is now so complicated that it surpasses most people's understanding." Banking, stock broking, insurance, mortgages, consumer credit, and other financial services have grown "increasingly porous at the same time as new markets in commodity, stock, currency, or debt futures have sprung up, discounting time future into time present in baffling ways" (161). It is not much more disconcerting to learn that, as Kurtzman notes, a major category of trade on the world's financial markets now consists of "derivative products"—not any actually existing products or commodities at all but merely possible, fictive ones, "a concept out of *Alice in Wonderland*" (19).

As a form of secular faith, credit from the outset has stood in an ironic relationship to weakening or waning religions and has adumbrated the emergence of postmodern negative sublimity. Thus Lyotard arrives at the "sublime" concept of the "Great Zero," "that is to say, of the negative, in the economy of desire . . . it is . . . capital, carried even into the sphere of passions . . . and yet again . . . it is piety that comes to take its course, the pulsional and passionate *dispositif* of religiosity, inasmuch as this is identified as the *force of lack*, capitalist religiosity, which is that of money engendering itself, *causa sui*" (*Libidinal Economy* 5). Money only "engenders itself" on the basis of credit, but this is apparently not an infinite self-engendering. As in MacEwan's account of national and international debt, the process of money's self-creation through credit appears to have limits, although the extent and type of these limits is unclear even to economists (including "libidinal" ones), who seem to disagree on this as on almost all other issues except that money matters. As to what has been produced by the Great Zero (or "capitalist religiosity," including commodity fetishism), Lyotard has many answers. It has paradoxically been enormously productive and disruptive, but certainly it has been imperialistic in its relentless pursuit of profits, territory, power, and exotic theatricality: "Hence voyages, ethnology, psychiatry, pediatrics, pedagogy, the love of the excluded: enter, beautiful Negresses, charming Indians, enigmatic Orientals, dreamers, children. . . . All this is theatre; it is the white innocence of the West in expansion, base cannibalistic imperialism" (*Libidinal Economy* 14).

Lyotard constructs his "libidinal economics" using a rhetoric of lack, which is simultaneously a rhetoric of consumerist desire, commodity fetishism, and "cannibalistic imperialism." But the positivist rhetoric of the "science" of economics has from the beginning also been constructed partly in the negative language of lack, as signified by the concepts of debt and credit. At least one distinction between "national debt" and "public credit," moreover, is both obvious and crucial: the former phrase refers to a major aspect of the financial insolvencies of all modern nation-states, whose founding moments are identical to the funding of their debts. The latter phrase, when it is not simply used as a synonym for national debt, refers to the faith a society or "public" has in itself to prosper or in the future—presumably eternal—power and glory of a given nation-state. In other words, public credit amounts to "capitalist religiosity" again, whose leading tenet is that financial investment in the public sector, including taxes to pay the interest on the national debt, will be secure and profitable. Public credit in this sense is an ideological, economic corollary of nationalism, patriotism, public opinion, and kindred terms. Public credit is not a concept that stands alone; it is relational, comparative, and thoroughly, reciprocally interwoven in other social and ideological processes such as imperialism, capitalist development or modernization, and the postmodern mushrooming of the global debt crisis.

MacEwan's metaphors for the global debt crisis offer a variation on the postmodern sublime; his otherwise rational argument also expresses the Lacanian production of "delusional metaphor"[15] in a social register:

15. Writing about the causes of psychotic behavior, Lacan declares: "It is the lack of the Name-of-the-Father in that place which, by the hole that it opens up in the signified, sets off the cascade of reshapings of the signifier from which the increasing disaster of the imaginary proceeds, to the point at which . . . signifier and signified are stabilized in the delusional metaphor" (Lacan 217). This production of "the delusional metaphor," fetishistically substituting fullness or presence for that which is eternally lacking, is precisely the mechanism of what Žižek calls "the sublime object of ideology." For "postmodern sublimity," besides Žižek's *Sublime Object*, see Lyotard, *Postmodern Condition* 77–82; Connor 201–223.

> The debt process is a bit like building a tower with a set of children's blocks. We cannot tell ahead of time how high we can go, how many blocks we can pile on top of each other, but we do know that there is a limit. If we keep going higher and higher, at some point the whole structure will come tumbling down. There are, of course, ways to extend the limit. We can widen the base of the tower, for example, or construct some support structures. There comes a point, however, where we are devoting all our efforts and resources to shoring up the tower. (31)

Certainly towers in the form of skyscrapers have been a major modernist architectural fetish; certainly, too, what goes up must come down, even the pyramids. But can "we" really "know that there is a limit" when "we" cannot tell what that limit is, and especially when the skyscraper (or perhaps, the phallocentric, many-storied erection) of modern society is so patently mythical and therefore fetishistic? So much a matter of blind faith (one synonym for public credit)? Like all fetishes, what MacEwan's skyscraper of children's building blocks metaphorically represents is invisible, quite literally insubstantial and nonpresent if not exactly nonexistent—a towering, imaginary debt with nonetheless real effects—Judt's "significant material consequences" again. As MacEwan's metaphor suggests, the national debt is the national phallus minus its clothes. Also, the higher the skyscraper of debt towers, perhaps the more mythical—certainly the more sublime—it grows, while the more inclined, perhaps, its worshiping, deluded public becomes to believe in the inevitability and eternality of its positive effects of national stability, progress, and prosperity and to believe in themselves as history's chosen people. But MacEwan argues instead that there is some indeterminate threshold beyond which blind faith or delusional metaphor turns into its opposite—into skepticism, anxiety, panic, terror, catastrophe (see Kindleberger, *Manias*).[16]

16. Maybe all economists would agree that today's general, global financial situation is "baffling." But so is the direct equation of national and international debt with social disorder and the poverty of the masses at home (putting to one side the obvious poverty of the "third world" masses). In *The Debt and the Deficit*, Robert Heilbroner and Peter Bernstein argue that the U.S. national debt is not a problem: it is not too big, given U.S. resources and productivity, and "the burden of the debt will not impoverish our grandchildren" (132). In contrast to Heilbroner and Bernstein's rosy picture, Lawrence Malkin contends that, if the debt continues to mushroom, the bankruptcy of "the American empire" is inevitable: America has already "crashed into a black hole" of debt, although "we can [still] crawl out of it" (see his subtitle). Malkin is certainly closer to economic orthodoxy, back through Adam Smith to the early eighteenth-century opponents of national indebtedness and sometimes of empire building, than are Heilbroner and Bernstein.

4

THOUGH IT is not a fact that many British historians have rushed to acknowledge, the "Enlightenment came first to England," to borrow Arthur Wilson's title (21). Perry Anderson argues that the bourgeois revolution against feudalism was in the British case premature (15–47). Occurring in the 1640s, with religion more at issue than class conflict, the earliness of that revolution, according to Anderson, left Britain without a strong tradition of radical philosophy. It also meant that British mercantilism or early capitalism would be less a bourgeois domain than one of a shifting alliance of aristocracy and a commercial (preindustrial) middle class—an alliance still evident in the financial institutions identified with "the City" of London (the Bank of England, the Treasury, the stock market). The pragmatic successes of Baconian empiricism and Newtonian mechanics in many areas, including military, navigational, and industrial applications, coupled with fear of revolutionary ideas going back to the Civil War, helped produce the stereotype of Britain as the land of steady practice and common sense rather than of rationalism and radical theory (supposedly France's role)—a stereotype that still holds sway.

An alternative way of explaining the stereotype would be to say that, at least from 1688 foward, the British upper classes, including both bourgeoisie and aristocracy, were such successful entrepreneurs and empire builders that they did not need to theorize about what they were doing—though of course they did theorize. One strain of their theorizing, from Locke down to John Stuart Mill and beyond, adapts empiricist epistemology to the analysis and advocacy of political liberalism. Another adapts that same epistemology to what has been called the earliest of the social sciences, economics. First venturers into Enlightenment, the British have never been bereft of political and economic theory, even when that theory—as in the case, for instance, of Edmund Burke's *Reflections on the Revolution in France*—can be described as anti-Enlightenment.

As an aspect of the Enlightenment, Jürgen Habermas claims, a protodemocratic "public sphere that functioned in the political realm arose first in Great Britain at the turn of the eighteenth century" (*Structural Transformation* 57). Here is another way in which early modern Britain was a vanguard nation-state. Habermas understates the extent of censorship and violence in eighteenth-century Britain; nevertheless, a "bourgeois public sphere," expressing itself through relatively uncensored journalism and "public opinion," did emerge there before it did in France or other nation-states (see also Calhoun 14; Chartier 20–37; Gunn). Habermas also downplays, though he clearly understands, the contradiction between economic self-interest and enlightened public reason that attended the birth of the public sphere in Britain. According to Habermas's Frankfurt Institute predecessors Theodor Adorno and Max Horkheimer in *Dialectic of Enlightenment*, mainly economic factors caused the Enlightenment's metamorphosis into instrumental reason, bureaucratic rationalization, imperialism, racism, mass culture, fascism, and totalitarianism. But in the early 1700s, Habermas claims, those economic factors did not yet outweigh public or collective interest, as they would come to do in the nineteenth century.

By Habermas's account, the public sphere in early-modern Britain was—at least partially and for awhile (for some of the people some of the time)—liberal and rational in an apparently undistorted sense. Nevertheless, liberal political theory, empiricist epistemology, and early capitalist economics were from the beginning interfused, in deeply conflicting ways. Contrary to the assumption that Enlightenment culture expressed an undistorted faith in human emancipation and perfectibility through the untrammeled exercise of reason, modern economic theory from its inception defined the concept of value both materialistically and relativistically; moreover, it defined the modern individual—"economic man"—as a bundle of needs, wants, passions, and lacks. Thus, in *The Leviathan*, Hobbes treats human nature as fundamentally vicious and avaricious. The perpetual insecurity and irrationality of the human condition is especially terrible in a state of nature, a situation of *bellum omnium contra omnes* making "the life of man" "solitary, poor, nasty, brutish, and short" (100). Hobbes's state of nature is a version of the stereotypical "savage" or "primitive" human condition that has perhaps always served as the antithesis of the rational, "civilized" individual in the ideological nexus nationalism-imperialism-racism. But Hobbes's natural human seems little different from the civilized "possessive individualist" that supposedly makes for economic and political progress (Macpherson 61–70). "The value of all things contracted for, is measured [only] by the appetite of the contractors," Hobbes believed (117). But because all individuals compete for the scarce goods to satisfy their appetites, a sovereign through government and laws must regulate the competition, which would otherwise be just the dog-eat-dog state of nature. Possessive individualism—Hobbesian human nature—is fundamentally antisocial or "savage" and therefore in desperate need of the social contract. So the possessive individualist does not vanish with the progress of "rational," "civilized" institutions but instead turns out to be the very goal of liberal, "Whig history": the good bourgeois as both *homo economicus and* public-spirited citizen of the modern, European nation-state.

Possessive individualism is basic to the emergence of modern economic thinking from Hobbes and Locke through George Berkeley and David Hume and on to Adam Smith, Thomas Malthus, David Ricardo, and the other ministers of the "dismal science" (as Thomas Carlyle called economics). With the identification of economic self-interest as the driving force of human activity, early bourgeois social theorists had to explain how that self-interest could be (indeed, in normal social conditions, under the rule of supposedly just laws, *was*) "enlightened" self-interest. Thus a key theme in early economic theory in Britain was the idea that out of "private vices" (especially avarice) comes the common good, a paradox that Bernard Mandeville expressed in *The Fable of the Bees, or Private Vices, Public Benefits* (1714). Moreover, the parceling out of human nature into distinct but perpetually interacting *and* conflicting motives (Hirschman's "passions" and "interests") that in early liberal theory *mainly* make for the common good of society—when coupled with empiricism of Hume's skeptical sort—issued in a series of dissolving views of personal identity or subjectivity which foreshadows psychoanalytic and poststructuralist deconstructions of "the subject" and of rational self-possession. According to Hume, because all knowledge derives from sense impressions, and because "self or person is not any one impression, but that to which our several impressions and ideas are suppos'd to have a reference," what individuals think of as their selves or egos "are nothing but a bundle of different perceptions, which succeed each other with an inconceivable rapidity, and are in a perpetual flux and movement" (*Treatise* 299–300). Though different in several ways from twentieth-century accounts of the philosophical subject-who-knows of the Enlightenment, Hume's decentering of personal identity is not far removed *either* from postmodernist dismantlings of "the subject" *or* from eighteenth-century descriptions of economic man, driven by "speculation" and "fantasy" as much as by the clear light of social reason (Pocock, *Virtue* 69).

For the development of eighteenth-century economic ideas, credit was a major catalyst, perhaps the key idea, in part because of its evident connections to equally major epistemological considerations (Rist 32–33). From Hobbes onward, economic theories, concepts, and metaphors are interwoven with, and in some sense inseparable from, philosophical discourse. In Locke's case, for example, questions of government and of the nature of money were not distinct from, but were instead intimately connected to, the deepest metaphysical and epistemological questions. "For Locke," says Constantine Caffentzis, "civil government has its origin and end in the regulation of money" (21). The problems posed by counterfeiting and coin clipping, Locke believed, amounted to "semantic crimes" against both truth and the state (Caffentzis 35). Lockean monetary theory thus suggests much more than merely a parallel or analogy between economic and philosophical discourses, and the same is true of later philosopher-economists such as Hume and Berkeley. According to Jerome Christensen, the eighteenth-century "man-of-letters" like Hume "invented an economics emancipated from history and politics and assigned himself the position of exemplary economic man," motivated by civilized or enlightened self-interest, "whose own history was a career designed to correspond in all its refinements with the economic mechanism" (12).

Discourse about public credit is one aspect, an especially symptomatic one, of the emergence of modern economic "science," with its central assumption of an economy operating by its own "laws," in relative isolation from the interconnected spheres of politics, culture, and morality (Polanyi 57, 71; Dumont 33–39). In precapitalist societies, the economic "is submerged in . . . social relationships"; under capitalism, this situation is reversed (Polanyi 46). Not only does the economy begin to stand apart as a self-regulating system, but economic categories and motivations begin to infiltrate and dominate all other categories and motivations, including politics and the law as well as "polite" culture and "letters" (i.e., "literature"). Another name for this gradual separating-out of the concept of the economy is its reification: economic discourse is the modern (and now postmodern) form of reified, and therefore also of fetishized, disciplinary discourse par excellence. No matter what the specific ideological orientation of a particular economist, the "science" of economics has been *the* dominant ideology associated with modernization and therefore with modernity. How far social critiques associated with postmodernity have subverted or at least exposed the empty inner workings of this economistic ideology remains to be seen.

Against religious and absolutist theories of human nature and of government, the idea of value as determined solely by economic causes—by the circulation of commodities and money—emerged as early as 1621 in *A Discourse of Trade* by Thomas Mun, one of the directors of the East India Company (Appleby 41). Two years later, in *The Circle of Commerce*, Edward Misselden claimed that money is what measures value, but money itself also circulates as a commodity and has only the value set for it by the marketplace. Value is nothing more nor less than "the plenty or scarcitie of Commodities, their use or Non-use" (Misselden 21). This thoroughly materialistic conception of value did not take root immediately and everywhere, but it gradually spread as the central thesis underlying modern economic thought. If value is determined only by the marketplace, and if money is the chief measure of value, it follows that societies and cultures are themselves superstructures resting only on the flux or "circle of commerce." What Mun and Misselden shadow forth is an early capitalist version of the Marxist base/superstructure paradigm, but with the stable-sounding metaphor of "base" itself destabilized, in perpetual motion or "circulation."

The destabilizing of questions of value through economic discourse, moreover, is exacerbated by the fact that money—modern money, at least—originates in debt and is always a statement of debt, even as it represents wealth. In *The Consequences of Modernity*, Anthony Giddens explains the relation of money both to debt and to state power in this manner:

> In its early form, money is identified with debt. "Commodity money" thus designated is a first step along the way in the transformation of barter into a money economy. A basic transition is initiated when acknowledgments of debt can be substituted for commodities as such in the settlement of transactions. This "spontaneous acknowledgment of debt" can be issued by any bank and represents "bank money." Bank money is recognition of a private debt until it becomes more widely diffused. This movement to money proper involves the intervention of the state, which acts as the guarantor of value. Only the state (which means here the modern nation-state) is able to transform private debt transactions into a standard means of payment—in other words, to bring debt and credit into balance in respect of an indefinite number of transactions. (23–24)

The modern nation-state may be the ultimate "guarantor of value," but it is also founded or funded on its own indebtedness, which makes it also dependent on the relatively unregulated ("free") economic activities of its citizens. What props it up—keeps it in power or, so to speak, in currency and circulation—is not gold and silver bullion locked up in its treasury vaults but merely public credit. Patriotism and nationalism underwrite public credit (and vice versa) but also the nation-state's own facilitation of (or noninterference with) the economy and, as well, the faith that the paper money it issues can be redeemed for the gold or silver supposedly locked in its treasury vaults. But modern paper money is not intrinsically valuable as was, supposedly, the gold or silver bullion it used to represent. Instead, modern and now postmodern money is a statement of a relationship of credit and debt, a statement of mere belief or of absence rather than of any substantial wealth or presence. This conception of money is rooted in the late seventeenth century in Britain and the rest of western Europe, when paper receipts and bills of exchange were coming into increasing circulation as convenient, safe forms of payment among the individual goldsmiths and moneylenders in the major cities and increasingly also for corporations such as the Bank of Amsterdam (founded in 1609) and the Bank of England (Vilar 213–222).

Freed from the encumbrances of religion and morality, but also from those of more general forms of public, political, and cultural rationality, the category of the economic does not merely assert the autonomy and truth of its own definitions of value (utilitarian, commercial, monetary) as so many "laws." As Habermas puts it, the economic "colonizes" all other value forms:

> In place of "false consciousness" we today have a "fragmented consciousness" that blocks enlightenment by the mechanism of reification. It is only with this that the conditions for a *colonization of the lifeworld* are met. When stripped of their ideological veils, the imperatives of autonomous subsystems [especially the economic] make their way into the lifeworld from the outside—like colonial masters coming into a tribal society— and force a process of assimilation upon it. (*Theory* 355)

On one level, commodity fetishism is consumers' worship of desirable objects; but it also involves a more far-reaching reification and fetishizing of the economic, whereby all value forms (cultural, moral, personal, etc.) come to have their price or are themselves, so to speak, taken to market. Such a process of reification, J. G. A. Pocock claims, was necessary in early-eighteenth-century British culture to stabilize what otherwise was inherently unstable (stock market "gambling," paper money, public credit, and the other phenomena associated with the "financial revolution"): "goods had to be reified, and the laws of the market discovered or invented, in order to restore reality and rationality to an otherwise purely speculative universe" that, to many of its critics, seemed quite "hysterical" and "pathological" (*Virtue* 69, 11). But it is partly this very process of the separation, reification, and gradual coming to dominance of the economic that writers such as Pope, Swift, and Berkeley expressed great anxiety about, an anxiety summed up in Bolingbroke's lament: "The power of money as the world is now constituted is real power" (quoted in Kramnick 28). That power put all values in flux, as "perceptions of individual worth came to [be] mea-

sured by the rise and fall of the stock market," notes Colin Nicholson
(10). It is the apparent consummation of that process—often represented as, for better or worse, the final triumph of late capitalism—
that now characterizes the postmodern condition.

5

MARX TRACES the evolution of capitalism from the Renaissance discovery of the Americas, "the beginning of the conquest and looting of the
East Indies," and the birth of the transatlantic slave trade. The relationship between early modern imperialism and national indebtedness
emerges as a key element in the economic history of *Capital.* The various stages of "primitive accumulation," Marx writes, occur "more or
less in chronological order," starting with Spain and Portugal and moving on through the seventeenth century to Holland, France, and finally
England, where "these different moments are systematically combined. . . . The combination embraces the colonies, the national debt,
the modern tax system, and the system of production" or mercantilist
monopoly. "These different moments depend in part on brute force,
for instance the colonial system. But they all employ the power of the
state, the concentrated and organized force of society, to hasten, as in a
hothouse, the process of transformation of the feudal mode of production into the capitalist mode. . . . Force is the midwife of every old
society which is pregnant with a new one. It is itself an economic
power" (1:915–916).

"Force," by which Marx means primarily the military and technological power that enabled England and the other European states to establish their global empires, does not itself arise unbidden or unpaid
for. "Primitive accumulation" through the exploitation of "the colonial
system" was the economic foundation of modern capitalism and industrialism. But Marx suggests that, underlying "primitive accumulation,"
there was another economic foundation, shadowy, negative, perhaps
thoroughly phantasmal, which he alternatively names "national debt"
and "public credit":

> The system of public credit, i.e. of national debts, the origins of which
> are to be found in Genoa and Venice as early as the Middle Ages, took
> possession of Europe as a whole during the period of manufacture. The
> colonial system, with its maritime trade and its commercial wars, served
> as a forcing-house for the credit system. . . . The national debt, i.e. the
> alienation [*Veräusserung*] of the state—whether that state is despotic, con-

stitutional or republican—marked the capitalistic era with its stamp. (*Capital* 1:919)

But was "the colonial system" the "forcing-house" for public credit, or vice versa? This issue is probably undecidable; they seem to have operated symbiotically, inseparably. Presumably *primitive* accumulation comes first, but Marx also writes, "The public debt becomes one of the most powerful levers of primitive accumulation" (1:919).

As the European nation-states modernized during the Enlightenment, with their economies and empires evolving through war and conquest from mercantilism to industrial capitalism, the thoroughly modern idea of public credit emerged. Insofar as this book is a genealogy of a key historical phenomenon and its cultural effects, it concerns public credit in the British context. Here again, as Marx recognized, England was the paradigmatic European nation-state, its vanguard status in regard to both the colonial and the credit systems apparent well before its leading role in the Industrial Revolution. In *The Sinews of Power*, John Brewer corroborates much of Marx's historical analysis. The British variant of the modern "fiscal-military state, with large [standing] armies and navies, industrious administrators, high taxes and huge debts," was a product of William III's wars and "of the political crisis which racked the British state after the Glorious Revolution of 1688." The "financial revolution" of 1688–1714 "had a profound effect on the subsequent history of the British state, enabling it to arbitrate the balance of power in Europe, to acquire its first empire and, when that was lost, to build another" (250). The victory at Plassey in 1757 secured British hegemony in Bengal, the first major military step toward British domination of India. With the later victory over France in the Napoleonic Wars, the national debt soared to £839,000,000, almost four times what it had been after the American Revolution. As S. G. Checkland points out, "In 1827 interest on the debt (£29 million) accounted for over one-half of the total of the public expenditure of the United Kingdom. . . . This greatly aggravated the taxation problem" (337). Domestically the symbiotic growth of empire and national debt meant *both* growing prosperity for many *and* new forms of social marginalization and poverty for the vast majority.

The series of major wars fought by Britain against Spain, France, and its own colonists in America, starting with the War of the League of Augsburg (1689–1697) and ending with the Napoleonic Wars (1803–1815), could not have been waged without the new financial institutions grounded in public credit and the national debt. Accumulating with interest paid through taxation, and despite "sinking funds" established to reverse or retard its growth, the mushrooming national debt was a domestic and also international problem caused mainly by Britain's overseas wars and adventures from the late seventeenth century forward. Ironically the national debt and the Bank of England were at first virtually identical, because the Bank was established as a private corporation in 1694 to fund the debt. Walter Bagehot, who called the early Bank a "Whig finance company," explained its origins in these terms:

> In 1694, the credit of William III's government was so low in London that it was impossible for it to borrow any large sum; and the evil was the greater, because in consequence of the French war the financial straits of the Government were extreme. At last a scheme was hit upon [to] raise "twelve hundred thousand pounds . . . at what was then considered . . . the moderate rate of 8%." In order to induce the subscribers to advance the money promptly on terms so unfavourable to the public, the subscribers were to be incorporated by the name of . . . the Bank of England. They were so incorporated, and the £1,200,000 was obtained. (92)

This seemingly simple scheme strengthened the allegiance to the new king of at least those wealthy investors willing to bet on the nation's economic future—that is, to bankroll the treasury for their personal gain. According to Swift, "Whoever were Lenders to the Government, would by the surest principle [self-interest] be obliged to support it" (*History* 68). Anything but a defender of the new system of government finance, however, Swift would certainly have agreed with Edmund Burke's later assessment: "Public credit . . . had its origin, and was cradled . . . in bankruptcy and beggary" (*Works* 5:294).[17] In any event, by investing in "the funds" and placing their faith in the Bank of England, both aristocratic and bourgeois profiteers (the "money'd interest" deplored by Bolingbroke and his allies) laid the economic foundation of the modern British Empire.

Built by warfare and looking for ways to fund new wars, the modern nation-state is always impoverished, even as it develops and thrives in imperial prosperity and glory. The contradiction is obvious: wealth founded on the absence of wealth. Empire entails the violent, but also always insecure or unstable, appropriation of somebody else's wealth. The national debt enabled Britain to move expansively, imperi-

17. For histories of the national debt and the Bank, see Burn, Clapham, Collins, Dickson, Hargreaves. On the relation between the national debt and the Bank, see also Horsefield 137–143.

alistically, and with increasing confidence into the future, though the confidence—the general prerequisite for public credit—was at first extremely fragile. Moreover, the establishment of the debt as a permanent, central fixture of government meant that the nation was mortgaging its future prosperity for present expediency. Britain became in Pocock's words, "the paradigm of a society now living to an increasing degree by speculation and by credit: that is to say, by men's expectations of one another's capacity for future action and performance" (*Virtue* 98). Among other cultural effects, these developments produced a new sense of temporality, including the "homogeneous, empty time" that Benedict Anderson also identifies with the rise of modern nation-states (22–26). "The growth of public credit obliged capitalist society to develop as an ideology something society had never possessed before, the image of a secular and historical future," Pocock points out (*Virtue* 98). Such an image is basic both to political liberalism and to nationalism. It is also basic to the modern money form as a statement of debt systematically misrecognized or fetishized as wealth. Unhinged from a metallic standard, a unit of paper money (or "promissory" notes in various forms, most obviously bank notes) promises only its future redemption, as Brian Rotman says, through "an identical copy of itself" (5). Since the seventeenth century, paper money has evolved unevenly away from metallic standards until, in the postmodern era, it has become completely "floating and inconvertible," signifying only "future states of itself," as in computerized "futures trading" through international stock exchanges (Rotman 95). The erosion of convertibility has increased the volatility of all currencies, weakening the belief in a "secure and historical future," which means a weakening of the fundamental form of "public credit." This weakening of confidence now characterizes the "postmodern condition," including postmodern British culture.

The ideological image of the future involved in public credit and the evolution of paper money is either catalyst or necessary ingredient in all modern beliefs about endless, inevitable social progress and secular perfectability: the future fictions that the "imagined communities" of modern nation-states tell themselves. Yet how can such beliefs arise from what is so patently *negative*—Lyotard's "Great Zero"—a foundation of national indebtedness? Paper money brings with it the "scandal" of its self-creation (Rotman 49), doubling the scandal of national indebtedness. The repayment of debts is always a matter of future-tense discourse, a postponement that only underlines the fragility of any prosperity (founded on scarcity and exploitation) in the present. Belief in progress as such is belief in overcoming the deficiencies, lacks, or debts of the present, which can never be repaid (if at all) by going backward (there is no retreat to yesterday) but can only possibly be repaid by forging ahead hopefully, expansively into the future. As the histories of Britain and other capitalistic nation-states based on the new financial system of national indebtedness and public credit repeatedly show, temporal expansion into the future entails a spatial, geographic expansion through exploration, war, and conquest: in Marx's terms, the "forcing-house" of "the colonial system."

The Faustian, alchemical paradox of creating something thoroughly substantial and imposing—the modern nation-state and its ever expansive empire—out of nothing was central both to Augustan satire and to the early realist novel. Marx himself has recourse to magical and alchemical metaphors, suggesting the mysteriousness as well as the insubstantiality of society's unreal real foundations: "As with the stroke of an enchanter's wand, [public debt] endows unproductive money with the power of creation and thus turns it into capital" (*Capital* 1:919). From the perspective of Augustan satirists such as Pope and Swift, the entire fabric of modern society seemed magical or illusory, not as it does on Prospero's island in *The Tempest* (the result of salutary magic) but as witchcraft or as a conjuror's cheap trick.[18] Counterfeiting became a familiar metaphor for modernity long before André Gide's *Les faux monnayeurs*. And from the repeated metaphors of illusion and fraud in works like *The Dunciad* and *Gulliver's Travels*, it is not a huge leap to Marx's acerbic analysis of "commodity fetishism" in the first chapter of *Capital*.

So-called Augustan satire, like eighteenth-century Britain itself, flourished insecurely on a foundation of debt—a contradiction expressed through its own sense of the bankruptcy or imaginative impoverishment of modern as opposed to ancient or classical poetry. Its "Augustan" qualities are largely emulative, of the imperial power and glory of the Roman Empire and its literature, of course, and therefore always, so to speak, in unending debt to the classical past. A key feature of the neoclassical "episteme," as Foucault calls it in *The Order of Things*, is precisely its awareness of *not* being classical, of having fallen from that earlier state of innocent reasonableness that neoclassical writers identified with ancient Greece and Rome. Satire, the main literary genre of the Enlightenment and perhaps also of both modernist neo-

18. See, among many examples, Swift's poem "The Magician Sid Hamet's Rod," in which, as later in *Faust*, financial conjuring is metaphorized as phallus worship.

classicism (as in T. S. Eliot's *Wasteland*) and postmodernism (as in Caryl Churchill's *Serious Money*), expresses this sense of fallenness: "The satirist is always demonstrating a failure," as Martin Price puts it (16).[19]

At just the same time that new fiscal constructions of public credit and national debt were emerging to support the modernizing nation-state, the word fetish entered the English language via the slave trade. The coin and coinage "guinea" came a bit earlier from the same source (Horsefield 73–90).[20] In *A Voyage to Guinea, Brasil, and the West Indies,* John Atkins, a Royal Navy surgeon, offered in 1735 a sympathetic account of many strange customs, including West African fetish worship, which he defined as belief in a "charm"; a "fetish" was any physical object treated as having a degree of localized supernatural power. "The word *Fetish* is used in a double Signification among the *Negroes*: It is applied to Dress and Ornament, and to something reverenced as a Deity ·. . . both so far agree, as to be regarded as a Charm. [A fetish] can *attract Good, or divert Evil.* . . . They sometimes hide the *Fetish* in secret parts of the Woods; on urgent Occasions [they] make a sort of Appeal to [it] . . . and keep within doors the whole day, in a Moaning, or what you may call a Devotion to it" (79). The etymology of *fetish* is not African, however, but Eurocentric. It leads back through Portuguese and Portugal's imperializing and slave trading to the Latin *facere* (to make or produce) and *facticius* (manufactured, artificial). Fetishism has always meant that something rationally produced by human skill or labor is alienated from the producer and irrationally misrecognized or idolized as endowed with superhuman powers.

In the Manichaean vision of imperialist ideology, fetishism is one of

19. Thus Pope's *Dunciad* is a forerunner of Eliot's *Wasteland* with its burden of ruinous footnotes: "These fragments I have shored against my ruin." As Claude Rawson notes, *The Wasteland*'s "method of playing off a decaying present against an ambiguously noble past derives partly from Augustan techniques of ironic literary allusion; and it shares with *The Dunciad* especially its great theme of cultural disintegration" (212).

20. Pietz's essays in *Res* offer the most complete history to date of the word and idea of fetishism, but see also Simpson; Manuel; and there is an important analysis of fetishism in relation to ideology in Mitchell 151–208. Apter and Pietz, *Fetishism as Cultural Discourse,* is the most important contemporary work on the general subject of fetishism. The first "guineas" were minted during the reign of Charles II. According to C. H. V. Sutherland, the royal "supplies of bullion were to be increased by the gold of African Guinea, brought back by the African Company, and by the silver from mines in the west of England and in Wales: these three metal-sources were specified on coins marked, respectively, by an elephant (later elephant and castle), a rose and plumes. It was the Guinea gold which gave its name to the new 20 shilling piece and subsequently (owing to the rising price of gold versus silver because much scarcer) to a piece that was finally stabilized at 21s. from the time of George I until that of George IV" (174).

the markers dividing the world into "savage" or "barbarous" versus "civilized" societies. The stereotype of the crazed, cannibalistic fetishist was offered up in countless nineteenth-century travelogues, ethnographies, and adventure stories, like R. M. Ballantyne's 1861 *The Gorilla Hunters*, in which a white trader tells Peterkin: "All the nigger tribes in Africa are sunk in gross and cruel superstitions. They have more fetishes, and greegrees, and amulets, and wooden gods, and charms, than they know what to do with, and have surrounded themselves with spiritual mysteries that neither themselves nor anybody else can understand" (73). These superstitions later underwrite the scenes of human sacrifice and cannibalism, savage practices treated as poles apart from "the white innocence of the West" (in this case, from the general slaughter of gorillas by Peterkin and his friends). Irrational (i.e., "uncivilized") human beings worship fetishes and false gods; rational (i.e., "civilized" or European) human beings recognize reality for what it is and worship only genuine deities. But over against this pervasive, double stereotype, a tradition of social criticism which Marx exemplifies discovers fetishism at the heart of civilization. Of course Marx's analysis of commodity fetishism does not question the negative stereotype of the savage fetishist; it merely locates it inside bourgeois consciousness. Similarly, in *Heart of Darkness*, Conrad does not challenge the stereotype but instead challenges, through the powerful theme of Kurtz's "going native," the assumption that European civilization is superior to African savagery and fetishism.

Nearly two centuries lie between Atkins's obviously political (imperializing) use of *fetish* in English and Freud's apparently depoliticized, psychoanalytic employment of *Fetisch* in German. There seems to be no connection between these two moments, but an obvious one lies through empire and the slave trade, by way of Marx's theory of commodity fetishism. Yet Freud's theory of fetishism seems to avoid politics by focusing on the individual. As Neil Hertz has remarked, however, politics crops up in an unexpected way in Freud's 1927 essay "Fetishism." There, Freud explains that when a little boy discovers that women lack penises he assumes that they have been castrated and fears that he also is in danger. This fear produces a displacement whereby an object, often another body part, becomes the unconscious surrogate for the woman's lost penis. Freud's argument then takes this odd turn: "In later life a grown man may perhaps experience a similar panic when the cry goes up that Throne and Altar are in danger" (153).

There are two more or less literal ways of interpreting this statement. Perhaps Freud is equating fetishism with whatever specific ideology he means by "Throne and Altar": monarchism, nationalism, or imperialism. Or he may be equating fetishism with *all* ideologies and therefore with politics in general. This second interpretation matches his reiteration, in *Group Psychology and the Analysis of the Ego*, of what Gustave Le Bon and other turn-of-the-century theorists called "crowd psychology": basically, the study of the irrational behavior of the masses, as in Ortega y Gassett's *Revolt of the Masses* or, glancing backward, as in Pope's *Dunciad*:

> And now the Queen [of Dullness], to glad her sons, proclaims
> By herald Hawkers, high heroic Games.
> They summon all her Race: An endless band
> Pours forth, and leaves unpeopled half the Land.
> A motley mixture! in long wigs, in bags,
> In silks, in crapes, in Garters, and in rags.
>
> (2:17–22)

The point of most crowd psychology from Pope forward is antidemocratic and sometimes antipolitical.[21] Party politics, both Pope and Swift declared, "is the madness of many for the gain of a few." Similarly, in response to the South Sea Bubble of 1720, Sir Isaac Newton declared, "I can calculate the motions of erratic stars, but not the madness of the multitude" (quoted in Bourne 292). Of course Pope, Swift, and Newton did not use the phrase "crowd psychology," a late-nineteenth-century coinage, but the idea of the insanity of "the mob" was endemic in Renaissance and Enlightenment thinking, as it is again in postmodernist theory. For Baudrillard, for example, "the masses" are "the abyss of meaning"; they represent the refusal of "systems of representation" (*Shadow* 6): "The masses function as a gigantic black hole which inexorably inflects, bends and distorts all energy and light radiation approaching it: an implosive sphere, in which the curvature of spaces accelerates, in which all dimensions curve back on themselves and 'involve' to the point of annihilation, leaving in their stead only a sphere of potential engulfment" (9).

Debt, fear of castration, and "mob" infantilism; these seem to be the opposites of wealth, potency, and the maturity of modern, industrialized nation-states with their empires (or perhaps supercrowds) called "commonwealths." Yet the paradoxical links between debt and empire, between poverty for the masses and the "wealth of nations" for the classes, were everywhere inscribed in European and, more specifically, British culture. Even at the climax of Britain's industrial and im-

---

21. See my analysis of crowd psychology in *Bread and Circuses* 154–183.

perial prosperity, in the mid-Victorian period often characterized by the plenitude of meaning and being in its great works of realist art and fiction, these paintings, poems, and novels are plenitudes full of magical or fetishistic transformations of debt into wealth and wealth into debt—at least for private individuals. The public realm—state and empire—for a while, though perhaps only for four decades (1848 into the 1880s), seemed to have the solidity, the solvency, of an entire worldful of gold bullion and sterling silver. Throughout the history of the novel, there is an at least covert analogy between money and fiction which is expressed (and repressed) in many ways by Victorian writers. But, as John Vernon shows, this equation is ultimately one of zeroes rather than of plenitude: "The failure of money, the fact that paper money is money but at the same time the absence of money, parallels in the realistic novel the failure of mimesis, which can never be a pure, homogeneous extension of its world" (19); that is, which can never be a plenitude of meaning and being.

Like money, the novel is simultaneously a form of debt and of wealth, and a commodity in search of buyers. "Life is a perpetual loan," exclaims Balzac's Mercadet. At the same time, as Pedro Salinas declares in relation to Balzac's Human Comedy, the novel is the "imperialistic genre" (quoted in Levin 161). Certainly Victorian novels are full of feckless Micawbers and Rawdon Crawleys who escape the bill collectors at home by decamping to the colonies. Abroad, many of these ne'er-do-wells succeed, strike it rich, and a few even return to pay their debts. Yet as in Magwitch's case in Dickens's *Great Expectations*, wealth gained in the colonies often proves to be fool's gold back in Britain. In a related connection, the much-satirized figure of the Anglo-Indian nabob in eighteenth-century literature foreshadows numerous vulgar, piratical financiers in Victorian literature, who make their insubstantial fortunes through fraudulent investment schemes abroad. Augustus Melmotte with his bogus Mexican railway in Trollope's *The Way We Live Now* can stand for the type; a variant is Thackeray's Colonel Newcome, who grows rich by investing in an Indian bank and then loses his fortune when, through oriental skulduggery, the bank fails. Fortunes made through empire were often lost through empire, which is what happened to Thackeray.

Behind the shady financier with his colonialist recipes for bankruptcy looms the specter of an empire founded on debt, both financial and moral, a prosperity and progress more shadow than substance, a metaphorical dialectic of enlightenment. Just here, where substance turns into shadow, or where inflationary sentiments about the progress of civilization prove to be alchemical mumbo jumbo threatening bankruptcy, as in the magical empire building in Part 2 of *Faust,* the idea of fetishism comes into play. Mark Shell offers an interpretation of the "paper money scene" in *Faust* which emphasizes the symbolic connections between debt, empire, and fetishism—the magical phallus worship, as it seemed to Goethe, involved in a system of public credit based on paper money (99–111). In the masquerade scene, Faust as Plutus, underworld lord of wealth, "shocks decency" and the ladies in the audience by kneading a lump of gold into an oversized phallus, which he lewdly brandishes (2.1.5780–5800). (As Shell also points out, Mephistopheles treats the pact, which he persuades Faust to sign in blood, "as a credit note, brandishing it during the drama as a deed entitling him to Faust's soul" [88]).

Later, in the paper money scene, Mephistopheles tells Faust:

> My recent journey over several states
> Showed me our Emperor is in sorry straits.
> . . . [But] with us at court
> Providing him false wealth of every sort,
> The entire world was his possession.
>
> (2.4.10242–10246)

In stressing the worship of gold as a form of fetishism, and empire building as promoting the production of "false wealth," Goethe echoes the satiric tradition that treats empire as the reverse of "commonwealth"—as both fueling and fueled by national debt. Binswanger shows that *Faust* is focused on the "alchemical" search for infinite wealth and power embodied in industrial capitalism and the modern fiscal regimes of paper money and public credit. Governed only by the "Faustian urge" for the ever increasing production of "surplus value," the modern economy is in quite literal ways "a continuation of alchemy by other means. . . . Faust's enterprise has become the global plan of the economy. It is *the* modern economy" (30–33).

Binswanger points to Goethe's interest in the various technological projects of the early Industrial Revolution (e.g., to his forecasts of the Suez and Panama canals) and also to Goethe's familiarity with such major works of the emergent "science" of economics as Adam Smith's *The Wealth of Nations* and Henry Thornton's *Paper Credit* (103–115). But there were earlier examples and sources for Goethe's critique of the unbridled pursuit of wealth and "alchemical" economic and imperial expansion. These include John Law, with his 1715–1717 Mississippi scheme and his over-speculative flotation of paper money to enrich the French treasury (Rist 43–77). Law was, however, by no means the first financier to discover "the scandal of paper-created money" (Rotman 49), which is also the scandal of the seemingly diabolic creation of wealth out of nothing: the founders of the Bank of England were Law's most important predecessors. The creation of the Bank in 1694 through the funding of the British national debt, Binswanger claims, was itself a prime example for Goethe of *successful* modern economic "alchemy" (31). Nevertheless, "Goethe's model for Faust as a creator of quick wealth" was Scotsman John Law, asserts Binswanger (30). The collapse of Law's monetary house of cards in France, moreover, was a prelude to the bursting of the South Sea Bubble in Britain in 1721. In any event, Goethe was by no means the first social critic to attack the funding systems of modern nation-states as alchemical and fetishistic. The origins of this critical tradition in British culture, focused specifically on the national debt, paper money, and public credit, go back to the Glorious Revolution of 1688. The Augustan satirists—Swift, Pope, John Gay, and others—were among the main early contributors to the demystification of modern economic forces as forms and results of practices close to counterfeiting and necromancy. Defending the new concept of public credit, Defoe called it "the best Philosopher's Stone in the World" (*Review* 6[31]: 14 June 1709, 122). That the word *fetish* entered the English language at the same time is not coincidental but dialectical.

2

The Assets of Lilliput
(1694–1763)

Ye *Britons*, who the Fruit of Commerce find,
How is your Isle a Debtor to the Wind,
Which thither wafts *Arabia's* fragrant Spoils,
Gemms, Pearls and Spices from the *Indian* Isles,
From *Persia* Silks, Wines from *Iberia's* Shore,
Peruvian Drugs, and *Guinea's* Golden Oar?
Delights and Wealth to fair *Augusta* flow
From ev'ry Region whence the Winds can blow.
—Sir Richard Blackmore, *Creation*

Barbarous nations cannot obtain loans.
—Ellis T. Powell, *The Evolution of the Money Market*

1

FOR MANY eighteenth-century British writers, the modern age was inherently counterfeit; it was inferior to, because in debt to, the past; and it was objectively, financially in debt as well, having through false public credit—itself a form of financial mumbo jumbo or mystification—mortgaged its future prosperity for the sake of mere present expediency. Augustan satirists deal obsessively with the financial revolution, involving the national debt, the nascent stock market, and public credit, often while referring to their own satires as commodified, prostituted, or bastardized literary works analogous to counterfeit money. As Isaac Kramnick points out in his study of Bolingbroke and his circle of Tory intellectuals (which included Pope, Swift, Dr. Arbuthnot, and John Gay), "The financial revolution of 1690–1740 was . . . the most meaningful social experience in [their] lives . . . it informs all their writings on politics and society, and it feeds their gloom, their satire, and their indignation. They saw an aristocratic social and political or-

48

der being undermined by money and new financial institutions and they didn't like it" (4). Yet they both unwillingly and willingly participated in aspects of the financial revolution. Thus, despite their frequent attacks on "the money'd interest," Swift, Pope, and Gay behaved like moneyed men; they invested and lost money in the South Sea Company (Nicholson 63–71), and they were close to Edward Harley, earl of Oxford, whose "transcendant Genius for publick Affairs," as Swift described it, had led to the creation of the South Sea Company in the first place (*Examiner* 44: 7 June 1711, 170).

It is not just incidentally, trivially in *The Drapier's Letters* and in his poems "The Bubble," "The Run upon the Bankers," and "The Bank Thrown Down" that Swift refers to national fiscal dilemmas and debacles. Dealing with William Wood's copper coinage scheme, which Swift believed would turn Ireland into a gigantic poorhouse, *The Drapier's Letters* emphasize that the Protean forms money takes—under post-1688 conditions, at least—are crucial to modern social and cultural experience. Wood's inflationary halfpennies are just an extreme instance of the fraudulence of modern money in general, which is an expression simultaneously of *both* debt *and* wealth, or of a prosperity founded precariously—both improbably and imperialistically—on debt. Swift understood post-1688 money as corrosive of all values and as the parasitic cause of the "disease" of modernity which affected everything and everyone, even himself (Montag 154). Throughout his poetry, Swift employs a satiric rhetoric that persistently undermines its own hypothetical poetic or cultural value by insinuating that the words on the page are equivalent to pieces of money perhaps as worthless as Wood's halfpennies would have been: counterfeit coinages or commodities traded for supposedly real (i.e., valuable) coins, or debts to an authentic cultural past that the fraudulent present can never repay.

A cultural Gresham's law meant that bastard forms had everywhere routed genuine, ancient ones. For the ancients, Swift believed, poetry transcended its social conditions, but not for the fallen moderns like himself. Thus "On Poetry: A Rapsody" stresses that poetry and empire are not separate endeavors but interdependent; in an age of universal "folly," empire will decline and fall and true poetry with it:

> Not *Empire* to the Rising-Sun,
> By Valour, Conduct, Fortune won;
> Nor highest *Wisdom* in Debates
> For framing Laws to govern States;
> Nor Skill in Sciences profound,
> So large to grasp the Circle round;

> Such heavenly Influence require,
> As how to strike the *Muse's Lyre*.

(ll. 25–32)

All of these activities, from empire building to poetry writing, require a "heavenly Influence," which under modern conditions is either hard to obtain or unobtainable. Further, by speaking of the "Dunce" poet's losing "your Credit all at once"; by mentioning "A *Statesman*, or a South-Sea *Jobber*" in the same breath with "A publick, or a private Robber"; and also by likening the printing and dissemination of poems to the minting and dissemination of the least valuable sort of money (farthings), Swift identifies modern poetry with public credit:

> Your Poem in its modish Dress,
> Correctly fitted for the Press,
> Convey by Penny-Post to *Lintot*,
> But let no Friend alive look into't.
> If *Lintot* thinks 'twill quit the Cost,
> You need not fear your Labour lost;
> And, how agreeably surpriz'd
> Are you to see it advertiz'd!
> The Hawker shews you one in Print,
> As fresh as Farthings from the Mint:
> The Product of your Toil and Sweating;
> A Bastard of your own begetting.

(ll. 105–116)

Analogously, in *The Dunciad*, according to Colin Nicholson, "Pope's Queen of Dulness embodies public credit as cultural agency" (10).

It would be a mistake to assume (as many historians and literary scholars have) that Swift, Pope, and other Augustan satirists merely damn the "dunces" of their age for producing "bastard" poetry while they themselves go blithely about their task of producing the legitimate article. Swift and Pope are condemning their entire age, and therefore themselves, for having lost touch both with "heavenly Influence" and with the "ancient" or classical principles that allowed for the production of genuine poetry, and therefore for a true not counterfeit coinage of words. A similar self-implication occurs in Gay's *Beggar's Opera*, with its condemnation of the age as generalized thievery (Nicholson 123–138). To put this point differently, there is no clearly genuine poetry that Swift is offering—or that Pope in *The Dunciad* or elsewhere offers (except in translations of Homer and other classical authors)—in counterpoise to the "trash" that Lintot, Curll, and other contemporary Grub Street booksellers were publishing or that the Grub Street hacks were spawning for money. "On Poetry: A Rapsody," *The Dunciad*, and *The Beggar's Opera* are all swept up in the very modern conditions, including the national debt, the stock market, and the commodification of literature, which, their authors believe, make genuine poetry an impossibility; and these conditions also make genuine wealth and genuine statesmanship impossible.

Britain may have entered an age of relative economic and political stability after 1688, but "the rage of party" continued down to 1725 and beyond (compare Plumb 173), and "relative" is the word to stress, much as Lemuel Gulliver declares that "undoubtedly Philosophers are right when they tell us, that nothing is great or little otherwise than by Comparison" (*Gulliver's Travels* 66–67). Labels such as "the age of order" and "the age of reason" are misleading derivatives from Macaulay's brand of Whig history, which celebrated Britain's supposedly smooth sailing into modern constitutional reasonableness and economic prosperity after the so-called Glorious Revolution of 1688. Yes, the period from 1688 through about 1750 seemed to many contemporary and later observers a great improvement over the turbulence of the Civil War period (though of course Macaulay and other Whig historians have been even more anxious to draw a contrast between 1688 and the French Revolution of 1789, a contrast Burke also stressed in his *Reflections on the Revolution in France*). But no, it was not a period of orderly, linear progress and sweet reasonableness; it was instead one of highly risky capitalist accumulation and development, of almost continuous warfare especially against France, and of empire building in various parts of the world, including the national-imperial building of "Great Britain" (see Brewer; Colley; Stone).

The formalist, academic scholars who once dominated eighteenth-century literary studies "came to a field already constrained," as Felicity Nussbaum and Laura Brown point out, "by . . . a heritage from the Whig historians . . . which viewed the eighteenth century as the tranquil haven of political stability in modern English history" (5). Translated from political to literary history, Whiggism gave rise to a long-standing orthodoxy that the neoclassical or Augustan age was preeminently one of moderate, progressive conservativism—the nonviolent fruition of British liberty that "broadens down / From precedent to precedent," in contrast to the revolutionary violence of France and the American colonies.[1] In *The Augustan World*, to take just one

1. In "You Ask Me, Why, Though Ill at Ease," Tennyson describes Britain as the land "that sober-suited Freedom chose. . . . A Land of settled government, / A land of just and old renown, / Where Freedom slowly broadens down / From precedent to precedent"

influential example, A. R. Humphreys contended that eighteenth-century British literature "reflected a society fairly stable in structure and expectations": "Literature, like society, was a more orderly spectacle than at any other time" (47). Heroic couplets perhaps offer an "orderly spectacle," but to project that orderliness onto Augustan society, Humphreys had to ignore much contrary evidence: "Even Swift's destructiveness is, with a few exceptions, the outcome of a wish to disentangle from bigotry and hypocrisy a healthily-conservative state of society" (49). This proposition and others like it are both tautological (Swift the conservative churchman and Tory wished ardently for "a healthily-conservative state of society") and, in Edward Said's phrase, also a version of the "housebreaking . . . of the tiger of English literature" (*World* 54), because nowhere in actuality did Swift see "a healthily-conservative state of society" to conserve.[2]

For Humphreys, political and economic events that caused writers like Swift, Pope, and Johnson much consternation form merely "the daily small talk of political zeal." Humphreys lists "the National Debt, Bubbles, the 'landed' or 'moneyed' interests, the increase or decrease of royal prerogative, the decadence or advance of the times, the dangers or benefits of luxury, the patriotic duty of urging wars with France and Spain if none were being waged, and of deploring them if they were" as topics of this "small talk of political zeal" (112). But far from trivial pursuits to Swift, Pope, Johnson, and many others, these topics are the main themes of their writings. And far from seeming like a model of orderly, rational civilization, their own society, despite or rather because of growing "luxurious," seemed thoroughly corrupt, deranged, and endangered from all sides, but especially from the internal dissensions of "party" and of such recent economic phenomena as the national debt, stock jobbing, and public credit. Here is Swift, writing

---

(ll. 6–12). The title of George Saintsbury's 1916 book expresses a depoliticized version of this standard, patriotic view: *The Peace of the Augustans: A Survey of Eighteenth Century Literature as a Place of Rest and Refreshment.* The title reflects a literary scholar's wishful fantasy, the Augustan period reduced to the peaceful dimensions of Saintsbury's library (see Rogers 1–3).

2. "The productive force of Swift's energy as a writer need not be portrayed as emanating from a vision we create of him as an Anglican divine whose life can be described as a [coherent] sequence of events over a period of time. On the contrary, we do him a greater service if we accept the discontinuities he experienced in the way he experienced them: as either actual or imminent losses of tradition, heritage, position, history, losses located at the center of his disjointed verbal production" (Said, *World* 65). In describing Swift's often violent reactions to "all the contradictions of [his] poisoned age," Warren Montag argues along lines similar to Said's (Montag 1–41).

about the wars and "corruption" caused by the "pernicious" system of Whig finance—the national debt and its corollaries:

> By this means the Wealth of the Nation, that used to be reckoned by the Value of Land, is now computed by the Rise and Fall of Stocks: And although the Foundation of Credit be still the same, and upon a Bottom that can never be shaken; and although all Interest be duly paid by the Publick, yet through the Contrivance and Cunning of *Stock-Jobbers*, there hath been brought in such a Complication of Knavery and Couzenage, such a Mystery of Iniquity, and such an unintelligible *Jargon* of Terms to involve it in, as were never known in any other Age or Country of the World. (*Examiner* 13: 2 November 1710, 7)

This passage represents Swift at his least satiric, Swift the (almost) uni-ronic journalist. It also approximates later diagnoses of capitalist mysti-fication and ideology ("such a Mystery of Iniquity"), including Marx's of commodity fetishism.

One has only to acknowledge with David Nokes that "the literature of the entire century from the Restoration of Charles II to the acces-sion of George III, is dominated by satire" (1) to recognize how mis-leading Whig historical accounts of that period are. Satire may be an inherently conservative genre, and much neoclassical literature is obvi-ously conservative in a variety of ways. But what were the satirists at-tempting to conserve, and what were they attacking? The Whiggish approach has tended to attribute the satiric bitterness of Pope and Swift (for instance) to two sorts of personal circumstance. One can be summed up as personal spleen related to Pope's physical deformity and Swift's "excremental vision." The other involves the claim that, as Tories, Pope and Swift felt disempowered, marginalized by "the Whig ascendancy" after Queen Anne's death in 1714. Moreover, runs this argument, Pope was further disempowered as a Roman Catholic, and Swift was further disempowered as an Irishman. So Whiggish literary criticism clears the way for the triumph of Augustan reason, order, and social progress (or modernization) by disempowering the period's most canonical writers, Pope and Swift. This is not to say that Pope and Swift were not neurotic, or in other words that they did not have per-sonal reasons for bitterness and cynicism. It *is* to say that the Whiggish view of the Augustan era as one of stability, prosperity, and reason, and also of steadily progressing Enlightenment, liberalism, and capitalism, is thoroughly problematic on the evidence of the most obvious features of the canonical literary texts of that era. And as both Isaac Kramnick and Colin Nicholson have demonstrated in detail, nothing was more upsetting to the leading Tory intellectuals of the age than the financial revolution that was empowering a new set of moneyed men, while threatening to disempower the landed interest.

2

FROM THE outset, the British national debt was controversial. In "The True Picture of a Modern Whig," written in 1701, Charles Davenant condemned it as "theft and rapine" (175), whereby "every little scoundrel got an estate" (154) while the nation veered toward bankruptcy (for more on Davenant, see Pocock, *Machiavellian Moment* 437–446). Annuities, mortgages, insurance, and stocks were emerging as new forms of property associated with the commercial middle class—or at least, "the money'd interest"—and challenging the traditional solidity and conservatism of landed property. In this early-modern version of class conflict, public credit also emerged as an important concept in political and economic discourse and as a main target of Augustan satire. Defoe defended public credit and the national debt from a Whiggish perspective, but the Tory *Moderator* headlined its twenty-eighth issue (21–25 August 1710) "The False Fits of Whiggish Credit Discovered; or, an Account of the Turns and Returns, Comings and Goings, Visits and Departings of that Subtle Pharisaical Lady Call'd Whiggish Phanatical Credit." Enter a misogynist's nightmarish Medusa, a "phallic mother," generativity gone haywire (see Ian; Gallagher, "Response").

The *Moderator* was partly mocking Defoe's own fanciful personification of "Lady Credit" in several issues of his *Review*. Defoe introduced Lady Credit, "the daughter of Prudence," in the 1 August 1710 *Review* (7[55]) as an allegorical tale to illustrate the workings of the new financial system. For the most part, Lady Credit is a sensible, well-behaved young woman, whom Defoe describes as "the whole Nation's Mistress" (*Review* 7[58]: 8 August 1710, 225). In normal circumstances, wherever you encountered her,

> she was always Smiling and Pleased, Gay and in Humour—Her walk was daily between the Bank and the Exchequer, and between the Exchange and the Treasury; she went always Unveil'd, dress'd like a Bride; innumerable were her Attendants, and a general Joy shew'd itself upon the Faces of all People, when they saw her; for the whole World was pleas'd with her Company:—She was a Chearing to our Spirits under the Weight of a Terrible War, a Support to our Hopes, under general interruptions of Commerce: Her Musick Charm'd us. (*Review* 7[58]: 8 August 1710, 226).

But Queen Anne's threatened change of Treasury ministers has also given Defoe's Lady Credit a bad case of "the Staggers." So she turns just as "vaporish" and inconstant as the *Moderator* declares her to be, coming down with a hysterical "distemper" that Defoe calls "the Falling-Sickness" (*Review* 7[58]: 8 August 1710, 226).

Even in its most positive incarnations, the gendering of "publick Credit" as female implies its frailty and irrationality. Pocock traces female personifications of public credit back to Machiavelli's accounts of *fortuna, fama,* and *occasione* and (perhaps less confidently) to Giovanni Cavalcanti's concept of the political function of *fantasia* (*Machiavellian Moment* 453; see also Pitkin). This last concept especially suggests some of the resonance between the economic idea of public credit on the one hand and, on the other, psychologistic and aesthetic categories such as "enthusiasm" and "sublimity," both precursors of Romantic "imagination." Moreover, as Paula Backscheider demonstrates, "Lady Credit" and similar female personifications are linked to the popular, patriotic imagery of Britannia: Defoe recast the familiar figures of "patron goddesses" as "Credit, an economic, everyday Britannia" (Backscheider 99). These personifications may also be a source of references to the Bank of England as the "Old Lady of Threadneedle Street" (Fig. 1; and see Burn 2; Dickens and Wills).

In the *Spectator,* Addison offered a Whiggish "allegory" or dream-vision involving a slightly less misogynistic heroine than the one in the *Moderator.*[3] Addison describes entering the Bank of England and seeing the directors hard at work. That night in his sleep he revisits the Bank and sees, not its all-male directors, but "a beautiful Virgin, seated on a Throne of Gold. Her Name . . . was *Publick Credit.*" Though lovely to behold, she is strangely fitful, perhaps owing to the "vapours." Yet she is surrounded by "heaps" of gold and also by acts of Parliament "written in Golden Letters" (*Spectator* 15). Like Midas, writes Addison, "she had the same Virtue in her Touch, and . . . could convert whatever she pleas'd into that precious metal" (16). The dream turns nightmarish when the Bank is invaded by "Tyranny and Anarchy . . . Bigotry and Atheism." Together with the Jacobite Pretender and his double, an illusory "Commonwealth," these antithetical demons reduce the Virgin's golden hoard to scraps of paper and empty moneybags. But then the demons of political and religious extremism are in turn banished by the entrance of "Liberty, with Monarchy at her right hand: . . . Modera-

3. Addison's essay-allegory on the Bank and public credit has been discussed by, among others, Pocock, in *Machiavellian Moment* 455–456, and Nicholson 45–47.

FIGURE 1. Prime Minister William Pitt "ravishing" the "Old Lady of Threadneedle Street" (James Gillray, 1797)

tion leading in Religion"; and the future George I "with the Genius of Great Britain. . . . At their . . . Entrance the Lady reviv'd, the Bags swell'd to their former Bulk . . . and Heaps of Paper changed into Pyramids of Guineas: And for my own Part I was so transported with Joy, that I awaked, tho' I must confess I would fain have fallen asleep again to have closed my Vision" (17). In all of these journalistic satires and countersatires, the central mystification that serves as the ideological basis of the modern nation-state—the foundational but phantasmal moment when public credit is mobilized to create the unifying economic power of the national debt—is treated as just that: mystification. Even in Whiggish defenses of the new financial institutions that formed the economic foundation of the modern state, metaphors of the alchemical transformation of nothing into something, paper into gold, and debt into wealth prevail.

Swift apparently had in mind Defoe's and Addison's allegories and perhaps the *Moderator*'s equivalent piece when in the *Examiner* (37: 19 April 1711) he wrote, "To hear some of these worthy Reasoners talking of *Credit*; that she is so nice, so squeamish, so capricious; you would think they were describing a Lady troubled with Vapours or the Cholick, to be only removed by a *Course of Steel*, or *swallowing a Bullet.* By the narrowness of their Thoughts, one would imagine they conceived the World to be no wider than *Exchange-Alley*. It is probable *They* may have such a sickly Dame among them; and it is well if she hath no worse Diseases, considering what Hands she passes through" (134). "Exchange Alley" was the locus of the early stock market in London, haunt of one of the most despicable, depraved creatures in all of Augustan satire, the "stock jobber," as in Thomas Shadwell's 1693 play *The Volunteers, or The Stock-Jobbers.* This loathesome creature, often associated with the devil in the writings of Defoe, Swift, Pope, and many others, was supposedly largely to blame for turning Addison's golden dream of "Publick Credit" once again into a nightmare of disaster and national ruin. Fewer than twenty years after its establishment as moneylender to the nation, and only a few years after John Law's financial debacles in France (on Law's monetary schemes and theories, see Rist 43–77), the Bank of England became embroiled in the imperialist phantasmagoria of the South Sea Bubble (Dickson 90–156).

The South Sea Company had originally been established to gain a share of the highly lucrative trade in the Caribbean and along the Pacific coasts of the Americas, a trade then dominated by Spain and France. The company was also a Tory response to the initial success of the Bank of England as moneylender to the nation. Except in relation to the slave trade, however, the South Sea Company's promises of creating a fabulously rich trade proved fabulously illusory. Yet by 1720 it had acquired a capital of thirty-six million pounds, more than three times that claimed by the Bank of England in 1776, when Adam Smith published *The Wealth of Nations.* And the South Sea Company had overtaken the Bank as the institution most involved in managing the national debt. "From its foundation," Eric Hargreaves explains in his history of the British national debt, the South Sea Company "bore chiefly the character of an institution formed for the administration of the public debt, a character which provided after 1720 its sole justification" (20).

Hargreaves's sober description does not begin to convey the hysteria caused by the swelling and bursting of the South Sea Bubble. In his authoritative account of the financial revolution of the late seventeenth and early eighteenth centuries, P. G. M. Dickson declares that "the public creditors [took] up the South Sea Company's offers with a blind enthusiasm reminiscent of the Gaderene swine" (133; see also Carswell; Glyndwr Williams; Kindleberger, *Manias* 31–39). According to a Dutch observer, it was "as if all the Lunatics had escaped out of the madhouse at once" (quoted in Charles Wilson 316).

> Thus the deluded Bankrupt raves,
> Puts all upon a desp'rate Bett,
> Then plunges in the *Southern* Waves,
> Dipt over head and Ears—in Debt.

So writes Swift in "The Bubble" (ll. 21–24), one of his poems about the South Sea crisis. Where debt and lunacy crop up in eighteenth-century satire, some version of fetishistic magic is sure to crop up as well, as repeatedly in Swift's writings:

> Conceive the Works of Midnight Hags,
> Tormenting Fools behind their Backs;
> Thus Bankers o'er their Bills and Bags
> Sit squeezing Images of Wax.

> Conceive the whole Enchantment broke,
> The Witches left in open Air,
> With Pow'r no more than other Folk,
> Expos'd with all their Magic Ware.

> So Pow'rful are a Banker's Bills
> Where Creditors demand their Due;
> They break up Counter, Doors, and Tills,
> And leave his empty Chests in View.
>
> ("The Run upon the Bankers," ll. 29–40)

In retrospect the South Sea Company seems more like a pyramid scam spawning other pyramid scams than like a stable financial institution, so for good reason Charles Mackay featured it in his 1852 *Extraordinary Popular Delusions and the Madness of Crowds*, a sort of anti–public credit compendium that offers a version of Tocqueville's theme of the tyranny of the majority while pointing ahead to Ortega's *Revolt of the Masses* (in short, Mackay like Tocqueville was a forerunner of "crowd psychology," the study of the idolatrous or fetishistic masses). "Men, it has been well said, think in herds; it will be seen that they go mad in herds, while they only recover their senses slowly, and one by one," observes Mackay (xx). In regard to the South Sea Bubble, he resorts to the by-then-hackneyed metaphors of magic, witchcraft, alchemy, delirium, and epidemic. "Visions of ingots" danced before the eyes of the South Sea investors (53). Among the smaller bubbles spawned by the great one were at least eighty-six get-rich-quick schemes or scams, ranging from imperialist proposals "for settling the island of Blanco and Sal Tartagus" to Laputan promises to "extract silver from lead" and to invent "a wheel for perpetual motion" (60–63). But the prize for mystification has to go to a promised company for "an undertaking of great advantage; but nobody to know what it is," to which more than one thousand foolish investors subscribed (the undertaker absconded with their loot) (55).

3

JOHN TRENCHARD, whose *Cato's Letters* made "the keeping *England* out of foreign Broils, and paying off the publick Debts" main themes (xliii), called for lynching the "Stock Jobbers" he held responsible for "the Bubble," in language that echoes the satirists' motif of magic and alchemy.[4] "A thousand Stock-Jobbers, well trussed up, besides the diverting sight, would be a cheap Sacrifice to the Manes of Trade" (8). Trenchard saw nothing less than the decline and fall of the British Empire as the result of the bursting of the South Sea Bubble, and he declared that "the Ruin is general . . . every Man has the miserable Consolation to see his Neighbour undone." Instead of establishing the nation-state on a solid economic foundation, the financial revolution, which had led to the South Sea debacle, would be its downfall. And above all others, the stock jobbers were to blame:

> For as to that Class of Ravens, whose Wealth has cost the Nation its All, as they are manifest Enemies to God and Man, no Man can call them his Neighbours: They are Rogues of Prey, they are . . . a Conspiracy of Stock-Jobbers! A name which carries along with it such a detestable and deadly Image, that it exceeds all human Invention . . . nay, it gains visible Advantage by the worst Comparisons that you can make: Your Terror lessens, when you liken them to Crocodiles and Cannibals, who feed, for Hunger, on human Bodies. (11–12)

Like the word *fetish,* Trenchard's reference to "Crocodiles and Cannibals" locates the savage antithesis of civilization—African "terror" or, rather, the European "terror" of Africa—in its metropolitan center. Robinson Crusoe's great terror of being eaten by cannibals is perhaps no more terrible than that aroused by the home-grown, monetary cannibalism of the stock jobbers. "Terror" in Trenchard's anti–public credit rhetorical arsenal also evokes the aesthetic terror that objects of sublimity supposedly arouse. In general, the antisublime (or "bathetic") discourse of Augustan satire, including *Cato's Letters,* attacks forms of supposedly excessive emotionality like terror and enthusiasm. But it

---

4. *Cato's Letters* were coauthored by Thomas Gordon, with "occasional" assistance from Lord Molesworth; but according to Gordon, the main author was Trenchard (Kramnick 246). I have therefore referred just to Trenchard in the text.

also responds with its own terroristic rhetoric to Africa, land of cannibalism and fetishism, as well as to that "sublime object of ideology," the
national debt, at home.

In later letters, Trenchard defines what public credit could be in a
healthy condition, but he still rails against the "Stock-Jobbers" or the
"Cannibals of Credit" (20) who have, he believes, turned the entire
nation "topsy-turvy." Similarly, Bolingbroke's journal the *Craftsman* lik-
ened both stock jobbers in general and the South Sea Company directors in particular to vampires, sucking the nation's blood (Carretta 66).
Besides cannibalistic metaphors, Trenchard and Bolingbroke also refer
to alchemy—and therefore to the magical, fantastic transformation of
valueless objects or substances into gold or value—to describe the
South Sea crisis. "If we have any State Chymists, who have Art enough
to make Millions evaporate into Smoak; yet I must beg Leave to doubt
their Skill at consolidating Smoak into Gold" (Trenchard 29). At the
same time, those who pursued the bait held out by the South Sea Company and by the many smaller "bubble" companies it spawned are, according to Trenchard, nearly as despicable as the profiteering stock
jobbers, because they are victims alike of the false claims of the "jobbers" and of their own gullibility in "pursuing gilded Clouds, the Com-
position of Vapour and a little Sunshine . . . fleeting Apparitions!"
(26).

For Trenchard, the South Sea catastrophe points to a major moral
lesson, one shared by all the Augustan satirists, about the sham or
counterfeit constitution of modern society or, indeed, of society in general: "What is human Life, but a Masquerade: And what is civil Society,
but a Mock-Alliance between Hypocrisy and Credulity?" (Trenchard
24). William Hogarth makes much the same point in his pictorial satire
"The South Sea Scheme," with its devils and its double version of the
wheel of fortune (Fig. 2). The central image is a lunatic merry-go-
round turned by South Sea Company directors, with a variety of social
types for riders, pursuing crazy illusions of wealth. So, too, Pope, Swift,
and Gay stress in innumerable ways in their satires that modern society
is nothing more than "a Mock-Alliance between Hypocrisy and Credulity" or a "masquerade" (see Castle). Moreover, "credulity" is near-allied
in those satires both to madness and to the tautological idea of crediting credit, that is, of believing that debt equals wealth or that a lack of
substance is really substantial (a contradiction implicit in the frequent
metaphors of smoke, apparitions, wind, and moonshine).

For much of the eighteenth century, false opulence or "luxury" was
also the false antithesis of debt, including the national debt (see

FIGURE 2. William Hogarth's "The South Sea Scheme" (1721)

Sekora for an examination of the concept of "luxury" throughout eighteenth-century literature). Further, commodity fetishism, or as Laura
Brown describes it, "the tendency for relations between people to be
mediated by and thus to be seen as relations between things," informs
Pope's "Rape of the Lock" as well as much other Augustan literature
(13). Margaret Doody claims that Pope's poem, and indeed Augustan
literature in general, expresses an "expansiveness" based on a triumphant, world-adventuring imperialism. Though it is true that, as Doody
puts it, "at times . . . Augustan poets . . . seem like millionaires totting
up their (nearly inexhaustible) assets aloud" (28; cf. Bunn)—a wealth
derived from mercantilist exploration and empire building—a different, ironic note is evident in Brown's emphasis on commodity fetishism
in Pope's mock epic. The irony arises not just because Pope extols the
"luxurious," fashionable "things" in Belinda's world, nor because of Belinda's fascination with the commodities by and through which she is
identified. The mock-epic contrast between "Belinda's world of things"
and classical epic's emphasis on heroic deeds and state formation "enables the poem to avoid the implication that imperialism produces a
fetishism of the commodity, a moral anarchy and degradation of culture," Brown writes; "The poem can thus attack commodities and their
cultural consequences while it extolls imperialism. It can praise the

battles of imperial expansion while it condemns the consequences of capitalist accumulation" and consumption (22). With the key exception of *Gulliver's Travels*, this contradiction pervades Augustan satire, a genre that, in form as well as content, often lays claim to a patriotic, imperial prosperity and reasonableness that, it also asserts, is directly threatened by the bankrupt, commercial society it satirizes.

The theme of luxury in much Augustan literature reveals this contradiction, one that simultaneously enables praise for Britain's imperial power and prosperity and expresses anxiety about the instability of that very power and prosperity. Luxury is a false or decadent sort of wealth that threatens the downfall of the very society powerful enough to create it in the first place:

> This mournful truth is ev'ry where confess'd,
> SLOW RISES WORTH, BY POVERTY DEPRESS'D;
> But here more slow, where all are slaves to gold,
> Where looks are merchandise, and smiles are sold.
>
> (ll. 176–179)

In these lines from "London," Samuel Johnson captures the central anxiety associated with luxury, an anxiety that he, too, connects to the new forms of moneyed property that had sprung up since 1688. Johnson's language, moreover, associates prostitution with the new dominance of "commerce" or of the category of the economic, thus approximating later discourse about the commodification and reification of all social relations (cf. William Blake's "youthful Harlot's curse" in his poem "London").

"London" deals with the triumph of what Johnson, in common with Pope, Swift, and Bolingbroke, viewed as the upstart moneyed interest:

> Here let those reign, whom pensions can incite
> To vote a patriot black, a courtier white. . . .
> Let such raise palaces, and manors buy,
> Collect a tax, or farm a lottery.
>
> (ll. 51–52, 57–58)

As John Sekora contends, "The Revolution of 1688 was a Pandora's box setting loose a spirit of luxury" that, according to many Augustan writers, "the natural order could not contain. . . . Luxury was fast begetting new, false, and artificial wealth, a new and noxious economic order, and a new and sinister breed of men whose sole office was to multiply by some nefarious means the new man-made [economic] values. Taxes, credit, public funds, stock-jobbing, a standing army—all of these misbegot, from nothing, the innovators, the moneyed men who set out to break the nation to their own ways" (68). "Public credit," David Hume declared in his essay on that topic, has bred "a stupid and pampered luxury" (98). And luxury, so the eighteenth-century consensus seemed to have it, had been one of the main causes (perhaps *the* main or even sole cause) of the decline and fall of all previous empires. Insofar as "luxury" named the false modern wealth that accrued to those who, like the stock jobbers, benefited from the nation-state's new fiscal arrangements (including the funding of the national debt), its critics can also be read as attacking the increasing influence of economic, commercial forces and values in general.

Pope's ambivalent attitude toward commodification and imperial power and glory, centered in the theme of luxury in "The Rape of the Lock," is evident as well in his ambivalence toward "the use of riches" (and therefore toward the new financial institutions, exemplified by the Bank of England and the South Sea Company) that he expresses in his "Epistle to Bathurst":

> The Sense to value Riches, with the Art
> T'enjoy them, and the Virtue to impart. . . .
> To balance Fortune by a just expence,
> Join with Oeconomy, Magnificence;
> With Splendour, Charity; with Plenty, Health;
> Oh teach us, BATHURST! yet unspoil'd by wealth!
>
> (ll. 219–220, 223–226)

Moderation and reason will, the poet hopes, cure whatever ails the overly luxurious nation-state, as also the too-wealthy individual. Yet moderation and reason, for much of the poem, seem inoperative in relation to the new economic phenomena associated with

> Blest paper-credit! last and best supply!
> That lends Corruption lighter wings to fly!
> Gold imp'd by thee, can compass hardest things,
> Can pocket States, can fetch or carry Kings;
> A single leaf shall waft an Army o'er,
> Or ship off Senates to a distant Shore;
> A leaf, like Sibyl's, scatter to and fro
> Our fates and fortunes, as the winds shall blow:
> Pregnant with thousands flits the Scrap unseen,
> And silent sells a King, or buys a Queen.
>
> (ll. 69–78)

A remarkable feature of this passage is how readily it can be interpreted not just as satire but as a thoroughly astute, clear-headed rendering of some of the cultural effects of the financial revolution. Pope is not merely saying that kings, queens, and all other powerful people are greedily dependent on money, or that those who depend too much on money fall prey to corruption and luxury. He recognizes what under-lies or, rather, constitutes *modern* money (and hence, modern power), namely, "paper credit" (for a detailed reading of *The Dunciad* in terms of public credit, see Nicholson 177–201). "Imp'd" in line 71 is an espe-cially magical pun in this context: imitated, implied, diminished, aped, and demonically possessed all fit into Pope's poetic analysis. (Or, be-cause of its imitative indebtedness to the supposedly genuine literary wealth and originality of its antique models, perhaps it is a *post*poetic analysis.) Even more impressively (and impishly and impiously), Pope underscores the analogy between such "paper credit" and literature (or perhaps, literacy—reading and writing in general—and therefore civili-zation in general). His own poetry is a sort of "paper-credit," imp'd, impowered, or "empired" only by individual fantasy or genius to be, like Sibylline prophecy, scattering fates, fortunes, kings, queens, and nations to the winds (just as Britain was an island "Debtor to the Wind", accord-ing to the unironic Sir Richard Blackmore in the first epigraph).

Though thoroughly, cynically astute about the new forms of wealth that had developed since 1688, Pope's "Epistle to Bathurst" is struc-turally and thematically old fashioned, even "medieval" (Carretta 76). Not only does Pope point insistently backward to the national trauma of the South Sea Bubble, but, as Vincent Carretta shows, he uses "medi-eval allegorical types, the pattern of rising and falling on Fortune's wheel, the importance of Christian values [especially charity], the ap-pearance of devils and wizards" (79), which are similar to the allegori-cal typology in Hogarth's satire (Fig. 2). Pope's concluding story of Sir Balaam is also at least "somewhat old-fashioned" (Carretta 79). And just as the ancient, fickle goddess Fortuna seems to foreshadow the female personifications of public credit in Augustan satire, so luxury was often personified as a perversely sensual woman, Luxuria (Sekora 44). But this widely used medieval, typological and misogynistic sym-bolism, with the idea of the unpredictable (or hysterical) but inevitably turning wheel of fortune at its center, framed by an imagery of witch-craft and black magic, continued to be used well into the nineteenth century and beyond. It can be detected in Marx's account of commod-ity fetishism, for example, and also in postmodern theories of the "hy-perreal" production and uncontrollable, if not exactly unpredictable, circulation of empty, fetishistic, diabolic or at least dystopian "sim-ulacra."[5]

5. I am, of course, alluding to Jean Baudrillard, who in *Simulations* declares: "Capital in fact has never been linked by a contract to the society it dominates. It is [instead] a sorcery of the social relation" (29).

4

THE THEMES of debt, fetishism, and empire building are nowhere more elaborately explored in Augustan satire than in *Gulliver's Travels*. At the height of the British Enlightenment, Swift seems almost to be looking ahead to Adorno and Horkheimer's *Dialectic of Enlightenment*. Swift's masterpiece both typifies his "Tory anarchism" with its corollary "discovery of the intellect's madness" (Said, *World* 55) and expresses, in however comic, neurotic, and fantastic a manner, the disturbances and absurdities of its culture. Beneath the orderly, rational surfaces of that culture, violence and irrationality reign supreme. After listening to Gulliver describe European warfare and its causes, the Master Houyhnhnm decides "that instead of Reason, we [European Yahoos] were only possessed of some Quality fitted to increase our natural Vices; as the Reflection from a troubled Stream returns the Image of an ill-shapen Body, not only *larger*, but more *distorted*" (215). This is exactly the sort of "distorted" reflection, Swift implies, that Gulliver's narrative offers. Questions of who and what to believe (or credit) underlie everything Gulliver says. Is it reasonable to believe a narrative that has so many of the features of reasonableness and that insists on its own truthfulness at every turn, when it is so patently preposterous, so monstrous? The Master Houyhnhnm's observation about a Yahoo faculty that only *seems* like reason but is really its opposite applies of course to Gulliver. The reader is forced to conclude that if this is not reason, then it is madness. Gulliver's entire world (i.e., supposedly stable, sane Augustan society) belongs to the realm of the Lacanian imaginary of impossible binary oppositions; or else it teeters precariously in some liminal space between the imaginary and the symbolic order—the mirror stage of emerging nation-states, perhaps, just as they are plunging through the looking glass into modernity.

If maturity or adulthood is somehow identical to truth telling, scientific objectivity, and rationality (growing up into the symbolic), then *Gulliver's Travels* is either infantile or adolescent, because the society it both expresses and represents is, according to Swift, immature—either infantile or adolescent. How could it be otherwise when it was based on public credit or debt, which was nothing more than "a device intended to beguile the taxpayer into thinking that he is getting something for nothing" (Tilden 230)? Kant's definition of Enlightenment as the progress of society out of *Unmündigkeit* (immaturity) fits Swift's satire at least negatively. Swift's religious and political conservatism does not allow him any clearer or more optimistic sense of the possibilities of

Enlightenment than the Houyhnhnms' utopian rationality; from this counter-Enlightenment perspective, he mercilessly anatomizes the foundationless foundations of his society. Especially in Gulliver's voyage to Laputa, Swift anatomizes the Enlightenment ideology of science and reason as major discursive powers in his society. That is, he dissects the irrational uses to which appeals to science and reason were being put, or the irrationality of overreliance on appeals to science and reason. The crazy "projects" of the Laputans and Lagodans—extracting sunshine from cucumbers, for instance—mock both the overweening faith in scientific Enlightenment in the age of Newton and Boyle and the sorts of "projects" or "bubbles" spawned by the South Sea Bubble of 1720/21 (Nicholson 99–100).

Swift wrote *Gulliver's Travels* in the wake of the South Sea fiasco, and it is imbued with the terrors of that irrational but highly symptomatic episode in socioeconomic history. As to his society's being well ordered and harmonious, Swift saw precious little evidence anywhere he looked, from Exchange Alley to imperialized Ireland. Moreover, behind all the questions about what if anything in Gulliver's narrative can be credited, lurks the question of public credit, and not just in the sense of how and whether the reading public will believe what Gulliver has to say. Informing Swift's satire is the newly emergent question, associated with the Bank of England and the national debt, of what it means to have even a modicum of faith or confidence in the present and future greatness of a nation-state recently born out of a catastrophic period of religious civil war and already plunged into a series of perhaps endless imperialist wars abroad.

Gulliver describes his conversation with one of the crack-brained political "projectors" at the Academy of Lagado in these questionably patriotic terms:

> I told him, that in the Kingdom of *Tribnia* [Britain], by the natives called *Langden* [England], where I had long sojourned, the Bulk of the People consisted wholly of Discoverers, Witnesses, Informers, Accusers, Prosecutors, Evidences, Swearers; together with their several subservient and subaltern Instruments; all under the Colours, the Conduct, and pay of Ministers and their Deputies. The Plots in that Kingdom are usually the Workmanship of those Persons who desire to raise their own Characters of profound Politicians; to restore new Vigour to a crazy Administration; to stifle or divert general Discontents; to fill their Coffers with Forfeitures; and raise or sink the Opinion of publick Credit, as either shall best answer their private Advantage. (163)

The modern phrase "publick Credit" does not occur incidentally or trivially in this passage. Here, in Lilliput, Brobdingnag, and the other countries he visits, Gulliver assumes the role of spokesman and supposed defender of his homeland, though at every turn what he says has the effect of sinking the "publick Credit" of Tribnia/Britain in the estimations of his auditors and readers. Further, when he is at home in England, he claims that his honest, credit-worthy or credible accounts will inform geographic science and future voyagers and that they may be of some service in the imperial aggrandizement of Britain, though everything he says is obviously incredible and though imperial aggrandizement is one of the main targets of Swift's satire.

In relation to the themes of both public credit and imperialism, the fact that two of Gulliver's four voyages take him to the "South Sea" is significant. The *Antelope* makes it to the South Sea somewhere northwest of Van Diemen's land (Tasmania), where it is shipwrecked in a storm and where Gulliver winds up beached in Lilliput. There, as "Quinbus Flestrin" the "Man-Mountain," Gulliver becomes serviceable to the state not just as a spectacle but, on two occasions, as its new-found tower or phallus or fetish of strength, so to speak. The Lilliputians are, of course, delighted when Gulliver wades over to Blefescu and captures its fleet; they are less than happy with him when he puts out the fire in the Queen's bedchamber by urinating on it. The question arises: Is Gulliver an asset or a liability to the government of Lilliput? All the comic imagery of the huge amounts of food and drink Gulliver consumes in Lilliput points to his being a liability. Like the wars and the standing army that had become a main source of the skyrocketing British national debt, Gulliver quickly becomes a gigantic burden to the rulers of Lilliput: "the Court was under many Difficulties concerning me" (15). Gulliver continues, "They apprehended my breaking loose; that my Diet would be very expensive, and might cause a Famine. Sometimes they determined to starve me, or at least to shoot me in the Face and Hands with poisoned Arrows, which would soon dispatch me: But again they considered, that the Stench of so large a Carcase might produce a Plague in the Metropolis, and probably spread through the whole Kingdom" (15).

In Gulliver's Lilliputian experience, feast or famine, bulimia or anorexia, are the corollaries of public credit. It is not just that Gulliver poses a colossal headache the Lilliputians don't know how to deal with. The problem is couched in economic terms ("my Diet would be very expensive, and might cause a Famine") and in such a manner that the analogy becomes unmistakable: Gulliver is to the Lilliputian kingdom what the effects of the national debt are to Tribnia/Britain. This analogy is especially evident in the arguments of Flimnap (supposedly Swift's caricature of the great Whig prime minister Robert Walpole). As the Lilliputian treasurer, Flimnap is keen on getting rid of Gulliver one way or another. Thus Flimnap "represented to the Emperor the low Condition of his Treasury; that he was forced to take up Money at great Discount; that Exchequer Bills would not circulate under nine *per Cent.* below Par; that I [Gulliver] had cost his Majesty above a Million and a half of *Sprugs*, (their greatest Gold Coin, about the Bigness of a Spangle;) and upon the whole, that it would be advisable in the Emperor to take the first fair Occasion of dismissing me" (45). To Flimnap's seemingly rational economic motives for "dismissing" or "dispatching" Gulliver are quickly added motives of jealousy, when "evil Tongues" and "Court-Scandal" propagate the malicious falsehood that Flimnap's wife has "taken a violent Affection for my Person" (45) and has been seen coming privately to Gulliver's lodgings (a fantasy, of course, adding to Gulliver's phallic/fetishistic stature). Quite apart from the question of his being an economic drain on the treasury, Gulliver's alleged romantic entanglement with Mrs. Flimnap seals his fate in Lilliput: "I lost all *Credit* with [Flimnap], and found my *Interest* decline very fast with the Emperor himself" (46; my italics).

Things come to a climax, so to speak, when a well-wisher secretly delivers to Gulliver the "Articles of Impeachment against *Quinbus Flestrin*" (48), no doubt an allusion to the charges of treason that were the basis for the impeachment of lords Oxford and Bolingbroke in 1715 and that led to Bolingbroke's escape to France, much as Gulliver escapes to Blefescu. But along with the articles, this anonymous friend describes to Gulliver the various arguments that have led up to their drafting, including Flimnap's renewal of his claim that "the great Charge his Majesty was at in maintaining you" will drain the treasury and impoverish the state, unless the Emperor would "provide against this Evil, by gradually lessening your Establishment" (51). Through slow starvation, Flimnap contends, Gulliver will be so reduced to skin and bones by the time he dies that "the Stench of your Carcass" would not then be "so dangerous . . . and immediately upon your Death, five or six Thousand of his Majesty's Subjects might . . . cut your Flesh from your Bones, take it away by Cart-loads, and bury it in distant Parts to prevent Infection; leaving the Skeleton as a Monument of Admiration to Posterity" (51). This drastic scheme Gulliver understandably wants no part of, any more than he wishes to be "dispatched" more quickly by poisoned arrows; and so he makes his escape to Blefescu.

There are many senses in which Gulliver the "Man-Mountain" challenges both the Lilliputians' and our credulity (or gullibility), even as he challenges the emergent meanings of "publick Credit." He is "a Monument of Admiration" and a goad to disbelief or skepticism not just in Lilliput but in every strange new "empire" where he becomes stranded. In Brobdingnag, Gulliver is no longer a drain on the state treasury nor a miracle of phallic stature; but he becomes a source of profit for the farmer who first discovers him, displays him as a freak of nature, and then sells him to the Queen as a sort of spectacular asset or commodity, like a perverse pet or crown jewel.

Beyond Gulliver's treatment as commodified spectacle, his relation to the concept of public credit surfaces when the Brobdingnagian King questions him about conditions in England. Gulliver begins his account patriotically enough, praising the laws, the institutions, the "prudent Management of our Treasury" (104), and so forth. But when the King scrutinizes this discourse, it quickly unravels because of the issue of national debt (cf. Nicholson 106). On the management of the treasury, the King concludes that Gulliver's memory must have failed him, because in contrast to "prudent Management" Gulliver has suggested that taxes do not pay nearly all of the state's bills. What follows is clearly aimed at the question of British public credit; "at a Loss how a Kingdom could run out of its Estate like a private Person," the King asked

> who were our Creditors? and, where we found Money to pay them? He wondered to hear me talk of such chargeable and extensive Wars; that, certainly we must be a quarrelsome People, or live among very bad Neighbours; and that our Generals must needs be richer than our Kings. He asked, what Business we had out of our own Islands, unless upon the Score of Trade or Treaty, or to defend the Coasts with our Fleet. Above all, he was amazed to hear me talk of a mercenary standing Army in the midst of Peace. (106)

All the issues mentioned in this passage (wars, imperialism, "a mercenary standing army") Swift understands as major causes of the national debt.

The King continues grilling Gulliver until his patriotic account of England is in shambles, its recent history reduced to a catalog of vice and crimes chargeable to a false sense of public credit: "He was perfectly astonished with the historical Account I gave him of our Affairs during the last Century; protesting it was only an Heap of Conspiracies, Rebellions, Murders, Massacres, Revolutions, Banishments; the very worst Effects that Avarice, Faction, Hypocrisy, Perfidiousness, Cruelty,

Rage, Madness, Hatred, Envy, Lust, Malice, and Ambition could produce" (107). Needless to say, this inventory of crimes, reminiscent of Voltaire's assertion that "history is nothing more than a tableau of crimes and misfortunes" (56), undermines any and all versions of economic public credit and of patriotic faith in the soundness and sanity of modern Great Britain. Swift offers the antithesis of Whiggish versions of Britain's progress toward stable, rational, and prosperous modernity. Having discredited Gulliver's praise of Britain, the King concludes that "the Bulk of your Natives [must] be the most pernicious Race of little odious Vermin that Nature ever suffered to crawl upon the Surface of the Earth" (108)—probably about what Swift believed.

By the end of his *Travels*, if the Houyhnhnms have as much trouble believing both what Gulliver is and what he says as do the Lilliputians and Brobdingnagians, that is not because of his size or even because of his physical resemblance to the Yahoos but because Gulliver seems to have done the very thing he accuses other writers of travel narratives of doing—fantasized, exaggerated, or lied: "it hath given me a great Disgust . . . to see the Credulity of Mankind so impudently abused" by "Books of Travels" (256). In contrast, the Houyhnhnms are totally virtuous creatures who cannot lie, or *"say the Thing which is not"* (214). The reader is left with only two interpretive possibilities in relation to Gulliver's (and Swift's) discourse: to imitate the King of Brobdingnag by rejecting everything Gulliver says as untrue (perhaps the "ravings" of a madman) or to assume that what Swift is saying through Gulliver is a form of ironic or satiric truth by indirection.

Everywhere he goes, Gulliver is asked to give some account of his own country, and while these accounts arouse greater or lesser degrees of incredulity among his auditors, they are all Swift's readers have to steer by, so to speak, to avoid shipwreck in the thoroughly delusional foreign island realms Gulliver describes—which may only be the thoroughly delusional realm of his own madness. So to the Master Houyhnhnm, Gulliver gives an account of the "Glorious Revolution" of 1688 that deserves comparison with Macaulay's Whiggish one a century later: "I related to him the *Revolution* under the Prince of *Orange*, the long War with *France* entered into by the said Prince, and renewed by his Successor the present Queen; wherein the greatest Powers of *Christendom* were engaged, and which still continued: I computed at his Request, that about a Million of *Yahoos* might have been killed in the Progress of it; and perhaps a Hundred or more Cities taken, and five times as many Ships burnt or sunk" (214). Swift's fantasy offers an extraordinarily powerful criticism of the social, political, and economic status quo in Britain in the early eighteenth century, a criticism that suggests there is no such thing as a status quo except in fantasy. Swift recognizes the fantastic basis of public credit on which all modern nation-states are funded and founded: Britain is perhaps no more real or unreal than Lilliput or than Laputa, Luggnagg, or Tribnia. *Gulliver's Travels*, precisely because of Swift's lack of credit in what Whig history sees as most substantial and creditable about the Glorious Revolution of 1688, reads like an inverted, negative version of *The Tempest*: magic is insanity rather than utopian wishfulfillment and statecraft, politics, and nation building are sheer irrationality and violence.

The various "crackpot materialists" (to use John Sitter's term, 125–154) Swift satirizes in Gulliver's account of Laputa and Lagoda are representatives of science, but perhaps science (or empiricist rationalism) is not the main issue. Rather, it is materialism as national "avarice," which for Swift includes the overweening desire for wealth, power, and imperial aggrandizement (as in the Balnibarbi episode) which he sees as motivating modern warfare and also as spawning the paranoid, phallocentric delusions of grandeur expressed in nationalism and imperialism. These national delusions are subjected to comic deflations in each episode. All the island kingdoms Gulliver describes are, like "Great Britain," "empires." Yet what is the state of their "public credit"? Who will even believe in their existence back in Britain? And is not Britain just as fantastic, as delusional?

In his utilitarian mode, aiming at "PUBLICK GOOD" (256), Gulliver declares that none of the places he has visited would be worth Britain's while to conquer or claim as parts of its rapidly expanding empire. Having asserted that those irrational, incredible realms would be unprofitable as sites of future warfare and conquest, Gulliver adds that he has "another Reason which made me less forward to enlarge his Majesty's Dominion's by my discoveries":

> I had conceived a few Scruples with relation to the distributive Justice of Princes upon these Occasions. For Instance, A Crew of Pyrates are driven by a Storm they know not whither; at length a Boy discovers Land from the Top-mast; they go on Shore to rob and plunder; they see an harmless People, are entertained with Kindness, they give the Country a new Name, they take formal Possession of it for the King, they set up a rotten Plank or a Stone for a Memorial, they murder two or three Dozen of the Natives, bring away a Couple more by Force for a Sample, return home, and get their Pardon. Here commences a new Dominion acquitted with a Title by *Divine Right*. Ships are sent with the first Opportunity; the Natives driven out or destroyed, their Princes tortured to discover their

> Gold; a free Licence given to all Acts of Inhumanity and Lust; the Earth reeking with the Blood of its Inhabitants: And this execrable Crew of Butchers employed in so pious an Expedition, is a *modern Colony* sent to convert and civilize an idolatrous and barbarous People. (258)

Such is the incredible, and incredibly evil, formula for national consolidation and progress through empire building which Swift's satire unmasks. "If a Prince send Forces into a Nation," says Gulliver, "where the People are poor and ignorant, he may lawfully put half of them to Death, and make Slaves of the rest, in order to civilize and reduce them from their barbarous Way of Living" (213).

There are few more clear-sighted, powerful indictments of the avarice, violence, and horror of the collective, self-legitimating or nationalistic piracy known as imperialism than Swift's; it merits comparison with Marx's accounts of the British domination of India and with Conrad's *Heart of Darkness.* On his voyages, Gulliver sets out innocently, as a ship's surgeon and/or captain and merchant in search of wealth through presumably pacific trade. When he is not shipwrecked by storms and waylaid by infantile and infantilizing natives, who take him captive and treat him as a slave, a freak, or an object of profitable spectacle, a sort of personified colony in relation to the empires he visits (and even Lilliput is an "empire"), then he is waylaid by pirates. In his diatribe on "the distributive Justice" of colonization, Gulliver/ Swift comes close to saying that another name for global empire building *is* piracy.

When Gulliver tries to explain to the Master Houyhnhnm "the State of *England,* under Queen Anne" (218), Swift explicitly condemns the moral, social, and cultural home results of imperial aggrandizement. Gulliver first has to explain "the use of *Money,*" which is completely foreign to the rational, virtuous Houyhnhnms, who believe that "all Animals had a Title to their Share in the Productions of the Earth" (218). Then, to justify his Yahoo breed and their global behavior, Gulliver has to admit that

> in order to feed the Luxury and Intemperance of the Males, and the Vanity of the Females [of Britain], we sent away the greatest Part of our necessary Things to other Countries, from whence in Return we brought the Materials of Diseases, Folly, and Vice, to spend among ourselves. Hence it follows of Necessity, that vast Numbers of our People are compelled to seek their Livelihood by Begging, Robbing, Stealing, Cheating, Pimping, Forswearing, Flattering, Suborning, Forging, Gaming, Lying, Fawning, Hectoring, Voting, Scribling, Stargazing, Poysoning, Whoring, Canting, Libelling, Free-thinking, and the like Occupations. (219)

Such were the home results of Britain's and Europe's imperializing piracy and warfare abroad. Britain's piracy did indeed breed "luxury," but it also swelled the national debt while simultaneously consolidating and rendering precarious the "invisible phantom," as Defoe called it, of public credit. At least the crimes and vices Gulliver enumerates appeared to be real. Even supposing that imperialism or colonization abroad led to the reduction instead of the phantasmal erection of the national debt, it also led to a host of moral obligations or debts— crimes or sins—that could never be repaid.

5

Gulliver's Travels is a hyperbolic version of the themes and tropes to be found throughout Swift's political journalism and histories in the *Examiner* and elsewhere and also throughout the journalism, speeches, and correspondence of Swift's Tory ally and patron, Lord Bolingbroke. In one of his letters written from exile in France in 1739, Bolingbroke, as if offering a pessimistic version of Kant's famous definition of Enlightenment as a social progress out of childishness into the maturity of public reason, writes that Britain is "in the dotage" of its "Commonwealth":

> Are we not in the second infancy, when rattles and hobby-horses take up all our attention, and we truck for playthings our most essential interests? In a first infancy there is hope of amendment, the puerile habits wear off, and those of manhood succeed; reason grows stronger and admits of daily improvement. We observe, we reflect, we hear, we persuade ourselves, or we are persuaded by others. But in a second infancy, what hope remains? Reason grows weaker; the passions, the baser passions, the inferior sentiments of the heart, avarice, envy, self-conceit, and obstinacy grow stronger, and the habits we have then accompany us to the grave. (Rose 2:182)

Bolingbroke's toy metaphor, "rattles and hobby-horses," points toward later applications of the concept of fetishism, as in Marx and Freud; but this is a "second infancy," wherein Bolingbroke sees a senile England in rapid decline. In his final essay, *Some Reflections on the State of the Nation* (1749), the great Tory intellectual "spoke of the new financial world with a bitterness not heard since the closing of Swift's *Examiner*" in 1711, writes Isaac Kramnick (*Bolingbroke*, 36). By midcentury the national debt had mushroomed to "the dizzying sum" of eighty million pounds apparently adding to a process of national ruin traceable to the original funding of the Bank of England and of William

III's wars. "Thus," explained Bolingbroke, "the method of funding and the trade of stock jobbing began. Thus were great companies created [besides the Bank, he has in mind the Royal African, the East Indian, and the South Seas companies among others], the pretended servants, but in many respects the real masters, of every administration" (2:443). Stock jobbing especially caused "the growth and spreading of that cancerous humor, which had begun to gnaw our vitals" (2:443).

Citing these remarks, Kramnick also cites Bolingbroke's quite contrary lost-cause slogan (though the cause can be declared finally lost perhaps only from a postmodern perspective): "The landed men are the true owners of our political vessel: the moneyed men, as such, are no more than passengers in it" (2:458; Kramnick 37). Lemuel Gulliver is a merchant but never a "moneyed man"—rather, a moneyless and frequently a shipwrecked man (note Bolingbroke's "political vessel" or ship-of-state metaphor). Gulliver's fortune and therefore identity are in continual flux and jeopardy (including the reader's resistances to giving any credit to his narratives of shipwreck and escape). Gulliver's sense of time and the future is thus also disoriented, uncertain, scrambled. In relation to the "politics of nostalgia" (to quote from Kramnick's subtitle) of Bolingbroke, Swift, Pope, and their Tory allies, all of them fixated on the past, Gulliver is perhaps also in some sense the ultimate exile, the landless rather than landed man—as rootless and restless as any of the countless sailors, traders, wanderers, explorers, adventurers, and pirates who helped to create and destroy the first and second British empires. Here is a different version of the same point: even though he is clearly not a "moneyed man," Lemuel Gulliver is nevertheless "a true bourgeois." Friedrich Engels uses the phrase "true bourgeois" not in relation to crazy Gulliver, however, but to his apparently sane and sober antithesis, Robinson Crusoe. Or more precisely, Engels applies this phrase to "Marx's Robinson" who is, Engels claims, "the *genuine*, original Robinson of Daniel Defoe, from which secondary features are also taken—the debris rescued from the shipwreck, etc. Later, he also had his own Friday, and was a shipwrecked merchant, who, if I am not mistaken, traded in slaves at one time. In a word, a true 'bourgeois'" (Marx and Engels, *Literature and Art* 318). Unlike Bolingbroke's senescent England falling into its "dotage," Defoe's Crusoe is a figure of resurrection, second life if not exactly new life, a figure who, even in the midst of his terror and isolation on his desert island, looks to the future. Perhaps he has always also been understood as representing both nascent capitalism and nascent imperialism, the characteristic bourgeois citizen of emergent Great Britain.

When Marx interpreted Crusoe as an ur-capitalist, he noted that he was following a long tradition; by the midnineteenth century, Crusoe's adventures had become a cliché among political economists (*Capital* 1:169). Defoe's novel has seemed to many commentators to offer a paradigmatic account of possessive individualism and even, perhaps in some more basic or prior sense, of primitive accumulation and imperialism (Hymer 12–13; Watt 60–92). But all Defoe's novels can be read in relation to modern and modernizing economic ideas and, perhaps especially, to the concept of public credit. If *Gulliver's Travels*, both in its explicit themes of debt, warfare, and empire building and in its structural challenges to the credulity or gullibility of its readers, is thoroughly imbued with the controversies surrounding public credit, that is equally true of Defoe's nonsatiric, realistic fictions, stories traditionally identified as the first full-fledged novels in English (Watt 9). Whereas Swift is appalled by the new attitudes and practices spawned by the financial revolution of his age, Defoe seems to approve and even to champion them. Unlike *Gulliver's Travels*, which is both incredible and made up of structurally repetitious but disjointed episodes that do not form a narrative progression into a clear, secure future, Defoe's novels are presented as unironic narratives for readers to credit as quite simply true—the straightforward accounts of their protagonists' trajectories, through many vicissitudes, toward the safe future havens from which they usually appear to be writing. Swift's fantasy points toward incoherence, insanity, and the loss of a secure future; Defoe's novels are individualistic success stories. For most of Defoe's main characters (Crusoe, Moll Flanders, Captain Singleton, Colonel Jack), the future turns out to be better, more prosperous and also more stable, than the stormy seas of the past through which they have navigated. For Swift, credit (and the future) is near-allied to madness; for Defoe, credit works, and the future in which credit is to be rewarded can already be represented as sober, commonsense reality.

All Defoe's essays as well as his novels are saturated with modern (early capitalist or mercantilist) economic language. "Writing," he declared in 1725, "is become a very considerable Branch of the English Commerce. The Booksellers are the Master Manufacturers or Employers. The several Writers, Authors, Copyers, Sub-writers and all other Operators with Pen and Ink are the workmen employed by the said Master-Manufacturers" (quoted in Watt 53). Just as Defoe understood modern literature to be a form of commercial activity and "manufacturing," so the main characters in his novels are representatives of the emergent capitalist ideology and commercial order he heralded in his *Essay on Projects*, his *Compleat English Tradesman*, and many of his other journalistic endeavors. This is as true of Roxana, Moll Flanders, Colonel Jack, and Captain Singleton as it is of Robinson Crusoe. As in Johnson's allusion to prostitution in "London," so in Roxana's "whore-dom," Defoe offers a paradigm of the new commercialization and com-modification of all social relations. The "fortunate mistress" or the mis-tress of fortune, she appears to be a realistic incarnation of such allegorical figures as Lady Credit and Fortuna. Elsewhere, Defoe per-sonified "trade" in general as a sort of "fortunate mistress." In the last issue of his *Review*, Defoe claimed that "writing upon Trade was the Whore I really doated upon, and design'd to have taken up with" (9[106]: 11 June 1713, 214). Though she winds up penitent, she also winds up poor, and in this regard she appears to be less "fortunate" than other Defoe protagonists. But she has nevertheless been able to live much of her life in security and even luxury.

Roxana's variable "fortunes" depend mostly on her ability to profit from her sexual prowess and her wits, though she is first and foremost a coolheaded businesswoman: "By managing my Business . . . myself, and having large Sums to do with, I became as expert in it, as any She-Merchant of them all; I had Credit in the Bank for a large Sum of Money, and Bills and Notes for much more" (170). True, on many occasions Roxana laments the "whoring" that has made her life one "full of prosperous Wickedness" (287), but her moral and religious misgivings are tallied up on the debit side of her autobiographical led-ger just as calmly and coolly as her Dutch merchant-husband tallies up his debts and assets. Much of *Robinson Crusoe* reads like a merchant's account book (after all, Crusoe like Gulliver is a merchant, willing to trade in slaves and anything else that comes his way), and *Roxana* is no different (cf. Watt 63–64). Thus the Dutch merchant's opening of his account books to Roxana can be taken as an analogue for the novel as a whole. In those account books, Roxana says,

> he shew'd me several Adventures he had Abroad, in the Business of his Merchandize; as particularly, an eighth Share in an *East-India* Ship then Abroad; an Account-Courant with a Merchant, at *Cadiz* in *Spain*; about 3000 *l.* lent upon *Bottomree*, upon Ships gone to the *Indies*; and a large Cargo of Goods in a Merchant's Hands, for Sale, at *Lisbon* in *Portugal*; so that in his Books there was about 12000 *l.* more; all which put together, made about 27000 *l.* Sterling, and 1320 *l.* a Year. (303)

At the same time, Roxana's husband is careful to point out that he has debts that must be subtracted from his wealth. These debts "are very great, *I assure you*; and the *first, he said,* was a black Article of 8000 Pistoles, which he had a Law-Suit about, at *Paris*" (303), and so forth. And when the merchant is done with presenting his accounts to Roxana, she returns the favor by listing in solid, solemn detail all of *her* financial assets.

In *Defoe and Economics*, Bram Dijkstra argues that the union between Roxana and her "honourable" Dutch merchant in part allegorizes an ideal union between the two great mercantile and imperializing nations of the early eighteenth century, England and Holland (65). At least it can be said that the pages describing their relationship by detailing their assets, "scintillating with astonishing four- and five-figure lists of rents, mortgages and securities . . . form the true climax of the narrative" (65). Dijkstra also argues that in *Roxana*, Defoe presents a narrational analysis of "the world of high finance and international monetary exchange, the world of the great merchants, of the bankers, and of the nobility. . . . As always," Defoe sets forth "in striking exempla both the fruitful methods of capital accumulation and management and the evil consequences of inadequate financial acumen" (13). *Roxana* offers its readers both "simple instruction" in "the secrets of good business practice," Djikstra says, and "a careful exposition of the central features of [Defoe's] economic theory" (13).

The parallels Dijkstra shows between *Roxana* and Defoe's explicitly economic writings such as *The Compleat English Tradesman* are too numerous and striking to dismiss as incidental either to this particular novel or to Defoe's practice of fictional realism in general. Yet Dijsktra finds himself swimming upstream against those critics who believe that Defoe is being ironic (Roxana as an embodiment of lust and avarice, the perfect prostitute) and who think that Defoe condemns, like the Tory satirists whom he often opposed, the economic motives of security and self-interest in favor of an otherworldly puritanism. Dijkstra sees Defoe instead as a multifaceted, intellectually rather sloppy writer who simply contradicts himself and covers his tracks—especially his approval of Roxana's profitable sexuality—by tacking on a "wages of sin" morality, as in the last paragraph of the novel. But whether the economistic, capitalistic Defoe is the true one, and the moralizing, puritanical Defoe is a hypocrite (or vice versa) is undecidable. Instead, the very undecidability of all of Defoe's fictions can hardly be overemphasized.

This undecidability corresponds to the overdetermined quality of early realist (empiricist) narratives like the stories of apparitions (e.g., Defoe's account of the ghost of Mrs. Veal) that, as Michael McKeon notes, are told with all the rhetorical armature of later, thoroughly secular or materialistic realism. "The great and tireless argument of a supernatural reality is maintained," McKeon writes, "within a succession of narrative frames and articulated there by a complex pattern of circumstantial and authenticating details—names, places, dates, events, eye- and earwitnesses, attentiveness to stylistic 'sincerity,' confirmations of good character, denials of special bias—all of which subserve the crucial claim to a natural existence; that is, to historicity" (85). What McKeon identifies as "the contradictory posture of the apparition narratives" (86) carries over into early realistic novels like *Roxana*, where empiricist "historicity" and at least distantly supernatural (or providential) "romance," purely materialistic economic motivations and religious fervor, swim together in a discursive medium in which they never quite fuse or synthesize. This uneasy, contradictory coexistence, McKeon argues, is the result of "an epistemological 'revolution' in early modern England" which produced "a categorical instability so acute that the condition of conceptual fluidity and process which characterizes all culture" was greatly exaggerated (87).

At the heart of this "epistemological revolution," moreover, was the question of epistemological credit, just as at the heart of the simultaneous financial revolution was the question of public credit. McKeon quotes Joseph Glanvill: "Now the credit of matters of Fact depends much upon the Relatours, who, if they cannot be deceived themselves nor supposed any ways interested to impose upon others, ought to be credited. For upon these circumstances, all humane Faith is grounded, and matter of Fact is not capable of any proof besides, but that of immediate sensible evidence" (85). One difficulty with such a formulation, quite apart from the question of whether "sensible evidence" can deceive, is that, whereas direct observers of nature or events have access to "immediate sensible evidence," in discursive situations people have to credit or discredit what others tell them. And the narratives that others offer of *their* experiences of "immediate sensible evidence"—the basic form of all discourse, culture, or ideology—can just as easily as not be exaggerated, distorted, or completely fabricated. Hence the contradiction on which "realistic" fiction builds its imaginary edifices, a contradiction that can only be offset or compensated for by credit in the form of what Coleridge would later call "the willing suspension of disbelief," granted by the reading public just as an investing public grants financial credit to a needy, imperious nation-state.

In *Roxana*, Defoe offers a detailed dramatization of one of the key metaphors of cultural modernism in relation to capitalism, namely, prostitution as in Johnson's "London," but also as later in Blake, Balzac, Dickens, Baudelaire, Zola, and many others. According to Walter Benjamin, in the "Hell," which is also the "Golden Age" of modernity associated with fashion, advertising, and the growing hegemony of commodity fetishism—a culture of "immediate sensible evidence" built on the phantasmagoria of consumerist desire—prostitution becomes the norm. In the capitalist metropolis, woman as prostitute "appears not merely as a commodity but as a mass-produced article" ("Central Park" 50–52). Benjamin was writing, of course, just a few decades before the appearance of Baudrillard's postmodern hell—or "achieved utopia" known as America—of hyperreality, simulation, and the supposedly total commodification and derealization of everything (for Benjamin, prostitution, and commodity fetishism, see Buck-Morss 96–109, 189–194; for Baudrillard, *America* 46, 77). In any event, though Roxana the "fortunate mistress" may adumbrate postmodern consumerism, she more immediately embodies, in her attainment of a "wicked Prosperousness," eighteenth-century ambivalence toward luxury which for Defoe as for Pope and Swift seems tantamount to successful prostitution.

In several other fictional and nonfictional narratives, Defoe offers similar dramatizations of another key economic metaphor, one that is more directly linked to imperialism than the prostitute: piracy, as in Swift and as in Defoe's *Lives of the Pirates* and also *The Life of Captain Singleton.* Defoe no more approves of piracy than he does of prostitution, and yet he recognizes that both forms of economic activity are central rather than marginal to modern economic activity and therefore to social and political reality. Moreover, they are forms of economic activity which, in a Hobbesian way, stem directly from the natural condition of scarcity and which therefore in some sense come before, underlie, or seem more basic than do "honourable" forms of trade, just as primitive accumulation underlies capitalism.

Prostitution and piracy are forms of economic activity that also in some sense underlie and largely determine the very identities of Defoe's characters. Though "the devil" tempts Roxana and Defoe's other protagonists on many occasions, the chief form temptation takes in his novels is "poverty" (or "necessity"). A secular, modernizing reader can therefore come away from *Roxana* or *Captain Singleton* with the thought that Defoe's characters behave exactly as a fickle, often not bountiful nature or "fortune" dictates in "her" interactions with even the most rational, calculating human nature. At the same time, a religious, antimodernizing reader can come away from the same stories with a puritanical wages-of-sin morality and a belief in providential design perhaps shaken but more or less intact. Thus from "wicked Prosperousness" Roxana devolves, in the final pages of the novel, to so low a point that she can merely, ambiguously declare, "My Repentance seem'd to be only the Consequence of my Misery, as my Misery was of my Crime" (379).

Defoe here seems to be saying that good and evil behavior depend on economic circumstance, not vice versa. Being good, honorable, or civil does not make a person prosperous; on the contrary, to become prosperous, and therefore to reach a safe haven in which it is possible to be morally upright, one may have to be dishonorable and wicked, a prostitute or a pirate. That so much economic activity, for Defoe, can be subsumed under the rubrics of prostitution and piracy does not contradict his Christian worldview, largely because no theologian has ever considered the world anything but a morally contested realm at best, and at worst, the devil's turf anyway. Thus as Blake said of Milton, it could be said of Defoe that he is of the devil's party without knowing it—or perhaps while partially knowing it. In any case, religion seems to be an afterthought for most of Defoe's characters, though perhaps that is only another way of saying that Defoe thinks of religion as applying mainly to an afterworld, whereas *this* world runs by rules that often mean that the wicked prosper while the honorable fall by the wayside. The moral credit of all humanity is apparently, for Defoe, more at issue than the credit of Providence.

There is another, related, but also fundamental idea at work in Defoe's novels, and that is that personal identity is dependent on, though perhaps not completely determined by, economic factors. If "misery" leads Roxana to repent at the end of her story, "poverty" pushes her into her life of "prosperous Wickedness" in the first place: "Poverty was my Snare; dreadful Poverty!" (73). Defoe's characters are the creatures of "fortune" and its antitheses: misfortune, bad luck, and lack of money. Roxana's identity, including her alias, which betokens her status as a "fortunate mistress," is ultimately a function of the economic ups and downs that constitute her narrative. In a sense, the emotional and erotic aspects of her story are the superstructure, thoroughly determined by an unpredictable, precarious economic base that, at almost every turn of the plot, attaches price tags to events.

Similarly, Captain Singleton has no self-history apart from his career as a fortune-seeking pirate; more than either Crusoe's or Roxana's, his identity is never secure or even exactly identifiable. Kidnapped as an infant, he winds up in the clutches of a female beggar who disposes of him for twelve shillings "to a gipsy, under whose government I continued till I was about six years old" (2). The gipsy calls him "Bob Singleton," but neither she nor he ever know "by what name I was christened"; and in any event, after his "good gipsy mother" is hanged for an unspecified crime, he shifts about from place to place for several years until he winds up on a ship bound for Newfoundland. But this voyage does not last long, because the ship is captured by "an Algerine rover" or pirate "man-of-war," though this act of piracy is also quickly undone when "the Turkish rover [is] attacked by two great Portuguese men-of-war, and taken and carried into Lisbon" (3).

So Captain Singleton's story begins with several violent, rapid displacements and scramblings of identity. The novel as a whole, moreover, is a web of piratical actions at sea and of captivity stories starting with the kidnapping of Singleton himself when he was a child. Among other versions of the captivity motif, there are the story of William Walters the Quaker, who is captured by Singleton and his pirate crew and who becomes an indispensable figure among them, an oxymoronic Quaker pirate; the presumably true story of Robert Knox's captivity in Ceylon (210), which Defoe mirrors in the fictional story of the Kurtz-like Dutchman of Ceylon (198); and the story of the slave ship that the pirates capture, only to discover that the slaves have mutinied, "murdered all the white men, and thrown them into the sea" (138). Singleton and William the Quaker take pity on the slaves but also take them to Brazil, where they sell them into bondage once again: everywhere in Defoe the profit motive prevails.

The world works by piracy, Defoe suggests; the strong capture, destroy, and sometimes even devour the weak; and only the lucky and adaptable manage to survive and, perhaps, become strong in their turn. At the same time, Defoe seems also to recognize that piracy is only a nonofficial version of the primitive accumulation and empire building of modern nation-states. When Singleton and his mates are marooned on Madagascar, they are at first "terrified exceedingly with the sight of the barbarous people" (12), whom they mistakenly assume to be cannibals. But the natives treat them civilly; indeed, "as for the inhabitants being cannibals, I believed we should be more likely to eat them than they us" (11). This is no more than what Defoe says elsewhere in relation to "desperate poverty." As Carol Flynn notes, "Cannibalism enters into Defoe's most vivid fantasies of a Hobbesian universe" (150), which is the normal universe at least under conditions of scarcity. The "cannibal fictions" of both Swift and Defoe "represent an imperialistic society that compromises their most compassionate instincts. . . . Defoe, ostensibly the professional booster of . . . a vigorous economy of expansion, points repeatedly to its cost, its dependence upon slavery, upon violence, and upon death," writes Flynn (150). "I tell you all, Gentlemen, in your Poverty, the best of you all will rob your Neighbour; nay, to go farther . . . you will EAT your Neighbour, *ay*, and say Grace to your Meat too," as Defoe put it (*Review* 8[75]: 15 September 1711, 303). True, the Madagascar natives are "only civil from fear" (*Captain Singleton* 13), though that Hobbesian/normal reaction applies also to the stranded mutineers. Indeed Defoe stresses at every turn the desperation of his European desperadoes, capable of virtually any "wickedness" and violence against the surprisingly more "civil" (if not "civilised") Africans, while he also stresses the commercial acumen that provides the Europeans with their true superiority over the benighted savages.

In contrast to Robinson Crusoe's great terror of the cannibals, and also to Crusoe's intolerant, violent episode of idol smashing in Siberia (on which, see Simpson 4–9), Captain Singleton and his mates travel among Africans who appear to be less dangerous and more rational than the stereotypical, fetish worshiping cannibals depicted by later European slavers and explorers. On the one hand, the pirates have guns and sabers, but they are so outnumbered that this technological advantage is negligible. On the other hand, the clever sailor who had been a "cutler, or worker in iron," devises a method that turns out to be the mutineers' ticket for crossing the entire continent of Africa (a feat not actually accomplished, so far as is known, by any European before David Livingstone in the mid-1800s). With a file and hammer, the cutler shapes pieces of eight into the images of "birds and beasts" and strings these apparently worthless "trinkets" into necklaces and bracelets, items the Africans find irresistably attractive. "Thus, that which when it was in coin was not worth sixpence to us, when thus converted into toys and trifles, was worth a hundred times its *real value*, and purchased for us anything we had occasion for" (25; my italics). Singleton seems almost to fathom the mystification that Marx would later name "commodity fetishism," though the relativity of value—the chief secret underlying the magical conversion of coins into fetishistic images in Defoe's text—escapes him as it perhaps also does Defoe. He, like his protagonist-narrator, seems to believe that all objects have a "real value" that can be designated by money.

Later in the story, close to the west coast of Africa, the pirates stumble on a "stark naked" Englishman living Kurtz-like among the natives (having been "a factor for the English Guinea Company at Sierra Leone" who had been "plundered" by the French). Though close to their goal, Singleton and his mates follow the Englishman's advice by panning great quantities of gold from the rivers. Here the clever cutler becomes especially busy, forming "all manner of images" out of gold—"elephants, tigers, civet cats, ostriches, eagles, cranes, fowls, fishes" (115)—"toys" that, because of the Africans' credulity, fetch far more in return in the form of large quantities of gold dust. Part of the secret of this seemingly irrational exchange appears to lie in the specifically *mimetic* quality of the images the cutler fashions. But in even the earliest accounts of West African fetish worship, there is a distinctly antimimetic relationship between the fetish and what it supposedly does. According to these accounts, a fetish is not a symbol, much less a mimetic reflection of some other object in either the real or the supernatural world. It is instead a charm with magical properties, capable of altering reality or of making wishes come true. A horseshoe or a rabbit's foot as a good luck charm is a fetish in this sense; but these objects are not symbols or images of something else. So what exactly does Defoe have in mind when he stresses the mimetic quality of the cutler's metal "toys"?

The Africans' interest in the cutler's artifacts is more aesthetic than superstitious, and perhaps Defoe intended the mimetic factor to associate the cutler's art with his own. Exchanging his realistic "toys" for peace, food, and gold dust, the cutler is like the novelist, making his living by creating simulacra of the world. In this allegorical relationship, Defoe's readers, when they buy and consume his stories, are like the innocent Africans—perhaps most like the Africans if they overvalue his fictions by believing them to be true. Although it is not possible to demonstrate that Defoe is self-consciously likening the cutler's realistic, economic, quasi-monetary artistry to his own, Defoe is well-aware of the mysterious and mystifying nature of economic value based on credit. He is also aware of the connection between economic credit and other forms of belief, including the willingness of gullible novel readers to credit fictional stories as true ones—and to buy them.

Why indeed should anyone believe the "true story" narratives of pirates and whores to begin with? What sort of credit are readers asked to exercise in relation to *Roxana* or *Captain Singleton*? Just as paper money is a form of debt that behaves like wealth (even if it represents gold or silver, it is itself as insubstantial as the paper it is made of), so the words in Defoe's narratives seem to be the voices of living, actual persons, though of course they are only the ventriloquism of Defoe. A realistic novel is only a counterfeit of the scientific empiricism and "true story" facticity that it mimes; fantastic or surrealistic stories at least announce their fictional status. But the "true story" narratives of thieves and pros-titutes—self-confessed uncreditworthy types—pose an extra epis-temological dilemma for the reader. And yet this extra dilemma, em- ˙phasized by the narrator's criminal past, a dishonesty that the narrator appears to be honestly confessing, spills over to narratives by appar-ently more trustworthy types. Though presumably an honest merchant with a stable identity, is Robinson Crusoe any less fictional than Roxana or Captain Singleton? It does not make Crusoe's story more creditable to point out that Defoe based it on the "true story" of Alexander Sel-kirk; he also based the story of Captain Singleton on several of the various supposedly "true stories" in his *Lives of the Pirates*. Defoe knew that firsthand, "sensible" observation of reality does not involve credit, at least not of the extreme sort required by the secondhand stories of others, which depend exclusively on the fidelity (verisimilitude, proba-bility, and so on) of their imitations of reality.

Throughout *Captain Singleton*, what constitutes both spiritual value and material wealth is called into question by the contrast between European and African behaviors, but also between the behaviors of pirates and (at least by implication) honest, law-abiding Europeans. At the same time, just as the social legitimation of value is called into question, so are standard conceptions of individual identity. Like Field-ing's Tom Jones, Defoe's Bob Singleton could be everyman or anyone. He does not know his original name, and the label "captain" is at first only a nickname, given him in his defiant, teenage days of mutiny and piracy by his equally piratical comrades. As in *Roxana, Robinson Crusoe, Moll Flanders*, and Defoe's other fictions, Bob Singleton's identity de-pends on fortune, and fortune is, if anything, an even more fickle and fantastic goddess than public credit. Before commerce or trade, more-over, can settle down to something like a normal, even-keeled, and civilized routine, kidnapping, robbery, piracy, and perhaps even canni-balism seem to constitute the normal if also violent, precarious mode of production—or rather, mode of survival—which in Defoe's always insecure world is also the mercantilist, imperialist mode of primitive accumulation.

The wealth of nascent capitalism, at least in the early 1700s, seemed to ride in the dark holds of ever imperiled ships, some doomed to fall prey to Britain's warring enemies or to pirates, and some doomed to shipwreck in storms as far distant as the East or West Indies. Many, though, would also be fortunate enough (like Roxana the "fortunate mistress," at least for awhile) to return to their home ports in England. Defoe also understood that every ship that sailed away from England on whatever venture—warfare, slave trading, gold or spice hunting, colonizing, pirating—was burdened not just with its physical cargo but also with an indebtedness to its owners and investors that it could only repay by returning to port with an even more valuable cargo than it had carried abroad. Given such conditions, shipwreck, as also in Swift and Bolingbroke, provides an obvious metaphor for the general insecurities and disasters that beset economic man (and woman) and that imperil the national ship of state:

> A Tradesman is never safe; his Condition is subjected to innumerable Casualties, and to unavoidable Disasters: No Estate is so big as not to be in Hazard; no Posture of his Affairs out of the Reach of Accidents; while he continues in Trade, like a Seaman, tho' he is at the Mouth of the Harbour, nay tho' safe in the Port, and come to an Anchor, he can never say he is entirely out of Danger, and perfectly safe, till he has set both Feet safe on Shore. (Defoe, *Tradesman* 2:1:91)

As with Gulliver, so with Captain Singleton, Roxana, Robinson Crusoe, and other Defoe characters: shipwreck is one of the few experiences that fortune can be counted on to provide for everyone. Yet this passage suggests the pattern in most of Defoe's novels: the Tradesman *will* return home safely, he *will* (at least, in many "fortunate" instances) "set both Feet safe on Shore." Above all, Defoe believed, no matter how unpredictable and hazardous, the future is where fortune and Providence ultimately coincide and is, for that reason, to be credited.

6

THE COMPLEX metaphorical connections between literature and money have often been traced; they are perhaps as old as literature and money, or even language and money. So Mark Shell points out that the Greek word *seme* doubled for both "word" and "coin" (2). It is at least clear that these connections were present at the birth of the modern novel, in such texts as *Roxana* and *Robinson Crusoe.* "In the language of trade, money is the alphabet that forms the sound," Defoe declared in his *Review* (3: 1706, 3); money is also an "alphabet" that is just as basic as language to Defoe's fictional realism. It remained for Addison, however, to write the autobiography of a shilling (with John Phillips's poem "The Splendid Shilling" in mind): the personified shilling describes how he "rambled from Pocket to Pocket" until he acquired "great Credit and Antiquity" (*Tatler* 249: 11 November 1710). Addison's fantasy in turn may have inspired what is without doubt one of the oddest and yet most symptomatic novels of the eighteenth century, Charles Johnstone's *Chrysal, or The Adventures of a Guinea*, in which through four volumes Chrysal, the "Spirit of Gold" conjured up by an alchemist in the opening chapter, narrates her picaresque life in the form of a guinea, traveling from owner to owner. Johnstone's fantasy literalizes the metaphorical relationships between gold and imagination (or credit in the sense of belief) and between money and novels. The fetishizing of money, in the personified form of the adventurous guinea, provides both the structure and the main theme of *Chrysal*, which along with greed takes as one of the main targets of its satire "the vanity of luxury" (1:x).

In a crudely phantasmagoric way, *Chrysal* thus anticipates the equation between money and fiction which informs nineteenth-century novelistic realism from Balzac and Scott through Zola and Hardy. The great realistic novelists often also complicate the money-fiction equation by suggesting that the novels they write are not true gold but the reverse—mere paper money or, carrying self-deprecation even farther, mere counterfeit money. As Derrida contends in his analysis of Baudelaire's short story "Counterfeit Money," the gold standard of fictional realism is riven through and through with the knowledge of its own fictiveness, its own status as something unreal, not genuine, not finally golden at all. The cutler in *Captain Singleton*, transforming gold into mimetic (realistic) trinkets, is one way in which Defoe also explored the analogy between his own fiction and (counterfeit) money. "Everything that will be said, *in* the story, *of* counterfeit money (and in the story of counterfeit money) can be said of the story, of the fictive text bearing this title ["Counterfeit Money"]. This text is also the coin [in the story], a piece of counterfeit money provoking an event and lending itself to this whole scene of deception," writes Derrida (*Given Time* 86). What is true of Baudelaire's story is for Derrida generalizable to literature itself as a system of credit or belief—a system, moreover, that he treats as coterminus with and, indeed, in some sense as identical to capitalism: "Everything is act of faith, phenomenon of credit or credence, of belief and conventional authority in this text which perhaps says something essential about what here links literature to belief, to credit and thus to capital, to economy and thus to politics. Authority is constituted by accreditation, both in the sense of legitimation as effect of belief or credulity, and of bank credit, of capitalized interest" (97). For Derrida as for the Romantics, literature is a matter of faith or imagination, but it is a faith (credit) that is always already contaminated or at least interfused with a capitalist materialism and commodification that ties it to money.

Citing the same equation between literary belief and monetary credit, Mark Shell adds that the confusion caused by paper money in "our 'natural' understanding of the relationship between symbols and things" has often been construed as "diabolical," as in *Faust* (Shell 7). But whereas paper money has a modern history, the always already capitalism in Derrida's argument (perhaps like the instrumental reason that, in *Dialectic of Enlightenment*, Adorno and Horkheimer identify with Odysseus), seems to be almost ahistorical, even essentialist. Yet just as for Derrida there is nothing beyond the text or beyond writing, so there is nothing prior to (or innocent of) the literature-as-credit, literature-as-money nexus—nothing prior to a certain literary capitalization that anticipates everything Defoe, Balzac, Dickens, Flaubert, and Trollope had to say about these antitheses (literature vs. money) that turn out to be identities (literature equals money). Because it both criticizes bourgeois materialism (or the fetishizing of wealth and respectability) and yet presumes to reproduce the gold standard of that materialism as its portrait of substantial social reality, fictional realism from Defoe forward is perhaps the most hypocritical of literary modes. It rejects the equations of fiction and reality and of literature and money while capitalizing on those very equations. For as Derrida rightly says, "the most apparently direct writing, the most directly concrete, personal writing which is supposedly in direct contact with the 'thing itself,' this writing [too] is 'on credit' " (*Given Time* 100).

3

Upon Daedalian Wings
(1750–1832)

> The commerce and industry of the country . . . though they may
> be somewhat augmented, cannot be altogether so secure, when
> they are . . . suspended upon the Daedalian wings of paper
> money, as when they travel about upon the solid ground of gold
> and silver.
>
> —Adam Smith, *The Wealth of Nations*

> Nations are wading deeper and deeper into an ocean of
> boundless debt.
>
> —Edmund Burke, *Reflections on the Revolution in France*

1

THE POLITICAL and economic storms that Swift and many others believed threatened the vessel of state with shipwreck did not dissipate
after the South Sea Bubble. Between Swift's age and the early 1800s,
Great Britain emerged as the vanguard European state in both empire
building and industrialization. It did so through the consolidating violence it exercised against Scottish and Irish resistance and against the
American and French revolutions. As "an invention forged above all by
war" (Colley 5), Britain was more successful but otherwise no different
from its continental rivals. From the Middle Ages onward, the main
activity of the European nation-states has been war (Tilly 74). But a key
difference between medieval and modern war making lies in the early
modern regularization of budgetary and revenue practices, including
the regularization of long-term debts based on mortgaging future
power and glory. "From the late seventeenth century onward budgets,
debts, and taxes arose to the rhythm of war," Charles Tilly notes. "All of
Europe's warmaking states had the same experience" (75; cf. Rasler
and Thompson). The mystification whereby the British national debt

was transubstantiated into the Bank of England, that symbol of rock-solid monetary stability and fiscal rectitude, had everything to do with the mobilization and triumphs of the state as war machine. Almost tautologically, key factors in forging public credit and confidence in Britain's future power and glory were the dual ideologies of nationalism and imperialism.

Britain's victories in the series of wars against Holland, Spain, and France down to 1815 entailed both an enormous expansion of the national debt and an enormous expansion of the British Empire (despite the loss of the American colonies). With Jacobitism brought to bay after the Battle of Culloden (1746), and with military and imperial victories in the Seven Years' War (1756–1763), "Great Britain," just at the onset of the Industrial Revolution, seemed triumphant over its enemies. Yet success in 1763 had its bitter consequences as Colley observes: "In part, this was because of the hangover that always follows excessive indulgence in major war. There was the predictable social strain of absorbing more than 200,000 demobilised men, most of them poor, some of them mutilated, all of them trained to violence. There was the hard, unpleasant fact of a massively inflated National Debt which led inexorably to a rise in taxation" (101). Colley notes that by the end of the Seven Years' War the debt had grown "so corpulent that it sucked in almost five-eighths of the government's annual budget in interest payments" (136). Partly in response to increased taxation fueled by the national debt, moreover, just on the horizon loomed the discontents of the American colonists which would soon erupt in the Revolutionary War and a new escalation of national debt (including the creation of the United States on the fiscal basis of paper money and of its own new, massive national debt).

War fueled the British national debt and taxation problems both at home and in the colonies, but success in war also fueled prosperity and the increasing domestic unity involved in the emergence of British as opposed to merely English nationalism. Colley points to the connection between nationalism and public credit when she notes that, along with its destabilizing effects, "credit's contribution to political stability also needs to be recognised. All credit systems rely on . . . confidence that interest payments will be made at the correct level and at the correct time, and confidence that debts will ultimately be repaid" (67). *Confidence* is the key term also in the first thorough, modern analysis of public credit in relation to monetary theory. In *An Enquiry into the Nature and Effects of the Paper Credit of Great Britain*, Henry Thornton declares, "Commercial credit may be defined to be that confidence which subsists among commercial men in respect to their mercantile affairs" (75). But such confidence arises only in societies whose governments provide both legal and military mechanisms for securing property against all forms of depredation, thereby enabling widespread commercial activities to flourish. "In a society in which law and the sense of moral duty are weak, and property is consequently insecure, there will . . . be little confidence or credit, and there will also be little commerce," maintains Thornton (76). But of course confidence or credit in the internal security of a nation-state can arise only when that state has no external enemies, has defeated its enemies in war, or at least can mount a sufficient military threat to hold them at bay.

Though less familiar than Smith's *Wealth of Nations*, Malthus's *Essay on Population*, or Ricardo's *Principles of Political Economy and Taxation*, Thornton's *Paper Credit* is one of the founding texts of economics, which during the Industrial Revolution achieved the status of the first widely recognized, modern social "science." Britain was in the vanguard in this respect also, in part because of its advanced practices in banking, monetary policy, and government finance. Key problems for early economics were the theorization, or rationalization, of the increasing national and international dependence on public credit and paper money which, as Adam Smith's "Daedalian wings" metaphor suggests, has always seemed dangerously unstable or volatile, if not downright diabolic.[1] The emergence of economics as a discreet, scientific discipline parallels—often as its antithesis or adversary—the emergence of romanticism in literature and the arts. How the major Romantic writers reacted to "political economy" is a familiar story (see, e.g., Bonar; Heinzelman); in general, they attacked the reification and fetishizing of the economic realm as (to quote Coleridge) "a self-regulating Machine" (*Lay Sermons* 205). Adam Smith's famous metaphor of the "invisible hand" that guides this machine is such an obvious symptom of this fetishizing that its phallic but also fantastic properties hardly need emphasis (Smith 423). But there are also ways in which economic discourse and literary romanticism share ideological terrain; romantic fetishizing of the nation-state as mystical organism is not completely antithetical to the fetishizing of the economy as mystical mechanism in Smith, Ricardo, and others. Ironically, at the same time that he condemned the fetishizing of the economic sphere, Coleridge developed a theory of the positive, religious effects of public credit and the national

1. According to Brian Rotman, "The Chinese called [paper money] 'flying money'" (50).

debt which echoed Thornton's *Paper Credit* with its matter-of-fact revelations of the "mysteries" of high finance. Before turning to Thornton and Coleridge, however, I examine the ideas of some earlier theorists both of public credit and of an important forerunner of romantic aesthetics, the eighteenth-century theory of the sublime.

Parallel to what might be called the early adventures in primitive accumulation of novelistic realism, the adventures both of philosophical empiricism and of the nascent science of economics reflect the central but decentering ambiguities and anxieties of the concept of public credit. Two key figures in the shaping both of philosophy and of economics in Britain before Adam Smith and the Industrial Revolution were George Berkeley and David Hume, both of whom, in the wake of the South Sea Bubble, had much to say about public credit. For both, that concept shades into or is in some sense even synonymous with public opinion, a key idea in the evolution of liberal-democratic theories of the public sphere and also of early theories of ideology.[2]

George Berkeley wrote "An Essay towards Preventing the Ruin of Great Britain" at the height of the South Sea public credit crisis and published it in 1721; *The Querist*, on Irish economic difficulties, first appeared in the next decade (starting in 1734) in Dublin and bears comparison with his friend Swift's satiric attacks on England's imperialist exploitation of Ireland.[3] "Industry is the natural sure way to wealth," Berkeley declares (71); "credit" is creditworthy, so to speak, only "as it promoteth industry . . . but money or credit circulating through a nation . . . without producing labour and industry in the inhabitants, is direct gaming" (71). Attacks on stock jobbing and stock market speculation often treated them as forms of gambling; in the case of the South Sea Bubble and the national debt, Berkeley argues, the entire nation is engaged in the "evident folly" of sitting down "to a public gaming table" and of risking the loss of everything that has heretofore made it powerful and prosperous. For Berkeley, moreover, "luxury" is another, virtually self-evident name for that avaricious, money-worshiping temptation that leads to sure national ruin: "We are doomed to be undone. Neither the plain reason of the thing, nor the experience of past ages, nor the examples we have before our eyes, can restrain us from imitating, not to say surpassing, the most corrupt and ruined people, in those very points of luxury that ruined them. Our gaming, our

2. On the eighteenth-century emergence of "public opinion," see Chartier 20–37; Gunn; Habermas, *Structural Transformation* 89–102; Palmer.

3. For Swift on Ireland, see *The Drapier's Letters* and "A Modest Proposal" in vol. 10 of the *Prose Works*. See also vol. 12, *Irish Tracts, 1720–1723, and Sermons*.

operas, our masquerades, are, in spite of our debts and poverty, become the wonder of our neighbours" (77). Luxury is the offspring of the new system of national finance based on public credit, which generates a false, insubstantial sort of prosperity that is really only debt disguised as wealth. Berkeley's litany of modern vices, all associated with luxury and public credit, swells until by the end of the essay he sounds like Swift's Master Houyhnhnm deploring the evil nature of the Yahoos. Berkeley ends by expressing the fear that his contemporaries, unlike their great, liberty-loving and creditable (or honorable) forebears, have all "degenerated" into "servile flatterers of men in power"; they have "adopted Epicurean notions" and become "venal, corrupt, injurious, which [may draw] upon them the hatred of God and man, and [occasion] their final ruin" (85).

Hume's 1752 essay "Of Public Credit" is more temperate than Berkeley's "Ruin," no doubt partly because it was written well after the South Sea crisis, and Britain had not collapsed but only grown stronger and more prosperous. Noting that "public securities are with us become a kind of money, and pass as readily at the current price as gold or silver" (93), Hume offers a careful benefits versus costs analysis of public credit. Among the benefits stemming from the establishment of a permanent national debt, "no merchant [now] thinks it necessary to keep by him any considerable cash . . . our national debts furnish merchants with a species of money, that is continually multiplying in their hands, and produces sure gain [interest], besides the profits of their commerce" (93). This facilitation of the merchants' business in turn brings down prices, increases both consumption and employment, and spreads "arts and industry throughout the whole society" (93–94). Further, public credit creates a new category of citizens whose interests are closely allied to those of the state: these capitalists are "half merchants, half stock-holders" (94). By multiplying the number of such capitalists with holdings in government funds, the system of public credit diffuses wealth and accelerates its circulation.

On this largely positive account, public credit is a source of potentially great profit and progress to the modern nation-state. But Hume thinks its positive results may be unimportant in comparison to the numberous drawbacks "which attend our public debts" (94). He lists five major disadvantages, which, by the conclusion of the essay, greatly outweigh the benefits.[4] First, national debts produce a prodigious in-

---

4. All the dangers of national debts which Hume identifies crop up again in postmodern analyses of both national and global debt crises. For instance, they can all be found, though couched in different terms, in Lawrence Malkin's *The National Debt: How America Crashed into a Black Hole and How We Can Crawl Out of It*; see also Davidson.

flux of both money and population to the cities, giving a metropolis like Paris or London far too much dominance over the provinces (with his preindustrial, agrarian outlook, Hume sees the country rather than the city as main source of the wealth of nations). Crammed into the great city, the masses seeking to make their livings in commerce and the new sources of wealth (e.g., stock jobbing) are likely to grow "factious, mutinous, seditious, and even perhaps rebellious" (95).

Second, in apparent contradiction of the chief benefit Hume says derives from public credit, "public stocks, being a kind of paper-credit, have all the disadvantages attending that species of money." The chief of these disadvantages is that paper money "banish[es] gold and silver from the most considerable commerce of the state" (95), and it is ultimately only gold or silver that can represent genuine wealth. While the state that depends on public credit may seem to be growing wealthier, it is in reality growing poorer by losing gold and silver. This is Hume's version of Gresham's law (named after Sir Thomas Gresham, who founded the Royal Exchange in the 1560s), according to which "bad money drives away good money" (Galbraith, *Money* 10).

Third, the taxes that must be imposed to deal with the interest payments on the "public debts" (Hume uses the plural throughout) are likely to push labor costs up and also to fall most heavily on the poor, or on those least able to pay new taxes who are also those with least stake in the system of public funding ("Public Credit" 96). This argument would become a key theme in the writings of nineteenth-century radicals and utopian socialists such as William Cobbett, Robert Owen, and Bronterre O'Brien. Here, too, Hume counters his earlier idea that public credit may lower the prices of commodities and increase employment, but the main point is that he believes the disadvantage outweighs the advantage.

Fourth, insofar as foreigners invest in the new public stocks and bonds, they are in some measure part owners of the nation-state without being its citizens. The nation becomes, Hume says, "tributary to them, and may in time occasion the transport of our people and our industry" overseas (96). This pattern suggests a reverse imperialism, rather than what Hume sees as healthy forms of emigration and colonization. Instead of dominating others abroad, the British may find themselves dominated, even shipped into servitude or slavery in foreign lands (this is the at least implicit threat in Hume's argument).

And fifth and finally, Hume declares, "the greater part of the public stock being always in the hands of idle people, who live on their revenue, our funds . . . give great encouragement to an useless and unactive life" (96). This is, once again, the theme of luxury as false or decadent wealth, and it approximates what Berkeley has to say about the debilitating effects of gaming, masquerades, and luxury. Despite his seemingly balanced consideration of benefits and costs, Hume reaches, partly through the theme of luxury in relation to gambling, a conclusion almost as apocalyptic as Berkeley's: "The seeds of ruin are here scattered with such profusion as not to escape the eye of the most careless observer" (98). If the national debt is increased much more, it will exceed its natural limit; the burden of taxation will outweigh profitable gains from productive commerce and agriculture. In a vision of future catastrophe reminiscent both of Berkeley's "Ruin" and of the writings of Bolingbroke and the Tory satirists, Hume declares that, through the system of public credit, all wealth is passing more or less rapidly into the hands of "the stock-holders . . . who have no connexions with the state, who can enjoy their revenue in any part of the globe in which they chuse to reside, who will naturally bury themselves in the capital or in great cities, and who will sink into the lethargy of a stupid and pampered luxury, without spirit, ambition, or enjoyment" (98).

If that sentence echoes earlier attacks like Berkeley's on luxury, Hume's next one adumbrates a later political and economic theorist for whom public credit was also a central issue, namely, Edmund Burke, with his elegy to "the age of chivalry," which is "gone. . . . That of sophisters, oeconomists, and calculators, has succeeded; and the glory of Europe is extinguished for ever" (Burke, *Reflections* 170). This is an outcome that in the French case Burke blames directly on what he sees as the ruinous new system of mortgaging the public estate to pay the revolutionary government's bills. Having sketched his own dystopian nightmare of national wealth passing into the hands of unproductive stockholders, many of whom may be foreigners, Hume likewise writes, "Adieu to all ideas of nobility, gentry, and family" ("Public Credit" 98). The decline of the landed interest and the rise of the moneyed interest, as Bolingbroke had argued and as Burke would reiterate, seemed, to Berkeley and Hume alike, to portend nothing less than national ruin or bankruptcy. The solution? According to Hume, "Either the nation must destroy public credit, or public credit will destroy the nation" (102).

2

USUALLY HUME employs the phrase "public credit" in a strictly economic sense, as synonymous with "public debts," "public funds," or the national debt. According to this usage, it hardly matters what an owner of shares in "the funds" believes in religious or ideological terms; he or she could be an inveterate critic of the nation-state and still look upon investment in its funds as making economic good sense. But that was part of the problem: the investors in the nation-state prepared to take advantage of public credit had, Hume believed, no better reason to be patriotic than the profit motive. If this was patriotism, it was cold blooded, self-interested, and very different from that associated with the other, presumably older virtues of citizenship based on landed property (see Pocock, *Machiavellian Moment* 423–461). For Hume, as Jerome Christensen declares, credit "begins to resemble every virtue. . . . The reification of virtue as credit is the hallmark both of the subjectivization of experience and of the commercialization of morality which were the ideological benefits bestowed by British empiricism; credit is the solvent that deidealizes the pieties of civic humanism" (206), just as both Hume and Burke held it to be the death knell of "the age of chivalry." But like most of the early critics and defenders of "public credit" such as Bolingbroke and Defoe, Hume also uses that phrase in a way that aligns it *both* with the sort of "popular madness and delusion" that seemed especially evident during the South Sea debacle *and* with an honorable patriotism ("Public Credit" 107). The conflicted meanings of public credit, both economic and patriotic, psychological and collective, and rational and insane, central to Berkeley's and Hume's politics but also to their epistemologies, make that phrase almost indistinguishable from the simultaneously emergent concept of public opinion.

Even though Hume advocates abolishing public credit (in the sense of the national debt), it is nonetheless *only* public credit (in the sense of faith in the economic future of the nation-state) combined with public opinion that binds any modern nation-state together. Berkeley, too, who in *The Querist* expresses a clear understanding of the arbitrary, relativistic nature of money (Vickers 143), shares Hume's double sense of the equally arbitrary, immaterial basis of both public credit and public opinion. Berkeley asks, "Whether it be not the opinion or will of the people, exciting them to industry, that truly enricheth a nation?" (*Works* 6:107)—phrasing that obviously identifies the concept of opinion with public credit's conversion of debt into wealth (when public credit works).

In "Of the First Principles of Government," Hume asserts that it is "on opinion only that government is founded" (24). The principles themselves are reducible to three sorts of opinion: the first concerns "public interest"; the second, legitmacy or sovereignty ("right to power"); and the third, the nature of property and ownership rights (25). In all three cases, it is only public opinion (majority, hegemonic belief or, perhaps, credulity) that holds a status quo in place, because "force is always on the side of the governed, [whereas] the governors have nothing to support them but opinion" (24). Hume is not saying that opinion per se is either irrational or rational; but he is saying that there is something irrational, or at least quasi-mystical, in the majority's allowing themselves to be governed, when they have "force" (in the sense of vastly superior numbers, anyway) on their side. Should the majority change their minds, "opinion" combined with "force" would overwhelm the rulers.

In these two essays, Hume does not directly compare public credit with public opinion, though the implicit differences between them are as important as the similarities. When it does not simply mean national debt, public credit for Hume is an abstract, anonymous, threatening monetary power. It emanates mainly from wealthy investors, who in the eighteenth century were a small minority of the general population of any nation-state. As Hume points out, these investors need not be citizens. Public credit is motivated first and foremost by the expectation of interest or profit; it is therefore relatively detached from specific political interests, issues, and causes; and if it can be described as rational, it is so only in terms of the rational self-interest of the individual investors. In contrast, public opinion is less abstract and anonymous because it arises from or consists of the circulation of individuals' opinions among a sizable number of the citizens of a nation-state, and it tends to be, Hume believed, more stabilizing than threatening. In the eighteenth century, again, the public was most often defined as a minority of educated, property-owning citizens, in contrast to the uneducated, supposedly irrational, or supposedly unopinionated general populace. Public opinion emanates from those citizens who, no matter whether they are voters and investors, take a direct interest in how the government is run. So public opinion is conservative, whereas public credit is radical, or at any rate is uprooting and restless (capitalism as incessantly destabilizing).

Like Gramsci's theory of hegemony, Hume's argument about opinion does not necessarily involve false consciousness: opinion may be quite accurate, logical, or at least commonsensical (cf. Gramsci on common sense, 419–425) in its assessment that a given regime is the best possible or that no better one is likely to emerge from its overthrow (public opinion as resignation to the status quo). Partly because of opinion's conservatism, and partly because Hume does not otherwise question the rationality of governments and therefore of nation-states in general, he does not recognize a distinction like Rousseau's later one between public opinion and general will (Rousseau 26–28), nor does he deal explicitly with the related phenomenon of state worship or patriotism that developed into the romantic nationalisms of the nineteenth century. In other words, though Hume may point ahead to Gramsci's theory of hegemony, he only partially recognizes the irrational possibilities inherent in public opinion, despite his dissection of the irrational possiblities inherent in public credit.

Hume's own conservatism leads him instead to approve of the apparent tendency of opinion to stick to the tried and true. Nevertheless, stressing opinion as the sole support of governments, he also stresses the fragility and insubstantiality of the legitimacy of all state institutions, all of which are based on nothing solider than what people think, or on the belief of the governed that their rulers and laws more or less deserve their legitimacy. The same rational irrationality is apparent in the idea of public credit. In both cases, Hume detects a certain reasonableness or common sense in terms of everyday practice but (especially in the case of public credit) nothing more than a version of Tertullian's *credo quia absurdum* underlying this apparent reasonableness. A similar tension is evident in Burke's stress, in *Reflections on the Revolution in France*, on the positive, conservative functions of "prejudice" in the foundation and maintenance of "the ancient constitution" of Britain, versus his abhorrence of new ideas generated by intellectuals. The exercise of reason in the present is merely corrosive, merely productive of skepticism or even nihilism; "prejudice," by definition prerational but, because historically tried and true, not necessarily irrational, is constructively effective in its support of communal traditions, established religion, and inherited laws.

For Berkeley, Hume, and Burke, belief is far more fundamental to the strength of the nation-state than anything that could be identified with material or, for that matter, economic causation. And indeed belief, opinion, or credit in an abstract sense is, for Berkeley and Hume at least, ultimately the only guide to knowledge or truth. As Gilles Deleuze writes:

> [Hume] established the concept of *belief* and put it in the place of knowledge. He laicized belief, turning knowledge into a legitimate belief. He asked about the conditions which legitimate belief, and on the basis of this investigation sketched out a theory of *probabilities*. The consequences are important: if the act of thinking is belief, thought has fewer reasons to defend itself against error than against *illusion*. Illegitimate beliefs per-

haps inevitably surround thought like a cloud of illusions. In this respect, Hume anticipates Kant. An entire art and all sorts of rules will be required in order to distinguish between legitimate beliefs and the illusions which accompany them. (ix)

In Hume's social theory, belief or opinion in some sense precedes and determines the forms of human sociality, including economic forms. But Hume's valorization of belief or opinion and its economic corollary public credit (in the positive sense of faith in the solvency or reputation of a business enterprise or a nation-state) itself arises from—is somehow shaped or determined by—the economic factors associated with the financial revolution and the nascent industrial one. Hume's philosophy and his economic ideas are not clearly separable; the hinge on which they turn is the concept of credit, which is in economic terms, Hume believes, both potentially ruinous and an "energizing surplus" without which economic activity would come to a standstill. For Hume, according to Christensen, credit "is wholly the 'product' of a mercantile rhetoric that persuades producers to believe in a system which they are not able fully to see, let alone understand—ever" (168). But economic credit parallels the reliance on belief rendered necessary by Hume's epistemological deconstruction of ideas about causation in particular. And it also parallels, Christensen contends, Hume's conception of himself as a modern "man of letters" and leading citizen of "the republic of letters." Throughout Hume's work, in his economic and political writings as well as in his grand *Treatise*, there is a convergence between the philosopher as "man of letters" and the economic theorist as merchant-capitalist. "It was Hume's project to generalize the distinction between trading and polite world into a virtual identity," Christensen says; further, as "middleman" between all "factions," and between theory and practice, Hume considered himself to be trading in ideas or turning "learning into a commodity" in such a manner that, inevitably, "knowledge has lost any claim to disinterestedness" (151 n). This may not be a result Hume fully intended, but it is one toward which his commercial metaphors and interests insistently point. "Hume's vulnerability stems from the uneasy status of philosophical autonomy as an epiphenomenon of credit, itself a simulacrum," concludes Christensen (205).

If philosophy is "an epiphenomenon of credit," it is inseparable also from what Søren Kierkegaard would later call the "phantom" of "public opinion," the key locus of those resentful or envious energies (as Kierkegaard thought of them) that propel "the abstract levelling process, that self-combustion of the human race" (55). Kierkegaard echoes

Burke's negative assessment of opinion, which aligns it with Hume's negative assessment of public credit. But for liberals such as William Hazlitt, John Stuart Mill, and William MacKinnon, enlightened public opinion was the basis of representative government and ultimately of all social progress. MacKinnon's 1828 *On the Rise, Progress, and Present State of Public Opinion* identified it explicitly with liberalism and the bourgeoisie; distinguished it from "popular clamour," which was based on "ignorance" rather than "information"; and defined it as the hallmark of both civilization and progress. MacKinnon's rosy view of public opinion, however, failed to take account of the problems and contradictions that Mill would later grapple with in *On Liberty* and elsewhere. Perhaps the most intractable of these problems is that, as Walter Lippman put it in *The Phantom Public*, "the more complex the collection of men [sic] the more ambiguous must be the unity and the simpler the common ideas" (49).

Following Burke, counter-Enlightenment thinkers such as Wordsworth, Carlyle, and Kierkegaard anticipated all of Lippman's cirticisms of public opinion. From Burke's or Kierkegaard's antidemocratic perspective, both opinion and credit are relativizing and destructive of all traditional values, while they incessantly create new, degraded but also inflationary values. "The public is . . . the real Levelling-Master," writes Kierkegaard, even though the public is also "a monstrous nothing."

> The public is a concept which could not have occurred in antiquity because the people *en masse, in corpore*, took part in any situation which arose, and were responsible for the actions of the individual, and, moreover, the individual was personally present and had to submit at once to applause or disapproval for his decision. Only when the sense of association in society is no longer strong enough to give life to concrete realities is the Press able to create that abstraction "the public," consisting of unreal individuals who never are and never can be united in an actual situation or organization—and yet are held together as a whole. (Kierkegaard 60)

This passage has numerous analogues in nineteenth-century British discourse—in, for example, Carlyle's assertion that "the true Church of England, at this moment [1829], lies in the Editors of its Newspapers" ("Signs" 241). And the characteristically modern emphasis on the role of the press and "print capitalism" not just in informing, guiding, or influencing but in actively constructing the public and with it the nation-state (Benedict Anderson 33–46, 61–65) points ahead to postmodernist claims that society consists only of mass-mediated simulations. For Baudrillard and others, society is nothing more than the commodified illusions that advertising, cinema, and television create to fill in the phantasmal void once positively identified (at least, in liberal political theory) with the public opinion of Habermas's democratic public sphere.

3

MODERN ECONOMIC orthodoxy begins with Adam Smith, whose *Wealth of Nations* ends, ironically enough, with a chapter entitled "Public Debts," which in turn ends with a discussion of colonies as sources both of public indebtedness and of potential wealth to pay that indebtedness. Smith's final sentence reads, "If any of the provinces of the British empire cannot be made to contribute towards the support of the whole empire, it is surely time that Great Britain should free herself from the expence of defending those provinces . . . and endeavour to accommodate her future views and designs to the real mediocrity of her cirumstances" (900). With the remarkable phrase "real mediocrity of her circumstances," Smith foreshadows Britain's twentieth-century fate: to be an economic and political mediocrity, a condition resulting partly from the economic contradictions inherent in empire as both source of the wealth of nations and source of the national debt and of the exploitation and impoverishment of the working class at home and abroad. The American colonies, Smith thought, were not profitable and were in any case bound to go their separate ways, but meanwhile the debt could at least be managed by loading Ireland, India, and the remaining colonies with new taxes. Smith's magnum opus appeared just at the start of the Revolutionary War, but he comes close to declaring, as Freeman Tilden notes, that the British national debt "cost [Britain] the American colonies" (Tilden 225). Whatever the home consequences of the national debt, Smith nevertheless believed that much of the burden could be shifted to the poor and powerless elsewhere in the world—one of the founding insights of the new "science" of economics, foreshadow today's global debt crisis.

Smith also adumbrates the anti-imperial emphasis among some Victorian advocates of free trade such as Richard Cobden and John Bright (Semmel 53–55). Smith is not happy about much of the expansion of the British Empire. The American and West Indian colonies provide revenue and markets for British goods, but the profits accrue only to a minority of British investors and merchants whereas the majority "have been burdened with the whole expence of maintaining and defending that empire" (Smith 626). The eighteenth-century series of wars mainly against the French have been fought at costs far higher than the returns from the colonial trade. In just the two most recent wars, Smith points out, "more than two hundred millions have been spent, and a new debt of more than a hundred and seventy millions has been contracted" (626). The interest alone on this new debt amounts to more than the profits coming from the colonies—according to Smith, to more even than the entire value of the colonial trade. But quite apart from the self-interest of the wealthy minority who benefit from that trade, there is another factor, Smith thinks, that will prevent Britain from relinquishing any of its colonies, no matter how unprofitable, without more warfare. Though he does not analyze this highly irrational factor in any detail, Smith identifies it as national "pride" (582).

Like Smith at the end of *The Wealth of Nations*, toward the end of the first volume of *Capital*, Marx analyzes the relations between debt and empire. "The only part of the so-called national wealth that actually enters into the collective possession of a modern nation is," he writes, the "national debt" (1:919). The ideological subterfuge whereby the majority of people are led to mistake national debt for national or common wealth—that is, "the modern doctrine that a nation becomes the richer the more deeply it is in debt [is] the *credo* of capital. And with the rise of national debt-making, lack of faith in the national debt takes the place of the blasphemy against the Holy Ghost, which may be forgiven" (1:919).

Identification of the nation-state as both source and guardian of the public's prosperity, when in reality it is grounded on nothing more solid or credible than its own national indebtness, Marx thinks, is the large-scale version of the mystification that occurs before the very eyes of an individual mesmerized by commodities. Marx goes on to argue that empire is tied to industry through "public debts, heavy taxes, protection, commercial wars, &c" and that these involve not only mystification to disguise exploitation, debt, and poverty as their opposites. What is more, they involve human sacrifice and cannibalism—fetishism again, in short, at least as most Victorians understood the term, as virtually a synonym for "savage" beliefs or superstitions. "The birth" of industry, Marx writes, "is celebrated by a vast, Herod-like slaughter of the innocents" (*Capital* 1:922), especially child factory workers offered up as sacrificial victims to the new Mammon or Moloch of capital. In comparison with these savage metaphors for what Zola in *Germinal* also referred to as the "cannibal god" of capital, the fetishism of commodities seems relatively harmless. But for Marx, it is the key to the clockwork that makes the modern nation-state and its empire tick, creating a living, breathing monstrosity produced by the "dream of reason" of the Enlightenment.[5]

From Smith's time forward, the debt continued to mount as Britain moved toward its climax of industrial and imperialist expansion, with the Bank of England pulling the purse strings. Successive governments struggled against what Gladstone in 1848 called "that great throttling monster, the Debt" (quoted in Matthew 624), but this monster was a much deflated threat by the mid-Victorian period. The British national debt, though never shrinking to eighteenth-century levels, had miraculously shrunk in relation to GNP and per capita income. For the expanding bourgeoisie, individual prosperity was on the rise. Even regularly employed urban workers including the factory proletariat were comparatively prospering. As Hobsbawn puts it, "The British middle-class citizen who surveyed the scene in the early 1870s might well have thought that all was for the best in the best of all possible worlds. Nothing very serious was likely to go wrong with the British economy. But it did" (*Industry* 126). In regard to what went wrong first, Hobsbawm has in mind the so-called Great Depression that began in 1873 and lasted until 1896. Though not a catastrophe like the 1929 crash and its global aftermath, it marked the beginning of the end of Britain's imperial and industrial hegemony, a decline that accelerated dramatically after World War I. Also, although through empire, industry, and the stock market, debt had miraculously turned into wealth for many, the burden of interest payments continued to be so great that the national debt has to be considered among the causes of Britain's decline in this century (see O'Brien; Veseth). After World War I, Britain had spent about twelve billion pounds, "less than half of which had been raised by taxation, the rest by internal borrowing. The National Debt rose elevenfold," writes Harold Perkin, "from £706 million to £7,876 million, and debt interest [absorbed] up to 40 per cent of state expenditures between the wars" (226). Just what overall impact the national debt had on the British economy may be unclear, but through taxation and interest payments it was part of a fiscal regulatory system that for years helped keep the economy on an even keel while also exacerbating the exploitation of labor and class conflict both at home and abroad.

5. I have in mind the etching by Francisco de Goya whose title in English translation reads: "The dream of reason produces monsters." In Spanish, the sentence is ambiguous; *sueño* means either "dream" or "sleep." Cf. Zizek: the ultimate "subject of the Enlightenment" is "the monster," as in that pioneer science fiction fantasy *Frankenstein* (*Symptom* 134–140).

Exploitation abroad involved the creation of debts for the colonies. Both Britain's industrial takeoff and its world hegemony, from roughly 1830 down to World War I, were attended by a mounting "deficits of payments" problem that successive governments managed partly to solve through the Indian revenue system. Perhaps two-fifths of British deficits in Europe and the United States were offset by the growing indebtedness of India to its imperial master (Doyle 265). Britain stayed prosperous partly by draining India of its wealth and undermining its indigenous textile industry along the way. Millions of Indian craftworkers were thrown back on the land, adding to the already crippling population problem and abetting a series of unprecedented famines starting in 1877. Indian indebtedness to Britain, to be paid from Indian taxes, stood at £51 million in 1857, the year of the mutiny; at £97 million in 1862; and at £200 million in 1901 (Dutt 5–7). After World War II, the situation was temporarily reversed: according to Cheryl Payer, Britain stood in India's debt "for unrequited exports which India had supplied . . . during the war, which in 1948 amounted to £1,200 million" (167). But this foreign exchange surplus was soon exhausted in independent India's drive to modernize (i.e., industrialize), and India is today one of the largest debtors to the World Bank and the International Monetary Fund (Payer 166).

After 1776, the fledgling United States also had to contend with the issues of national debt and public credit, which formed its initial economic base, or Great Zero. Even more radically than its imperialist "mother country" and enemy, the United States was both founded and funded through the creation of its national debt, and that insolvency, despite the country's territorial aggrandizement and modern prosperity, has never been eradicated.[6] In *The Federalist Papers* and elsewhere, Alexander Hamilton argued for responsible management of the national debt, but by the time of his "First Report on the Public Credit" to the House of Representatives (14 January 1790), the total indebtedness of the United States was approximately $77,124,464 (Stabile and Cantor 19). Hamilton did not believe that the debt should be entirely eliminated; on the contrary, when not excessive, national debts were stimulants to progress (Stabile and Cantor 16). But this position led him into the reiteration of the tautological proposition that it was necessary to restore and maintain "confidence" or "faith" in "public credit" (that is, to restore confidence in public confidence): "If the mainte-

6. For still another example of the creation of a new nation-state out of a former British colony on the economic foundation of a large and growing national debt, compare New Zealand (see Sinclair, esp. the chapter "The Frontier of Debt" 151–171).

nance of public credit, then, be truly so important, the next inquiry which suggests itself is: By what means is it to be effected? The ready answer . . . is, by good faith" (Hamilton 5).

Hamilton is less conservative on the issue of public credit than Burke, Hume, or many other commentators. He just thinks that the national debt needs to be held in check, while the interest on it is paid in "good faith," so that it can swell the "confidence" of the public, rather than cause that confidence to collapse. In an equally ambivalent manner, Tom Paine argued, on different occasions, *for* the U.S. public debt as a source of national unification and loyalty and *against* the British "funding system" as a thoroughly iniquitous, ruinous cause of its empire building and its attempt to retain the American colonies. A key text here is Paine's 1797 pamphlet *The Decline and Fall of the English System of Finance*, from which William Cobbett (among others) learned that "the Nation must destroy that monster the Debt: or that the monster must destroy this form of government" (*Autobiography* 130). Paine also employed metaphors of monstrosity, delusion, and religious gullibility to describe how, through "public credit," England had been led to mistake the national debt for national wealth: "Do we not see that nature, in all her operations, disowns the visionary basis upon which the [English] funding system is built?" (302). *Credit* is, of course, the operative term here, identical to what Paine sees as the falsely "visionary basis" of the "funding system"; the contrary meanings of "credit" as indebtedness and as belief or faith, whether positive or delusory, pervade modern and now postmodern economic and social-theoretical discourse.

Jeremy Bentham's positive, utilitarian, and imperialist attitude toward public credit offers a striking counterpoint to Berkeley's, Hume's, and Cobbett's negative ones. "Among the effects resulting from the national debt in the *early* stages of its existence," Bentham writes, "was the security it afforded to the old established constitution, by engaging the *purses* and *affections* of the *monied interest* in the service and support of the new-established government" (145). Bentham goes on to propose that the system of "public credit" be extended to include the poor as well as the rich (so that "every poor man might be his own banker") and even to include the empire, or at least India: "What a sheet-anchor to British dominion . . . if by insensible and voluntary steps the population of that remote . . . branch of the British empire, should be led to repose the bulk of their fortunes and their hopes on a paper [bank note] bearing the image and superscription of a British governor!"

(146).[7] Establishing a system of investment in the nation-state's (and its empire's) future which the poor—even the Indian poor—would worship in place of their old forms of non-useful superstition, Bentham believed, might be a backdoor route to an ever more egalitarian but also secure and glorious prosperity at home *and* to increasing imperial hegemony abroad. Given both the economic exploitation and impoverishment of colonial India and the huge national debt that now burdens independent India, Bentham's rosy schemes seem like the cruelest of historical ironies.

4

As a Whig who made one of his major themes the contrast between the "Glorious Revolution" of 1688 and the French Revolution, Burke was in an uneasy position regarding the questions of the British national debt and public credit. He was unwilling to attack the original funding of the debt, but he worried greatly about its excessive expansion. Among other factors, the French Revolution, he thought, was largely caused by national indebtness run amok. "In England we feel the [stabilizing] influence of the bank," but in France "a paper circulation [the assignats], not founded on any real money deposited or engaged for," meant that "the spirit of money-jobbing and speculation" was "volatiliz[ing]" and eroding stable value in landed property and "assum[ing] an unnatural and monstrous activity" sure to prove ruinous to the nation (*Reflections* 307–308). Although Burke may have been right about the assignats through which revolutionary France tried to support itself, in 1797, just a few years after he wrote *Reflections*, the Bank of England itself would suspend cash payment and usher in Britain's own twenty-four year era of paper money.

Employing the key metaphor in Berkeley's "Ruin of Great Britain," Burke claimed that revolutionary France was the first nation-state in history to be founded "upon gaming": "The great object in these politics is to metamorphose France, from a great kingdom into one great play-table; to turn its inhabitants into a nation of gamesters; to make speculation as extensive as life" (*Reflections* 310). Moreover, it was not just stock jobbers and financiers who were transforming France into a disastrous, diabolic version of the wheel of fortune: "Along with the

7. It may be worth comparing Bentham on the possibility of supplying an imperial currency (and thereby debt) for India with the first book published by the most important twentieth-century economist (British or otherwise), John Maynard Keynes's *Indian Currency and Finance.*

monied interest, a new description of men had grown up, with whom
that interest soon formed a close and marked union; I mean the political Men of Letters" (211). These treasonous intellectuals Burke saw as
the hirelings of "the monied interest" or as "a sort of demagogues" who
"served as a link to unite . . . obnoxious [monetary] wealth to restless
and desperate poverty" (214). Among other results, this alliance between the philosophes and the moneyed interest had produced a new
sort of revolutionary bookkeeping or accountancy. In a passage rife
with metaphors of credits and debts, Burke writes:

> No theatric audience in Athens would bear what has been borne, in the
> midst of the real tragedy of this triumphal day; a principal actor weigh-
> ing, as it were in scales hung in a shop of horrors,—so much actual
> crime against so much contingent advantage,—and after putting in and
> out weights, declaring that the balance was on the side of the advantages.
> They would not bear to see the crimes of new democracy posted as in a
> ledger against the crimes of old despotism, and the book-keepers of poli-
> tics finding democracy still in debt, but by no means unable or unwilling
> to pay the balance. (176)

"The book-keepers of politics" is an apt metaphor for all economists
from Adam Smith down to Milton Friedman. Moreover, Burke's image
of "scales hung in a shop of horrors" vividly recalls Hogarth's "The
South Sea Scheme," with its "Devil's Shop, / Who Cuts out Fortunes
Golden Haunches, / Trapping . . . Souls with Lotts & Chances" (Fig.
2). In his belief in an alliance between the Enlightenment philosophes
and the moneyed interest, Burke also approximates the interweaving of
economic and philosophical themes in Hume's writings. Hume seems
in retrospect to have been mainly a philosopher who sometimes wrote
on economic issues, whereas Adam Smith was mainly an economist
who sometimes wrote on philosophical issues. But for both Hume and
Smith—as well as for many of the French philosophes from Montesquieu and Voltaire through Turgot and Rousseau—there was no sharp
division between economics and philosophy like that which delimits
those discourses today. As Christensen suggests, however, the interweav-
ings of economics with philosophy in Hume (and Smith) were also the
inner workings of the dialectic of Enlightenment in its early stages,
compromising the supposedly disinterested, rational discourse of philosophy at every turn. Burke paints that subtle process of reason's commodification in the unsubtle terms of a conspiracy between the "men
of letters" and the men of money. It was, in his view, a conspiracy to
bring about the downfall of France (and then Britain and the rest of
Europe) and to turn its once peaceful, religious, and virtuous people

into gamblers and fetishistic witches: "We are taught to look with horror on those children of their country who are prompt rashly to hack that aged parent in pieces, and put him into the kettle of magicians, in hopes that by their poisonous weeds, and wild incantations, they may regenerate the paternal constitution, and renovate their father's life" (*Reflections* 194).

With the conspiracy of the philosophes and money as the chief source of its woes, Burke held, France was doomed to suicidal violence and chaos. Meanwhile Britain would have to look carefully to its own increasingly perilous financial situation:

> Nations are wading deeper and deeper into an ocean of boundless debt. Public debts, which at first were a security to governments, by interesting many in the public tranquillity, are likely in their excess to become the means of their subversion. If governments provide for these debts by heavy impositions, they perish by becoming odious to the people. If they do not provide for them, they will be undone by the efforts of the most dangerous of all parties; I mean an extensive discontented monied interest, injured and not destroyed. (*Reflections* 264)

Whether or not Burke believed that Britain was in immediate danger of going the way of France, he saw something like the same process at work in India. Warren Hastings and the other East India Company employees whom Burke attacked in his many speeches on India during the Hastings trial Burke saw first and foremost as economic parasites, a moneyed interest sucking the "vitals" out of the Indian body politic.

This motif of imperialist parasitism or vampirism is evident in Burke's 1785 speech on the Nabob of Arcot's debts. Burke accuses Hastings and his underlings of building up a huge edifice of indebtedness to themselves which "there is strong reason to suspect . . . is wholly fictitious, and was never created by money *bonâ fide* lent" ("Speech" 93–94).[8] Thus has an honest British government managed to compromise its own public credit and, by shrouding its financial, military, and also sexual crimes in secrecy, to transform its entire enterprise in India "into a mystery of state." The "Indian mystery" is more than a conspiratorial cover-up, however; it extends to all the effects of "this gigantic phantom of debt" (108) throughout India, a debt fueled by "the golden dreams and sanguine speculations of avarice run mad" (143), which is already proving ruinous to India's prosperity and security.

The "fictitious" or "phantom" indebtness that the East India Com-

8. Cf. John Hobson's analysis of "the economic parasites of imperialism" in *Imperialism: A Study* (46–63).

pany was loading on the Nabob of Arcot and other Indian princes Burke treats in explicitly sexual terms—as the "rape" of India, for one thing: "This was the golden cup of abominations; this the chalice of the fornications of rapine, usury, and oppression, which was held out by the gorgeous eastern harlot; which so many of the people, so many of the nobles of this land had drained to the very dregs. Do you think that no reckoning was to follow this lewd debauch?" ("Speech" 169; cf. Suleri 24–75). In metaphorical terms similar both to *Faust* and to Freud's theory of fetishism, Burke treats the debt as a monstrous substitute for a phallus, rising and falling, shrinking or regaining its "plumpness" in relation to the "terror" of exposure: "When you pressed this sensitive plant, it always contracted its dimensions. When the rude hand of inquiry was withdrawn, it expanded in all the luxurious vigour of its original vegetation" ("Speech" 134). India, raped by the false phallus of debt, is doomed to fall prey to an "unnatural infection, a pestilential taint" leading to death: "and instead of what was but just now the delight and boast of the creation, there will be cast out in the face of the sun, a bloated, putrid, noisome carcase [sic], full of stench and poison, an offence, a horror, a lesson to the world" (176).

Burke's metaphors for national debts and their effects, like most of his rhetoric about the French Revolution, he himself must have regarded as "sublime," in one or more of the meanings of that word that he analyzed in his 1756 *Philosophical Enquiry into the Origin of Our Ideas of the Sublime and the Beautiful.* Peter De Bolla has observed a correspondence between the "discourse of debt" and the efflorescence of theories of the sublime, including prominently Burke's *Enquiry,* at the time of the Seven Years' War (De Bolla 103–140); and Burke's ideas about both debt and sublimity represent elaborations of this correspondence. The national debt and the public credit on which it was based were generally viewed, by both supporters and opponents, as irrational, mysterious or inexplicable, and virtually unrepresentable. As a Whig who could neither criticize nor directly, enthusiastically defend the British national debt, and yet who saw plainly enough the disastrous effects of the abuse of public credit in France and India, Burke had more than one reason to treat the financial mysteries of state as sublime objects of terror, combining the properties of immensity, obscurity or darkness, difficulty, power, privation, and pain into a towering phallic menace that could only dimly be apprehended through imagination and a suitably terroristic rhetoric.

"Whatever is fitted in any sort to excite the ideas of pain, and danger," writes Burke in his *Enquiry,* "that is to say, whatever is in any sort terrible, or is conversant about terrible objects, or operates in a manner analogous to terror, is a source of the *sublime*" (58). Through Greek and Roman epics, and through Shakespeare and Milton, Burke associates sublimity with "the ruin of monarchs, and the revolution of kingdoms" (106). The seemingly private, psychologistic categories of the sublime, the beautiful, and aesthetic taste which he explores in the *Enquiry* thus have, at least in his illustrations and metaphors, a public aspect that becomes especially clear when he discusses the connections between "superstition" and sublimity. Considering the effects of danger and obscurity, Burke notes "how greatly night adds to our dread" and then goes on to say "how much the notions of ghosts and goblins, of which none can form clear ideas, affect minds, which give credit to the popular tales concerning such sorts of beings." He then mentions the closely related manner in which "despotic governments, which are founded on the passions of men, and principally upon the passion of fear, keep their chief as much as may be from the public eye" (99).

Burke implies that despotism depends on superstition—a frequent theme among the Enlightenment philosophes whom he was later to lambaste as themselves purveyors of the new superstition of reason. In any event, for most religions as well as for despotic regimes, according to Burke, darkness and dread are highly instrumental: "Almost all the heathen temples were dark. Even in the barbarous temples of the Americans at this day, they keep their idol in a dark part of the hut, which is consecrated to his worship. For this purpose too the druids performed all their ceremonies in the bosom of the darkest woods" (*Enquiry* 100). He is here discussing what he believes to be the case with superstition or idolatry among all "barbarous" societies, but a similar emphasis on sublime terror in relation to idolatry occurs in his later examination of the role of public credit in what he declares to be the barbarous and despotic regime of revolutionary France:

> Laws overturned; tribunals subverted; industry without vigour; commerce expiring; the revenue unpaid, yet the people impoverished; a church pillaged, and a state not relieved; civil and military anarchy made the constitution of the kingdom; every thing human and divine *sacrificed to the idol of public credit,* and national bankruptcy the consequence; and to crown all, the paper securities of new, precarious, tottering power, the discredited paper securities of impoverished fraud, and beggared rapine, held out as a currency for the support of an empire, in lieu of the two great recognized species [gold and silver] that represent the lasting conventional credit of mankind, which disappeared and hid themselves in the earth from whence they came, when the principle of property, whose creatures and representatives they are, was systematically subverted. (*Reflections* 126; my italics)

As J. G. A. Pocock has shown, Burke saw the French revolutionaries' expropriation of land belonging to the church, which it then made "security for the issue of a national loan whose paper *assignats* were to be . . . legal tender everywhere," as a main cause of the catastrophes that followed 1789. Pocock contends that it is impossible "to read Burke's *Reflections* with both eyes open and doubt that it presents this action—and not assaulting the bedchamber of Marie Antoinette—as the central, the absolute and . . . unforgivable crime of the Revolutionaries" ("Burke's Analysis" 334). Certain it is that, for Burke, the idolatry of—or the idolatry named—"public credit" is a major aspect of that enormous historical crime. What more sublimely terroristic object of ideology did history have to show than the great French Revolution, with its thoroughly delusory, unfathomable basis in the fetishism of a perverted public credit?

Yet "the lasting conventional credit of mankind," as represented for Burke by the Bank of England and the British national debt, was no more grounded on a real or substantial basis than the French revolutionary paper currency: the "principle of property," like the identification of gold and silver as the ultimate grounding of all money and consequently all value, is as dependent on a kind of faith (idolatry or ideology) as France's "discredited paper securities." The only difference is that, for Burke, one faith (or form of public credit) is valid and the other is sheer, terroristic superstition. In 1797, by royal proclamation, the Bank of England would cease to exchange its paper bank notes for metallic coins or bullion; through the Napoleonic Wars and well beyond (until 1821), Britain itself would be dependent on (merely) "paper credit," to use Henry Thornton's term, or paper money. A sublime conception, perhaps, but for Burke it was one of utter abhorrence, suggesting the toppling of the mightiest thrones, the decline and fall of the greatest empires of both the past and present.

5

No DOUBT Prime Minister William Pitt was only putting a positive spin on the fetishistic metaphors evoked by the national debt when, in his 1792 speech to Parliament announcing the creation of a "sinking fund" to reduce the debt, he declared, "I am proud to flatter myself that my name may be inscribed on that firm column now about to be raised to national faith and national prosperity" (*Speeches* 1:235). But though Pitt's sinking fund restored public confidence for awhile, "that firm column" sank rapidly when Britain went to war once more against France and when its wartime expenditures through 1815 swamped the sinking fund and more than quadrupled the national debt. Moreover, the banking crisis of 1797 led to the suspension of cash payments by the Bank of England, a suspension that was supposed to be only temporary but lasted twenty-four years and caused numerous critics and satirists to treat their age as a counterfeit one of mere paper money.

The emergence of "political economy" as the first widely acknowledged social science was as much the result of debates surrounding the Bank of England's suspension of cash payments, including the "bullionist controversy" of 1809–1811, as it was of the Industrial Revolution (Houghton 90–125; Langer 103). But for many contemporary observers, these economic developments seemed inseparable. The destructive social impact of "England's dark satanic mills" (to quote Blake) coincided with what seemed to be the most dangerous—vertiginous, sublime, delusional—monetary policy imaginable. This was, at least, how many Romantic radicals including Blake viewed what they saw as Britain's cliff-hanging financial peril.

In *The Economics of the Imagination*, Kurt Heinzelman situates Blake's writings in relation to the historical and economic context of war, industrialization, and the paper money era of 1797–1821. For Blake, the Golden Age would not return until the "gold" of an honest people's affections and deeds should be recognized as the only true wealth; and yet he also believed in the gold standard as the only sound basis for Britain's economy. Heinzelman notes that, in Blake's fallen realm of experience, "to record the cost of a thing is to lament an absence." The word *price* thus "always indicates a labor lost. . . . As an indicator of loss, money has become the only word of value" (124). Though written before 1797, some lines from Blake's "Song of Los" express his view of the relationship between the destructive politics and the equally destructive economics of the modern world. "In bitterness of soul," he declares, the "Kings of Asia" cry out:

> "Shall not the King call for Famine from the heath,
> Nor the Priest for Pestilence from the fen,
> To restrain, to dismay, to thin
> The inhabitants of mountain and plain,
> In the day of full-feeding prosperity
> And the night of delicious song?
>   "Shall not the Councellor throw his curb
> Of Poverty on the laborious,
> To fix the price of labour,
> To invent allegoric riches?"

(ll. 61–70)

Blake seems to have considered all forms of contemporary wealth—from golden guineas to investments in the national debt, and from the rich man's "fix[ing] the price of labour" to goods alienated from the laborers who produce them—as counterfeit "allegoric riches."

In contrast to Blake's radical critique, Thornton in his 1802 *Paper Credit* presented the ablest analysis and defense of modern monetary and credit policy that had yet appeared. Great-great-grandfather of E. M. Forster, Thornton was M.P. for Southwark from 1784 until his death in 1815; he was also, with William Wilberforce, one of the leading lights of the evangelical, antislavery Clapham Sect. Like his brother Samuel, who served on the board of directors of the Bank of England between 1770 and 1833, Henry was a banker, familiar with all the details of monetary circulation, interest, and credit (Houghton 49–53).

In *Paper Credit,* Thornton specifically defended the Bank of England's history and policies, including its 1797 suspension of cash payments. A French invasion scare in that year had caused a general run on banks, which threatened to deplete the Bank's bullion reserve. The Bank's officials intended to resume cash payment immediately after the crisis, but full resumption did not occur until 1821. Thornton's defense of "paper credit" aligned him with the "antibullionists," who contended that the money supply need not necessarily be directly based on, or convertible into, gold or silver; but as a member of the 1810 Bullion Committee, Thornton shifted his position (though not his basic views), arguing that the Bank should return to full convertibility, which would help restore the Bank's public credit. Thornton knew very well that the general populace, just so long as it had confidence in the Bank's solvency, would only rarely demand coin or bullion for their bank notes. Afterall, since 1694, the latter had always amounted to far more than the Bank's metallic reserve, so that if everyone suddenly demanded specie for paper, the result would necessarily have been bankruptcy (cf. Smith, *Wealth of Nations* 277).

Thornton points out that, when the Bank ceased to exchange its notes for coin or bullion, it did not crash, nor did the growing prosperity of the country flag. The secret is that the strength of the nation-state does not depend on how much gold and silver are stored in its bank or treasury vaults. It depends instead on public credit, or the confidence of the public in the soundness of its affairs. More clearly than Adam Smith before him or John Stuart Mill after him, Thornton recognizes the insubstantiality—indeed, the fictiveness—of most forms of wealth, which ultimately amount to forms of credit/debt exceeding the existing material wealth (gold bullion, for example, though all desirable commodities and properties count) that represents the conversion of fiction into reality. Like the concept of exchange, the concept of credit, Thornton realizes, erodes the boundaries between real and fictive or between existing and potential wealth. At one point, Thornton analyzes the standard banking distinction between "fictitious" bills or notes and "real" ones and finds it wanting: both categories are forms of "paper credit" and therefore, he concludes, "to determine what bills are fictitious and what are real, is often a point of difficulty" (Thornton 89).

The greater the amount of existing, material wealth or capital, the more credit can be generated upon its basis: past performance breeds confidence in the future. But the unanswerable (sublime) question that pervades all discourse about public credit also pervades Thornton's analysis: what is the limit beyond which public credit—both in the sense of the national debt and in the sense of faith in the legitimacy of the nation-state—turns into its opposite? In Thornton's *Paper Credit*, as in all earlier and later analyses of monetary policies, of national debt, and of public credit, a key issue is the appropriate ratio between existing wealth and credit, which is always an estimate of the return that the two together can be expected to generate if they are invested in one way rather than another. For many analysts from Hume and Smith through Thornton, J. S. Mill, and beyond, the surest illustrations of how credit turns into substantial wealth are the presently wealthy, the successful "men of credit" who, like Thornton himself, have mastered the secret of credit and thereby made their fortunes. But these models—exemplary, often self-made men of business—because of their *practical* success and experience, can sometimes take unfair advantage of the mysteries of credit. That is, credit as confidence rubs shoulders with con games: fraud, forgery, and the magical or fetishistic conversion of "faith" in mere "paper" into substantial wealth.

There is more than a hint of such fetishism when Thornton speaks of the "mystery" in which the affairs of the Bank of England have traditionally been cloaked (111) or of the "magic influence" of new forms of paper credit (240). Further, he believes that it is only members of the vulgar "lower class" who worry about converting bank notes into gold or silver; well-to-do "men of credit" like himself are much more inclined to have faith in the more ethereal (or fictitious) forms of "paper credit." These, including Bank of England notes which, whether convertible or not, "are always in high credit" (97), are what have made them wealthy in the first place. The vulgar class mistakes existing material wealth, especially gold coin or bullion supposedly in the Bank's vaults, for imaginary and potential wealth; "men of credit" like

Thornton, in contrast, recognize that real as opposed to existing material wealth consists in economic activity and exchange. The "speed" or "velocity" with which money, credit, and commodities circulate is just as important as industrial and agricultural productivity. "The power of manufacturing at a cheap rate is far more valuable than any stock of bullion," Thornton writes; "Even the greatest quantity of gold which we can be supposed at any time to possess, bears but a small proportion to our extraordinary expenditure in time of war, and affords a security which is extremely slender in comparison of that which we derive from the commercial capital, the manufacturing skill, and the other resources of the country" (275). Thornton might have added, of course, "the other resources" of the empire as well. But there seems little doubt that to all of Thornton's seemingly calm, rational defense of the Bank of England and of "paper credit," Blake would have applied his scornful phrase, mere "allegoric riches."

Blake's own responses to the political and economic controversies of his age were themselves often allegorical, so there is no easy distinction between the way he uses "allegoric" in conjunction with "riches" to mean "unreal" and the way he declares his own writings to be "sublime allegories" (*Letters* 57). In any event, two Romantic poets who responded more directly (or less allegorically) than Blake to the issues of the national debt and the paper money of 1797–1821 were Coleridge and Shelley. Coleridge probably read *Paper Credit*; he voiced many of Thornton's arguments in favor of the Bank of England's history and policies both in his essays on the bullionist controversy for the *Courier* and in *Lay Sermons*. In contrast, Shelley hewed to a radical line close to Blake's, one that, on economic questions, was heavily influenced by William Cobbett.

6

CERTAINLY THERE is much in Shelley's "A Philosophical View of Reform" that echoes Cobbett on the national debt and paper money (see Cameron). In his *Autobiography*, Cobbett declares that "the great subject of 'The [Political] Register' always was, the Paper Money" (128) and also that the turning point in his career as a social critic came when he realized that paper money was virtually identical with the national debt: "I soon began to perceive that the fate of the Kingdom must finally turn upon what should be done with regard to the accursed thing called the National Debt. . . . I saw how it had been the instrument of putting unbounded power into the hands of the Government; I saw how it had drawn the wealth of the country into masses, how it had destroyed the lower and middle classes of farmers, how it had added to the list of paupers, how it had beggared and degraded the country" (129).

Besides numerous attacks on paper money and the national debt in the *Political Register*, Cobbett in 1815 published his two-volume *Paper against Gold and Glory against Prosperity*, which Shelley probably read and in which is exposed "the whole art and mystery of making loans and funds and stocks and national debts" (1:30). For Cobbett, this was the delusive mystery of making something out of nothing, or the wealth of a few out of the poverty of the many. The directors of the Bank of England, he writes, are "the Gods of the country" (2:34–35), and literary works depicting "fine benevolent *Jewish characters*" are "offerings . . . at the shrine of Mammon" (1:151). It scarcely needs pointing out that Cobbett's brand of economic populism entailed anti-Semitism in relation to the "mysteries" of high finance, including government finance, or that he resorts to "Jewish" (or Old Testament) analogies of idolatry and golden calves, not far removed from charges of fetishism. According to Bernard Semmel, Cobbett "saw the Jewish bankers of the London Exchange as the principal enemies of a benevolent and caring society" (87).[9]

For Cobbett, high finance including government funding mainly involves deluding the unwary masses through monetary hocus-pocus. He says that the government "funds" or "stocks" are erroneously thought of by many as "a PLACE, where money is kept. A place, indeed, [with] a sort of mysterious existence; a sort of financial Ark" (*Paper* 1:31). But these funds or stocks are not a place where wealth is stowed like a mine or a miser's pile of gold; they are nothing more nor less than the national debt (1:31). Both Cobbett and Tom Paine thought that, with the transition to paper money, "public credit" had been transformed into "public credulity." Also employing religious metaphors to describe the shaky condition of public credit in 1797, Paine writes, "Every English stock-jobber and minister boasts of the credit of England. Its credit, say they, is greater than that of any country in Europe. There is a good reason for this: for there is not another country in Europe that could be made the dupe of such a delusion. The English funding system will remain a monument of wonder, not so much on account of the extent to which it has been carried, as of the folly of believing in it" (303).

9. On anti-Semitism in nineteenth-century economics in general, see Semmel, 85–102.

For his part, Shelley condemns the "financial subterfuges" by which the majority of Britons have been impoverished ("Reform" 235). Since 1688, Shelley declares, the "power" that has increased is not that of the entire nation-state of Great Britain but only the oligarchic "power of the rich" (243). With William III came the institutionalization of public credit, a "device" that is "one of those execrable contrivances of misrule which overbalance the materials of common advantage produced by the progress of civilization and increase the number of those who are idle in proportion to those who work, while it increases, through the factitious wants of those indolent, privileged persons, the quantity of work to be done" (243). Echoing Paine's two main categories of misrule, "force" and "fraud," Shelley adds that "the rich, no longer being able to rule by force, have invented this scheme [of public credit] that they may rule by fraud" (243). Confidence as public credit has been nothing more than a hugely rapacious, imperialist con game. At least the ancient despotic empires like Persia and Rome, Shelley says, were free of "the modern scheme of public credit [which] is a far subtler and more complicated contrivance of misrule" (though also more violently rapacious) than the direct extortion of wealth through force and slavery (244). For the vast majority, Britain's imperial and industrial progress since 1688 has brought only destitution, misery, illiteracy, and starvation. "The cause of this . . . misery is the unequal distribution which, under the form of the national debt, has been surreptitiously made of the products of their labor and the products of the labor of their ancestors" (247). Furthermore, the national debt has been built up chiefly during "two liberticide wars"—the American Revolution and the Napoleonic War—"undertaken by the privileged classes of the country" and benefiting only those classes. The main reforms Shelley advocates to deal with these economic injustices might have come directly from Cobbett's *Political Register.* "We would abolish the national debt. We would disband the standing army. We would . . . abolish sinecures. We would . . . abolish tithes, and make all religions, all forms of opinion respecting the origin and government of the universe, equal in the eye of the law. We would make justice cheap, certain, and speedy" (249).

Shelley often expresses these Cobbett-like views in his poetry. In "The Masque of Anarchy," written in response to the Peterloo Massacre of 1819, Hope tells the "Men of England, heirs of Glory" that, though they do not yet know what freedom is, they know well enough what "slavery" is, and among other things it is

> . . . to let the Ghost of Gold
> Take from Toil a thousandfold
> More than e'er its substance could
> In the tyrannies of old.
>
> Paper coin—that forgery
> Of the title-deeds, which ye
> Hold to something of the worth
> Of the inheritance of Earth.
>
> (ll. 176–183)

In Part 3 of "Peter Bell the Third," entitled "Hell," there is a similar accounting of the main features of the British political landscape that includes the "public debt": "Which last is a scheme of paper money, / And means—being interpreted— / Bees, keep your wax—give us [the rich] the honey" (ll. 167–169).

"Oedipus Tyrannus, or Swellfoot the Tyrant" is Shelley's most elaborate poetical application of the lessons he learned from Cobbett and Paine. Like Mephistopheles in *Faust*, Mammon, chief priest to the Goddess Famine, can show the King the way to easy wealth:

> Does money fail?—come to my mint—coin paper,
> Till gold be at a discount, and ashamed
> To show his bilious face.
>
> (1.104–106)

It turns out that Mammon has had to disinherit his son Chrysaor, who

> Attended public meetings, and would always
> Stand prating there of commerce, public faith,
> Economy, and unadulterate coin,
> And other topics, ultra-radical.
>
> (1.197–200)

Chrysaor may well be a stand-in for the "ultra-radical" Shelley himself, though he sounds more like an orthodox political economist advocating free trade and the gold standard than Shelley ordinarily does. In any case, having disowned Chrysaor, Mammon entails his estate, "called the Fool's Paradise," upon his daughter "Banknotina, / And married her to the gallows." The estate consists of "funds in fairy-money, bonds, and bills" (1.201–204). Foreshadowing George Orwell's *Animal Farm*, all these foolish kinds of pseudowealth go to feeding the "imperial

Pigs" (1.304), who are not the laboring masses but the "drones" growing rich by expropriating the labor of those masses. Or rather, there are lean, starving pigs (Shelley throughout has in mind Burke's famous diatribe against "the swinish multitude" in *Reflections*, 173) and fat, truly piggish ones, the "Gentlemen and Boars" who subsist on "public burthens" (i.e., debts) and on "the taxes, that true source of Piggishness" (2.1.1–6).

Cobbett's and Shelley's Mammons look forward to Thomas Carlyle's diatribes against "the gospel of Mammonism" in *Past and Present* and elsewhere: "Industrial work, still under bondage to Mammon, the rational soul of it not yet awakened, is a tragic spectacle. Men in the rapidest motion and self-motion; restless, with convulsive energy, as if driven by Galvinism, as if possessed by a Devil; tearing asunder mountains,—to no purpose, for Mammonism is always Midas-eared!" (207). In British culture throughout the last century, fetishism was usually equated with the supposedly lowest forms of primitive religion, whereas empire was usually seen as the outcome of enlightenment, civilization, and progress. Yet fetishism and its various synonyms—idolatry, devil worship, ideology—were often turned back on Britain in those versions of social criticism that attacked the substitution of material for spiritual values: Carlyle's Mammonism, Ruskin's "Goddess of Getting On," Emma Robinson's "gold worshippers" (Reed 187), Matthew Arnold's "fetishism" of "machinery" in *Culture and Anarchy* (Simpson 20). Such metaphors carry straight through from the Augustan satirists to the political analyses of Edmund Burke and the graphic satires of James Gillray during the 1790s. (Thus Gillray's cartoons dealing with stupid John Bull, paper money, and the national debt are always about public gullibility or credulity/credit and usually represent that credulity in images that suggest fetishism; see Figs. 3 through 6). "Peter Bell the Third" and "Oedipus Tyrannus" belong to the same satiric tradition, and so does much of the work of Shelley's friend Thomas Love Peacock.

Also apparently an avid Cobbett reader (for he sent copies of the *Political Register* to Shelley in Italy), Peacock too was drawn to write about public credit and the Bank of England's suspension of cash payments. Just as idiosyncratic and yet symptomatic as "Oedipus Tyrannus," Peacock's 1825/26 *Paper Money Lyrics* read like an updated version of Swift's poetical attacks on the South Sea Bubble. Author of satiric novels of ideas such as *Nightmare Abbey* and *Headlong Hall*, Peacock was also, from 1819 forward, an East India Company employee like the Mills (he was not just an administrator; he designed the first armored steamboats used by the Royal Navy). Thus, unlike Shelley, he

FIGURE 3. Prime Minister Pitt and other ministers bilking John Bull with French invasion scares (James Gillray, 1796)

was directly involved in business and government, and yet he remained something of a radical. Anyway, Peacock offers an odd counterpart not only to Swift's attacks but also to Goethe's masquerade and paper money scenes in *Faust*. He was writing in response both to the banking crisis of 1825 and to the controversy surrounding the stoppage of cash payments by the Bank between 1797 and 1821, a period when the gap between paper money and genuine wealth, and between credit in the economic sense and imagination in the poetic sense, seemed unbridgeable to Romantic radicals like Blake and Shelley.

In damning paper money, Peacock employs metaphors of alchemy and devil worship just as do Swift, Gillray, Goethe, and Shelley. Like the critique of imperial politics in *Faust* or in Burke's speech on the Nabob of Arcot's debts, *Paper Money Lyrics* attacks as fetishistic the idea of conjuring something out of nothing, of turning debt into wealth, and of creating empires by magic. In Peacock's parody of Coleridge's "Rhyme of the Ancient Mariner," the three wise men of Gotham, all "paper-money men," go to sea in a tub to fish for the golden or at least silvery moon and return empty handed. Their tale, informed by the "Scottish science" of political economy, offers an allegorization of the financial mysteries of empire:

FIGURE 4. Prime Minister Pitt consuming gold and issuing paper money (James Gillray, 1797)

FIGURE 5. John Bull taking paper money instead of gold (James Gillray, 1797)

> Three men were they who science drank
> From Scottish fountains free;
> The cash they sank in the Gotham bank,
>   Was the moon beneath the sea.
>
> The breaking of the imaged moon
> At the fishing-net's first splash,
> Was the breaking of the bank as soon
> As the wise men claimed their cash.

(ll. 56–64)

Peacock perhaps borrows from Swift here; in "The Bubble," Swift writes:

> One Night a Fool into a Brook
> Thus from a Hillock looking down,
> The *Golden* Stars for Guinneas took,
> And *Silver Cynthia* for a Crown;
>
> The Point he could no longer doubt,
> He ran, he leapt into the Flood,
> There sprawl'd a while, and scarce got out,
> All cover'd o'er with Slime and Mud.

(ll. 125–132)

FIGURE 6. The Daedalian "Sinking Fund" to lower the national debt: "But is it going down or up?" (James Gillray, 1802)

Peacock is not another Swift, however, much less another Goethe: aesthetically and intellectually, of course, *Paper Money Lyrics* cannot compete with *Faust*. In a way, that is part of Peacock's message. What is remarkable about his verses is not their high cultural value but their deliberate lack of it. Peacock obviously knows that his "lyrics" ring false, that they are small zeroes or travesties just as, in his opinion, paper money counterfeits genuine wealth. One issue the contrast between Goethe and Peacock evokes is the relation between a literary or aesthetic scale of values and monetary values, between pricelessness and prices, and between conceptions of "the higher good" and the material "goods" of the market-place. Peacock was perhaps just as disturbed as Shelley by the increasing influence of "political economy," with its reduction of all value forms to the economic. Like Swift and Pope before him, he satirizes the inauthenticity of his age partly by blurring the distinction between poetry and money—because, in his satiric view, that distinction has ceased to exist. The ideology of possessive individualism and the marketplace had long ago begun to reduce the different "symbolic registers" of value, as Jean-Joseph Goux calls them, to money and market relations.[10] Literature and the other arts, emancipated— according to liberal, Enlightenment ideology—from aristocratic patronage and repression, were emancipated through the processes of commodification that also reconstructed them as hypothetically independent discourses, like economics. Capable of expressing revolutionary ideals, literature and the other arts were simultaneously invested with the signs of money and exchange value everywhere colonizing or subverting aesthetic value. The concept of culture, along with that of the artistic imagination, emerged in the early 1800s as a romantic "an-

10. Goux's "numismatics" compares categories of value as seemingly far apart and unchanging as the monetary and the aesthetic. Avoiding the monocausal implications of the base/superstructure paradigm in orthodox Marxist cultural theory, Goux emphasizes the homologies among four "registers" of symbolic expression: the economic, the political, the sexual, and the linguistic. The genealogy of the value form in each register reveals, according to Goux, the emergence of a "general equivalent" (the gold standard, the father/king, the phallus, and logocentric speech) through a series of stages that invariably include fetishism: "In the passage from fetish to symbol and from symbol to sign, value is gradually taken over by transcendence" (49). But this process leading to "transcendence" is illusory from the start, Goux suggests, because fetishism "originates in the erasure of a genesis, the obliteration of a history" (33), even though the process of "obliteration" is "history itself." The gold of the gold standard is always already a substitute for a presence that cannot be recaptured or even remembered. So in Goux's terms, it is possible to understand all forms of representation as involving a kind of absence or debt that is, as it were, the negative general equivalent (or common denominator) underlying the positive general equivalents of all symbolic registers.

tithesis to the market," but that was because of the increasing "subjection of art to the laws of the market" (Raymond Williams, *Culture and Society* 35, 34).

7

EIGHTEENTH- AND nineteenth-century histories of religion define *fetishism* as the original, most primitive, or basic form of belief but also as almost the antithesis of religion—as the false, antireligious worship of material objects regarded as magical or invested with supernatural power. These conceptions are not alternatives but can appear as emphases within a single history or discourse about religion. From the second emphasis arises the ironic inversion that Marx adapted in his analysis of commodity fetishism, namely, the idea that fetishism is not religion but is instead a deluded materialism: the idolatry of golden calves or even of mere stocks and stones. As Frank Manuel points out, Pierre Bayle and other early commentators on fetishism thought of it as "a vulgar, stupid adoration of *mere things*, an affront to the dignity and rationality of man" (28).

Revising Hume's *Natural History of Religion* in part by substituting the neologism "fétichisme" for Hume's "polytheism," Charles de Brossis in his 1760 *Du culte des dieux fétiche* gave the concept its cachet among the philosophes (Manuel 186–188). For most eighteenth-century commentators as later for Marx, fetishism was a negative, "stupid" form of delusion, at best a subreligion for peoples (Africans were the chief culprits) supposedly unable to think abstractly and therefore unable to form proper ideas about divinity. But fetishism also appears in an affirmative light in the writings of at least one important contemporary of Marx's: Auguste Comte.

Marx ironizes what Comte, in his elaborations of "positive religion," treats nonironically. Like de Brossis, Comte views fetishism as the earliest of "primeval" beliefs during the "theological" stage of history. Its originary status and its naïve lack of rituals and theological or superstitious baggage give it a "spontaneity" that, Comte argues, makes it an obvious candidate for "incorporation with positivism" (452). "In fact, religion in fetishism was worship, and nothing more. It was so absolutely spontaneous that its dogmatic element was a mere matter of intuition, and its regime was limited to the exercise of our sympathies, such was the then rudimentary condition of human activity" (462). The postivist religion of the future, Comte declares, "is but the systematization of the instinctive practice of the first childhood of the race"

(463). The fetishist, he adds, "worships materials," whereas the positivist "worships results," but otherwise "both alike invoke the protection of the same Supreme Power" (463). On this affirmative construction, then, fetishism emerges as a nondogmatic, reverent or worshipful materialism; Comte wants merely to transfer the reverence from material or natural objects to human activities and to society itself as the ultimate "Supreme Power" or "Great Being."

Marx, of course, does not question the philosophes' critical view of fetishism as the most irrational form of belief or ideological mystification. Insofar as fetishism—at least, according to many of its European interpreters—was a sort of primitive materialism, it suited perfectly to describe the deluded worship of the commodity spawned by the capitalist mode of production. But, then, in an irony Marx failed to recognize, it perhaps also suited *any* materialism, including Marx's own historical or supposedly scientific materialism. Certainly "fetishism" suits economism, or the worshipful reification of things economic practiced by the bourgeois economists from Adam Smith to Milton Friedman. This is another way of saying that "fetishism" has come to serve as a synonym for ideology, even when ideology takes the supposedly non-ideological form of social-scientific objectivity and materialism.

Public credit is to bourgeois economics what public opinion is to bourgeois liberalism. The emergent distinction between them, not yet systematized in Berkeley and Hume, is symptomatic of economism, or the reification of economic practices and theories as a realm of seemingly natural "laws," more or less divorced from the processes of political criticism, decision making, and reform or revolution that could change those practices and theories. "The unleashed market economy was both the actual form of reason and the power which destroyed reason," as Adorno and Horkheimer put it (*Dialectic of Enlightenment* 90). Again, Smith's metaphor of the "invisible hand" expresses the idea of the independent functioning of a capitalist economy working harmoniously for the good of everyone, but the metaphor also captures the fetishizing of the economy and of economic causation in history that parallels the fetishizing of the state through the dual ideologies of nationalism and imperialism. As historians of economics and the social sciences sometimes claim, moreover, the concept of the invisible hand was crucial for the development of social science in general (Vaughn 997). In short, as it emerges from economism, and insofar as it assumes the givenness and independent functioning both of the economy and of the state, the idea of a science of society is already a thoroughly fetishistic one.

Even more clearly than Blake, Cobbett, and Shelley, Coleridge identified economism, or the separation and gradual domination of economic rationality, as a key factor in what ailed the modern nation-state. Paradoxically, at the same time that he defended both public opinion and public credit as twin pillars of the state, he accused those who treat economics in isolation from other aspects of society or other forms of value as establishing a new sort of secular idolatry, a fetishism of the economic sphere itself: "I dare affirm, that few superstitions in religion have been so extensively pernicious to the intellectual and moral sanity of this country and France, as those of (so-called) Political Economy" (*Letters* 18). To the "idol" of the economy, the blindly worshiping economists "make bloodier sacrifices than ever the Mexicans did to Tescalipoca" (*Friend* 1:299). Those learned in "the mysteries of political oeconomy," according to Coleridge, mistake economic value for ultimate worth, but "men . . . ought to be weighed, not counted. Their *worth* ought to be the final estimate of their valuè" (*Lay Sermons* 211).

Just as Burke attacked the "mechanic philosophy" of the philosophes, so Coleridge attacks that of the economists, including Smith, Malthus, and Ricardo: "The histories and political economy of the present and preceding century partake in the general contagion of its mechanic philosophy, and are the *product* of an unenlivened generalizing Understanding" (*Lay Sermons* 28). Here Coleridge distinguishes between a lower, calculating or rationalizing faculty (the "understanding") and a higher "reason" (or "imagination") central also to Hegel's philosophical politics. Isolated from imagination, economics was mere rationalized avarice (Calleo 17). For both Coleridge and Hegel, the effects of the understanding, when divorced from the higher reason, are similar to those that Adorno and Horkheimer would later attribute to technological or instrumental rationalization, "the rationale of domination itself" emanating from "the coercive nature of society alienated from itself" (*Dialectic of Enlightenment* 121). In *Lay Sermons, On the Constitution of Church and State*, and elsewhere, Coleridge contends that the political principle that corresponds to the higher reason and that, in a healthy condition of society, should operate to countervail mere economic self-interest is the state. Hegel similarly identifies the "civil society" of commerce, self-interest, and economics for which the lower faculty of understanding is sufficient as standing over against the state, which appeals to the ethical ideals of community and self-sacrifice (as in war) and for whose full comprehension the higher, philosophical or

transcendent faculty of reason is necessary (*Right* 175).[11] For both Coleridge and Hegel, the lower sphere of commerce (for which the "science" of economics suffices in practical affairs) should be subordinated
to the higher sphere of the state, or rather of "church and state" (a
unity that economics or the mere "understanding" cannot compre-
hend or explain). But in the modern era, according to Coleridge, that
subordination has been abandoned, with devastating results (Calleo
105–124).

In *The Friend*, Coleridge develops a general account of materialism
as idolatry or fetish worship, an account that, as David Simpson notes,
applies to all forms of representation that disconnect subject from object and understanding from reason (Simpson 11–20). In relation to
ideas of causality, humankind

> is inevitably tempted to misinterpret a constant precedence into positive
> causation, and thus to break and scatter the one divine and invisible life
> of nature into countless idols of the sense; and falling prostrate before
> lifeless images, the creatures of his own abstraction, is himself sensu-
> alized, and becomes a slave to the things of which he was formed to be
> the conqueror and sovereign. From the fetisch of the imbruted African
> to the soul-debasing errors of the proud fact-hunting materialist we may
> trace the various ceremonials of the same idolatry, and shall find selfish-
> ness, hate and servitude as the results. (*Friend* 1:518)

The fetishism of materialism (for Coleridge, these terms are virtually
synonymous) was more than an intellectual disease, however; it was a
general one, evident everywhere in nineteenth-century European society: "Could we emancipate ourselves from the bedimming influences of
custom, and the transforming witchcraft of early associations, we
should see as numerous tribes of *Fetisch-Worshippers* in the streets of
London and Paris, as we hear of on the coasts of Africa" (1:106).

Guided only by the "invisible hand" of the economy, or in other
words by the materialistic idolatry of the economists, "the spirit of
trade" was producing not prosperity, but the impoverishment of the
masses. The economists, Coleridge believed, measured the progress of
wealth by the increase in the number of wealthy individuals and not in
relation to "commonwealth" (*Church and State* 64). The modern fetishism of materialism—or the worship of nothing greater or more sub-

---

11. On the understanding versus reason in relation to Hegel's theory of the state, see
also Avinieri 141–147. Coleridge elaborates on this distinction in many places, including
On the Constitution of Church and State 58.

lime than individual self-interest—had subverted the old, generous "constitution" of the nation, with tragic results,

> when the old Labourer's Savings, the precious robberies of self-denial from every day's comfort; when the Orphan's Funds, the Widow's Livelihood, the fond confiding Sister's humble Fortune, are found among the victims to the remorseless mania of dishonest Speculation, or to the desperate cowardice of [commercial] Embarrassment, and the drunken stupor of a usurious Selfishness that for a few months' respite dares incur a debt of guilt and infamy, for which the grave itself can plead no statute of limitation. (*Lay Sermons* 208)

This is the stuff of Victorian melodrama, perhaps, but it is also that of Burke's melodrama, both in *Reflections* and in his Indian speeches with their lurid metaphors of rape and of the towering, sublimely phallic properties of debt.

Both Coleridge and Burke understand the state as necessarily based on religion, more particularly on an "established church" (specifically, of course, the Church of England). But whereas Burke defends "prejudice" as the sort of belief vital to the maintenance of social order, Coleridge stresses "imagination" or "vision," as when, in *On the Constitution of Church and State,* he writes, "And of the many political *ground-truths* contained in the Old Testament, I cannot recall one more worthy to be selected as the *Moral* and L'ENVOY of a Universal History, than the text in Proverbs, WHERE NO VISION IS, THE PEOPLE PERISHETH" (46). The total body politic or social organism—"the state" in its highest meaning both as the ideal union of "church and state" and as "commonwealth"—is divinely, mysteriously ordered, ultimately comprehensible only through "vision" or the imagination. For Hegel, too, the state is nothing less than the incarnation of the World Spirit: "The state is the divine will" (*Right* 166); it is the ultimate "destination" of world-historical nations as the realization of "freedom" (*History* 59, 19). Moreover, for both Coleridge and Hegel, the state is intimately connected to the development and dissemination of a national culture. Rightly conceived, the state "is the Spirit of the People itself" as expressed in "the whole of that cycle of phenomena which constitutes the *culture* of a nation," according to Hegel (*History* 50). And while religion expresses the state's highest ethical and spiritual truths, the worldly vision or religious embodiment of the ultimate "ethical Idea" of the state is "patriotism" (*Right* 155–164).

To counteract the havoc wrought by industrialization and "the self-regulating economic Machine" that he saw as an immediate threat to culture, Coleridge offers a totalizing vision of the welfare of the whole

society under the benevolent supervision of "church and state," including the national "clerisy," or the clergy expanded to include all intellectuals who have or should have both the welfare and the "cultivation"
(or education) of all the people as their primary responsibility (*Church
and State* 46–54): "The CLERISY of the nation, or national church, in its
primary acceptation and original intention comprehended the learned
of all denominations . . . in short, all the so called liberal arts and
sciences . . . which constitute the civilization of a country, as well as the
Theological" (46). As Matthew Arnold was later to do, Coleridge pins
his hopes for "culture" on "the Spirit of the State" as opposed to "the
Spirit of Commerce" (*Lay Sermons* 223). The state itself is virtually identical to the higher reason (or vision) capable of imagining its own ideal
lineaments and thereby of expressing itself in the creation and dissemination of a unified, worshipful, and patriotic culture of all the people
(Raymond Williams, *Culture and Society* 49–70).

The Hegelian-Romantic separation of the poetic imagination and
the higher reason from the mere materialist calculus of the understanding was an attempt to overcome the insidious commodification of
reason (and therefore of philosophy) that Christensen detects already
at work in Hume's corrosive skepticism. But Coleridge like Hume declares that public opinion rather than the decisions or deeds of "the
great" is "the true proximate cause" of all "national events" (*Lay Sermons* 13). This is because public opinion, Coleridge claims, is not the
creature of mere self-interest. It is instead, at least in its ideal guise, the
reflection of the remote, first cause of "national events," namely, ideas.
"It would not be difficult, by an unbroken chain of historical facts,"
Coleridge writes in *The Statesman's Manual*, "to demonstrate that the
most important changes in the commercial relations of the world had
their origin in the closets or lonely walks of uninterested [i.e., disin-
terested] theorists" (*Lay Sermons* 14). These "commercial relations" in
turn have produced Britain's great success in war, in empire building,
and in domestic progress and prosperity.

In this sequence, at least, the ideas of "uninterested theorists" are
the primum mobile of history. But these ideas can take effect only
through the mediation of public opinion and its near ally, "commercial
relations." In short, although Coleridge is trying to argue the opposite
case, he suggests that the "uninterested" ideas of isolated genius can
act on the world only by entering the marketplace as commodities to
be bought and sold. Sounding very much like Macaulay on the grand
material results of Bacon's empiricism, Coleridge points to "discoveries
and improvements in the mechanic arts" as leading the way and yet as

emanating from "the visions of recluse genius. . . . All the *epoch-making* Revolutions of the Christian world . . . have coincided with the rise and fall of metaphysical systems" (*Lay Sermons* 14–15). Coleridge does not fully examine how "the visions of recluse genius" get disseminated into the lower-order reflection of those visions known as public opinion (nor does he suggest their diffusion through the medium of "culture" in the sense of education). But clearly the process is *both* facilitated by "commercial relations" *and* analogous to the origin and spread of religions: "WE . . . LIVE BY FAITH" (*Lay Sermons* 18).

In *On the Constitution of Church and State*, Coleridge argues that public opinion can be deluded or misled but also that, when truly led, it is nothing less than "the voice of God": "God is the unity of every nation; . . . the convictions and the will, which are one, the same, and simultaneously acting in a multitude of individual agents, are not the birth of any individual; '. . . when the people speak loudly and unanimously, it is from their being strongly impressed by the godhead or the demon. Only exclude the (by no means extravagant) supposition of a demoniac possession, and *then* Vox Populi Vox Dei" (31; cf. Hegel, *Right* 201–205). But if public opinion is religious or mystical in its workings, a reflection of demon or godhead, and also of "the visions of recluse genius," much the same can be said about public credit. Private or merely self-interested commercial credit, Coleridge thinks, is decidely *not* an offshoot of vision (much less of orthodox religious faith) but rather of merely worldly understanding. In *Lay Sermons*, it is the fluctuations of such private commercial credit that Coleridge was one of the first to understand as "cycles" or "revolutions" of economic activity. "Within the last sixty years," he writes, "there have occurred at intervals of about 12 or 13 years each, certain periodical Revolutions of Credit. Yet Revolution is not the precise word. To state the thing as it is, I ought to have said, certain gradual expansions of credit ending in sudden contractions" (202).

These expansions and contractions Coleridge then refigures in terms of mythical sublimity. Credit in good times soars "to a certain utmost possible height, which has been different in each successive instance; but in every instance the attainment of this, its ne plus ultra, has been instantly announced by a rapid series of explosions (in mercantile language, a *Crash*) and a consequent precipitation of the general system." In an extended analogy, he likens the cycles of credit, or of commercial boom and bust, to the story of Icarus trying to reach the sun on his Daedalian wings: "For a short time this Icarian Credit, or rather this illegitimate offspring of CONFIDENCE, to which it stands in the same relation as Phäethon to his parent god in the old fable, seems to lie stunned by the fall; but soon recovering, again it strives upward—" only to crash again, in cycles that mimic the wheel of fortune in medieval and Renaissance discourse and that Coleridge likens both to madness and to gambling (*Lay Sermons* 202–203). Fueled by "Want of principle" and by "Confederacies of false credit," he writes, "the movements of Trade become yearly gayer and giddier, and end at length in a vortex of hopes and hazards, of blinding passions and blind practices, which should have been left where alone they ought ever to have been found, among the wicked lunacies of the Gaming Table" (204).

At this point in his second *Lay Sermon*, Coleridge sounds utterly hostile to "the spirit of commerce" with its often ruinous revolutions or cycles of credit. On the contrary, he is critical only of unregulated or unbalanced credit, in need of some sort of state intervention. He does not describe such intervention in detail, but implicit in his argument are both his idea of the primary negative and positive functions of the state and a distinction between private and public credit. The negative functions of the state are military and policing, "the protection of person and property for all its members" (216). The three positive functions are "to make the means of subsistence more easy to each individual. . . . To secure to each of its members THE HOPE of bettering his own condition or that of his children. [And to help to develop] those faculties which are essential to his Humanity, i.e., . . . his rational and moral Being" (216–217). Directly inimical to fulfilling these positive functions is a "system of credit" that operates only for the potential gain of private "speculators" (those who indulge in "the wicked lunacies of the Gaming Table") rather than for the collective good. In his remarks on credit cycles, Coleridge is distinctly *not* attacking public credit in its usual identification with the national debt. It is only "the overbalance of the commercial spirit in consequence of the absence or weakness of the counter-weights" that causes boom-and-bust cycles. Provide the right counterweights—apparently chiefly religion and the education of the "lower orders"—and prosperity and progress will be assured, Coleridge thinks, through the vitality and growth of "the commercial spirit."

In contrast to private speculation and stock market gambling, public credit is a key element in Coleridge's theory of what unifies a healthy society—perhaps just as key as religion and, indeed, similar to religion in its invisible, mysterious operations. Besides the myopia of the economists, Coleridge finds the preachings of radical "demagogues" like Paine and Cobbett directly threatening to public credit: "Wretches!

they would without remorse detract *the hope that is the subliming and expanding warmth of public credit,* destroy the public credit that is the vital air of national industry, convert obstruction into stagnation, and make grass grow in the exchange and the market-place . . . !" (*Lay Sermons* 168; my italics). Here Coleridge is echoing arguments that he had offered earlier in *The Friend,* especially in the essay "On the Vulgar Errors Respecting Taxes and Taxation." The essay rejects Paine's thesis that taxes are "so much money actually lost to the people; and a nation in debt [is] the same both in kind and consequences, as an individual tradesman on the brink of bankruptcy" (*Friend* 1:229).

It is also a rejection of Hume's account of public credit, which like Paine's was based, Coleridge points out, on the false analogy between a nation and an individual, so that "a debt of a nation was the same as the debt of an individual" (1:234). On the contrary, the national debt has "more than quintupled" since Hume wrote, but with exactly the opposite effect from the one Hume predicted. Not national calamity but national prosperity and, indeed, imperial power and glory has been the result that Coleridge considers virtually self-evident: "Instead of being poorer and poorer, we are richer and richer. Will any man in his senses contend, that the actual labour and produce of the country has not only been decupled within half a century, but increased so prodigiously beyond that decuple as to make six hundred millions a less weight to us than fifty millions were in the days of our grandfathers?" (1:234). The chief cause of "this stupendous progression of national improvement," Coleridge says, is precisely "that system of credit and paper currency, of which the National Debt is both the reservoir and the water-works" (1:234).

The national debt is "the cement" that binds together all the members of the "body politic"; and credit is the transparent or invisible blood that flows through the arteries of that miraculous organism. Indeed, public credit has something about it virtually supernatural; Coleridge implies that it is nothing less than the "soul" of the body politic: "The cause and mother principle of this unexampled confidence [in the Bank of England], of this *system* of credit, which is as much stronger than mere positive possessions, *as the soul of man is than his body,* or as the force of a mighty mass in free motion, than the pressure of its separate component parts would be in a state of rest—the main cause of this, I say, has been our NATIONAL DEBT" (*Friend* 1:233; my italics). Throughout his astonishing essay on taxation, Coleridge seems to be echoing Thornton's *Paper Credit,* with which he was surely familiar. He certainly sounds less like a philosophical conservative than like a fellow traveler of Macaulay's liberal chauvinism. The present is better than the past; the "British Empire" is the mightiest in the world (1:231); no country is more prosperous than Britain; and Coleridge, in a thoroughly Macaulay-like assertion, "boldly challenge[s] the whole world to shew a Peasantry as well fed and cloathed as the English, or with equal chances of improving their situation, and of securing an old age of repose and comfort to a life of chearful industry" (1:238).

In his Indian speeches as well as in *Reflections on the Revolution in France*, Burke took to an extreme the rhetoric of insanity, rapacity, black magic, and fetishism which the Augustan satirists had visited upon the British national debt. And, as in *Gulliver's Travels*, this rhetoric is directly associated with a powerful critique of imperialism. Coleridge now adds to Burke's criticism a theory of commercial cycles, connected to a forceful attack both on economism and on the effects of industrialization. But the attack is paradoxically linked to a defense of both public credit and public opinion, which ideally are versions of secular faith or vision diffusing themselves—circulating together with money—and giving life to the body politic. Moreover, Coleridge's defense specifically of public credit and the national debt comes as part of his general program of refuting the political economists, who themselves, as in the last chapter of *The Wealth of Nations*, tended to view the debt as a major threat to the future stability and prosperity of Britain— one that should be either gradually or immediately diminished or eradicated. Idiosyncratic though his position may be, Coleridge's surprising alignment with both Thornton and Macaulay in the controversy surrounding the national debt is also a foreshadowing of Victorian attitudes: the size of the national debt is a measure of prosperity, not the reverse; private debt and speculation, but not public credit, are a danger to national solvency; and the Bank of England, even when issuing only paper money, is a rock of stability—a golden rock—in the turbulent seas of world history.

8

IN HIS *History of England*, Macaulay sees the funding of the debt and the creation of the Bank of England as examples of Whig genius and foresight which illustrate what was glorious about the Glorious Revolution of 1688: "If the most enlightened man had been told, in 1792, that, in 1815 the interest on 800 millions would be duly paid to the day at the Bank, he would have been as [hard-pressed to believe it] as if he had been told that the government [was] in possession of the lamp of Aladdin or of the purse of Fortunatus" (3:514). Moreover, "from a period of immemorial antiquity, it had been the practice of every English government to contract debts. What the Revolution introduced was the practice of honestly paying them" (1:217). Both Coleridge and Macaulay deploy metaphors found in Augustan satire (the workings of the national debt are magical; the South Sea investors are possessed or insane; speculators on the stock market are reckless gamblers). Yet both see the national debt and the Bank of England as sources of progress and prosperity rather than the reverse. But before, perhaps, the mid-1840s, Macaulay's brand of Whiggish optimism in regard to the national debt was far from hegemonic. And Coleridge's analysis seems like one of the visions of "recluse genius" in the context of the social criticism of most other Romantic intellectuals.[12]

The shared concerns expressed in Cobbett's *Paper against Gold* and Peacock's *Paper Money Lyrics* suggest a pre-1832 moment when working- and middle-class politics more or less coincided around taxation and monetary issues. The Reform Bill of 1832 marks a parting of the ways between radical and liberal economic as well as political views. The widening gap between middle- and working-class discourse is evident in the growth and demise of Chartism in the 1840s. For the Chartists, the national debt continued to be a major issue, as expressed in the 1842 Chartist Petition: "Your petitioners complain that they are enormously taxed to pay the interest of what is called the national debt—a debt amounting at present to 800,000,000 of pounds—being only a portion of the enormous amount expended in cruel and expensive wars for the suppression of all liberty" (in Maccoby 136). But radical and working-class criticism of the national debt recedes into the background in mid-Victorian culture, though later it received some new life in the modern economic theory of imperialism developed by J. A. Hobson and elaborated by Rosa Luxemburg, Lenin, and others. Like Adam Smith, Hobson argued that while colonies might be profitable for individuals and private companies, they were not necessarily or even usually profitable for the home country. Instead, they contributed to domestic social problems that can themselves be understood as forms of debt more or less both caused and alleviated by empire until empire erodes. It was the purpose of "the psychology of jingoism," Hobson contended, to mask as false "commonwealth" the impoverishment of the nation and its colonies for the profit of the few.

12. For Wordsworth's relationship to "the economy of debt," including the national debt, see Alan Liu 325–341.

In general, however, throughout the Victorian period, the burgeoning empire was seen as a source of prosperity at home and often also abroad, in the colonies. The connections between the national debt, war, and the empire were suppressed, though they continued to lead a subliminal life both in radical discourse and in the "political unconscious" of the Victorian novel. A surprising exception among the novelists is Benjamin Disraeli, who in *Sybil* recaptured some of the satiric energy of the first, Tory critics of the national debt; and *Sybil* is the only major novel in English in which the national debt figures as a crucial controversy.[13] Disraeli dates the decline and fall of England from 1688 and the introduction of "the system of Dutch finance"—that is, of the Bank of England and the national debt (William III was the "Dutch king"). The "demoralizing" Dutch "funding system," Disraeli asserts, sounding like Cobbett or Shelley, "has ended in the degradation of a fettered and burthened multitude. . . . It has made debt a national habit; it has made credit the ruling power, not the exceptional auxiliary, of all transactions; it has introduced a loose, inexact, haphazard, and dishonest spirit in the conduct of both public and private life; a spirit dazzling and yet dastardly" (45). A century and a half of "Dutch finance" has almost proved "fatal"; and "since the passing of the Reform Act the altar of Mammon has blazed with triple worship. To acquire, to accumulate, to plunder each other by virtue of philosophic phrases, to propose an Utopia to consist only of WEALTH and TOIL, this has been the breathless business of enfranchised England for the last twelve years, until we are startled from our voracious strife by the wail of intolerable serfage" (56). These are strong words indeed to come from a future Conservative prime minister and clever manager of the national debt, who did as much as any Victorian politician to promote a Coleridgean, quasi-religious nationalism and imperialism and who in 1876 was to recrown the Queen of the land of Mammonism and "voracious strife," eaten up by "Dutch finance," "Empress of India."

13. Cf. Harriet Martineau's *The Farrers of Budge Row*, which instructs its readers that "the same rule of morals which requires state-economy on behalf of the present generation, requires, on behalf of future generations, that no effort should be spared to liquidate the National Debt" (136). I am grateful to Johanna Smith for this example.

Banking on Novels
(1800–1914)

"Public credit means the contracting of debts which
a nation never can pay."

—William Cobbett, *Advice to Young Men*

"I pass my whole life, miss, in turning an immense
pecuniary Mangle."

—Jarvis Lorry in *A Tale of Two Cities*

1

PUBLISHED IN Robert Owen's *New Moral World* newspaper for 30 January 1836, was this bit of angelic doggerel titled, "The Bank-Note, or, Divine Promises":

> Should all the banks in Britain break,
> The Bank of England squash;
> Bring in your notes to Jesus' bank,
> You're sure to get your cash.
>
> Nay, if you have but one small note,
> Fear not to bring it in;
> Come boldly to the bank of grace,
>   The Banker is within. . . .
>
> But, ah! my bank can never break,
> My bank can never fail;
> The firm's THREE PERSONS IN ONE GOD,
>   Jehovah, Lord of all.
>
> *The Infant School Melodist,* 1836; in Silver 149

No doubt national debts are unheard of in the plenitude of heaven. There, money and grace, wealth and virtue are indistinguishable. But for the worldly philosophers of economics, secular variants of these equations often also seem almost self-evident: profitability translates into respectability, and the possession of increasing money translates into the command of ever expanding credit. From the standpoint of economics, moreover, what is true for individuals is true for nation-states and their empires. Though to a William Blake industrializing Britain might seem the antithesis of the New Jerusalem, to the successful man of business (or credit) it might appear to be a close approximation; as Macaulay put it in his essay on Bacon, "An acre in Middlesex is better than a principality in Utopia" (129).

Yet from 1694 down to World War I and beyond, Bishop Berkeley's apocalyptic theme was often repeated: the national debt threatened national bankruptcy and ruin. The classical economists usually balanced their own books by treating the debt as a source of prosperity in the short run which *might* become detrimental in the future, though Ricardo for one saw it as a much graver dilemma. In 1822, William Spence wrote, "[David] Hume and . . . Adam Smith, laid it down, that if the national debt increased to two or three hundred millions, it must ruin us. It increased to upwards of eight hundred millions, our prosperity all the while increasing. Yet all *sound* political economists still firmly believe in the ruinous effects of national debts" (xxiv). Spence himself called the national debt a "wen," but a "wen . . . too intimately connected with the main blood-vessels to admit of the surgeon's knife," though appropriate fiscal medicine might help to shrink it (xix). So, too, James Mill thought the debt a grave immediate danger, but his son disagreed, while still insisting that it should be gradually reduced—a view that both Gladstone and Disraeli expressed in their mid-Victorian budgets (see Matthew; Hirst 161, 215, 225–227).

Ricardo recommended the immediate elimination of the debt through a levy on capital, because the burden of taxation to pay the interest on it fell on the "laboring classes"; because wealth locked up in the debt could be more productively invested; and because debt was immoral, as its very existence gave an "encouragement to gambling" (Shoup 165). This last, moral argument reverberated through the Victorian era, as it had through the eighteenth century (as in Berkeley and Hume). Thus, both Carlyle and Ruskin thought that a nation in debt was like an individual in debt, parasitically thriving on the hard work of others. In condemning the national debt, Ruskin specifically recommended the creation of a "national store" of goods and services to replace it; such a store would deserve to be called genuine wealth or value, whereas the debt belongs in the death-dealing category that, in

Unto This Last, Ruskin calls "illth."[1] Carlyle and Ruskin would have declared immoral and yet understood exactly what Balzac's Eugene Rastignac means when he says, "Borrowing is the best way of sustaining credit." This policy Rastignac calls "the English system" (149). The moral undertow, expressed by Ricardo as well as by Carlyle and Ruskin, belongs with the range of cultural phenomena that both Michael Veseth and Martin Wiener consider in their attempts to explain Britain's industrial decline after the mid-Victorian boom years (Veseth offers his thesis specifically in relation to the history the national debt; see also O'Brien). In any event, other bourgeois economists disagreed with Ricardo's drastic remedy but not with his diagnosis; at least in the British experience, defenders of the national debt have been few and far between.

For Coleridge and Macaulay, however, as for Henry Thornton and the other economists and bankers who approved of the Bank of England's suspension of cash payments between 1797 and 1821 (see Houghton), the idea of credit assumed an almost utopian aura. In France, in the context of revolution, romanticism, and philosophical idealism that opened the nineteenth century, the St. Simonians also treated credit as a social-mystical category, as later did Auguste Comte and Pierre-Joseph Proudhon (see Marx's critique in *Grundrisse* 115–127 of Proudhonist "free credit" proposals). Credit was the spiritual energy that fueled materialist, industrial progress. For the St. Simonians, bankers and financiers were the high priests of the new quasi-mystical dispensation of industrial capitalism. It was two former St. Simonians, Isaac and Emile Pereire, who with the backing of Napoleon III founded the Crédit Mobilier in 1852, a general investment company for floating new business enterprises. "An apostolic band of one-time St. Simonians became promoters everywhere. The shift from Utopian dreaming to daring business adventure was the counterpart of the general change of outlook in Europe after 1848," explains Robert Binkley (97). In a similar manner, in his 1865 *History of . . . Rationalism in Europe,* W. E. H. Lecky echoed Coleridge and Macaulay by declaring that "the system of credit" was one of the major causes of industrialization and, moreover, was "one of the great moralising influences of society, by the immense importance it has bestowed upon character, and one of the great pledges of peace, by the union it has established be-

---

1. For Carlyle, see, e.g., the section on "dishonored bills" in *The French Revolution,* chap. 1, bk. 3. For Ruskin, see letters 7, 8, 58, and 61 of *Fors Clavigera* and also the section called "Store-Keeping" in *Munera Pulveris.* On death, "illth," and mid-Victorian "bioeconomics," see Gallagher's essay on *Our Mutual Friend* 47–49.

tween different nations." But Lecky quickly adds that credit has also been "the most powerful of all the engines of warfare" (2:332), so that he leaves the exact nature of the "moralising influence" of credit in some doubt.

In literary and artistic terms, the shift toward viewing both industry and credit in comparatively positive terms corresponds to the waning of romanticism and the rise of realism (Courbet opened his Pavillon du Réalisme in 1855; the word *realism* first appeared in English also in the 1850s). Ironically, the era of realism, including historical, scientific, and economic materialism and leading through Mill, Marx, and Darwin into the second Industrial Revolution and the new imperialism, was also the era of the final generalization—and general acceptance—of credit as a basic, unavoidable aspect of modern money and modern economic processes. This evolution corresponded to yet another general shift from the early industrial stress on production to the fin-de-siècle emergence of "consumer society." Zola's naturalistic novels—narrative realism taken to its reified extremes—are often about labor and class conflict, as in *Germinal*, but just as often about aspects of the new consumerism, as in *Au bonheur des dames*. Much the same emphasis on both consumption and credit can be detected in such late-Victorian and Edwardian novelists as George Gissing (*In the Year of Jubilee*, *The Whirlpool*) and H. G. Wells (*Tono Bungay*).[2]

In the brief period in modern British history—roughly 1846 to the 1880s—during which it seems at all plausible to speak about a plenitude of meaning and being in, for example, the great Victorian works of literary and artistic realism, working-class discourse about many issues including the national debt was relatively muted, whereas in middle-class discourse, debt became the negative property, so to speak, mainly of spendthrift, shiftless individuals. The banking crises of 1825 and 1837 seemed to repeat aspects of John Law's Mississippi scheme and the South Sea Bubble; the 1825/26 crisis especially was often recollected in Victorian fiction. During that crisis, numerous investment schemes or scams in South America, triggered by the revolutions in Spain's former colonies, gave "the late Regency get-rich-quick mania," to use Richard Altick's phrase (640), an imperialist emphasis. But the bank reform acts of 1826, 1833, and 1844, coupled with the growing

2. A similar stress on consumerism is evident in American naturalism (Frank Norris, Theodore Dreiser) and perhaps even more significantly in that influential protomodernist and aesthetic theorist of the novel Henry James. For Zola, Gissing, and Dreiser, see Rachel Bowlby. For the American naturalists, see Walter Benn Michaels. For Henry James, see Jonathan Freedman.

security of the Bank of England in contrast to the weaker credit of the
so-called country banks (like the one that fails in Elizabeth Gaskell's
Cranford), helped create a new sense of economic stability, at least
among the middle and upper classes.

The free trade victory of the Anti-Corn Law League (1846) followed
by the demise of Chartism (1848) also opened the way to an era of
high confidence and credit extending into the slow depression that
began in 1873. Gladstone's socially stabilizing budgets reduced the national debt slightly, while the GNP soared (Crouzet 10; Hirst; Matthew). In the 1880s, economic and labor troubles, Fenianism, and the
new industrial, military, and imperial competition from Germany, the
United States, and France marked the beginning of the end of the
high-Victorian period of apparent plenitude and confidence. But for
perhaps thirty years, from 1846 into the mid-1870s, it seemed, according to Marx, "as if Fortunatus's purse had been discovered"; no other
period of "modern society [was] so favourable for the study of capitalist
accumulation" (*Capital* 1:802). And Britain provided "the classical example" of capitalist accumulation at its most expansive and powerful,
"because it holds the foremost place in the world market, because capitalist production is fully developed only in [Britain], and finally because the introduction of the free-trade millennium since 1846 has cut
off the last retreat of vulgar economics" (*Capital* 1:802), which from
that date forward subscribed to capitalist orthodoxy.

For perhaps the first time in European history, moreover, in Victorian Britain "money became reliable. The major problems of its mis-
management seemed solved," as John Kenneth Galbraith asserts in *The
Age of Uncertainty* (163); he has in mind the entire nineteenth century
and perhaps other nations as well as Britain. But elsewhere Galbraith
makes two observations: both the American and French revolutions,
like the later Russian one, could not have succeeded except on the
highly volatile fiscal basis of paper money and huge public debts; and
America especially seemed paradoxically to be the thriving flotation of
a welter of different currencies and monetary experiments down to the
Civil War, at the outbreak of which there were approximately seven
thousand different supposedly valid currencies in circulation along
with perhaps some five thousand counterfeit ones (*Money* 89). Compared with the monetary craziness of the United States, France, and
Britain's other rivals for industrial and imperial hegemony, British sterling seemed like the incarnation of sanity and sobriety. Even during the
paper money era of 1797–1821, the bank note issues of the Bank of
England had remained relatively stable and uninflationary.

The Bank Act of 1844 required the Bank of England's note issues to be directly tied to its gold and silver holdings and also made the Bank the official lender of last resort, poised to bail out faltering country banks and other financial institutions in times of crisis (Fetter 165– 197; Clapham 2:186–270). There were further monetary crises in 1847, 1857, and 1866 during which the Bank Act was suspended, but gradually banking techniques improved (Rees 99), and the Bank of England itself remained solvent, even while country banks and invest- ment firms went under, as did Overend, Gurney, and Company in 1866. Coupled with Britain's increasing industrial and imperial hege- mony and, starting in 1847, with the influx of gold from both Califor- nia and Australia, the Bank of England emerged on a foundation of seemingly rock-solid credit that made it the leading financial power in securing and maintaining the international gold standard between 1867 and World War I. Throughout that period and beyond, sterling became virtually a global currency against which all other currencies were measured (Kindleberger, *Financial History* 77–96).

The gradual erosion of British economic growth and imperial power, of which the 1873 onset of the long depression was an early symptom, nevertheless coincided with the second Industrial Revolution and the emergence of modern consumer society with its credit econ- omy, which together with the jingoist expansionism of the new imperi- alism helped to extend modified, increasingly self-doubting aspects of high-Victorian culture, scientific materialism and novelistic realism among them, down to World War I and beyond. Though themes of decadence and degeneration begin to be heard as early as the 1870s, there was no cataclysmic rupture or downturn of the general confi- dence the British middle-class public had in the greatness of their cul- tural heritage, their racial prowess, and their economic and political world leadership. That public confidence is evident in the privatization of the theme of debt that occurs in Victorian novels; a typical work of Victorian fiction is likely to involve, or in some sense even to be, "a complex of money-laundering operations" from public into private capital and from the "possession" of empire into the "possession" of domestic security, centered on hearth and home, as Jeff Nunokawa points out (12).

The satiric tradition that from 1694 down to Gillray, Blake, Cobbett, Peacock, and Shelley had excoriated the government's dependence on public credit and national debt is overshadowed by the tendency of most Victorian writers (again, Disraeli in *Sybil* is an exception) to treat debt as a matter mainly of personal culpability. In Thackeray's *Vanity Fair* and Trollope's *The Way We Live Now* (among many others), charac- ters are often judged by the solvency/salvation equation. Often, too,

142 FICTIONS OF STATE

society at large is found to be deficient (lacking credit, or in a condition of moral indebtedness), but usually the institutions officially connected to money and the national debt—the Bank of England and the Treasury—are deemed both economically and morally solvent. An early example of the privatization of the theme of debt is Samuel Warren's 1841 bestseller, *Ten Thousand A-Year*, in which a lowly draper's clerk, Tittlebat Titmouse, is the beneficiary of a fraudulent inheritance cooked up by the law firm of Quirk, Gammon, and Snap. Although Warren treats the lawyers as little better than con artists, and though loopholes in British law help render the fraud believable for most of the novel, Warren nonetheless lards his text with officious quotations from Blackstone's *Commentaries on the Laws of England* without suggesting (as Dickens was later to do in his attack on Chancery in *Bleak House*) that there is much about the law that needs reforming. Nor does Warren hint that money and property may be categorically counterfeit. On the contrary, Titmouse (innocently enough, it seems) becomes himself the ultimate fraud, upstaging the lawyers—the vulgar clerk in gentleman's clothing.

Similarly, if politics is a sort of frivolous game in Trollope's Palliser novels, that is because the fiscal, legal, cultural, and religious machinery of Great Britain is mostly in order; there is apparently not much, in Trollope's view, that is in serious need of fixing. In *Phineas Finn, the Irish Member*, "Workmen were getting full wages. Farmers were paying their rent. Capitalists by the dozen were creating capitalists by the hundreds. Nothing was wrong in the country, but the over-dominant spirit of speculative commerce" (1:333). As it is precisely the "spirit of speculative commerce" that floats more and more capitalists who in turn pay their workmen "full wages" and that is also responsible for the phenomenon of "farmers . . . paying their rent," Trollope as a social critic has little to say (though he tries to say what he can about the "over-dominance" of the "spirit of speculative commerce" in *The Way We Live Now*). In his early incarnation as chancellor of the Exchequer, Plantagenet Palliser's great reform cause is to put Britain's money on the decimal system. Trollope views this cause as merely a comic crotchet of Palliser's, on a par with the labors of Phineas Finn's "potted peas" committee in Parliament: not much is wrong with Great Britain, and nothing is wrong with her money, even if it is a bit difficult to count.

Novels like *Phineas Finn* and *The Prime Minister*, meanwhile, along with newspapers and related discursive forms including money, helped to produce, as Benedict Anderson contends, the illusion of "homogeneous, empty time" basic to the "imagined community" of the nation-state (23–36)—specifically, to the powerful sense of national/imperial plenitude known as Great Britain. Indeed, although it is not one of the discursive forms that Anderson emphasizes in his book on the origins and spread of nationalism, money is of at least equal importance with novels, newspapers, maps, museums, and statistics in reinforcing a sense of national identity. In the nineteenth-century era of high capitalism, moreover, there is a symbiosis between money and novelistic realism that seems especially significant in making it also the era of high nationalism and imperialism. During the Victorian period in Britain, the forms of narrative discourse including the novel express public credit both more directly in their self-confident forms and more indirectly in their themes than in previous periods, including the first period of fictional realism in the early 1700s. Starting sometime after 1848, moreover, there is a decided shift away from social criticism as in the industrial novels of Disraeli, Elizabeth Gaskell, Dickens, and Charles Kingsley toward a stress on the "moral currency" of culture, as in Matthew Arnold's *Culture and Anarchy* and also in George Eliot's *Felix Holt* and, even more prominently, *Daniel Deronda*, with its related theme of a quasi-utopian, quasi-religious nationalism (Gallagher, *Industrial Reformation* 252–267).[3] This mid-Victorian shift away from social criticism focused on industrialization and the working class and toward the "moral currency" of culture parallels the increasing privatization of issues of debt and (monetary) credit.

Fictional realism in Britain and elsewhere has eroded since the 1880s into the forms of mass culture, while literary modernism rejected its bankrupt conventions in favor, as Fredric Jameson puts it, of a "characteristic indirection [that] circumscribes the place of the fantastic as a determinate, marked absence at the heart of the secular world" (*Political Unconscious* 134). Yet this absence or lack—the minus sign at the center of a society underwritten by ever accelerating national debt and declining industrial and imperial hegemony—was already inscribed in eighteenth-century satire, which condemned national debt as the antithesis of public wealth and which looked askance on public credit, public opinion, and stock market speculation as forms of the "madness of crowds." In Defoe's age as in today's "postmodern condition," it seemed specious to put too much credit in language, that is, to create illusions of reality out of mere words. But largely because of the frailty of mere words (prayers, promises, IOUs), Defoe repeatedly equates salvation with solvency, even though this equation nostalgically bespeaks only an impossible plenitude of meaning and being.

3. "Debasing the Moral Currency" is the title of one of George Eliot's essays in *Theophrastus Such* 81–87.

From Defoe forward, just this equation between financial solvency and personal salvation, at least in the secular sense of honor or credit, reputation or respectability, informs the great, canonical works of realist fiction that have often been described oxymoronically as bourgeois epics. Moreover, the realism that composes these prosaic, fallen or ignoble (commercial and commodified) epics is a linguistic medium that posits the direct convertability of reference into referent, or of a sort of paper credit (words on pages) into the gold standard of reality (cf. Goux, *Coiners* 3–22). "As money was becoming more fictional," John Vernon writes, "fiction was becoming more profitable, not merely more concerned with economic themes, but also more mediated, more representational, more omniscient—in a word, more realistic" (18). The increasing capitalization and commodification of novel production and of the nineteenth-century literary marketplace (see Feltes) corresponds to the rise and dominance of realistic fictional techniques, with their seeming triumph over "the failure of mimesis" (Vernon 19). Yet even at its most self-confident, novelistic realism is haunted by the ghost of that failure, which on one level is nothing more than awareness of its debt to, or difference from, the real. On another level, by its insistence on the substantiality and power of money and commodities, as opposed to the (mere) "moral currency" of culture (and therefore, of fiction), novelistic realism announces its inability to do anything other than mimic the real—that is, its failure to transcend the very conditions of its commodification.

2

MONEY AND fiction, both representational systems relying on credit, are also often interchangeable: money as the fiction of gold or of absolute value; fiction as a commodity, exchangeable for money. And from Defoe forward, realistic fiction, at least, is always in some sense about money. The cultural distance between the Midas-like piles of gold in Addison's dream vision of Publick Credit enthroned in the Bank of England and the piles of gold hoarded by Victorian fictional misers such as Scrooge and Silas Marner is thus not great: the Augustan age of satire was also the first great age of novelistic realism, and even the most avowedly mirrorlike, supposedly unironic versions of realism among the Victorian novelists often have satiric (and frequently self-mocking) tendencies, as in *Vanity Fair* and *The Way We Live Now*.

Nevertheless, throughout Victorian discourse, private misers, creditors, and debtors tend to replace the Augustan themes of public credit and national debt. In Victorian novels, individual bankers like Bulstrode in Eliot's *Middlemarch*, Bounderby in Dickens's *Hard Times*, or Richard Hardie in Charles Reade's *Hard Cash* (1863) may be capable of deceit or fraud, but in *The Banker's Wife* (1843), Catherine Gore treats the profession of banking as more respectable than either stockbroking or manufacturing (Russell 62–75; see also Altick 648–649 for an account of Gore's personal experience with banks and bankers). Private or country banks may fail, as they do in *Cranford* and in Dinah Mulock's *John Halifax, Gentleman* (1856), but the Bank of England is the rocklike support of British credit, national identity, and imperialism. As Altick notes, however, along with elections, bankruptcy was one of the two "most pervasive" of "the broad topical themes in Victorian fiction," but it is the bankruptcy of individuals rather than of governments that is at issue. Bankruptcy "was the Victorian version of Fortuna's wheel, the vulnerable power figures being no longer princes and conquerors but bustling, astute, and above all sanguine English merchants, bankers, speculators, investors—the new plutocracy who amassed wealth and then calamitously lost it" (Altick 638; cf. Reed; Russell; Weiss).

The 1840s—the "Hungry Forties"—especially seem to have been a liminal period for relationships between literary culture and monetary credit. In novels such as Dickens's *Martin Chuzzlewit* and Warren's *Ten Thousand A-Year*, "fortunes" swell and burst with bubblelike fragility, and plots are often based on the question of the authenticity of the major characters' claims to wealth. A similar sense of the insecurity and, perhaps, insubstantiality particularly of the wealth of the nouveaux riches is evident in other narrative forms, such popular stage successes, for example, as Edward Bulwer-Lytton's *Money* (1840) and Dion Boucicault's *London Assurance* (1841). In these plays, most of the characters engage in monetary frauds or deceptions of one sort or another, especially pretending to wealth they do not have. *London Assurance* ends with a symptomatic dialogue among Sir Harcourt Courtly, his son, and the impudent Mr. Dazzle, all of whom have manipulated others with the thoroughgoing "assurance"—both confidence and credit—of "City men" (i.e., of financial wheelers and dealers). When Sir Harcourt asks Dazzle, "Who the deuce are you?" the latter replies, honestly enough, "I have not the remotest idea," though he immediately adds, "Simple question as you may think it, it would puzzle half the world to answer. One thing I can vouch: Nature made me a gentleman—that is, I live on the best that can be procured for credit. I never spend my own money when I can oblige a friend. I'm always thick on the winning horse. I'm an epidemic on the trade of tailor. For further particulars, enquire of any sitting magistrate" (Boucicault 125–126). Sir Harcourt gets the last word, however, which is that "barefaced assurance is the vulgar substitute for gentlemanly ease. . . . No, sir. The title of gentleman is the only one *out* of any monarch's gift, yet within the reach of every peasant. It should be engrossed by *Truth*, stamped with *Honour*, sealed with *good feeling*, signed *Man*, and enrolled in every true young English heart." In short, "gentlemanly" status is a matter entirely of credit, but not the sort of fraudulent monetary credit that carries the day for the likes of Mr. Dazzle.

A time of greater prosperity and financial security emerged after the 1840s in much of western Europe and the United States. Both in Britain and in the France of the Second Empire, the period from 1848 down to the early 1870s has been often described both as the "age of realism" and as the era of "high capitalism." It was, of course, during this era that Marx gave final shape to his theories of historical materialism and of commodity fetishism. Even after the phase of industrial fiction, however, realistic fiction is also often highly critical of such generalized social evils as avarice and materialism (as in Pip's guilty sense of being loaded with "chains" of gold and silver in *Great Expectations*), but its rhetorical conventions and structures involve the reification of the social status quo. Novels by Dickens, Trollope, or Eliot both criticize and underwrite the seeming naturalness and stability of the capitalist social realm and, at least by implication, of the nation-state and its empire. Thus, in *Middlemarch* and *Felix Holt*, Eliot seems more critical of what she regards as the reformist illusions of her characters than of the societal forces of inertia and conservatism that her liberal social Darwinism treats as natural and, perhaps, inevitable. Realism as narrative reification, moreover, is related to commodification not just because novels are commodities written, manufactured, and marketed for profit but because the social realm depicted in them consists largely or wholly of commodities and commodified relations: of goods to be purchased and owned; of forms of property to be bought and sold, inherited or lost; and of characters who themselves either behave like commodities or, if they are good, honest, and at least semiheroic, struggle not to behave like commodities.

The initial signs of modern consumer culture appeared in such characteristic phenomena as the first World Exhibitions in London (1851) and Paris (1855) and, foreshadowed by the Parisian arcades that so fascinated Walter Benjamin, the opening of the first department stores, starting in 1852 with Aristide Boucicault's Bon Marché in Paris (see Michael Miller). In *Charles Baudelaire: A Lyric Poet in the Era of*

High Capitalism, Benjamin correlates emergent consumer culture with the artistic and literary modernisms and avant-gardes initiated by Baudelaire and his contemporaries. The new urban characters Baudelaire depicts and Benjamin anatomizes—the bohemian, the *flâneur,* the prostitute, the dandy—are creatures of the capitalist marketplace; the prostitute as seller/commodity; the *flâneur* and the dandy as prototypal consumers; and the bohemian as the artist/celebrant and at the same time critic/rebel against the regime of bourgeois "fashion" and novelty, which is also the regime of "exhibition," advertising, and commodity fetishism.[4]

Benjamin connects Marx's analysis of commodity fetishism with Freud's analysis of sexual fetishism especially through the figure of the prostitute, the double incarnation, as it were, of "the prostitution of the commodity-soul" (*Baudelaire* 56). The prostitute is the urban type who, in the writings of both Baudelaire and Balzac, most obviously points to the link between commodity and sexual fetishism in modernist culture. But insofar as the *flâneur* and the dandy invest the object world of commodities with aesthetic and erotic value, they also suggest that the two fetishisms are on some level indistinguishable.[5] For Marx, fetishism involves an emotional investment in commodities in excess of both their use-value and their exchange value. His analysis uncovers an *additional* amount of surplus value—a supplement, as Derrida would say, to surplus value. Benjamin suggests the emotional and sexual excess implicit in commodity fetishism when he writes, "If the soul of the commodity which Marx occasionally mentions in jest existed, it would be

4. Cf. Thomas Richards, "The Great Exhibition of Things," *Commodity Culture* 17–22. Benjamin writes, "The world exhibitions erected the universe of commodities. Grandville's [the French caricaturist's] fantasies transmitted commodity-character onto the universe. They modernized it. . . . Fashion prescribed the ritual by which the fetish Commodity wished to be worshipped, and Grandville extended the sway of fashion over the objects of daily use as much as over the cosmos. In pursuing it to its extremes, he revealed its nature. It stands in opposition to the organic. It prostitutes the living body to the inorganic world. In relation to the living it represents the rights of the corpse. Fetishism, which succumbs to the sex-appeal of the inorganic, is its vital nerve; and the cult of the commodity recruits this to its service" (*Illuminations* 166). Much more could be said about Grandville, especially in relation to the satiric iconography of Hogarth, James Gillray, and the Cruikshanks. Like George Cruikshank in Britain, Grandville portrays the general effects of a diffuse and increasingly powerful capitalism, capable of such fantastic effects as transforming people into commodities and commodities into the simulacra of people (as in his numerous cartoons of clothes, the creatures of fashion, behaving like their absent owners).

5. As already indicated, the two forms of fetishism are distinct (Žižek, *Sublime Object* 49). But they are nevertheless intertwined in the commodity form and its correlate, the advertising image.

the most empathetic ever encountered in the realm of souls, for it would have to see in everyone the buyer in whose hand and house it wants to nestle" (55)—like Johnstone's magical guinea in *Chrysal.* The "soul of the commodity" resembles in this regard *both* the soul of the modern, Baudelaire-like poet who gives himself up entirely to "the crowd," just as the *flâneur* "abandons himself" to its "intoxication," *and* the soul of the prostitute who can, for a little cash, "empathize" with anyone and everyone.

The "secret" or "mystery" of commodity fetishism is thus partly that it allows fetishists (or fashionable consumers) to "abandon" themselves and to partake of the "inorganic" realm of the dead, while investing that realm with the fantastic vivacity of alienated vision that brings the dead to life or that personifies objects like guineas. Thus a table, whose production and use-value are obvious to its maker, as a commodity becomes animated, apparently "transcendent": "It not only stands with its feet on the ground, but, in relation to all other commodities, it stands on its head, and evolves out of its wooden brain grotesque ideas, far more wonderful than if it were to begin dancing of its own free will" (*Capital* 1:163–164). The illusory world of commodity fetishism is, like the world of ideology in general, inverted: the inanimate object acquires simulacral properties while its consumers/fetishizers grow more and more lifeless, more and more like the object—or, better, like the objectified realm of the dead, of corpselike objects—they empathize with or long to possess, consume, incorporate. This bringing to life of the dead is one of the reasons Derrida, in *Specters of Marx*, calls Marxist materialist ontology itself a "hauntology" (10) while also insisting that nobody understood better than Marx "the logic of the ghost" (63) that underwrites the seemingly so stable, substantial realms of capital and commodification: capitalism as premature (narcissistic) celebration; and, therefore, also as covert, inadequate mourning.

For conceptions of modernism and now postmodernism, there is no more influential passage in all of Marx's writings than the fourth section of Chapter 1 of *Capital,* "The Fetishism of the Commodity and Its Secret." What is sometimes overlooked in later accounts of commodity fetishism is that Marx thought of money, "the universal commodity," as productive of even greater "fetishism" than the products of labor sold in the marketplace. Capital is also, of course, a commodity form; it is nothing but money invested in the "forces of production" in anticipation of two sorts of return, direct profits derived from surplus value and interest derived from the various forms of borrowing and lending, or credit. The "fetishisms" of money and capital as dominant, universalizing commodity forms are especially "mysterious" (even more arcane and impenetrable than in the case of a coat or a wooden table), arising as they do from the already highly abstract, quasi-religious mechanisms of banking, stock market speculation, and the national debt. Citing Dr. Richard Price, whom Burke had challenged in his *Reflections* and whose recommendations influenced Pitt's sinking fund schemes to pay off the national debt, Marx writes, "The conception of capital as a self-reproducing and self-expanding value, lasting and growing eternally by virtue of its innate properties . . . has led to the fabulous fancies of Dr. Price, which outdo by far the fantasies of the alchemists; fancies, in which Pitt believed in all earnest, and which he used as pillars of his financial administration in his laws concerning the sinking fund" (*Capital* 3:386). Marx points here to the national shape taken by what he earlier calls "the fetish form of capital and the conception of fetish capital" (3:385), which is most mystifying as "interest-bearing capital" (3:383). Invested in stocks, loans, annuities, and bonds underwritten by the state, "capital appears as a mysteriously self-creating source of interest—the source of its own increase" (3:384). Here is the seemingly alchemical formula of money as "potentially self-expanding value" which had been condemned as diabolic usury in the Middle Ages but which under capitalism had turned into an "automatic fetish" (3:384) worshiped by nearly everyone. In short, this is one version of Marx's account of the production of something from nothing, gold out of paper or mere credit, and prosperity out of its apparent opposite that the Augustans had also exposed and satirized as idolatry, alchemy, and mystification. But Marx is now dealing with a fetishism so pervasive and profound that it affects everything and everyone: there is no longer any clear outside to the belly of the whale called "capitalism"; the moneyed interest detested by Pope, Swift, and Bolingbroke has conquered everything in its path.

Implicit in Marx's comments on the fetishizing of capital and its relation to public credit is a further, in some ways even more mystified and mystifying form or, perhaps, level of fetishism known as nationalism. This further sort of fetishism entails the worship of the state apparatus that performs fiscal miracles by creating prosperity out of its own indebtedness. These fiscal miracles in turn both purchase and are rendered possible by the ever expansive military and economic conquest of much of the rest of the world—the voracious incorporation of more and more nonnational territory into the nation-state's empire. With British India specifically in mind, Marx declares, "The results of the bourgeois epoch . . . resemble that hideous pagan idol, who would not drink the nectar but from the skulls of the slain" (Marx and Engels, *Colonialism* 87).

3

THE REALIST novel as practiced by Defoe, Fielding, and others—seemingly so substantial, commonsensical, and veracious—was from the outset a creature of "credit" in at least two senses. First, it was a commodity, produced to be transformed into money in the increasingly capitalized and bourgeois literary marketplace—Hume's "republic of letters." Second, it begged to be "credited" or taken at face value as true, even though its contents were fabricated and therefore, despite their probability and typicality, as fantastic as any "romance"—a contradiction that seems especially strained in apparition narratives. Those prose fictions that continued to be identified by their authors as "romances" stressed their fictionality, their improbability, and their difference from everyday reality through a variety of familiar rhetorical devices that also marked them as quasi-aristocratic and traditional. In contrast, those prose fictions that, like Defoe's, tended to efface the difference between themselves and everyday reality tended also, as in the case of *Roxana*, to take on the formal features of business account books or ledgers—or better, to adopt some of the formal qualities of money itself. It is just this tendency that *Chrysal* pushed to its logical (or rather, illogical, fetishistic) extreme by presenting money—a magically "possessed" guinea, whose spirit of greed in turn "possesses" its owners—as the protagonist.

Mikhail Bakhtin argues that the novel form is so protean, so "dialogic" and, indeed, "novelistic," that "the experts have not managed to isolate a single definite, stable characteristic" of the genre (8). But the commodity status of modern prose fiction, coupled with the realistic novel's tendency to represent money and economic exchange both thematically and structurally, means that the novel has at least one "definite, stable characteristic": its tendency to behave like money. Further, the novel's "dialogic" or "heteroglossic" openness to or "empathy" with all sorts of "voices" and perspectives, in contrast to the closed, "monologic" worlds of epic and romance, mirrors the capitalist marketplace, with its bourgeois but empathic (or prostitute-like) openness to every kind of exchange that can be mediated by money. *Chrysal* approximates the money form more overtly (and yet fantastically and fetishistically) than does, say, *Great Expectations*. Nonetheless, like Defoe's novels, *Great Expectations* is very much a novel about money, about possessions and possessiveness, and therefore also about the making and breaking of its characters' "fortunes." So, too, are most of the other great, more or less realistic nineteenth-century novels, from *Waverley* and *Pride and Prejudice* through *Jude, the Obscure* and *Tono-Bungay*. For many novelists from Scott through Wells, moreover, novel writing was of course a way of earning money, both a "profession" and a demonstration of how, through imagination, poverty and debt could be overcome.

The story of Scott's catastrophic investment in Ballantyne and Company, his refusal to declare bankruptcy or default on his personal indebtedness, and his attempt to write his way out of debt offers a familiar, extreme, but in several ways also typical pattern. One can, for instance, substitute Balzac for Scott with nearly the same general results. "The shadow of bankruptcy, which had darkened . . . Scott's career, hung over Balzac's from the very beginning," writes Harry Levin; "happily for Balzac, financial failure was the beginning of literary success" (154). Levin's assertion can be applied to quite a few other novelists in various languages and more generally to a sizable number of artists in many genres and states of bohemian rebellion against bourgeois values and materialism as they struggled to succeed in the marketplace. This contradiction is reflected in divers ways in nineteenth-century realism, most obviously in its simultaneous critique and reproduction of materialism.

Levin notes that it was the "dollar-conscious" Henry James who said of the Human Comedy that its protagonist "is the twenty-franc piece, [although] it is rather the villain than the hero; its ubiquitous and diabolical fascination . . . is Balzac's *moteur social.* The Golden Calf has indeed usurped the altar and the throne" (191). *The Wild Ass's Skin* is a Faustian romance, which, like all of Balzac's novels, is centrally concerned with money and its effects; it seems to carry the demoniac fetishizing of money that informs *Faust* and *Chrysal* to its grotesquely realistic, and simultaneously fantastic, conclusion. The magic talisman that makes Raphael's dreams come true for a while is the obvious equivalent of the fetishized guinea in Johnstone's tale, but in other Balzac novels there are other equivalents, for example, the miser Grandet's pile of gold coins.[6] Balzac himself, however, remained a debtor to the

---

6. Also noting the importance of money in all Balzac's fiction, F. W. J. Hemmings points to the analogy between the moneylender and the novelist: "In the ordinary course of business, the money-lender necessarily found himself the recipient of so many strange and lamentable confessions that the novelist could not help envying him. . . . The would-be borrower, like the doctor's patient or the soliciter's client, cannot afford to be reticent, even about those secrets he is most ashamed to divulge." Hemmings quotes Bal-

last; as in Scott's case, writing novels was his alchemical way of converting the creatures of his imagination into hard cash. "The crown of [Balzac's] exhausting labors was not to die a bankrupt," writes Levin; "Bankruptcy and solvency, as no one more keenly felt, were to middle-class morality what dishonor and honor had been in the code of chivalry. 'To go bankrupt,' declares the miser Grandet, 'is to commit the most disgraceful of all actions that can disgrace a man'" (154–155). Among English-language novelists, Scott, the young Disraeli, Thackeray, Dickens, Martineau, the Brontës, the Trollopes (mother and sons), George Meredith, and George Gissing all waged literary combat against the specter of debt and disreputability or fiscal disgrace, and throughout their novels this combat is also waged by many of their characters. For all of them, moreover, the analogy between the fictions they write and the money that comes to them through selling those fictions seemed disturbingly self-evident.

Scott set the pattern for later novelists in several ways. He had pretensions, both for himself and for literature, to a higher social status than that associated with bourgeois commerce, but the novels he wrote sometimes seemed to him closer to counterfeit than to genuine money. Thus in regard to his completion of *The Antiquary* so soon after publishing *Waverley* and *Guy Mannering*, Scott wrote to John Ballantyne (11 October 1817): "I am afraid the people will take me up for coining. Indeed these novels while their attractions last [that is, while they continue to be popular and to sell] are something like it" (Letters 1:522).[7] Though stopping short of the counterfeiting metaphor, Scott in the "Introductory Epistle" to *The Fortunes of Nigel* (1822) portrays the still-anonymous "Author of Waverley" defending himself from the charges of "Captain Clutterbuck" that he is just a "mercenary" hack and that his rapidly written productions are no different from those of "a calico-manufacturer." The Captain asks whether the Author is aware that "an unworthy motive may be assigned" to the rapidity with which he produces novel after novel, namely, that the Author writes "merely for the lucre of gain." The Author's semi-ironic response is that, yes, he writes for money, but that in doing so he helps to support the productive labors of many others:

zac's character Gobseck, from the story of the same name: "'My eye is like the Eye of God, which can look into the hearts of men. Nothing is hidden from me. No one has anything to refuse to the man who can tie or untie the strings of the money-bag'" (57).

7. Scott also took an active interest in banking and currency reform; see his *Malachi Malagrowther* letters.

If the capital sum which these volumes have put into circulation be a very large one, has it contributed to my indulgences only? or can I not say to hundreds, from honest Duncan the paper-manufacturer to the most snivelling of the printer's devils, 'Didst thou not share? Hadst thou not fifteen pence?' I profess I think our Modern Athens much obliged to me for having established such an extensive manufacture; and when universal suffrage comes in fashion, I intend to stand for a seat in the House on the interest of all the unwashed artificers connected with literature. (*Prefaces* 53)

The Author suggests how private fantasy can contribute to public credit and also how substantial wealth, adding to the employment and support of "hundreds," can be "manufactured" out of thin air. The argument thus rubs two ways: literature is the miraculous production of something out of nothing (or out of imagination), *and* literature is no different from any other materialistic, commercialized "manufacture" of commodities. In response to the Captain's further charge that this is "the language of a calico-manufacturer," the Author adds, "A successful author is a productive labourer, and . . . his works constitute as effectual a part of the public wealth as that which is created by any other manufacture. . . . why are the author's bales of books to be esteemed a less profitable part of the public stock than the goods of any other manufacturer? . . . to this extent I am a benefactor to the country" (53).

Insofar as the Author's (or any author's) productions are indistinguishable from those of a "calico-manufacturer," their status as literature or art, transcending the economic realm of mere material necessity and self-interest (the realm also, Scott feared, as did Blake and the other Romantics, of encroaching and perhaps eventually universal commodification), was at best dubious. The self-contempt that pervades this apology of Scott's for his too-rapid but nonetheless lucrative novel writing exemplifies the ressentiment that becomes a more overt theme in later, more autobiographical fiction or portraits-of-artists such as *David Copperfield* and *Pendennis*. Among nineteenth-century English-language novels, the culminating expression of such ressentiment is undoubtedly Gissing's *New Grub Street*. The inability of Edwin Reardon and the other struggling author-characters to keep literature from degenerating into a mere trade (and thereby to maintain a clear distinction between artistic and mercenary values, or between novels and money) is the main source of their galling self-contempt (for Gissing and ressentiment, see Jameson, *Political Unconscious* 185–205).

"Literature nowadays is a trade," the successful but cynical Jasper

Milvain acknowledges (Gissing 8). In the new, sordid, Darwinian version of "the battle of the books" which Gissing depicts, popularity triumphs over aesthetic merit, actual over "moral currency," profits over taste and intelligence. The narrative realism that he himself practices Gissing treats as a literary dead end—"the spirit of grovelling realism," as a critic writes of Harold Biffen's failed magnum opus, *Mr. Bailey, Grocer* (Gissing 401). Of course Gissing is practicing the same sort of documentary, slice-of-life realism that Biffen practices, only he is practicing it on would-be novelists and literary hacks and journalists who (like Gissing himself) can no longer distinguish ideas (or ideals) from reality, fiction from money (or from debt and poverty), or even book reviews from groceries (or grocer's bills, at any rate). But in so collapsing the realm of imagination (or art, or idealism) into the squalid realm of necessity (money, poverty, and "circumstance," including both biology and environment), Gissing paradoxically also produces one of the most self-reflexive, albeit resentfully "grovelling," novels of the nineteenth century. In a sense, *New Grub Street* is *Chrysal* turned inside out. Johnstone's fantasy depends on the fetishizing of a piece of money, a thing "possessed" or personified. Gissing's realistic but nonetheless self-reflexive, even narcissistic narrative depicts a world in which such fantasy or magic is not possible (there are no genies in bottles, or spirits in guineas) but a world nevertheless also "possessed" by a reifying commercialization so absolute that nothing escapes: struggling artists and their productions are even worse off than commodities like cat's meat, which at least sell.

4

THE NOVELS of Thackeray and Dickens are often also more or less explicitly concerned both with money as a theme and with money as an analogous form of fictiveness. And as often as not, Thackeray and Dickens treat money in terms of credit and debt rather than stable, substantial wealth. But money, credit, and debt are also ordinarily matters of private concern to individual characters rather than issues of public or national solvency. Thus in *Vanity Fair*, being in debt is the norm for individual characters. Rawdon Crawley, for example, fits Eugène de Rastignac's modern formula ("the English system") of gaining credit through borrowing: "He lived comfortably on credit. He had a large capital of debts, which laid out judiciously, will carry a man along for many years, and on which certain men about town contrive to live a hundred times better than even men with ready money can do" (*Vanity*

Fair 165). The narrator then both moralizes (living on credit is wrong) and suggests that Rawdon's behavior is thoroughly typical of "Vanity Fair": "Indeed who is there that walks London streets, but can point out a half-dozen of men riding by him splendidly, while he is on foot, courted by fashion, bowed into their carriages by tradesmen, denying themselves nothing, and living on who knows what?" (166). Later in the novel, Chapters 36 and 37 explore "How to Live Well on Nothing A-Year," with Rawdon and Becky as the main illustrations.

Becky's gold-digging is more than a match for her husband's gambling and loose ways with "credit." At first they manage to live comfortably among their mounting debts, but during that time the wealthy stockbroker Mr. Sedley, Amelia's father, goes bankrupt, jeopardizing his daughter's future. Though the wicked and unfair do not always get their comeuppances, the worth of both the wicked and the morally upright (or at least, semiupright) characters can often be measured in *inverse* monetary terms, if not in exact pounds and shillings. The old baronet is a boor and a miser; meanwhile, his somewhat worthier (or at least, more affable) brother, the Reverand Bute Crawley, "was always in debt" (94). Having barely managed after ten years to pay off his college bills, he lost a small fortune betting on the wrong horse at the Derby, and so—religion mixing with wishful thinking—his "great hope" is that his rich sister will die and leave him half her fortune, although she seems intent instead on giving most of her money to her ne'er-do-well nephew Rawdon (she does not). And so it goes in "Vanity Fair," where debt is the norm and nothing is ever quite fair and square.

When Rawdon asks his older brother to take care of his son should he, Rawdon, be killed in a duel, the young baronet thinks at first that Rawdon is begging again. He refuses to lend Rawdon any more money and recommends instead that his younger brother declare bankruptcy: "'But as for paying your creditors in full, I might as well hope to pay the National Debt'" (520). This mention of the national debt is as close as Thackeray comes to connecting the fiscal failings and duplicities of his characters to the larger public issues of credit and debt; indeed other allusions to the national debt are generally to the security of the money that a few characters have invested in "the funds." Miss Crawley, for instance, refuses to lend her brother Sir Pitt, the old baronet, any of her "large fortune," preferring instead "the security of the funds" (86). Meanwhile her fortune, like "secure" money throughout *Vanity Fair*, "would have made her beloved anywhere. What a dignity it gives an old lady, that balance at the banker's!" (87).

In similar terms, Thackeray (or the narrator) claims for his narrative something like the same security and dignity that accrue to Miss Crawley. Unlike the sensational stories told by Italian or French "brother[s] of the story-telling trade" (80), the narrator declares that "it is not from mere mercenary motives that [he] is desirous to show up and trounce his villains; but because he has a sincere hatred of them" (81). In this passage, sincerity and the secure investment of the reader in the truth of the story are metaphorically linked. The reader can give as full credit to the narrative as to "the funds," because it will contain nothing extravagantly romantic, sensational, or improbable *and* because Thackeray's motives are higher than the merely "mercenary." But this nexus of metaphors simultaneously identifies the narrative with moneymaking and with the monetary problems of the characters (and the author); with questions of credit and financial security or insecurity; and with an honesty (or realism) that supposedly rises above the merely mercenary, or upon which no price can be set, and yet which produces the commodity novel. The reader can rely on the truth of the novel because it transcends the greed and possessiveness that are the major failings of nearly everyone in "Vanity Fair." *Or*, the reader can rely on the truth of the novel because its narrator is thoroughly materialistic (or realistic) and worldly wise; he knows at each moment exactly what each character is worth, both morally and monetarily. Suspended between these two contrary interpretations, the commodity novel itself, the details of which (as in Defoe) so often concern quite precise amounts and exchanges of money and indebtedness, possesses many of the qualities of a growing "balance at the banker's."

The scene of the auctioneers with their "Hebrew" henchmen selling the Sedleys' belongings is a typical one for Thackeray, who himself worked awhile as a bill collector (and was teased in *Fraser's Magazine* with the name "Bill Crackaway"). More important, in 1833, Thackeray, along with his stepfather, Major Carmichael-Smyth, had lost a fortune through the collapse of some Indian "agency houses," or investment firms. Gordon Ray notes the similarity between this experience and Thackeray's portrayal of the rise and fall of the Bundlecund Bank in *The Newcomes*—a fraudulent enterprise in which Col. Newcome invests and loses his considerable fortune (1:162). Thackeray's treatment of the Bundlecund Bank appears to examine the questions of credit and debt in a public, political light. But he displaces financial fraudulence onto the oriental (if not quite "Hebrew") machinations of one person, the sinister Rummun Loll, a "confounded old mahogany-coloured heathen humbug" (*Newcomes* 2:331), whom Thackeray's resentful racism charges with the entire blame for innocent Col. Newcome's bankruptcy.[8]

In *Vanity Fair*, a similar loss of fortune through a fraudulent Indian investment scheme is represented when Jos Sedley, the tax collector of Boggley-Wollah, rents a house and buys furniture for it from "the assignees of Mr. Scape, lately admitted partner into the great Calcutta House of Fogle, Fake, and Cracksman, in which poor Scape had embarked seventy thousand pounds, the earnings of a long and honourable life" (579). Fogle and Fake had escaped with fortunes intact, the narrator points out, and "Sir Horace Fogle is about to be raised to the Peerage as Baron Bandanna" (579), whereas Scape and his family have, like many English bankrupts, "faded away to Boulogne, and will be heard of no more" (579).

At least in his late novels, Dickens also almost connects the monetary failings and foibles of his individual characters with the larger questions of public credit, the currency, and the national debt. But as Thackeray does in *The Newcomes*, Dickens usually reduces these larger questions to the machinations of individual frauds, villains, and skinflints. For Samuel Weller and his father, the mysteries of "the monetary system of the country" (*Pickwick Papers* 779) may require the expertise of the likes of Solomon Pell and Wilkins Flasher to fathom. But the senior Weller has no other difficulty, with either the stock exchange or the Bank, in translating his late wife's shares in "the funs" into hard cash. The privatization of debt in Dickens's novels, moreover, is not inconsistent with Grahame Smith's argument that all of Dickens's social criticism follows the same thread through the social labyrinth to the monster named money. But Dickens tends to portray the destruction wrought by money in terms of its private effects, whereas he ultimately exonerates or misrecognizes the public institutions charged with the production and regulation of money—above all, the Bank of England—as virtuously constructive.

Grahame Smith writes that Dickens "saw beneath the anarchic, shapeless surface of his civilization to what seemed to him the controlling principle, the role of money." Money alone "formed the cement of

8. "Until the last months of 1833 Thackeray was a young gentleman of substantial prospects . . . worth between £15,000 and £20,000," Ray tells us. "Though the nature of the catastrophe that overtook him is not altogether clear, it seems reasonable to suppose that the bulk of Richmond Thackeray's estate was lost in the collapse of the great Indian agency-houses. . . . A hint in a letter to his mother suggests that the sum which [Thackeray] lost totalled £11,325" (1:162). For a fuller analysis of *The Newcomes*, see my *Rule* 73–107.

a society no longer held together by human bonds. . . . The details of plot, character, and action which make up the complex structures of Dickens's later novels reflect the web of financial interdependence that holds individuals and classes in modern society in a grasp as isolating as it is inescapable" (221). What Smith fails to recognize, however, are the many ways in which Dickens *avoids* treating money as the main official and yet counterfeit text or discourse, so to speak, uttered or authored by the government of Great Britain. Nevertheless, he attacks money's private abuses, consumptions, corruptions, or, to continue the textual metaphor, its best-selling commodity status. Dickens's later novels, at least from the time of his account of Mr. Dombey as made out of money, without any identity apart from money, might all be described as "Books of the Insolvent Fates," to borrow a phrase from *Our Mutual Friend* (815). And money in Dickens is, as in Balzac, both the engine of society and its ultimate mystery. Thus when little Paul Dombey asks his father, " 'What's money?' " the elder Dombey, who of all people ought to know the answer, is taken aback: "Mr. Dombey was in a difficulty. He would have liked to give [Paul] some explanation involving the terms circulating-medium, currency, depreciation of currency, paper, bullion, rates of exchange, value of precious metals in the market, and so forth; but looking down at the little chair, and seeing what a long way down it was, he answered: 'Gold, and silver, and copper. Guineas, shillings, and halfpence. You know what they are?' " (*Dombey and Son* 92). Yes, Paul knows what coins are, but this redundant answer does not satisfy him; he persists in asking, " 'What's money after all?' " much to the perplexity of his father, who is reduced to saying, mysteriously enough, that money is something that " 'can do anything' " (92).

As Humphry House long ago noted, "Dickens points a debt at a man's head much as G. P. R. James points a pistol: his heroes are unarmed because they are poor" (59). Moreover, debtor's prison looms large in his imagination from *Pickwick Papers* through *Little Dorrit*—an equally familiar point. And Dickens's novels both early and late are full of misers like Jonas Chuzzlewit or Scrooge and of financial cheats and scoundrels like Wilkins Flasher in *Pickwick Papers* or Fascination Fledgeby in *Our Mutual Friend.* They are also full of fraudulent companies and investment schemes or scams—all the way from the United Metropolitan Improved Hot Muffin and Crumpet Baking and Punctual Delivery Company in *Nicholas Nickleby* to the shady financial dealings of Merdle the great financier in *Little Dorrit.* Again, as House points out about the early novels, at least:

The finance of investment has hardly become, in these early novels, a recognized system: it is rather an elaborated form of private enterprise, and the investing public is a mere flight of gulls. The typical financial business-man is not a stockbroker or jobber or company promoter or speculator, but a man who specializes in notes-of-hand, mortgages, and loans for personal expenses: he buys and sells debts. . . . Speculation, as with Nicholas Nickleby's father, is a form of suicide rather than a way of getting on in the world. (59)

"Speculation" also turns into a literal "form of suicide" in *Little Dorrit*, in which Dickens's depiction of "the finance of investment" is just as individualistic and not much more complicated than in *Nicholas Nickleby*. Merdle's shadowy financial wheeling and dealing and his suicide, based on the real-life case of John Sadleir, who poisoned himself after the failure of the Tipperary Joint-Stock Bank, in which he was a partner, foreshadows Augustus Melmotte's suicide in Trollope's *The Way We Live Now*. In both cases, moreover, the great, greedy financiers are themselves the object of an idolatry by equally greedy worshipers: the moneyed man as fetish. In Merdle's case, "All people knew (or thought they knew) that he had made himself immensely rich; and, for that reason alone, prostrated themselves before him, more degradedly and less excusably than the darkest savage creeps out of his hole in the ground to propitiate, in some log or reptile, the Deity of his benighted soul" (*Little Dorrit* 556).

Like the characters in *Vanity Fair*, the denizens of Marshalsea Prison in *Little Dorrit* "had come to regard insolvency as the normal state of mankind, and the payment of debts as a disease that occasionally broke out" (88). Though Dickens's novels of the 1850s and 1860s privatize debt by identifying it mainly with uncreditworthy types like Wilkins Micawber or William Dorrit, Dickens nevertheless *almost* identifies the Circumlocution Office, run or at least overrun by the Barnacle family, who cling parasitically to "the national ship as long as they" can (*Little Dorrit* 121), with "the Funds" and therefore with the national debt. But banking and the Bank of England are clearly exempt from Dickens's assaults on financial speculation and on governmental inefficiency and corruption. The banker Mr. Meagles is a good-hearted fellow, and Little Dorrit praises Maggy for being "as trustworthy as the Bank of England" (101). Yet, just as all money and financial transactions pass through the Bank of England, "all the business of the country went through the Circumlocution Office, except the business that never came out of it; and *its* name was Legion" (106). Similarly, Tellford's Bank in *A Tale of Two Cities* may be an antiquated, mystifying institution, and British law may be mired in an equally antiquated, mystifying penal code; but Jarvis Lorry, representative of the emergent bourgeoisie as well as of Tellford's, is the soul of (commercial) honor. True, he tries to excuse himself from emotional engagement in the story on the grounds of "business," telling Lucy Manette that he has "no feelings" because "'I have no time for them, no chance for them. I pass my whole life, miss, in turning an immense pecuniary Mangle'" (21). Yet he is closer to Meagles or to Wemmick in *Great Expectations* than to any of Dickens's misers or financial scoundrels. Bankers may be strange characters to invest with feelings, but both Meagles and Lorry have the right sort of feelings—only, perhaps, underdeveloped.

If, in *Little Dorrit*, Dickens's analysis of the sources of insolvency, both personal and societal, brushes against the possibility that the Bank of England is part of the problem, Dickens just as abruptly steers away from that thought. It has sometimes been said that he criticizes every institution of his time except the police, but there are at least two other major exceptions: the Post Office and the Bank. Thus the article "The Old Lady of Threadneedle Street" in *Household Words* (6 July 1850), which Dickens coauthored with W. H. Wills, echoes the satiric tradition of Addison and Swift which personified public credit as a vaporish, fickle woman—except that, for Dickens and Wills, the Old Lady (i.e., the Bank of England) is both the soul of honesty and the reverse of fickle or unstable. The opening sentence announces: "Perhaps there is no Old Lady who has attained to such great distinction in the world, as this highly respectable female" (123). The tone is at times gently mocking, at times also fulsomely patriotic and even quasi-religious and awe struck, as when "we" enter "the Bank Parlour, the inmost mystery—the *cella* of the great Temple of Riches": "It is no light thing to send in one's card to the Foster-Mother of British commerce; the Soul of the State; 'the Sun,' according to Sir Francis Baring, around which the agriculture, trade, and finance of this country revolves, the mighty heart of active capital, through whose arteries and veins flows the entire circulating medium of this great country" (126). Though the national debt gives cause for a moment of anxious rumination (133), the "wonderful Old Lady! threading the needle with the golden eye all through the labyrinth of the National Debt" (134) magically transforms that apparent problem into no problem at all, just more British power and prosperity: "With all her wealth, and all her power, and all her business, and all her responsibilities, she is not a purse-proud Old Lady; but a dear, kind, liberal, benevolent Old Lady; so particularly considerate to her servants, that the meanest of them never speaks of her otherwise than with affection" (134).

Perhaps Dickens expresses greater pessimism about money and monetary institutions in *All the Year Round* and in such late novels as *Great Expectations* and *Our Mutual Friend*. In assessing Dickens's "ambivalence" toward money in the 1860s, Will Dvorak notes that there is a "rash of articles on speculation and investment" in *All the Year Round*, "especially between 1864 and 1865" (90). Most of these were written by Malcolm Laing Meason, who was, according to Dvorak, one of the "harshest critics" of new financial developments that included limited liability for joint-stock companies and banks; the rise of investment firms like Overend, Gurney in Britain and the Crédit Mobilier in France; and rampant stock market speculation (90). But Dvorak also notes that Meason, presumably in accord with his editor Dickens, emphasized that "'on the Stock Exchange, there is a legitimate business to be done, there are tangible securities to transfer, which afford a legitimate science to men of high character and honour'" (Meason quoted by Dvorak, 90). The titles of two of Meason's books illustrate the same ambivalence; the first title in particular appears to mingle legitimate with illegitimate business in a manner that makes it difficult to separate the counterfeit from the genuine. In 1865, Meason published *The Bubbles of Finance: Joint-Stock Companies, Promoting of Companies, Modern Commerce, Money Lending, and Life Insuring, by a City Man*; the next year, he published *The Profits of Panics: Showing How Financial Storms Arise, Who Make Money by Them, Who Are the Losers, and Other Revelations of a City Man.*

In *Our Mutual Friend*, Dickens again approaches dealing with the connections between private and public debt, or between individual poverty and national insolvency; he offers his fullest account of "the curiously death-centered bioeconomics" endemic to Victorian culture (Gallagher, "Bioeconomics" 53). Of course Dickens's account is a poetics, not an economics (not even an alternative economics, as Ruskin's ideas about wealth versus "illth," and so on, can be called). In Dickens's narrative, the national debt is mentioned prominently and early in connection with those "bran-new people," the Veneerings, and with their friend Twemlow; among those at a party they attend is "a Payer-off of the National Debt" (*Our Mutual Friend* 7). Further, "paper currency" is offered as a metaphor, together with Boffin's dust mounds, for counterfeit wealth or value: "That mysterious paper currency which circulates in London when the wind blows, gyrated here and there and everywhere. Whence can it come, whither can it go? It hangs on every bush, flutters in every tree, is caught flying by the electric wires, haunts every enclosure, drinks at every pump, cowers at every grating, shudders upon every plot of grass, seeks rest in vain behind the legions of iron rails" (144). Though this "mysterious paper currency" is literally only scraps of waste paper blowing around the streets, Dickens suggests that all forms of money are worthless either if selfishly hoarded (the dust mounds) or if squandered (waste paper blown about the streets). Almost nobody does anything that could be called productive labor: Gaffer Hexam fishes for corpses; Eugene Wrayburn loafs; Boffin inherits valuable "dust"; and so on. Only Jenny Wren produces—dolls' clothes. Those engaged in the production and circulation of valuable "waste paper" (423) are private persons—Fascination Fledgeby and his employee Mr. Riah, who buy and sell "dishonoured bills" (424); the impecunious Lammles; Silas Wegg, vendor of "street literature"; and others. Blackmail is a similarly nonproductive but pervasive business. Nonetheless, Dickens never explicitly connects the motif of "waste paper" with the governmental institutions responsible for producing the paper currency of bank notes or for creating and managing the national debt.

A *Household Words* essay just as symptomatic of Dickens's attitudes as "The Old Lady of Threadneedle Street" is W. H. Wills's "Review of a Popular Publication," in which the literary work under review is the bank note, praised for "the power, combined with the exquisite fineness of the writing. It strikes conviction at once. It dispels all doubts, and relieves all objections" (426). Like *New Grub Street*, the article offers an interesting contrast to *Chrysal*: instead of personifying a coin as the spirit of gold or greed, it treats a piece of paper money as equivalent to a best-selling novel. By erasing the distinction between bank notes and works of literature, "Review of a Popular Publication" renders explicit the equation between money and fiction which informs novelistic realism from *Roxana* down to *New Grub Street* and beyond. Moreover, cited as the chief authority on this "golden," highly popular publication is J. F. Francis, whose *History of the Bank of England* Dickens owned and apparently read (the assertion in "Old Lady of Threadneedle Street" that the Bank is "the Soul of the State" is a phrase straight out of Francis's book: 1:220). Francis offers a Whiggish account of British financial institutions similar to Macaulay's in his *History of England*. The Bank went through many crises in its early days, but particularly since the Bank Act of 1844, Francis claims, it has been on a secure footing and is in turn the secure footing of the ever expanding power and prosperity of the glorious British Empire.

5

JUST AS Dickens found his childhood experience of debtors' prison and the blacking warehouse traumatic, so Anthony Trollope declares that his father's genteel values and ambitions, coupled with "ruinous" naïveté about how to earn a living, made "boyhood . . . as unhappy as that of a young gentleman could well be." At Winchester, Anthony was taunted for being a debtor, and the various tradesmen who catered to the other boys "were told not to extend their credit to me." So miserably poor and alone did he feel that he contemplated suicide: "But, ah! how well I remember all the agonies of my young heart; how I considered whether I should always be alone; whether I could not find my way up to the top of that college tower, and from thence put an end to everything?" (*Autobiography* 8). Meanwhile his father went from bad to worse and "was always in debt to his landlord. . . . Our table was poorer, I think, than that of the bailiff who still hung on to our shattered fortunes" (11).

The inability of his father to make ends meet caused Anthony's energetic and intelligent mother to decamp to America in 1828, where she joined an abolitionist commune, opened a bazaar in the frontier town of Cincinnati, and though the bazaar did not prosper, returned to Britain three years later with a manuscript that, when published as *Domestic Manners of the Americans*, sold well enough to earn her approximately six hundred pounds. Thus her husband's impecuniousness launched Frances Trollope on a literary career during which she published thirty-five novels. This was an example of turning literary make-believe into money which both Anthony and his brother Thomas Adolphus followed. And it is precisely this sort of commercial exchange— novels into pounds, shillings, and pence—that Anthony soberly offers in concluding "the record of my literary performances,—which I think are more in amount than the works of any other living English author" (*Autobiography* 311). He means that he has written more volumes than anyone else—"I have published much more than twice as much as Carlyle" (311)—though he could also mean "more in amount" as monetary worth, because he proceeds to list each of his books by title, year of publication, and "total sums received" for them, in some cases down to the last penny (e.g., "*The Macdermots of Ballycloran*, 1847, £48, 6 shillings, 9 pence" [312]). To this ledger book of his literary career, his version of the solvency/salvation equation, Trollope adds: "It may interest some if I state that during the last twenty years I have made by literature something near £70,000. . . . I look upon the result as comfortable, but not splendid" (314).

Trollope thus echoes the equation between realistic commodity novels and business account books established by Defoe. Further, Trollope's account of his success at turning fiction into hard cash can be read as a variant of a favorite Victorian genre, the story of a self-made man, as in Samuel Smiles's best-selling *Self-Help* (1859). But from this perspective, Trollope's *Autobiography* necessarily sounds boastful; for how else can a self-made man narrate his own success? From a high-cultural perspective, however, the *Autobiography* can be read as merely a creditable, modest description of a best-selling author who, despite his *quantitative* success, measured in numbers of publications and money received for them, makes no claims about the *quality* of his "literary performances." Trollope portrays himself as a successful literary businessman whose success is measured by the fact that people buy and read his commodities. He seems to have no pretensions to being a high-cultural figure, the artist as genius, transcending the material realm of economic self-interest. Trollope might well have agreed with Scott that authorship is similar to calico manufacturing. But he might just as well have disagreed with Scott, or indeed with Thackeray and Dickens, that there is another, higher level, where the novelist transcends worldly motives and where great novels somehow cease to be mere commodities. He is instead closer to Gissing's view that literature, at least in a commercializing age, is just a "trade." To say so and get on with business is what any honest realist should do.

If by his own account Trollope is typical of realistic novelists, they necessarily write for "mercenary" reasons because writing is their way of making a living, just as a clergyman's way of making a living entails acquiring a church "living." (What the clergyman believes—what any of the clerical characters in Barsetshire believes, except in relation to comic conflict—is more or less beside the point.)[9] Further, for Trollope, the most honest (i.e., realistic) way of writing for money is writing about money, or in other words writing about those economic circumstances, desires, and transactions that, in combination with sexual desires and transactions, account for most human motivation and activity. Sex and money, money and sex: one might add ambition, status, power, and honor; but for the thorough-going realist like Trollope, these are

9. Trollope's Barsetshire novels are textual elaborations of Pascal's wager: they simultaneously downplay or take for granted questions of religious belief *and* take the business of religion quite seriously. The identical reduction (or reification) happens to politics in the Palliser novels: nothing is at stake; reaffirming the business of politics is at stake.

all translatable into love or cash or their opposites, forms of emotional and financial bankruptcy. And for a "comfortable, but not splendid," somewhat puritanical Victorian novelist, money, in the novels but even more in his autobiographical account book, counts larger than sex. So the *Autobiography* is perforce a modestly boastful book by a self-made man about worldly success and therefore about making money, which means that it is a book about converting fiction into cash, paper pages into paper bank notes into (implicitly) solid gold. Or the equation can be rewritten: realistic fiction supposedly reflects reality; if novels are genuinely realistic, then readers will credit them as real or genuine and authors can quite literally bank on them.

But starting in the 1870s, a number of things happened on the way to the bank. The bourgeois-realistic hegemony represented in and by such novels as *David Copperfield* and *Barchester Towers* began to erode. In part, the sense that if realism faithfully represented the world it could not also criticize it helped cause the erosion by stimulating the antireal-ist literary movements of symbolism, aestheticism, and "the deca-dence"—the immediate predecessors of the literary modernisms of the first half of the twentieth century. If Michael Sadleir is correct, Trol-lope helped put his own reputation in the shade for half a century by portraying himself as just as comfortably mercenary as any of his char-acters.[10] Only with the waning of high modernism did it begin to seem worthwhile (monetarily as well as literarily) to reprint Trollope's novels and to refigure Trollope himself, if not quite on a par with Dickens or George Eliot, as an author of literary works of *almost* the highest cul-tural value. The question lingers, however: How can a work of realism achieve the highest—that is, the most ideal—cultural value when to be realistic it must reject idealism for a thoroughgoing, commodified ma-terialism complete with price tag?

Like his *Autobiography*, Trollope's novels, and none moreso than *The Way We Live Now*, dramatize the underlying identity, based on credit, between the commodity forms of fiction and money. Lady Carbury's struggle to make money by writing parallels Trollope's much more suc-cessful efforts; the opening paragraph highlights the "many hours" she

---

10. Sadleir lists the *Autobiography* itself as the first of the causes of "the collapse of Anthony Trollope as a literary reputation": "He speaks of an author as a workman, com-paring his labour to that of a shoemaker. He asserts again and again that the profession of letters should be as loyally subject as are other professions to the laws of contract, to commercial integrity, to duty towards the public and to industry. He refers a little skep-tically to genius. That literary men write without thought of money he genially disbe-lieves" (ix).

spends at her desk writing "letters . . . also very much besides letters. She spoke of herself in these days as a woman devoted to Literature, always spelling the word with a big L" (1:1). In the letter she writes to Nicholas Broune, influential reviewer who she hopes will publicize her work in *The Morning Breakfast Table*, she mentions her production of a literary work called *Criminal Queens*. But perhaps that is a status which might be claimed for Lady Carbury, the narrator suggests, because she tries to conquer Mr. Broune by sexual allure: "She used her beauty not only to increase her influence . . . but also with a well-considered calculation that she could obtain material assistance in the procuring of bread and cheese, which was very necessary to her" (1:3). So Trollope's novel opens with a hint, at least, of the ways in which "popular authorship" (1:10) and prostitution are similar.

Of course Lady Carbury is a sympathetic and even somewhat admirable character (insofar as any of the characters in *The Way We Live Now* can be called admirable). She is, for example, "true to her children,—especially devoted to one of them [the perpetually insolvent Felix]—and . . . ready to work her nails off if by doing so she could advance their interests" (1:11). At the same time, she is good at novel writing, in part because "from the commencement of her life she had been educated in deceit" (1:12): "Lying," the narrator later says, "had become her nature" (1:285). As a novelist who bears some resemblance to Trollope's mother, moreover, Lady Carbury bears just as much resemblance to Trollope himself. The texts she produces in perfectly cold-blooded, mercenary fashion, *Criminal Queens* and *The Wheel of Fortune*, are analogues to the novel that Trollope has produced. As in the *Autobiography*, in Lady Carbury's dealings with "Literature," business questions about advertising, reviews, and profits are more distinct than characters and plots. In writing *The Wheel of Fortune*, for instance, when Lady Carbury chose that title, "She had no particular fortune in her mind [except her own] . . . and no particular wheel . . . but the very idea conveyed by the words gave her the plot which she wanted. A young lady was blessed with great wealth, and lost it all by an uncle, and got it all back by an honest lawyer, and gave it all up to a distressed lover, and found it all again in a third volume" (2:366). Lady Carbury does not think very highly of "the literary merit of the tale," but if it can attract readers and bring in the cash, and thereby also help to rescue Felix from his creditors, then that is the height of her ambition (2:366).

Lady Carbury's literary profiteering (or prostitution) is not clearly different either from Trollope's own or from two other sorts of fraudulent or counterfeit writing which occur prominently in *The Way We Live Now*. The first of these sorts are the IOUs that change hands in place of bank notes among Felix and his gambling cronies at the Beargarden and elsewhere. For Felix, Miles Grendall, Dolly Longstaffe, and the rest, there is no thought of paying off one's own IOUs but every thought of collecting from one's debtors. The second sort of counterfeit writing is Melmotte's many forgeries, including the phony stock in the great (nonexistent) railway to Veracruz, his speeches during the election and in Parliament, his disguise of his shady background (partly hiding his Jewishness), down to his literal forging of his daughter's and Mr. Croll's signatures in his last, desperate act to save his plummeting fortunes. Like Merdle's suicide in *Little Dorrit*, even Melmotte's suicide is, in a sense, counterfeit, not only because he is a fake (what does it mean for a fake to cease to exist?) but also because, instead of actually paying his debts, this was "the way in which the Financier had made his last grand payment" (2:342). But if Melmotte's house of cards or of counterfeit wealth collapses, not so that of his henchman, the American con artist Hamilton K. Fisker, for whom "the work of robbing mankind in gross by magnificently false representations, was not only the duty, but also the delight and ambition of his life" (2:394–395).

Can Melmotte's and Fisker's promotions of imaginary railroads and industries in the far reaches of the empire be distinguished ethically or epistemologically from Felix's more trivial but no less corrupt penning of IOUs, or from his mother's penning of imaginary stories for strictly mercenary motives? Lady Monogram, for one, has only "a confused idea of any difference between commerce and fraud" (2:99–100), but this is true of others in the story and also apparently of Trollope himself. That is, there is finally no way to distinguish between genuine and counterfeit money, or between fortunes legitimately made and those made like Melmotte's. And if the "commerce" in question is the production of literature, then again it is difficult or impossible, in an age when commerce and money dominate and corrupt everything, to tell the true from the false, the meritorious from the meretricious. The publishers and critics whose business it is to distinguish good literature from counterfeit are themselves mercenary hacks, morally no better, with their "system of [literary] puffing" (1:10), than Melmotte or Fisker. In Lady Carbury's case, all the narrator can say in her defense is, "The woman was false from head to foot, but there was much of good in her, false though she was" (1:17). In an age of general corruption, who can expect anything better from novelists than novels that act like money, or in other words that are thoroughly commodified and therefore bogus "Literature" with a capital *L*—just more or less "successful" or "popular" ways of "robbing mankind in gross by magnificently false representations"?

Trollope's apparently general indictment of the fraudulence of his society in *The Way We Live Now* seems to contradict the opinion expressed in the Palliser novels that "nothing was wrong in the country, but the over-dominant spirit of speculative commerce" (*Phineas Finn* 1:333). Because "speculative commerce" produces the prosperity that pays the bills, and yet because it conflicts with the traditional, genteel values based on land ownership which Trollope prizes, *and* because it is ultimately based on nothing more substantial than credit and debt (or the "gambling" implied by "speculative"), Trollope can only be ambivalent or negative about it. He is thus led simultaneously to portray the substantiality and healthy prosperity of his world *and* to portray its values, behaviors, and wealth as counterfeit. In the dark glass of individual indebtness, falsehood, and bankruptcy, even the most upbeat realistic fiction begins to look paper thin, hollow, like pages and pages of overdue bills or of debts to a "real" that can never be paid. The form of this doubleness—this self-betrayal of novelistic realism in Victorian fiction—is adumbrated by Peacock in *Paper Money Lyrics* and, indeed, by the satiric tradition extending back to Pope and Swift. That tradition involves the subversion of the antithesis between money and poetry, between the (real but supposedly false) realm of material values and the (unreal but supposedly true) realm of aesthetic and spiritual values. Likewise, the realistic novel always undermines its own foundations because it both announces in its materialist form and denounces as counterfeit or as fetishism the substitution of material for spiritual values. Realistic novels like *The Way We Live Now* and *New Grub Street*, which represent the writing and selling of novels in their plots, beg to be read as declarations of literary bankruptcy. Melmotte's or Edwin Reardon's and Harold Biffen's bankruptcies and suicides are analogues for the spiritual bankruptcy of the age and also of a novelistic realism that, the more successful it becomes at effacing the boundaries between imagination and reality, and between fiction and money, the less aesthetic or literary value it seems to have.

6

IN BEHAVING like money, the realistic novel is a perfect simulacrum of a social order based on nothing more substantial than public credit and "speculative commerce." When the money/fiction equation is closest to the surface or is most self-reflexively rendered, as in *The Way We Live Now* and *New Grub Street*, fictional realism seems both to undo itself and to be most cynical, resentful, or subversive in its social criticism. Yet these novels can also be read as substantiating, or perhaps substantializing, a social reality that, though they disapprove of it morally and perhaps even politically, is massive, overwhelming, and for better or worse and to greater or lesser extent, *determining* in the sense of operating as a final cause or an absolute horizon. A realistic novel structurally and metaphorically implies that it is a signifier completely determined by (or faithful to) its signified—social reality—just as a photograph seems exactly to reproduce its subject, without mediation or interpretation. In this way, the realistic novel claims not to be like paper credit or counterfeit money but, rather, like gold bullion itself. Paradoxically, however, its very success at conveying truth (or social reality) reduces its discourse to the level of money.

Realistic fiction is the cultural commodity form that utters the truth—which is simultaneously the falsehood, the mystification—of commodity fetishism. Both the massive substantiality and the finality of the (imagined) social reality that a novel like *Vanity Fair* or *Little Dorrit* signifies is typically rendered by a minute inventory of worldly goods and commodities. The "thingification," that is, reification, suggested by the etymology of the term *realism* (Levin 34) becomes a poetry of the object world—Marx's fantastic table again, with its "wooden brain" full of "grotesque ideas." Individuals are not just surrounded by and dependent on the things they or other characters own or disown but are themselves objectified and look or behave like things.[11] Grandville's fetishized fashions and Cruikshank's dance of the commodities are given endless variations in Dickens's novels, as for example in *Hard Times*, which is both about the economic "hardness" and hardheartedness of the times and about the "hardness" of a world of pure "facts," stripped of "fancy": "'Now, what I want is, Facts. Teach these boys and girls nothing but Facts.'" Dickens's critique of utilitarianism both attacks that philosophy's materialistic stress on "facts" and represents people as reduced to "facts," or rather to objects, as are the schoolchildren who are numbered rather than named and treated as so many empty vessels into which facts must be poured. The critique valorizes "fancy" and "fairy tales," but these are weak counters to a social reality that itself seems to have entirely "hardened" through reification. The treatment of characters as commodity-like objects is the corollary to the fetishizing of money and of Midas figures like Bounderby the banker. "Facts

11. See Andrew Miller on the commodified object world of *Vanity Fair*.

too," writes David Simpson about *Hard Times*, "are but fetishes" (49). In the reified social domain of his later fiction, Dickens "chronicles the *energetic* creation of deadness and fixity, the passionate reduplication of fetishized representations," Simpson concludes (41).

That Dickens's "fetishized representations" are linked both to money and to sexuality is perhaps especially apparent in *Our Mutual Friend*, which is, notes Eve Kosofsky Sedgwick, "the only English novel that everyone *says* is about excrement in order that they may *forget* that it is about anality" (164). In her interpretation, she portrays Dickens as a predecessor of "Freud, Ferenczi, Norman O. Brown, and Deleuze/ Guattari, among others, in seeing digestion and the control of the anus as the crucial images for the illusion of economic individualism" (170). She then quotes Brown's claim that "the category of 'possession,' and power based on possession, is apparently indigenous to the magic-dirt complex" (170). The anal fixation Sedgwick detects in *Our Mutual Friend* and more generally in capitalist or "possessive individualism" leads precisely to the fetishized "energetic creation of deadness and fixity" that Simpson describes. In the Dickensian version of the capitalist body politic, maintains Sedgwick, "the relation of parts to wholes becomes problematic; there is no intelligible form of circulation; the parts swell up with accumulated value, they take on an autonomous life of their own, and eventually power comes to be expressed as power over reified doubles fashioned in one's own image from the waste of one's own body. Power is over dolls, puppets, and articulated skeletons, over the narcissistic, singular, nondesiring phantoms of individuality" (170). In *Hard Times*, the underemployed but overworked Coketown "hands" (i.e., the factory workers like Stephen Blackpool) are the most obvious instance of metaphorical, detached body parts "energetically" demonstrating, apparently, some of the flaws inherent in Adam Smith's fetishistic model of the "invisible hand" at work in the capitalist marketplace. So "energetically" does Dickens go about his novelistic work that there seems to be no outside to the total reification and fetishizing (which is also the imaginary dismemberment) of the social realm except "fancy" and a kind heart. But perhaps all this suggests is that Dickens was the ultimate capitalist-with-heart-of-gold, or the ultimate good bourgeois liberal, who is able *to be good* only so far and no more.

In contrast to Thackeray and Dickens, Trollope does not usually provide an elaborate inventory of characters' material surroundings or possessions. Yet houses, estates, fortunes, and wills play just as prominent a role in *Barchester Towers* or *The Eustace Diamonds* as in *Vanity Fair* or *Great Expectations*. With occasional, dramatic exceptions like the Eustace diamonds, specific fetish objects or portable commodities are less important in Trollope's novels than amounts of money and, more significantly, the imagined geography of real estate—landed property—that can be extended to include the entire map of Great Britain and, indeed, the empire. Just as Dickens often provides something close to a detailed street guide of London, so Trollope provides a detailed map of Barsetshire, which connects metonymically to any actual map of England and beyond. What Scott represents diachronically in his "historical romances"—the story of the progressive unification of Great Britain—Trollope represents synchronically as the imagined geography of both real and fictive territory woven together as the ultimate possession of the public, the unified, taken-for-granted nation-state with its almost equally taken-for-granted empire. This ultimate real estate is also the ultimate "real" for Trollope, his "sublime object of ideology" or "Big Other" about which, to which, and for which he writes.

The ultimate form of wealth for Trollope is not money but land, the main material property possessed by or coterminous with the nation-state. Far from challenging public credit or its institutional workings, he like Dickens assumes its normality as the medium through which his novels function both as reflections of its effects and as commodities that translate easily into money, which can in turn be used to purchase real estate. Social criticism in *The Way We Live Now* is close to Augustan criticism of the "money'd interest": Melmotte represents counterfeit forms of wealth—above all, stock market speculation—not tied to land or to Britain's aristocratic traditions. "The genuine dialectic of land and money that generates much of the tension in [Jane] Austen's novels becomes in Trollope a mock battle, a ritual, because in fact money has already won," observes John Vernon (44). This is true in *The Way We Live Now*, but it is not the case that Trollope has ceased to think of land as genuine and money as fraudulent. The victory of money (or "speculative commerce," or capitalism) over the aristocratic values associated with land has produced a world "whose values have become decorative," in Vernon's phrasing (44), though perhaps a better word than "decorative" might be *commodified*. In another sense, however, "decorative" is apt: even in *The Way We Live Now*, Trollope never explicitly condemns, as does Gissing in *New Grub Street*, an entire social order that reduces art and all other values to money or commodity status; he condemns only what he perceives to be the (mostly commercial) diseases of the social order. That "speculative commerce" is hard to distinguish from "fraud" does not, Trollope believes, mean that commerce is always fraudulent. The marketplace must be cured of rampant borrowing and stock exchange "gambling" in order to function properly, to become once again the trustworthy servant of secure, clearly honorable wealth based on land. This is the social significance of the one clearly honorable, creditworthy character in *The Way We Live Now*, Roger Carbury, incorruptible member of the squirearchy.

The socially critical dimensions of Thackeray's, Dickens's, and Trollope's novels (Gissing's ressentiment tells another story) are best understood as loyal, moralizing opposition to the status quo (and therefore to the Big Other or the Big Brother of the nation-state). The narrator of *Vanity Fair* insists that he is only a moralist of the private realm, unable to comment on politics, war, or the larger institutional workings of society. The character inside the story most analogous to the narrator (or the novelist) is Becky Sharp, whose manipulative acuity about others' motives and weaknesses rivals the omniscient Puppeteer's string pulling. Becky's power, says Amanda Anderson, produces the "uneasy apprehension that the author is himself fallen," a prostitute (10–11). In contrast, Dickens's gentle mockery of the Old Lady of Threadneedle Street moves easily into patriotic hymn singing; even more contradictory shifts between social criticism and jingoism characterize his novels. And Trollope's suggestion that *The Way We Live Now* is artistically no more meritorious than Lady Carbury's gold-digging productions deflates that novel's social criticism, even as it makes its indictment of the fraudulence of its age all encompassing. If Trollope's tale of the corruption of "the way we live now" both represents and is a product of that corruption, then why should the reader grant it any more credit than, say, *The Wheel of Fortune*, or than the IOUs that circulate at the Beargarden and the racetrack? It is as real or unreal, as truthful or untruthful, as its social context. And most of the time in most of Trollope's novels (*The Way We Live Now* is more cynical *and* more self-deflating than usual), that society is comfortable and comforting, mostly decent, and solidly middle class, prosperous, and quite "real" indeed, like beefsteak and ale. Thus the net effect of both the Barsetshire and the Palliser series, despite the corruptions of individuals and the triviality of most of the political issues dealt with by Phineas Finn and Trollope's other parliamentary characters, is intensely patriotic and conservative.

7

ONE WAY to examine the symbiosis between novels and nations is by viewing it through the subgeneric lens of the "political novel," like the

Palliser series. As defined by Morris Speare in *The Political Novel*, that "genre" (Speare considers it a distinct species of literary animal) deals with characters directly engaged in the workings of government. Besides the Palliser novels, Disraeli's Young England trilogy and a few other individual texts like Meredith's *Beauchamp's Career* are Speare's main examples, from which it follows that the "genre" is quite small.[12] Also, the political novel is apparently uniformly nationalistic: Speare himself lauds the British genius for (he claims) democracy at home and nonviolent (*sic!*) empire abroad, as represented by Disraeli's Tory-Radical imperialism.

But Speare could have increased the size of his genre by including novels that at least touch on the workings of state machinery and political processes: *Pickwick Papers*, with its description of the Eatanswill election; *Oliver Twist*, with its trial and prison scenes; and so on; every one of Dickens's novels is political in at least this partial sense. Moreover, a huge number of nineteenth-century novels could be considered political because they describe the workings of state apparatuses in the Althusserian sense, that is, because they deal more or less deterministically with the relations of individuals to political and social institutions. But many of these novels—Dickens's again, for instance—are highly critical of aspects of the status quo. A novel like Gissing's *Demos* perhaps fits within Speare's definition; Christopher Harvie includes Gissing in his recent study of British political fiction (124–126). But Gissing's disillusioned stance toward *all* political activity puts *Demos* toward the negative end of a spectrum that would situate Trollope's *The Prime Minister* (for instance) at the opposite pole.

Demos belongs to the type of political fiction, or perhaps *anti*political fiction, that is deeply suspicious of political power in general (Dickens once more comes to mind, as does also George Eliot, especially in *Felix Holt*). Whereas Speare's political novelists including Trollope celebrate political activity in relation to state power, Dickens, Eliot, and Gissing do virtually the opposite: for them, politics is the real-world equivalent of tragedy, not comedy.[13] Like *Demos*, moreover, many more or less

12. In *The Centre of Things*, Christopher Harvie basically follows Speare's definition. Harvie's keyword is *parliamentary*; any novel that deals with parliamentary activities qualifies as a political novel. Harvie also, like Speare, treats the political novel as a genre unto itself; he enlarges it considerably, however, both by including novels only parts of which are "parliamentary" and by claiming to have identified some six hundred examples from the time of John Galt's *The Member* (1832), which Harvie claims as the first political novel, down to 1990.

13. This is the sort of pessimistic fiction Irving Howe deals with in *Politics and the Novel*: Dostoevsky's *Possessed*, Conrad's *Nostromo*, Orwell's *1984*. Of course many political

tragic political novels are works of social realism which may or may not include explicit depictions of characters involved in running state apparatuses but which deal with the individual's connection to the state if only because, as Eliot declares in *Felix Holt*, "there is no private life which has not been determined by a wider public life" (45). In both Eliot and Gissing, and throughout much late-Victorian social realism, something like Georg Simmel's or Max Weber's tragic vision of life in modernizing societies is dominant: the individual sacrificed on the altar of the social.[14]

Besides comic and tragic, there is at least one other type of political novel: utopian romances that, like William Morris's *News from Nowhere*, describe and often seek to enact some radical alternative social design (Speare ignores both tragic and utopian types). In the postrevolution, classless society depicted by Morris, the apparatuses of state power have been dismantled, and nationalism and imperialism have therefore gone the way of other ideological dinosaurs such as religion and novels. That the inhabitants of Nowhere have done away with money parallels the fact that they have done away with novels, except as curiosities or (in the case of writing them) as a hobby.[15] Paradoxically, what takes the place of money, novels, and both "ideological" and "repressive" state apparatuses in *Nowhere* could be defined as the sublime universalization of public credit—a mutual trust among all its inhabitants that forms the sole bond of their community. This universalization of credit is made possible by the eradication of inequality and the transformation of labor into art, or into aesthetic forms of production and exchange.

Through their examinations of national identity, two other Victorian novelists at least approximate the utopian diffusion of credit in *News from Nowhere*. From a perspective that is simultaneously orientalist, proto-Zionist, and romantic, both Disraeli's *Tancred* and George Eliot's *Daniel Deronda* explore ordinary nationalism in ordinary Great Britain and find it wanting. Yet for both Disraeli and Eliot, patriotism, with the self-sacrifice for the good of the nation-state that it implies, is an indis-

---

novels are also satiric, though such satires can move in either tragic or comedic directions. *Little Dorrit* combines satire with the tragic mode (at least, in relation to politics); W. H. Mallock's *The New Republic* combines satire with the comic mode.

14. For Weber, the famous example is the "iron cage" passage that concludes *The Protestant Ethic and the Spirit of Capitalism*; for Simmel, see *Sociology* 32.

15. Such romances are rarer than novels that celebrate parliamentary politics, perhaps in part because they fall out of the novel genre altogether: elsewhere I have argued that *News from Nowhere* is an antinovel that condemns ordinary novels as both symptoms and forms of capitalist oppression (Brantlinger, "*Nowhere*").

pensable worldly religion, in part because materialism cannot fill the void left by the (gradual, uneven) disappearance or death of God. For Disraeli, "Young England" idealism—patriotic, conservative, and yet adjustable to a sort of positive orientalism (or an affirmation of his Jewish roots)—provides the cure for the increasing faithlessness of the age. For Eliot, something close to the positivists' "religion of humanity," as expressed in the idealized proto-Zionism (a sort of displaced or alienated nationalism) of Daniel Deronda, provides a surprisingly similar solution.

Disraeli's Young England trilogy—*Coningsby, Sybil*, and *Tancred*—develops a "Tory-Radical" history of Britain as a counter to hegemonic Whig history. Disraeli locates the sources of Britain's contemporary difficulties primarily in the Reformation (Henry VIII's appropriation of church lands and wealth) and in the creation of the national debt—the "demoralizing" Dutch "funding system" (*Sybil* 30)—in 1694. In the course of his political education, Coningsby, the first of Disraeli's Young England heroes, learns to reject Tory-Whig money laundering and power mongering just as vehemently as he rejects utilitarianism, in favor of a utopian (albeit Tory) politics of imagination to be realized through a rejuvenated aristocracy. Disraeli's anti-Whig history is also joined to a theory of racial essences which, however, does not lead to the sort of chauvinistic Anglo-Saxonism expressed by Scott, Kingsley, and many other British novelists. Instead, Disraeli identifies the Jews with the purest of "Caucasian races," an identification both embodied and explained by Sidonia (Coningsby's mentor, an idealized portrait of Disraeli himself). "'The fact is you cannot destroy a pure race of the Caucasian organization,'" Sidonia tells Coningsby; it turns out that the Caucasian races Sidonia has in mind are Semitic, both Arabic and Jewish (263). Disraeli/Sidonia's assertion of the superiority of "Hebrew intellect" is partly an egoistic defense against anti-Semitism, in which he incongruously tries to fight racism with racism. But Disraeli also insists on the visionary character of all principled political theory and practice because human nature is not motivated primarily by narrow, utilitarian aims or self-interest. And the source of all visionary nations and empires has been "the East," whither Disraeli's third Young England hero, Tancred, travels in search of vision.

According to Sidonia, "'Man is made to adore and to obey: but if you will not command him, if you give him nothing to worship, he will fashion his own divinities and find a chieftain in his own passions'" (*Coningsby* 253). Such an elitist, authoritarian doctrine of charismatic leadership, especially when coupled to belief in racial essences, can be labeled, as Carlylean hero worship has been, protofascist (Saab 564–565; Vincent 44). However that may be, against this leadership doctrine, Disraeli juxtaposes his account of British history, illustrating the triumph of "Dutch finance" and bureaucratic routine over charisma. Coningsby's discovery that "he was born in an age of infidelity in all things" (130) raises the question of how Britain has fallen into its present faithless condition. The answer lies in the bad leadership provided by the fraudulent aristocracy, created during the Reformation through Henry VIII's "spoliation" of the church and solidified by the so-called Glorious Revolution of 1688, with its ruinous wars and national debt, followed by Whig hegemony.

Unlike the fraudulent conservatism of "Tory men and Whig measures," which would merely keep things as they are, Disraeli's Young Englandism promises to undo the entire course of the nation's past, back to 1534 and the founding of the Church of England. But of course Young Englandism never meant—much less accomplished—so much. *Coningsby* ends not with a counter-revolution that undoes the Whig "oligarchy" but with the election of the hero to Parliament, as a Tory, indeed, but also as the candidate sponsored by the idealistic liberal manufacturer Millbank (whose daughter Coningsby marries). It also ends with a paragraph of questions about the future careers of Coningsby and his young, equally idealistic friends: "They stand now on the threshold of public life. . . . What will be their fate? Will they maintain in august assemblies and high places the great truths which . . . they have embraced?" and so forth. Of course the answers will come in the sequel (whether that sequel is the rest of the Young England trilogy or the careers of Disraeli and his political allies in actual public life). But the trilogy does not pursue Coningsby's career; it takes up instead the political educations of two similar young aristocrats, Egremont and Tancred.

Also, in *Sybil* and *Tancred*, there is a noticeable shift away from parliamentary politics through a sort of "operatic" analysis of class conflict, Chartism, and "the Condition-of-England Question" in *Sybil*, to a thoroughly improbable, ironic, romantic glance toward religious issues in *Tancred*, which for the not very religious Disraeli takes the form of an exciting travelogue to Palestine, with the possible domination of the entire planet at stake.[16] *Tancred* transports its hero to the Middle East,

16. Arnold Kettle long ago observed that *Sybil* is an "operatic" novel (see 176). An even more romantic forerunner of *Tancred*, which takes up Zionist themes, is Disraeli's 1833 novel *Alroy*, about the medieval would-be liberator of the Jews, David Alroy. And in his *Life of Lord George Bentinck* (1847), Disraeli included a chapter on the historical significance of the Jewish "race" and of Judaism as the basis for Christianity.

identified as a region of mysterious powers and prospects, and does not return him to England. Named after a crusading ancestor, Tancred begins his political career by rejecting it: he refuses to run for Parliament and instead, with the blessing of Sidonia, goes on an oriental pilgrimage like Disraeli's own eastern tour of 1830/31. Tancred shares with Coningsby the sense of living in "an age of infidelity"; he hopes that his "new crusade" to Jerusalem will renew his own faith before he engages in politics at home.

In the "Holy Land," Tancred's political education proceeds under the tutelage of two other mysterious Orientals (Sidonia, of course, is the first of his tutors). One is "the Angel of Arabia," who comes to Tancred in a vision (or maybe it is just a regular dream) on Mount Sinai, to teach him—not exactly Christian, but—"*Arabian* principles" (my italics). Christianity, the Angel suggests, is only a subset of those world-governing principles: "'The thoughts of all lands come from a higher than man, but the intellect of Arabia comes from the Most High'" (299). Here is the superiority of "Hebrew intellect" again, in an apparently more universal ("Arabian") guise, as the source of the world's main religions: the Angel seems indifferent about which religion may be the true one; his stress is on inspiration and moral idealism rather than orthodoxies, presumably in the same way that the Tory-Radical idealism of all the Young England novels is antagonistic to political and historical orthodoxies.

The other character from whom Tancred learns in the Middle East is Fakredeen, a young Christian emir bent on becoming a Syrian Napoleon and conquering the world. But Tancred teaches Fakredeen more than the other way around; at least Tancred gets Fakredeen to agree that "'the world was never conquered by intrigue; it was conquered by faith'" (267). Once Fakredeen has accepted this proposition, he and Tancred join forces—more visionary than actual—in a world-conquering scheme, or at least a scheme to overthrow the Ottoman Empire and place most of Asia within the British Empire. "'We wish to conquer [the] world, with angels at our head,'" Tancred tells the Queen of the Ansaray, who of course falls in love with him (434). Caught up in the endless political intrigues of Fakredeen, however, this ambition seems merely farcical.[17] Yet *Tancred* offers at least three serious political lessons, and all three run at least partly against the grain of an unreflective or unselfconscious nationalism. The first is that nationalisms pro-

17. Harvie is right that "Tancred the man is even duller than Coningsby" (44), but Tancred is also the most quixotic of Disraeli's three Young England heroes, and Disraeli seems as much amused by, as serious about, his youthful idealism.

duce imperialisms: nationalisms are universalizing and world conquering in their aspirations. The second is that the main source of religions, and hence of nationalisms, and hence also of world-conquering
aspirations, has been "the East," not Europe. And the third is what
Tancred teaches Fakredeen: world conquest depends on faith and passion more than on intrigue, money, or any other merely worldly deter-
minant. As Sidonia tells Coningsby, "'Man is only truly great when he
acts from the passions, never irresistible but when he appeals to the
imagination. Even Mormon counts more votaries than Bentham'"
(*Coningsby* 253).

In her last novel, George Eliot invokes a proto-Zionist nationalism
through Deronda's discovery of his Jewish heritage, in part because
she, too, wishes to challenge the naturalness and narrowness of given
institutions (including state apparatuses and national boundaries) and
thereby also of given social, national, religious, and gender identities.
The romantic nationalism of *Daniel Deronda* works against a host of
provincial interpellative powers and beliefs, including the nationalis-
tic/racist proposition that it is better to be an Englishman than a Jew.
In *Middlemarch* the social organism (as represented by the provincial
town itself) engulfs the central characters and their various reformist
idealisms within its narrow limits, which is also the pattern in *Mill on the
Floss* and *Felix Holt*. But *Daniel Deronda* verges on being the sort of positively political—because quasi-religious—novel that Disraeli produced
in *Tancred*, and in both cases romantic liberation from provincial con-
finement comes in the paradoxical form of Judaism and oriental mystery.

The *Tancred*-like positive orientalism of *Daniel Deronda* is what most
differentiates it from Eliot's earlier novels, moving it onto a plane that
is simultaneously nationalist and internationalist. Harvie believes that
Eliot's turn to Zionism involved "a sort of flight" from practical politics
at home: "Eliot, like her Positivist friends, retreated from democracy"
at a time when British politics were becoming "increasingly pluralistic"
(111). Eliot had already taken a dim view of reformist projects and
radicalism in *Middlemarch* and *Felix Holt*. What is new in her last novel is
the cosmopolitanism of the Zionist cause that expresses her wish to
restore Britain, suggests Mary Wilson Carpenter, "to the great river of
human history by Hebrew prophetic vision. The narrative solidly identifies the downward progress of worldly empire with the English 'half,'
whereas the Jewish 'half,' dominated by Daniel, Mordecai, and Mirah,
represents visionary growth and progress" (135). In other words, Eliot
paints Britain as decadent or fallen; Daniel's conversion, more to an

idealized nationalism than to Judaism as a religion, expresses a fictional exhortation to spiritual rebirth. But what possible impact could Eliot have hoped to make on most of her readers by connecting her theme of the need for spiritual rebirth to Judaism? She seems thereby to guarantee that she and both the Jewish and gentile characters in her novel will continue to wander through a "landscape of exile" or alienation. As Jean Sudrann declares, "To a striking degree, *Daniel Deronda* is a novel of rootless human lives, lives lacking 'homestead,' 'native land,' and a family relation to the heavens" (436).

But Eliot had still other goals than the spiritual rebirth of Britain, or for that matter than the writing of a novel that affirms prophetic history along biblical lines. For one thing, she had Disraeli in mind, no doubt in part to show how a positive orientalism could be more reasonably expressed. She mentions Sidonia in one of her letters as a contrast to Mordecai (*Letters* 467), and in an earlier letter she accuses Disraeli of "writing more detestable stuff than ever came from a French pen. . . . [He] can do nothing better to bamboozle the unfortunates who are seduced into reading his *Tancred* than speak superciliously of all other men and things" (42). About six months after this 1847 letter, Eliot penned a third in which she offers a detailed critique of Disraeli's Young England novels (among other things, *Tancred* is "very 'thin' and inferior" compared with the others) and of his "theory of 'races,'" which "has not a leg to stand on. . . . The fellowship of race, to which D'Israeli exultingly refers the munificence of Sidonia, is so evidently an inferior impulse which must ultimately be superseded that I wonder even he, Jew as he is, dares to boast of it. My Gentile nature kicks most resolutely against any assumption of superiority in the Jews. . . . Everything specifically Jewish is of a low grade" (*Letters* 45). Though in this letter she praises Disraeli as an able man with some genuinely democratic attitudes, where he is concerned she verges on the very anti-Semitism that she repudiates in *Daniel Deronda*; and her anti–anti-Semitic novel seems written as a deliberate contrast to *Tancred* and Disraeli's other Young England fictions.

Further, through making her hero discover his identity in a "nation" or "race" that was not a state, but which had kept its unity through faith and poetic traditions down the ages, and which was also a main source of modern, European national cultures, Eliot was contesting her friend Herbert Spencer's social Darwinism, according to which nations develop like individuals: strong ones grow up and survive as modern, empire-building states; weak ones go to the wall. The concept of Jewish nationhood thoroughly scrambles social Darwinist categories (Paxton

212–224). As Eliot presents that concept through Deronda and her other Jewish characters, it also thoroughly scrambles false notions of racial purity. Like the musician Klesmer, who combines German, Slavic, and Semitic strains, "Deronda is enriched by the multiple past, both genetic and cultural," as Gillian Beer puts it (201). Whereas Disraeli/ Sidonia stresses an impossible racial purity, Eliot stresses the reverse; *race* is still an operative term for her, but as a sort of healthy mongrelization or miscegenation.

In *The Impressions of Theophrastus Such*, Eliot has this to say about the moral uplift to be gained by an idealistic nationalism, functioning as a second or substitute religion:

> Not only the nobleness of a nation depends on the presence of [a] national consciousness, but also the nobleness of each individual citizen. Our dignity and rectitude are proportioned to our sense of relationship with something great, admirable, pregnant with high possibilities, worthy of sacrifice, a continual inspiration to self-repression and discipline by the presentation of aims larger and more attractive to our generous part than the securing of personal ease or prosperity. And a people possessing this good should surely feel not only a ready sympathy with the effort of those who, having lost the good, strive to regain it, but a profound pity for any degradation resulting from its loss. (147–148)

What is incompatible here with social Darwinism is partly the stress on moral idealism and self-sacrifice; Eliot offers a version of Arnold's connection of the "best self" with the "moral currency" of an ideal nation-state. According to Theophrastus, the Jews are remarkable for maintaining their "national" identity over centuries, despite dispersal and persecution and also despite the historical tendency "towards the quicker or slower fusion of races" (160). National solidarity, even without a metropolitan center and a state, is the very source of all morality. But does such nation-based sentiment moralize in an anti-imperialist or an imperialist manner? Against the positive results of nationalism, Theophrastus weighs such phenomena as racism and the conquest of weaker by stronger nations (Britain's dominion over India, for instance). So in what sense can Eliot's liberal nationalism—seemingly far removed from Disraeli's Tory romanticism as well as from Kingsley's jingoism and Spencer's social Darwinism—work toward the liberation of *all* nationalities? Or is liberation—and therefore liberalism—only for a few, or only for one, chosen people? Or perhaps for none at all? Theophrastus is not quite clear about these questions.

At the end of Eliot's last novel, Deronda is headed for Jerusalem and perhaps his own encounter with the Angel of Arabia. And what is he leaving behind? The society of peasants and landowners around Wancester and Diplow in Eliot's final novel represents the same provincial, merely *English* narrowness that Eliot criticizes in *Mill on the Floss* and *Middlemarch*. Deronda's discovery that, as his grandfather's friend Joseph Kalonymos puts it, he is "something more than an Englishman" (669)—that in fact, deracinated though he has been through his mother's actions, he has a *double* "national" identity and heritage—points beyond local and also national boundaries as well as beyond the selfish, limited perspectives of the present to the world and to a future that potentially includes all peoples. It is the vocation of liberal nationalist, in the cause of Israel and on the pattern of Mazzini and Young Italy, that Deronda accepts at the end of the novel as his "life's task" (697). This is an *international* nationalism, and one moreover that Eliot expresses in terms of *racial* unity or community, even though no race can be pure in the physical sense, so that the only possible unity is spiritual—that is, cultural:

> "Since I began to read and know, [Daniel tells Mordecai,] I have always longed for some ideal task, in which I might feel myself the heart and brain of a multitude—some social captainship, which would come to me as a duty, and not be striven for as a personal prize. You have raised the image of such a task for me—to bind our race together in spite of heresy. You have said to me—'Our religion united us before it divided us—it made us a people before it made Rabbanites and Karaites.' I mean to try what can be done with that union—I mean to work in your spirit. Failure will not be ignoble, but it would be ignoble for me not to try." (698)

Theophrastus Such says much the same thing about nationalistic/racist idealism in the essay Eliot entitles, with more than a twinge of self-contradictory but self-reflexive irony, "The Modern Hep! Hep! Hep!"[18]

Just as Eliot wants to find in an idealized or spiritualized nationalism a way to counteract merely parochial, merely English chauvinisms, Disraeli looks to a theory of racial essences for weapons to combat Whiggish political and historical orthodoxies, including anti-Semitism. So neither Eliot nor Disraeli escapes the ideological nexus of nationalism-imperialism-racism; both are instead practicing what Michel Pêcheux has called "counter-identification," a mode of discourse which resists by inverting the terms of ideological interpellation without otherwise altering those terms (Pêcheux 157). But perhaps all nationalisms always involve counteridentification: insofar as every supposedly independent, sovereign nation-state has to defend its independence against the

18. According to Nancy Henry, editor of *Theophrastus Such*, "Hep! Hep! Hep!" was an anti-Semitic war cry and "the name given to a series of anti-Jewish riots which broke out in Germany in 1819" (184 n 1). That phrase can also be read as racist or nationalistic drum beating in general.

claims of rival nation-states, the basic ideological mechanisms of national identity and loyalty will be everywhere the same (compare Slovenia-Croatia-Bosnia-Serbia in the 1990s).

Eliot and Disraeli had no reason to expect that an idealized nationalism, racism, or imperialism could be clearly separated from its real incarnations, or that it would behave any differently if it were so separated. Yet by inscribing their positive orientalisms in their novels, they also dramatized some of the limitations and dangers of those real incarnations. The selfless dedication and faith of Mordecai and his Jewish friends contrasts sharply with the selfishness and infidelity of most of the merely Christian, merely English characters in Eliot's last novel. And the Angel of Arabia may not be made out of the same visionary fire that Moses saw, but the Angel's romantic smoke-and-mirrors, at least, are well calculated to scandalize the Mr. Podsnaps and Lord Monmouths of England. Positive orientalism for both Disraeli and Eliot expresses the desire to infuse the seemingly inevitable, inescapable ideologies of nationalism, imperialism, and racism with a cosmopolitan idealism that looks beyond St. Ogg's and Middlemarch, and beyond merely Whig histories of the fame and glory of "the island race"—whoever that "race" may be.

As an antinationalistic antinovel, *News from Nowhere* may only be the exception that proves the rule: most novels most of the time are intrinsically nationalistic; whether unconsciously or not, they speak the language of the Big Other. Many English historical novels offer quite explicit versions of the founding of the modern British state. The "bourgeois epic" is certainly epic, that is, about the founding of nation-states, in Scott's historical romances. *Ivanhoe* deals with the emergence of modern England through the reconciliation of Anglo-Saxons and Normans in the persons of the protagonist and Richard the Lionhearted (meanwhile the Jews, moneylending Isaac and his daughter, Rebecca, are tender-heartedly exiled from England, just slightly before, historically speaking, the Jews of York were massacred). *Waverley* deals with the more recent chapter in the emergence of modern *Britain* through the union of Scotland and England and the last stand of the Jacobites. Similarly, Kingsley's *Westward Ho!* celebrates the derring-do of Sir Francis Drake and the other English sailors who defeated the Spaniards and went forth to conquer empires—natural outcomes, Kingsley believed, of the naturally puissant "race" of English heroes.[19]

19. *Westward Ho!* was partly a reaction to sour news coming from the Crimean War and meant to resurrect the heroic "Saxon" spirit that, along with the weather, had smashed the Spanish Armada in 1588. Kingsley may have been an ordained Anglican

This is no more than to say that yes, of course, many novels have been quite explicitly nationalistic, though not always explicity racist, imperialist, and warmongering like Kingsley's. There are conflicting nationalisms, and novels that express Scottish or Irish or Nigerian nationalisms—or positive orientalisms like Disraeli's and George Eliot's—are in different ways and degrees critical of standard British nationalism and jingoism. What happens in these cases to Benedict Anderson's thesis about the intrinsic, structural interdependence or ideological complicity of all novels with nation-states and with nationalism? Perhaps nothing: the ideological sublimity (including darkness, terror, superstition, and fetishism) of the nation-state forms the invisible subtext, context, or horizon of *every* "English" novel (if not every novel "in English" or "broken English"), no matter how domestic, privatistic, or perhaps even overtly antinationalistic it may be.

Yet as Bakhtin might have put it, far from being unified, coherent ideological constructions, novels are intrinsically *novelistic.* Bakhtin's model of heteroglossic discourse treats the novel as generically subversive of the coherent hierarchies and ideologies of all previous literary genres. As against the state-founding theme of the epic, Bakhtin stresses the novel's "entrance into international and interlingual contacts and relationships" (Bakhtin 11). The novel works to undermine linguistic exclusiveness and therefore also the "univocal" quality of epic. In contrast to "the national heroic past" that constitutes "the world of the epic," the novel tends to deal with contemporaneous social processes; it is antinationalistic to the extent that these modern processes work against the solidarities and univocal ideologies of nation-states and ruling classes. Thus, the novel may even be said to have a *utopian* internationalist dimension, via its corrosive treatment of linguistic isolation and of ideologies of linguistic and racial purity.

But Bakhtin's multilinguistic internationalism is not clearly different from the internationalism or, at least, nation blindness of money and credit, able to cross every boundary, negotiable and exchangeable anywhere in the world, and also corrosive of linguistic, cultural, religious, and ethnic differences. From Bakhtin's own dialectical perspective, the internationalizing tendencies of the novel can be seen to stem not just from its linguistic dialogism but from its commodity form and therefore from its structural homology to money. And wherever money reigns supreme, so do social inequality, class conflict, and patterns of

---

priest, but he accurately called his novel a "most ruthless, bloodthirsty book" (*Life* 1:330), a Victorian *Rambo*, in short.

domination. So the antithesis that the dialogism of the novel is corrosive of nationalisms must be weighed against the thesis that, because of its likeness to money, the ordinary novel, and therefore the genre of prose fiction in general, does not open onto the utopian terrain depicted in *News from Nowhere,* with its universalization of credit, but instead onto the terrain of modernizing imperialisms.

Further, the novel is not merely a simulacrum or "mirror in the roadway" of a society based on public credit; it is also a powerful instrument for eliciting public credit, or a reading public's belief in itself as a coherent "imagined community," the ruling class of the modern nation-state and its empire. In this abstract sense, all novels are political or have a political effect in reinforcing public credit, even when they do not explicitly deal with politics. Along with newspapers and other modern and now postmodern forms of discourse (including money in all its proliferating forms), novels help to weave the fictional webs that constitute public credit. And just as obviously, the fictive, ideological filaments that bind the nation-state together through public credit extend beyond national boundaries to the world, or at least to the farthest reaches of empire. (But there is no crediting a New World Order that continues to be wracked by class and racial conflict; by gender injustice; by environmental devastation; by the political and economic violence of nation-states and rival nationalisms; and by endemic poverty aggravated by a global debt crisis and insolvency of sublimely terrifying proportions.)

5

CONSUMING MODERNISMS,
PHALLIC MOTHERS (1900–1945)

> "At the heart of the earth sleeps a great serpent. . . . Those that
> go down in mines feel the heat and the sweat of him, they feel
> him move. . . . And if he died, we should all perish. Only his liv-
> ing keeps the soil sweet, that grows [the] maize. From the roots
> of his scales we dig silver and gold."
>
> —D. H. Lawrence, *The Plumed Serpent*

> "Society it seems was a father, and afflicted with the infantile fixa-
> tion too."
>
> —Virginia Woolf, *Three Guineas*

1

STARTING WITH *The Wealth of Nations*, many liberal economists read a
salutary lesson in the American Revolution: colonies should be decolonized *either* when they become unprofitable *or* when they can govern
themselves, or both.[1] At the same time, territories that can *not* govern
themselves (from the British perspective, India, Africa, and so forth)
should remain or perhaps become colonies. The "colonies of white
settlement" such as Canada and Australia "mature" into independent
nation-states, a metaphor that recalls Kant's famous answer to the question What is Enlightenment? According to a fairly standard Victorian
view, white colonies, like the European nation-states that created them,
"mature" automatically. But the "maturing" of the nonwhite areas of

---

1. Historians sometimes used to claim that the bourgeois economists from Adam
Smith to John Stuart Mill were opposed to imperialism, but what they mainly opposed
was the old colonial system based on mercantilism. Donald Winch describes the shift
from the early free trade phase, well-expressed in Bentham's 1792 *Emancipate Your Colonies*, to that of the so-called colonial reformers of the 1830s and 1840s, who included the
advocate of the "systematic colonization" of New Zealand, Edward Gibbon Wakefield.

the world calls for European intervention, even when such intervention cannot be directly squared with the profit motive.

The distinction between white (or "civilized") and nonwhite (or "uncivilized") colonies is central to nineteenth-century British economic discourse, which depends on a more or less phantasmal ethnography. (For example, David Ricardo speculates about societies with "abundance of fertile land" but suffering from "all the evils of want and famine" because of "ignorance, indolence, and barbarism"; these, he says, need to be "better governed and instructed" [56].) From the early 1700s, "fetishism" was woven into such ethnographic fantasies. For Smith, Ricardo, and the Mills, the civilized/uncivilized dichotomy is one between behaviors that match and those that do not match economic rationality, and fetishism obviously does not match it. There are Rousseauistic moments in most of the early economists, as also in Marx's conception of "primitive communism." But usually, despite the Hobbesian character of *modern* economic individualism, the bourgeois economists see non-Europeans in Hobbesian terms. Thus, instead of recognizing tribal cooperation or primitive communism, J. S. Mill declares that "the savage cannot bear to sacrifice . . . the satisfaction of his individual will," whereas "civilization" arises from "the power of cooperation" ("Civilization" 152). Whether cooperative or not, "savage" societies are held to be inferior because they are uneconomical, *not* productive, profitable, and progressive from a western, supposedly scientific (i.e., economistic) perspective.

Harriet Martineau's 1845 free trade, Anti-Corn Law League fable *Dawn Island* offers an exact fictional representation of these economistic views. Martineau describes a society where, before the coming of the British, the "savages" are so very savage that they threaten their own extinction. In a reversal of the Malthusian nightmare, warfare, cannibalism, and infanticide will soon depopulate the island; fortunately the "dawn"—the arrival of a British ship signaling "the advent of commerce" (the economistic version of enlightenment)—saves the islanders from their collective suicide.[2] The fantasy of what might be called autogenocide, a self-inflicted slaughter that Martineau equates with savagery, is a form of blaming the victim through which the liquidation of "primitive races" by European invaders is frequently rationalized. The "vanishing" of "savages" owing to "savagery" is viewed as inevitable, unless the opposite of "savagery"—"civilization"—intervenes.

2. I offer a more detailed account of *Dawn Island* in *Rule of Darkness* 30–32.

Unlike the Tasmanian aborigines (supposedly extinct by 1876), Martineau's Dawn Islanders are lucky, because their fate is to become civilized through the practice of "commerce," the true dawn in Martineau's materialistic religion of free trade.[3] The unprogressive fetishism ("superstitions") of the Dawn Islanders will be replaced by the commodity fetishism of British "civilization." Discovering that they can acquire axes, cloth, mirrors, and spectacles from the seemingly divine white men if they can offer food or other goods in exchange, the Islanders are immediately converted to economic rationality (common sense according to the economists, which makes it difficult to explain seemingly irrational "savage" customs including fetish worship). But this happy ending does not alter the Manichaean vision that Martineau shares with the major economists of her era: either savages must be saved from themselves by becoming civilized (that is, they must cease to be savages) or they must cease to exist.

In contrast to autogenocide, genocide as the direct result of imperialism is not a theme in economic discourse. But this silence is only a symptom of the disease; another symptom is the reduction, through economism, of all possible value forms to the economic. By identifying value as such with material wealth or, more specifically, with property and profits, economics denies value to "uncivilized" societies. To be nomadic is to fail to understand "civilized" land use and barbed wire. To practice seemingly inefficient, uneconomical activities like Kwakiutl potlatches is to be "savage." This supposedly scientific *subtraction* of value from nonwestern cultures has allowed economics to function as the political unconscious for the imperialist *extraction* of wealth from colonies.[4]

---

3. For Darwin and the Victorians, the Tasmanians represented the purest or most total instance of what later came to be called "genocide"; see my " 'Dying Races.' "

4. In his 1821 *Essay on the Production of Wealth*, Robert Torrens argued that because "the territories in which colonies are generally established are inhabited by tribes of savages, possessing neither the inclination nor the skill to render their soil productive; [therefore] before any beneficial divisions of employment can be established with such territories, they must be taken possession of by a civilized people" (230). This argument is similar to that of the Mills for the maintenance of British rule in India. Though they claimed that that rule was not profitable to Britain, India "is not fit to govern itself"; it is therefore Britain's "duty" to govern it (J. S. Mill, *Representative Government* 257). An obvious example of the reduction of all value forms to the economic is James Mill's definition of civilization as "utility" in his 1817 *History of British India*: "Exactly in proportion as *Utility* is the object of every pursuit, may we regard a nation as civilized. Exactly in proportion as its ingenuity is wasted on contemptible or mischievous objects . . . the nation may safely be denominated barbarous" (224). Given Mill's puritanical standard of what is "useful," it seems at least consistent for him to assert that "the English government in

From the Renaissance forward, in response to poverty and population pressures at home, overseas territories that had previously seemed valueless to Europeans—mere "wilderness" or "desert"—came suddenly to look valuable. The fact that these "wastelands" were already populated with indigenous peoples was, economically speaking, irrelevant. "Waste" or "wilderness" only meant land that was uncultivated, or not yet in European possession.[5] So what was to be done with savages who failed to understand or refused to learn the concepts of property and productive labor? In his 1894 best seller *Social Evolution*, Benjamin Kidd provided a common social Darwinist answer: having "exterminated the less developed peoples with which he has come into competition," the "Anglo-Saxon" marches relentlessly forward "to develop the natural resources of the land" and to convert them into profits and civilized property. Those "natives" who do not submit to the regime of work and development of the land should and will inevitably disappear. "In the words [of] a leading colonist of [South Africa], 'the natives must go; or they must work as laboriously to develop the land as we are prepared to do'" (Kidd 49–50). Thus the juggernaut of economic progress—what economists still refer to as "modernization" or "growth" (the "maturity" metaphor again)—must and will roll on, over the bodies not just of its blind worshipers but of all who stand in its path. Besides "economic progress," an alternative name for this juggernaut is imperialism, and one of its most important products has been genocide. "The bourgeoisie," declare Marx and Engels, "by the rapid improvement of all instruments of production, by the immensely facilitated means of communication, draws all, even the most barbarian, nations into civilization. The cheap prices of its commodities are the heavy artillery with which it batters down all Chinese walls. . . . It compels all nations, *on pain of extinction*, to adopt the bourgeois mode of production" ("Manifesto" 477; my italics).

Genocide and "development" have marched together through modern and now postmodern history, as Zygmunt Bauman argues in *Modernity and the Holocaust*. The ideological formations that mystify the

India with all its vices, is a blessing of unspeakable magnitude to the population of Hindustan. . . . Even the utmost abuse of European power is better . . . than the most temperate exercise of Oriental despotism" (*Economic Writings* 387).

5. An extreme ideological outcome of the economic concept of "wilderness" coupled to the great nineteenth-century emigration engine was the Australian legal doctrine of *terra nullius*, the doctrine that Australia was empty land that belonged to nobody before the British invasion. This doctrine continued in force until June 1992, when the Eddie Mabo land rights case led the Australian High Court to abolish it, for the aboriginal rights movement a major victory.

tragic links between "civilization," imperialism, and genocide are often highly sophisticated in terms of economic "science." But at the heart of that heart of darkness lurks commodity fetishism and its corollary, a Eurocentrism that identifies value with property and enlightenment mainly or exclusively with industrialization and the endless production line of modernity."[6] Orthodox economics as the locus classicus of what Adorno and Horkheimer call "instrumental reason" involves the reification of all values into the fetishized forms of commodities and money. The infinite range of possible human relations and communal affiliations shrinks to that of property and the profit motive. At the same time, relentless change ("progress")—the search for the ever-new, or for the future magical products to fill the lacks of the modern consumerist psyche—gives to modernity a fetishistic structure that pervades even the most critical cultural modernisms. By 1900, mass-mediated advertising was rapidly becoming the dominant form of capitalist culture, simultaneously promoting commodity fetishism and jingoism. Ads for Pear's Soap (for example) featured pickaninnies washed white by that sterling product, and also Soudanese warriors idolizing a "Pear's Soap is the Best" sign painted on a boulder. The caption for the latter ad reads: "The Formula of British Conquest." "The real significance" of the claims made by this specific advertisement lies in the way British imperialists were able "to represent commodities as a magic medium through which [British] power and influence could be enforced and enlarged in the colonial world," observes Thomas Richards (*Commodity Culture* 121–123; for the symbiosis of advertising and imperialism, see also MacKenzie 25–36).

Since the Renaissance, the rise of "the religion of nationalism" and its corollaries of racism and jingoism have involved a fetishizing of the grand properties of the nation-state and its imperial satellites which Marx understood as linked both to commodity fetishism and to the illusion of national debt as national wealth. But the "*credo* of capital" would not have deluded the vast majority in Britain (or anywhere else) without paying some of the public bills and fulfilling at least some of the private dreams of both the middle and the working classes (*Capital*

6. "'Modernization', like 'development' itself, is a myth-word in whose name any destruction, and any expenditure, may be undertaken with impunity," writes Susan George. She speaks of the "*mal*-development model," which "never seeks to enhance the specific, generic, original features of 'undeveloped' countries and their peoples, treating them as if they were a kind of undifferentiated clay to be moulded to the standard requirements of the world market and of world capital, to the uniform tastes of international bureaucrats and national ones trained in their image" (15).

1:919). Throughout western Europe, the last quarter of the nineteenth century witnessed both the new imperialism and "the second Industrial Revolution," which also marked the advent of modern "consumer society" (Barraclough 44–50; Hobsbawm, *Industry* 109–133). In Britain, the long depression from 1873 into the 1890s marked the beginning of a slow decline from imperial and industrial hegemony which was accompanied by the emergence of socialism and the Labour Party, the women's suffrage movement, the strengthening of Irish and the stirrings of Indian and South African (or Boer) nationalisms, and the appearance of major new rivals on the international horizon. A consolidated Germany and the United States, reunited after its Civil War, especially challenged British imperial and industrial-economic hegemony. Such international competition intensified jingoism and led to wars that made the Crimean War of 1853–1856 and the Indian Mutiny of 1857/58 seem like the minor skirmishes of a golden age. But the long depression of trade was far from catastrophic: it brought on a deflationary lowering of prices which caused average real incomes for workers to increase (so long as they stayed employed). New technologies and industrial processes (e.g., electrification) produced a proliferation of new commodities and services on an equally new mass scale. From the start of the first Industrial Revolution in the late eighteenth century, the period of greatest overall improvement in British working-class living standards was probably 1880 to 1895, despite increased unemployment.

Contributing both to the new consumerist orientation and to imperialist expansion, developments in communications and transportation were powerful shapers of cultural productions of all sorts, from music hall to professional sports, amateur photography to the birth of cinema. Despite the depression and its accompanying anxieties, improved living standards, increasing leisure, a proliferation of new commodities, and such technological marvels as the dynamo (celebrated by Henry Adams) and the automobile (celebrated by Bernard Shaw) characterized the late-nineteenth-century "democratization of luxury." That phrase "stood for a market that was now prepared to turn practically any retail article into a mass-consumer good. And thus . . . it stood for the realization that bourgeois culture was coming more and more to mean a consumer culture," as Michael Miller points out (165). The subject of Zola's 1883 novel *Au bonheur des dames*, the department store, typified a culture that seemed increasingly dominated by advertising and the new, mass "yellow journalism" deplored by Matthew Arnold, George Gissing, Henry James, and many other intellectuals (Carey 6–10).[7]

The cultural shift in emphasis from production (the early stages of industrialization) to consumption (corresponding to the second Industrial Revolution) was marked in economics by the "marginalist revolution" associated with William Stanley Jevons in Britain and Leon Walras and Carl Menger on the Continent. Jevons's 1871 *Theory of Political Economy*, according to which "value depends entirely on utility" and more specifically "on the final degree of utility" (165), necessarily focused economics on consumption, distancing it from the more "political" or sociocritical labor theory of value. Jevons insisted on dropping the first word in the old phrase *political economy*, preferring to call his supposedly objective, apolitical "science" "economics." He also defined *utility* so abstractly that he could apply differential calculus to its measurement. His belief that economics, to be scientific, must be mathematical has been orthodoxy ever since (Schabas 229, 247). But that belief, like the focus on "marginal utility" and, hence, on consumption, has involved what Regenia Gagnier calls the "normative evisceration" of orthodox economics ("Insatiability" 125). The sociocritical dimension of older "political economy," weak though it may have been, drops away; in Britain, only Marxists or socialists such as H. M. Hyndman and maverick liberals such as J. A. Hobson continued to treat economics as a sociocritical "political" science.

At the same time that Jevons and others were giving economics a new consumerist emphasis, social Darwinism inflected both economics and political theory in several conflicting ways, valorizing war, empire, and also competition among individuals and businesses in one direction but leading to a sort of organicist anarchism or antistatism in another. For Herbert Spencer, for instance, every apparent gain by mass democracy was immediately contradicted by the cancerous growth of

7. Though advertising agents operated on a small scale in western Europe and the United States from about 1800 on, only with the expansion of markets and consumer goods from the 1870s forward did advertising emerge as a big business and a primary shaper of culture. By 1900, there were several hundred advertising agencies in London alone, conducting a far larger volume of business than fifty years earlier (Fraser 138; Richards, *Commodity Culture* 6–8). Much advertising relied on and reinforced imperialism, although empire was portrayed both defensively and nostalgically as "a means of arresting national decline" (MacKenzie 10). But the flourishing of advertising was itself often seen as a symptom and even cause of the national and imperial decline it strove to counteract. This is one of the ways in which "advertising . . . signifies the modern predicament. . . . The debates over mass culture and consumption so constitutive of twentieth century thought often converge in an assessment of advertising, usually to mourn its presence among us," notes Jennifer Wicke (593).

government. Acting as blind instrument and idol of the masses, the modern nation-state itself seemed to be the Frankenstein's monster now threatening its creators. This is the main theme in Spencer's 1884 *The Man versus the State*, as it is later in Hilaire Belloc's 1912 *The Servile State*. Anticipating the postmodern theme of state fetishism, Spencer declared that "the great political superstition of the present" (151) equaled the false worship of the state, which threatened to repress individual liberty, healthy competitiveness, and even identity. Spencer identified war and imperialism as "the religion of enmity" (187), politically atavistic phenomena resulting from the survival of aristocracy and king worship. These would disappear in the progressive, pacific future that industrializing, free-trading nation-states had in store for their citizens. Yet he fused his laissez-faire individualism, which was close to anarchism, with an organicism that fetishized society rather than the state. For Spencer, government interference was a form of parasitism or disease, almost directly antithetical to J. A. Hobson's theory of "economic parasitism" by bankers, financiers, and munitions makers (Hobson, *Imperialism* 46–63). Get rid of the state, Spencer believed, and the economy (Hegel's civil society) would function productively and progressively for the good of the entire social organism (cf. Hayek).

2

RESPONSES TO new cultural patterns ranged from a facile technological optimism to diagnoses of physical and mental degeneration and "the dusk of the nations" (Nordau 2).[8] In *The Lost World*, expressing the ultimate social Darwinist nightmare, Sir Arthur Conan Doyle writes: "Suddenly it rained apes" (221). These are "ape-men" similar to Swift's Yahoos—"'Missin' Links,'" as Lord John Roxton puts it, "'and I wish they had stayed missin''" (Doyle 221). But these Yahoos are precisely contemporary "missing links." For conservative intellectuals such as Doyle, industrialized mass culture threatened traditional forms of high-cultural authority and social control, including both religion and state. Amid striking evidence of technological and economic progress, many British artists and intellectuals shared Nietzsche's pessimistic view that mass conformity was subverting higher, aristocratic cultural standards. For radicals such as William Morris, it threatened indigenous, tradi-

---

8. According to Paul Kennedy, the "mood" of the Edwardian period bears "uncanny similarities" to the "growing mood of anxiety" in the United States today, though perhaps the current American pessimism needs to be remeasured against a postmodern British nihilism (529).

tional forms of popular culture, which contained at least the potential for true class-consciousness and progressive social change. The new "age of the masses" was also the era of the decadent movement and of the British *l'art pour l'art* modernisms that echoed Baudelaire, Mallarmé, and Huysmans in France. These early modernisms expressed critical reactions to, but often also parodic, satiric, or sometimes just unwitting assimilations of, the new forms of communication and massification. Oscar Wilde's poses and self-promotions, for instance, both mocked and sought to capitalize on the practices of sensational journalism and advertising.

The aestheticism of the 1890s was rooted in "the beginnings of modern spectacular and mass society and depended upon image and advertising," asserts Gagnier (*Idylls* 8). The corollary to Wilde's or Beardsley's *épater le bourgeois* stance was the aesthete's adoption of the glitter of high fashion and a rarefied consumerism. Huysman's decadent hero Des Esseintes vehemently rejects the bourgeois life-style of materialist consumption and conformity, yet his very aestheticism, says Rosalind Williams, is an "attempt to create an authentic style in consumption uncontaminated by the marketplace" (133). A "final aristocrat" like Count Dracula, Des Esseintes is also an exemplary consumer, in the avant-garde of perpetually new and therefore perpetually jaded tastes, fashions, and sensations. The new is never new enough; and it is anyway, in Walter Benjamin's terms, the recurrence of the always-the-same.[9] So the literary and artistic decadence simultaneously condemned and participated in the general diffusion of the dual fetishisms associated with mass consumerism.

If the decadent artist simultaneously rejected and adopted mass cultural, fetishistic tendencies through pose, parody, and satire, various avant-garde movements celebrated technological change. The automobile, blazing the trails of tomorrow, was the special symbol of modernity both in Shaw's *Man and Superman* (1903) and in the "Futurist Manifesto" of 1909: "A roaring motor car which seems to run on machine-gun fire is more beautiful than the Victory of Samothrace" (Ma-

---

9. In his archaeology of early industrial society in France, Benjamin sought, according to Richard Wolin, "to demonstrate how the phantasmagorical proliferation of new commodities which distinguished urban life under conditions of nineteenth-century capitalism in reality constituted a regression to the notion of 'eternal recurrence' or 'mythical repetition'; i.e., it represented a return to the notion of *cyclical time* dominant in prehistoric life, insofar as the novelties themselves were thoroughly interchangeable. When viewed from the vantage point of consumption, full-scale commodity production signified the reversion to a Great Myth: the reproduction of the always-the-same under the semblance of the production of the perpetually new" (174).

rinetti 211). Just as significant for modernist culture as the Futurists'
love affair with the automobile and speed were the numerous assimilations between avant-garde movements and cinema. If photography was
a major influence on nineteenth-century realisms, likewise cinema on
twentieth-century modernisms and now postmodernisms, as in Joyce's
keen interest in film. In these and many other ways, the boundaries
between high and low, elite and popular, "auratic" and "mechanically
reproduced" forms of culture were permeable, ambiguous, and often
transgressed long before postmodernism came to be defined as the
erosion or collapse of the distinction between high and mass culture.[10]
  In the American context, Thorstein Veblen identified the "habits" of
"conspicuous consumption" and "pecuniary emulation" bred by capitalism as survivals of "barbarism" in the midst of "civilization." War and
imperialism, he argued, were also "barbaric," atavistic features of a
global political landscape rapidly being steamrollered by the industrialized, western nation-states. The relentless, wasteful production and
consumption of commodities at home was matched by the relentless,
wasteful rivalry among nation-states for imperial power and glory
abroad. In "Veblen's Attack on Culture," Adorno writes, "Culture,
which today has assumed the character of advertising, was never anything for Veblen but advertising, a display of power, loot, and profit"
(79). Veblen therefore "does not shrink from using the crudest rationalism to expose the universal domination of the fetish over the ostensible realm of freedom" (80).[11]
  Various turn-of-the-century British social critics also recognized, as

10. Perhaps the chief difference between the two periods or conditions is that,
whereas modernism sought to define and maintain hierarchical cultural boundaries,
postmodernism often promotes and celebrates their erasure. "Modernism," says Andreas
Huyssen, "constituted itself through a conscious strategy of exclusion, an anxiety of contamination by its other: an increasingly consuming and engulfing mass culture" (vii; cf.
Jameson, *Postmodernism* x). But though Huyssen rightly identifies modernism's most significant other as mass culture, he does not fully recognize the many ways in which avant-
garde movements all the way back to the Fourierists and St. Simonians identified with,
depended on, or even advocated industrialization and democratization. If some versions
of modernism seek to avoid the contamination of the masses and the mass produced,
avant-garde movements have tended instead to strive to erase or transgress distinctions
between art and everyday life. And some versions of postmodernism are just as elitist or
just as dependent on some sort of distancing, albeit often through parody or ironic
forms of exaggeration and mimicry, from, say, advertising or television as were some
versions of modernism.
  11. For an analysis of postmodernism which takes Veblen as its starting point, see
Mestrović. There is at least a good case to be made that Veblen is to economics what
Nietzsche is to poststructuralist cultural theory, though it goes without saying that,
among orthodox (positivist) economists, Veblen gets no more attention than does Marx.

did Veblen, that capitalism, both domestically and internationally, was the driving force of a new "barbarism." Some (e.g., William Morris, Olive Schreiner, and Edward Carpenter) further recognized that capitalist economism, reinforced by social Darwinism, provided supposedly "scientific" legitimation for jingoism and war. Against the mounting disciplinary scientizing or reification of economics, J. A. Hobson seems to have been the first British social critic to link imperialism both to what Rudolf Hilferding would later call "finance capital" and also to a "crowd psychology" that treated jingoism as a disease of "public opinion" or mass "credulity" closely related to fetishism. At the same time, Hobson offers a modern elaboration and synthesis of themes to be found in the anti-imperialist, anti–national debt tradition extending back through Marx, Shelley, and Cobbett to Swift and Bolingbroke. In *The Psychology of Jingoism,* his 1901 prelude to his classic *Imperialism: A Study,* Hobson adopted the "crowd psychology" approach of Gustave Le Bon to explain "popular pugnacity" and its role in international affairs, especially South Africa. In his modern "Dunciad," Hobson hoped to explain "the quick ebullition of national hate termed Jingoism" (*Psychology* 2) which, although not a new phenomenon at the turn of the century, nevertheless had emerged with a new intensity and destructive irrationality in response to, and indeed as a cause of, the Boer War.

Hobson saw jingoism as a "neurotic disease" of public opinion, one that involved what Freud, also following Le Bon, would analyze as "a regression to an earlier stage such as we are not surprised to find among savages or children" (*Group Psychology* 49). The phenomenon of jingoism belongs, Hobson writes, to "the province of the subconscious. Whatever qualities of deliberation and calculation may have been present in the conduct of the politicians, financiers, and journalists who were the direct conscious agents in bringing about the [Boer War], the popular approval of, and enthusiasm for, the war were not roused by any ratiocinative process. The British nation became a great crowd, and exposed its crowd-mind to the suggestions of the press" (*Psychology* 18–19). Like Conrad's Kurtz in *Heart of Darkness* (and, indeed, like many other characters in late-Victorian and early-modern literature), the supposedly civilized citizen "goes native," or reverts to savagery. "The superstructure which centuries of civilization have imposed upon the ordinary mind and conduct of the individual gives way before some sudden wave of ancient savage nature roused from its sub-conscious depths," Hobson declares; "the war-spirit, as displayed in the non-combatant mass-mind, is composed of just those qualities which differentiate savage from civilized man" (19) and children from adults (67).

Among the key causes of the late-century upsurge of jingoism, Hobson identified the superficial stimuli of "town life" and the impact on culture of new technologies, especially such forms of communication as the cablegram, the telephone, and the mass daily press. "Mechanical facilities for cheap, quick carriage of persons, goods, and news" (*Psychology* 6) might be technological marvels, but they were also prone to a sensationalism that, Hobson believed, had degraded all "popular culture."

Hobson sounds like Matthew Arnold, Robert Lowe, and the many other critics of the Education Act of 1870 and its aftermath when he writes:

> A large population, singularly destitute of intellectual curiosity, and with a low valuation for things of the mind, has during the last few decades been instructed in the art of reading printed words, without acquiring any adequate supply of information or any training of the reasoning faculties such as would enable them to give a proper value to the words they read. A huge press has sprung into being for the purpose of supplying to this uneducated people such printed matter as they can be induced to buy. (*Psychology* 9; cf. Carey 5–20)

Although Hobson analyzes music hall, "khaki Christianity," and other aspects of "popular culture" and "the mass mind," he is most worried about the effects of the new mass journalism. This emphasis may be partly because of his own work as a journalist in South Africa, but it is also because of his belief that the very developments that should be making for the greater enlightenment of public opinion are doing the opposite: "The popularization of the power to read has made the press the chief instrument of brutality" (*Psychology* 22).

In a similar manner, "the physical and mental conditions of . . . town-life" tended, "for the majority of its population . . . to destroy strong individuality of thought and desire" and to substitute instead that modern nervousness or neurasthenia that Le Bon in France, George Beard in the United States, and Georg Simmel in Germany also diagnosed. "In every nation which has proceeded far in modern industrialism," Hobson wrote, "the prevalence of neurotic diseases attests the general nervous strain to which the population is subjected" (8). This was again the paradox of material, scientific, and educational progress as decadence (or the identity of "civilization" with new forms of "barbarism") that serves as a refrain in critiques of industrialism, capitalism, and urbanization from Coleridge and the utopian socialists, through such Victorian social critics as Carlyle, Arnold, and Ruskin, and on to decadent writers and artists including Wilde, Morris, and the young Yeats.

Whereas Veblen is mainly concerned with patterns of conspicuous consumption in the leisure class, Hobson identifies "underconsumption," or the maldistribution of wealth, as what drives capitalism relentlessly to seek markets abroad and therefore to press for imperialist expansion as a solution to its periodic crises. Capitalism in general is not to blame, however. The wealthy who benefit from war and empire are by no means the entire upper classes, but a "parasitic" subgroup. The latter's profits derive directly from such malign instruments of expansionist foreign policy as the national debt and credit and banking mechanisms that support shipbuilding, arms manufacturing, and such colonialist concerns as diamond and gold mining in South Africa. Hobson's analysis thus points to a financial, colonial, and industrial oligarchy, like the moneyed interest abhorred by Bolingbroke, Swift, and Pope, whose motives conflict with genuine national interest and "commonwealth." The economic side of Hobson's argument, moreover, approximates the sort of conspiracy theory that underwrites Ezra Pound's ideas about usury, banking, and "social credit" (and therefore that underwrites that paradigmatic modernist poem, *The Cantos*). In both Britain and America, versions of economic populism, often antagonistic to imperialism, were often also anti-Semitic and anticipated or, as in Pound's case, turned into fascism.[12]

As does his cultural analysis in *Imperialism*, Hobson's analysis in *The Psychology of Jingoism* becomes a conspiracy theory especially in relation to the ways South African financiers and expansionists such as Cecil Rhodes ("the little group of men who . . . own or control the diamond mines at Kimberley, the gold-fields of the Rand, and the government and resources of Rhodesia" [112]) have bought and manipulated the press both in South Africa and at home in Britain. Prostituted by this financial clique, the South African press has "instructed the readers of the London *Times* in the necessity of war" (111). Because the press is "by far the most potent instrument in the modern manufacture of public opinion" (109), moreover, Hobson views its corruptions and distortions as especially dangerous and as leading directly to the false worship or idolatry of "the tribal God" known as the British race or nation (41). "A biassed, enslaved, and poisoned press has been the chief engine for manufacturing Jingoism" (125).

12. Hobson identifies the imperialist controllers of "international capitalism" as a virtual cabal composed "chiefly by men of a single and peculiar race" (*Imperialism* 57). On anti-Semitism in relation to the theme of "the international usury of finance capital" in nineteenth-century economic theory, see Semmel 85–102; on Hobson's anti-Semitism in particular, see Semmel 111–115. Pound's economic theories, as these connect both to his fascism and to his interest in Major C. H. Douglas's advocacy of "social credit," are well described in Chace 3–36.

The results of jingoism would be less brutalizing and dangerous, Hobson believes, if the new mass journalism affected only the half-educated masses. But, though in lesser degree, it also influences the well educated: "The most astonishing phenomenon of this war-fever is the credulity displayed by the educated classes. . . . The canons of reasoning which they habitually apply in their business or profession . . . are superseded by the sudden fervour of this strange amalgam of race feeling, animal pugnacity, rapacity, and sporting zest, which they dignify by the name of patriotism" (*Psychology* 21). When not indulging in jingoism, moreover, the educated classes are failing to show the masses any cultural leadership to offset regressive beliefs and warmongering "passions." Modern civilization has produced a condition of "scepticism and . . . dilettantism" among the educated, "while among the masses it has produced a loss of curiosity and indiscriminate receptivity" (13). Similarly, with World War I in mind, Yeats in "The Second Coming" would write,

> The best lack all conviction, while the worst
> Are full of passionate intensity.

Whereas the high literary culture and even the journalism of past ages had produced high truths and enlightenment, or at any rate had encouraged readers in the exercise of reason, the sensational, "spectatorial" journalism of the 1890s was undermining the very possibility of a generalized enlightenment or a rational public opinion. The new mass journalism was not just intellectually poisonous; it also involved the counterfeiting of the "intellectual currency" of authentic culture. With the "unscrupulous . . . debasing of the intellectual currency of print" (*Psychology* 124), mass "credulity" was taking the place of genuine cultural "credit." "What is at stake . . . is nothing less than *the credit of printed matter*" (123; my italics):

> Even among the educated classes there survives a certain tendency to believe printed statements of fact in a newspaper or a book; and uneducated persons are far more profoundly impressed. . . . As large new masses . . . are brought within the range of the newspaper or the book, the aggregate intellectual credit of the press has expanded, until it represents a vast sum. This intellectual credit may either be economized and maintained by careful and accurate use of the press, or it may be squandered. The war-press, having this immense fund of popular confidence to draw upon, has recklessly abused its trust, pouring misstatements into the public mind. (123–124)

Hobson repeated the main themes of *Psychology of Jingoism* a year later in *Imperialism: A Study.* There he also offered a more elaborate economic analysis of imperialism which influenced Lenin's and many later attempts to explain the relationship between capitalism and the expansionist policies of Britain, the United States, Germany, and other modernizing nation-states at the turn of the century. "From the standpoint of the recent history of British trade," Hobson writes, "there is no support for the dogma that 'Trade follows the Flag'" (*Imperialism* 33). The new imperialism involving the late-Victorian "scramble for Africa" and much of Asia was not generally profitable to Great Britain, or for that matter even to the majority of Britain's commercial interests, though it clearly *was* profitable to a powerful fraction of those interests: "These great businesses—banking, broking, bill discounting, loan floating, company promoting—form the central ganglion of international capitalism. . . . To create new public debts, to float new companies, and to cause constant considerable fluctuations of values [of stocks and currencies] are three conditions of their [profiteering]. Each condition carries them into politics, and throws them on the side of Imperialism" (56–57). One tragic result was the Boer War, fomented by the press manipulations of Rhodes and other South African financiers. A further result was the general acceptance by both politicians and public of Rhodes's commodification of patriotism through his "famous description of 'Her Majesty's Flag' as 'the greatest commercial asset in the world'" (61), a commodification that, as national policy, could only lead to future wars. So the imperial profiteering of a moneyed elite, disguised as national interest, was being enforced at the cannon's mouth. In general, Hobson saw the financial oligarchy as virtual traitors, the exploiters of true "public credit." Rhodes and his kind were "harpies who suck their gains from every new forced expenditure and every sudden disturbance of public credit" (58). The "parasites of patriotism" (61) had managed, largely through advertising and mass journalism, to warp "public credit" into the race hatred, bloodthirsty "war-spirit," and irrational worship of the nation-state that constituted jingoism.

3

THE CONCEPT of fetishism stands at the crossroads of late-Victorian and early-modern literary, artistic, and scientific cultures. The etiology of the sexual "perversions" or "inversions" in the work of such investigators as Jean-Martin Charcot in France and Havelock Ellis in Britain meant that, for the first time, it was possible to articulate Marx's analysis of commodity fetishism with early (pre-Freudian) accounts of sexual fetishism. By dissolving belief in the uniformity of heterosexuality while demonstrating the wide range of human sexual behaviors and desires that it identified as fetishistic, the new "sexology" implicitly aligned this range with the cravings of the individualistic consumer (Birken 51), who, rather than either the capitalist or the worker, now appeared to be driving if not exactly steering the economy. The so-called marginalist revolution in orthodox economics also emphasized the proliferation of consumer desires. With or without benefit of either sexology or marginalist economics, moreover, advertisers in the last quarter of the nineteenth century were beginning to exploit the double jeopardy of commodity and sexual fetishisms.

A recent issue of the *James Joyce Quarterly* is devoted to analyzing how, in *Ulysses* and elsewhere, Joyce deploys the fetishistic language of commodities and advertising (Bloom is an adman; ads are everywhere). Joyce, it appears, was both critic and purveyor of commodity fetishism. This contradiction is structurally analogous to that which informs Victorian novelistic realism: materialism as critique of materialism. Cultural modernists deal self-consciously, critically with both sexual and commodity fetishisms, though their works are themselves often fetishistic. The literary and artistic modernisms of this century are marked by a sense of loss and of nostalgia as much as by any positive sense of the new, or of surpassing or supplanting past insufficiences and lacks. "Primitivism, formalism, alienation—these are only chief among the incongruent categories through which we try to organize what we mean when we say modernism," writes Perry Meisel. "Modern literature acts out the loss of something primary that it wishes to regain" (1).

That modernist "primitivism" in particular expresses a fetishistic fascination with certain ancient or nonwestern cult objects is a point reiterated in Marianna Torgovnick's *Gone Primitive* and Chris Bongie's *Exotic Memories*. "Hardly the flight toward immediate vision that we think it is . . . modernism is instead a structure of compensation, a way of adjusting to the paradox of belatedness that is its precondition," asserts Meisel (3). For Torgovnick and Bongie also, modernism is first and foremost "a structure of compensation." Analyzing modernist writers such as Conrad and modernist artists such as Gauguin, whose works utilize "imperialist exoticism" to critique modernity, Bongie notes, "In the age of the New Imperialism, the exotic necessarily becomes, for those who persist in search of it, the sign of an aporia—of a constitutional absence at the heart of what had been projected as a possible alternative to modernity" (22). As "a structure of compensation," moreover, cultural modernism is closely allied to fetishism: modernists such as Conrad and Gauguin "engage in a double game" by being at once fetishistic and critically aware of fetishism. Bongie calls this a "conscious fetishism" for Conrad and several of the other primitivizing modernists he analyzes; the exotic otherness to the modern condition which they seek has, they at least half-recognize, already vanished (if it ever existed). "Vitally aware that the 'outside' they so desire has been fully inscribed within the global network of colonialism, these exemplars of the fin de siècle imagination persevere in search of it" (77). But the double awareness expressed by a writer such as Conrad is perhaps less critical of his own fetishism than Bongie suggests, because that awareness seems only to reproduce the fetishist's standard disavowal: "I know very well that such-and-such is not the case, but all the same. . . ."

As sexology developed, so did increasingly sophisticated versions of ethnography and mythography, which, as in the work of Bloomsbury art critic Roger Fry (Torgovnick 85–104), stimulated a new, appreciative fascination with "primitive art." Among various studies of myth and the "primitive mind," Sir James Frazer's *The Golden Bough* (1890) became a major influence and source book for modernist writers including W. B. Yeats, T. S. Eliot, and D. H. Lawrence—and also for Freud, Jung, and psychoanalysis, which itself began to be discussed in British intellectual circles shortly before the outbreak of World War I. (The Hogarth Press, a Bloomsbury project established in 1917, commenced publication of James Strachey's translation of Freud's writings in 1924.) The links among Frazer's mythology, sexology including psychoanalysis, and fetishism are especially apparent in Lawrence's phallocentric version of modernism (or, more accurately, his phallocentric version of modernist primitivism). "Like Frazer's selections from myth, Lawrence's myth and ritual focus upon male revival. The phallus may be Lawrence's ultimate character," notes Bonnie Kime Scott (221).

The central modernist contradiction—attempts to critique, transcend, or evade fetishism which are themselves deeply fetishistic—is evident in the frequent resort to inevitably nostalgic versions of myth (as in *Ulysses*, Eliot's *The Wasteland*, Yeats's *Mythologies*, and so forth) as a means of combating modern materialism, fragmentation, and alienation. The contradiction perhaps reaches its absurd extreme in Lawrence's *The Plumed Serpent*, in which Don Ramon seeks, through a renewal of faith in Quetzalcoatl, "a supposedly indigenous form of ritualized phallus worship," as Marcia Ian calls it (109). Against Kate Leslie's (and Lawrence's) feeling that "white" civilization, along with its religion, has exhausted itself "in attempting to convert the dark man to the white man's way of life," the rebirth of Quetzalcoatl promises a rebirth also of genuine sexuality, "the one mystery" (*Plumed Serpent* 86,

162). Quetzalcoatl, the great bird-snake or serpent god, represents nothing more nor less than the fulfillment of "the dream of the phallos" (189).

In the religion of Quetzalcoatl, Lawrence wanted to believe, the fear of castration or of the loss of the phallus, basic to Freud's theory of fetishism, could be overcome. The male characters in Lawrence's Mexican fantasia, Ian observes, "solemnly ritualize their own symbolic embodiment *as* the phallus," involving the illusion, at least, of "the momentary unity of signified and signifier" (109). As Kate loses herself in a renewal of her own sexuality (for Lawrence, feminine passivity as the antithesis of masculine, phallic domination), she experiences a renewal of the dark, primal world of ancient myth itself, as opposed to the superficial, crumbling hegemony of "white," Eurocentric values: "Ah, how tired it made Kate feel; the hopelessness, the cynicism, the emptiness. She felt she could cry aloud, for the unknown gods to put the magic back into her life, and to save her from the dry-rot of the world's sterility." She thinks of returning to Europe, but Europe is the problem, "all politics or jazzing or slushy mysticism or sordid spiritualism," a civilization from which "the magic had gone" (Lawrence 112). Instead, she discovers, salvation lies in the dark, mysterious sexuality of Don Ramon and Don Cipriano and in the mysterious phallic power of the serpent-god of the Aztecs.

From the revival of *masculine* energy, identified with Quetzalcoatl, emerges one of Lawrence's major post-1915 themes, his "leadership politics," akin to fascism (the other novels that express this authoritarian turn most clearly are *Aaron's Rod* and *Kangaroo*). Although Lawrence "was critical of the fascists from the time he became aware of them," Cornelia Nixon argues, he nevertheless advocated a politics that shared much with Ezra Pound's explicit support of Mussolini, including Pound's anti-Semitic conspiracy theory of economics (183–184). For a while at least, he, like Pound, thought of "the Force of Finance" as "a great Secret Society," a machine for coining money owned and operated by a cabal of "Jewish financiers" (*Movements* 264–265; *Kangaroo* 217).

Ian sees Lawrence as extreme but also typical of literary modernism, many of whose influential shapers turned toward fascism. Moreover, literary modernism is, she demonstrates, haunted by the fetishistic figure of the "phallic mother." This fearsomely sublime figure "symbolizes both the unique claims to aesthetic autonomy made by the literary modernists and the specific fantasy of corporeal completeness (the symbolic reunion with mother), which Freud claimed lurked deep in every psyche" (xi). The impulse toward symbolic or mythical, and therefore phallic, wholeness in modernism seems manneristic, self-conscious, or contrived in ways unlike and often actively opposed to the apparent naturalness or solid common sense of Victorian novelistic realism. This is so despite the underlying anxieties of impotence that inform, for instance, "the *energetic* creation of deadness and fixity" in Dickens, as David Simpson suggests (41). Joseph Conrad's and Virginia Woolf's literary impressionisms are intended to overcome (or compensate for) the deficits in Victorian realism and materialism; Yeats's and T. S. Eliot's symbolist poetics are likewise intended to restore or recapture a lost artistic, cultural, and psychic unity (in Eliot's famous formulation, a wholeness lost through the post-Renaissance "dissociation of sensibility"). But it is possible to understand all these variations on modernism as fighting fetishism with fetishism. Ian contends that literary modernism offers numerous versions of the phallic mother; this may be *both* because it is more aware of fetishism as a universal process *and* because it is more fetishistic than previous forms of literature. In short, modernism's attempts to defetishize the social realm or to overcome alienation, as in *The Plumed Serpent,* are themselves highly fetishistic; perhaps this is even true of psychoanalysis, "itself a genre of literary modernism" (Ian xi).

If cultural modernisms are informed or infected by sexual and commodity fetishisms, even as they analyze and seek to resist them, they cannot function as clear alternatives to the new consumerism and imperialism of the 1890s and early 1900s. Nevertheless, Hobson was hardly alone in suggesting that the chief modern, secular substitute for religion as well as Enlightenment was a mutually self-supporting system of jingoism and commercial advertising. Lawrence himself agreed with many of Hobson's criticisms of "the psychology of jingoism"; indeed, through his modernist primitivism, Lawrence seems to be far less Eurocentric than Hobson: "In attempting to convert the dark man to the white man's way of life, the white man has fallen helplessly down the hole he wanted to fill up" (86). Lawrence's view of the complete bankruptcy of "the white man's way of life" is very different from, and in a reactionary direction far more radical than, Hobson's liberal anti-imperialism. In *Civilization and Its Discontents,* with World War I in mind, Freud would write of a generalized "return of the repressed," a "barbarism" (or social infantilism) that only seemed to reemerge more destructively from the graves of history, the more "civilization" tried to bury it. Freud is not saying much that Hobson had not already said in *The Psychology of Jingoism*—that civilization tragically reinvents barbarism—whereas Lawrence invested his anticivilizing hopes in the renewal of a genuine sort of barbarism.

Though Marx's theory of commodity fetishism would only later become a major influence in cultural criticism, a main theme of British intellectuals from Hobson, Wilde, and Lawrence through I. A. Richards, F. R. Leavis, and Cyril Connolly and on to Richard Hoggart and Raymond Williams was the subordination or subversion of supposedly authentic (high) cultural forms by commercialism and consumerism, signaled by the triumph of advertising as the new mythology. In one of his Arnoldian books on culture, industrialization, and education, G. H. Bantock writes, "Modern popular culture in its purest form is . . . manifest in the advertisement, which involves the selection of words and images (photographs) for the sole purpose of salesmanship. All popular culture must sell . . . and we can see something of its essence in the deliberately created dream world of the ad man" (52). The idea of advertising as a modern, secular, materialistic, and yet infantilizing form of mythology is basic alike to Walter Benjamin's "archaeology" of consumer capitalism in Baudelaire's Paris and to Roland Barthes's readings of twentieth-century French culture in *Mythologies*. It is, furthermore, already everywhere inscribed in late-Victorian and Edwardian critical responses to consumerism. These responses say, in effect, that advertising dictates or constitutes the culture of the vast majority, the masses. Between primitive mythology like Aztec serpent worship, moreover, and consumerist self-worship in the magical mirrors of advertising, there is apparently a great gulf fixed. "The great myths were founded on profound human truths; they expressed in symbolic form permanent human conflicts, brought order into many of man's ethical dilemmas," Bantock asserts (52). But it is different today, with the "petty myths" of the advertisers, which "rest on nothing more substantial than dreams and fantasies, unanchored to any sort of reality other than the power aspirations of an ill-educated democracy used to seeing its material longings fulfilled with little effort from itself, and deprived of any genuine emotional pattern of happening and events which will serve to bring home some of the deeper truths of mankind" (55).

Bantock comes close to saying that, as the apparent quintessence of capitalist culture, advertising is capitalist "mythology" and perhaps something more: its ultimate, most spectacular, and also most insidious form of ideological imposition on the deluded masses. Further, the Frankenstein's monster of false consciousness that looms up from the pages of Marx and Engels acquires, so to speak, a mate, once late-Victorian sexologists begin to map the sexual "perversions" including fetishisms. The unholy union of commodity and sexual fetishisms has generated both conservative and radical accounts of ideological mystification in modern and now postmodern cultural theory. This union has also, of course, abetted the rise of vast new image-making industries and media with their cadres of more or less noncritical intellectuals—the advertising and public relations agents, for instance, the cynical priests of commodity fetishism.

The connections of advertising and consumerism to a new, almost exponential level of individual as well as corporate and national reliance on credit and debt are also aspects of late-Victorian and early-modern culture in Britain. Accompanying the so-called consumer revolution at the turn of the century was a vast expansion of credit mechanisms for purchasing the new proliferation of goods. In 1983, Raymond Williams noted "the immense involvement of a majority of the population in what used to be called debt but is now called credit" and claimed that this was a new situation; but it was a situation already emergent in the 1890s, as was the "mobile privatization" that Williams associates with individual dependence on credit (*Resources* 170–171). Along with the diffusion of individual credit mechanisms came new attitudes toward individual indebtedness and bankruptcy, and also new arguments about the nature of money and banking, as in Henry Dunning Macleod's 1889 *Theory of Credit* (a sort of Scottish parallel to Simmel's *Philosophy of Money*) or in John Maynard Keynes's first writings, including his 1913 *Indian Currency and Finance*.[13]

As Walter Benn Michaels has suggested in relation to American naturalism, the reification of fictional realism in the novels of Gissing, Arnold Bennett, John Galsworthy, and others may be homologous with rigid belief in the gold standard. At the same time, the emergence of the new psychological impressionism from Henry James to D. H. Lawrence, James Joyce, and Virginia Woolf may be homologous with the new relativistic complexity in monetary and credit theory and also the (gradual, uneven) modern abandonment of the gold standard. This is Jean-Joseph Goux's thesis in *The Coiners of Language*:

> Was it purely by chance that the crisis of realism in the novel and in painting coincided with the end of gold money? Or that the birth of

13. McLeod believed, according to Freeman Tilden, that there had been no scientific analysis of "the juridical and mathematical principles of the colossal system of credit"; he proposed to supply that lack. But, continues Tilden, that "he did not satisfactorily encompass the phenomenon of debt was perhaps due to two principal reasons: first, that it may be that nobody *can*; and second, that although he knew perfectly well that credit is debt . . . he constantly dealt with credit as though it were not debt" (29).

"abstract" art coincided with the shocking invention of inconvertible monetary signs, now in general use? Can we not see in this double crisis of money and language the collapse of guarantees and frames of reference, a rupture between sign and thing, undermining representation and ushering in the age of the floating signifier? (3)[14]

Goux analyzes the shift from "the gold language" of nineteenth-century fictional realism to the "inconvertibility" of modernist literary discourse, as in André Gide's *Les faux monnayeurs*. This shift Goux relates to all four main "registers" of value—money, language, the king or the father, and the phallus—whose relationships he maps in *Symbolic Economies*.

Goux's insistence on the importance of the shift from the gold standard to inconvertible "token money" is perhaps simplistic, in part because it suggests a monocausal explanation of cultural change not much different from the old Marxist base/superstructure paradigm (money changes, so culture changes). As Britain's early paper money era (1797–1821) suggests, the movement away from the gold standard for most modern nation-states has been gradual and uneven, rather than a sudden, turn-of-the-century affair. Thus, Britain has continued to move in and out of the gold standard in the twentieth century; Churchill's *resumption* of the gold standard in 1925, for instance, was fraught with disastrous consequences, the British prelude to the 1930s global depression. Still another major shift occurred beginning about 1970, with the emergence of international currency markets entailing "futures" trading divorced from trading in commodity gold, from individual nation-states, and even from commodity production. The introduction of paper money going back to 1694 and before already signaled "the loss of transcendental origin, the end of a 'grounding' of money signs in some natural thing imagined to have a pre-monetary worth," notes Rotman (96), which is why it seemed alchemical or diabolic to the Augustans and, indeed, to many later critics of its use such as William Cobbett. The abandonment of the gold standard was a three-centuries-long process involving much vacillation and debate. Nor, except in an economistic, base/superstructure sense that Goux

14. Goux's argument should be carefully compared with Michaels's different account of the interplay between literary naturalism and the gold standard in the American context. Also Derrida provides an interesting critique of Goux in *Given Time* (109–110). In contrast to Goux's historicist attempt to provide too definite a causal connection between the abandonment of the gold standard and the stress on the fictive status of all discourse in literary modernism, Derrida goes to the opposite extreme by simply asserting the obvious: namely, that all discourse, including money, is fundamentally always already fictive.

appears to resist, is it clear why the monetary should be privileged over the other three registers of value.

But Goux nevertheless clearly demonstrates how literary modernism involves new metaphors, springing from a new awareness by such writers as Gide, Yeats, Conrad, and Lawrence of the interplay between the dual fetishisms and therefore among sexual and economic categories and indeed among Goux's four registers of value. Furthermore, taken in conjunction with other aspects of the emergence of consumerism and cultural modernism, the movement away from the gold standard, as theorized by Simmel, Keynes, and others who define money in increasingly relativizing terms as a mode of signification that works independently of gold or any specific signified, can indeed be interpreted as a general "crisis of representation." For Gide as perhaps for other modernists, maintains Goux, "counterfeiting becomes the central metaphor for the historical crisis of a certain type of value-form. Values—not merely economic but also semantic, ethical, religious, and juridical—[become] riddled with suspicion" (*Coiners* 11). Whether or not modernist writers emphasize that crisis in their own themes and styles, modernist forms of representation differ from those most characteristic of the Victorian era by being far more relativistic or less sure of their epistemological power to reflect or represent reality.

4

MODERNISM IN fiction starts with the rejection of nineteenth-century realism, but late-Victorian and Edwardian realistic novels often themselves announce the bankruptcy of the literary conventions they employ. This self-reflexive pattern is very evident in Gissing's *New Grub Street* and in many later novels, including H. G. Wells's 1908 "condition of England novel" *Tono-Bungay*. For Wells's protagonist, George Ponderevo, both advertising and shopping, those hallmarks of modern consumerism, loom large. George's narrative also replays, with both comic and cosmic overtones, the financial boom-and-bust themes and patterns of *Little Dorrit* and *The Way We Live Now*. The quack patent medicine for which the novel is named, and its many equally fraudulent derivatives, are analogous to Merdle's shady financial dealings in Dickens or to Melmotte's Veracruz railway scam and numerous other frauds and forgeries in Trollope. Moreover, to his aviation-minded nephew George, Teddy Ponderevo's "comet-like transit of the financial heavens" (10) is a Daedalus-and-Icarus story that parallels the commercial-imperial flight and fall of Britain itself.

Aristocratic Bladesover, where George's story commences, is abandoned for the modern, vulgar architectural bricolage and chaos of Uncle Teddy's never completed Crest Hill, "which grew and changed its
plans as it grew, and bubbled like a salted snail, and burgeoned and
bulged and evermore grew. I know not what delirium of pinnacles and
terraces and arcades and corridors glittered at last upon the uplands of
[Teddy's] mind; the place, for all that its expansion was terminated
abruptly by our collapse, is wonderful enough as it stands,—that
empty instinctive building of a childless man" (221). Like modern society in general, Crest Hill is at once a miraculous and a cancerous
growth of something out of nothing. Both architecturally and cultur-
ally, Wells implies, modernity creates its own ruins or, in other words, is
simultaneously creative and destructive. The "romance of commerce"—a phrase of Uncle Teddy's applicable to his career, to the
novel, and to modern British history—is thus more than a comic oxymoron. But besides Tono-Bungay, Crest Hill, and the activities of advertising and shopping, the items in the novel that are most characteristic
of modernity are machines. Most significant are the gliders and air-
planes George designs and flies and, even more pointedly, the naval
destroyer he also designs and rides down the Thames at the end of the
novel: the total horror of mechanized war, that ultimate ruinous and
ruin-making activity of modern society, was in 1908 just on the horizon.

More explicitly related to the financial condition of England, however, is the story of how George attempts to rescue the tailspinning
Ponderevo fortune by sailing to Africa to steal "the heaps of quap"
from Mordet Island. As Bernard Bergonzi and others have pointed out,
this end-game tale makes frequent allusions to Conrad's *Heart of Darkness*.[15] Although George does not venture into the mainland of Africa,
he does murder a native who comes too close to the quasi-mining operation. The very superficiality of George's African encounter, including
its seemingly irrelevant moment of homicidal violence, is an aspect of
Wells's commentary on imperialist exploitation and the late-Victorian
"scramble for Africa." In any event, George's story of stealing the quap
from Mordet Island parodies such standard imperialist adventure stories as Robert Louis Stevenson's *Treasure Island*, H. Rider Haggard's
King Solomon's Mines, and John Buchan's *Prester John*.

The "heaps of quap" that George tries to bring home in his wooden
brig are the parodic equivalent of the gold or diamonds that earlier
imperialist adventurers had sought in Africa and elsewhere. But like

15. See Bergonzi's introduction to *Tono-Bungay*.

Uncle Teddy's boom-and-bust in contrast to the pastoral calm and prosperity of Bladesover, quap is a far more unstable, dangerous item than
the gold of the gold standard. An outcome of the fraudulent, tumes-
cent commercial "growth" represented both by Tono-Bungay and by
Crest Hill, the radioactive quap is diseased, "cancerous" (268). Indeed,
it rots in transit, and rots George's brig along with it, so that he returns
empty handed. George associates the "mysterious decay" of his would-
be mineral wealth with the general decay of British culture and society.
He writes that "radioactivity is a real disease of matter" and that quap
carries this "contagious disease." He then adds, "It is in matter exactly
what the decay of our old culture is in society, a loss of traditions and
distinctions and assured reactions. When I think of these inexplicable
dissolvent centres [whether of quap or of mass culture] that have come
into being in our globe . . . I am haunted by a grotesque fancy of the
ultimate eating away and dry-rotting and dispersal of all our world"
(268).

Like the quack medicine for which the novel is named, quap is a
kind of counterfeit wealth or fools' gold. Based on such illusory wealth
(or, rather, on the absence of real wealth), modern progress is itself an
illusion, decadence disguised as its opposite. After his uncle's bankruptcy, the modern ruins of Crest Hill strike George "as the compactest
image and sample of all that passes for Progress, of all the advertise-
ment-inflated spending, the aimless building up and pulling down, the
enterprise and promise of my age" (284). Uncle Teddy's "romance of
commerce," which, as the novel itself, George says he came close to
titling "Waste" (311), is thus a morality tale about the wasteful "conspicuous consumption" of the late-Victorian and Edwardian "plutocracy"—Thorstein Veblen's "leisure class":

> For this the armies drilled, for this the Law was administered and the
> prisons did their duty, for this the millions toiled and perished in suffer-
> ing, in order that a few of us should build palaces we never finished,
> make billiard-rooms under ponds, run imbecile walls round irrational
> estates, scorch about the world in motor-cars, devise flying-machines, play
> golf and a dozen such foolish games of ball, crowd into chattering dinner
> parties, gamble and make our lives one vast dismal spectacle of witless
> waste. (284)

While George tries to redeem the plummeting Ponderevo fortune
through quap, Uncle Teddy tries to redeem it through forgery. In this,
Teddy follows the downward spiral of Trollope's Melmotte, which was
also the fate of the real-life financier Whittaker Wright, who in 1904,
while on trial for fraud, committed suicide. As in *The Way We Live Now*,

moreover, forgery and fraud seem to spread until they infect the novel itself, implying the bankruptcy of the realistic conventions Wells employs. Thus *Tono-Bungay* is an even more suggestive title than *Waste*: by giving his novel the same label that is pasted on every bottle of quack medicine produced in Uncle Teddy's factory, Wells issues a *caveat lector*; like Swift and Pope, he implies that the only literature that can be written in a fraudulent age will also be fraudulent. This is the same self-indicting trope, of course, that Gide utilizes in the title and one of the central tropes of *Les faux monnayeurs* and that, in *The Coiners of Language*, Goux analyzes as symptomatic of cultural modernism.

Wells's "romance of commerce," as in the instance of the Mordet Island adventure, is in several senses a counterfeit or parody "romance." It is above all a story of modern illusions of wealth and prosperity (and of imperial power and glory) that are tantamount to fetishism, in the sense of a false or degraded (*barbarian* was Veblen's term of choice) worship of material things: money, commodities like Tono-Bungay (and like *Tono-Bungay*), possessions like Crest Hill—or better, the worship of substitutes for material things or genuine wealth, a worship based ultimately on false commercial credit:

> At the climax of his Boom, my uncle . . . must have possessed in substance and credit about two million pounds' worth of property to set off against his vague colossal liabilities, and from first to last he must have had a controlling influence in the direction of nearly thirty millions. This irrational muddle of a community in which we live gave him that, paid him at that rate for sitting in a room and scheming and telling it lies. For he created nothing, he invested nothing, he economised nothing. I cannot claim that a single one of the great businesses we organised added any real value to human life at all. Several, like Tono-Bungay, were unmitigated frauds by any honest standard, the giving of nothing coated in advertisements for money. (180)

Uncle Teddy is well aware that his and his nephew's fortunes depend ultimately on nothing more substantial than public credit, more "moonshine" than "substance" (181). As he tells George, their chief product isn't Tono-Bungay at all, but illusion: "'We mint Faith, George,' said my uncle one day. 'That's what we do. And by Jove we got to keep minting! We been making human confidence ever since I drove the first cork of Tono-Bungay.'" George, however, immediately translates this highly "romantic" idea into the production of counterfeit money: "'Coining' would have been a better word than minting! And yet, you know, in a sense he was right. Civilisation is possible only through confidence, so that we can bank our money and go unarmed about the streets. The bank reserve or a policeman keeping order in a jostling multitude of people, are only slightly less impudent bluffs than my uncle's prospectuses" (181).

If soaring and crashing, as in Adam Smith's "Daedalian wings of paper money," is one traditional metaphor for what happens to such "impudent bluffs," and hence for what happens to entire civilizations based on nothing more substantial than debt and public credit, the swelling and bursting of a "bubble" is another. The Tono-Bungay fortune is a "bubble" analogous to the old South Sea Bubble, and Uncle Teddy, "the modern man of power" (220), is bubbledom incarnate, a sort of walking, talking balloon full of hot air that bursts in the end. As George's Aunt says, life "'puffed him up and smashed him—like an old bag—under my eyes'" (300). That Wells means the bursting of the bubble that is Teddy Ponderevo to be emblematic of the imminent bursting of the bubble of modern commercial civilization—or, more specifically, of Great Britain and its empire—is made quite explicit in the novel's conclusion, which offers additional echoes of *Heart of Darkness*. As George rides his destroyer into the darkening future, he writes, "Light after light goes down. England and the Kingdom, Britain and the Empire, the old prides and the old devotions, glide abeam, astern, sink down upon the horizon, pass—pass. The river passes—London passes, England passes" (316).

5

NUMEROUS ACCOUNTS of literary and artistic modernisms emphasize the critical perspectives those modernisms adopt toward economic, technological, and political modernization. In *All That Is Solid Melts into Air*, for example, Marshall Berman identifies cultural modernisms first with the great critical writings of such nineteenth-century figures as Marx and Nietzsche, Baudelaire and Dostoyevsky. The distinctively "modern landscape" of the nineteenth century, Berman writes, is one of "steam engines, . . . factories, railroads . . . of teeming cities that have grown overnight, often with dreadful human consequences; of daily newspapers, telegraphs, telephones, and other mass media; of increasingly strong national states and multinational aggregations of capital . . . [and] of an ever-expanding world market embracing all, capable of the most spectacular growth, capable of appalling waste and devastation, capable of everything except solidity and stability." The first great cultural modernists, Berman goes on to say, were passionate critics of this environment of continual upheaval, even though they also found themselves "remarkably at home in it, alive to its possibilities, affirmative even in their radical negations, playful and ironic even in their moments of gravest seriousness and depth" (19).

Against those first, nineteenth-century modernist critics of modernity, however, Berman pits numerous twentieth-century modernists most of whom strike him as failing to combine a critical attitude toward modernity with an affirmative sense of its excitements and possibilities. Critical modernisms ranging from T. S. Eliot's and Ezra Pound's to Herbert Marcuse's and Michel Foucault's are, for Berman, too critical, too totalizing in their rejections of the present and, more particularly, of capitalism. Yet "pop modernism" ranging from Marshall McLuhan and John Cage to a few postmodernists, while recreating "the openness to the world, the generosity of vision, of some of the great modernists of the past" (Berman here names the odd assortment of Baudelaire, Whitman, Apollinaire, Mayakovsky, and William Carlos Williams) have failed to "recapture their critical bite" (32). In general, Berman thinks, "all of the modernisms and anti-modernisms of the 1960s . . . were seriously flawed" by being either too upbeat or too dystopian, and it was the lack of "generous visions and initiatives that made the 1970s such a bleak decade" (33). Therefore, the chief purpose of his book is to return to "the modernisms of the past," to "our own modern roots" (35).

But if modernity is characterized by a destabilizing dynamism that, in Marx's phrase (and Berman's title), causes "all that is solid [to melt] into air," there can of course be no return, no going back to "our own modern roots" (an oxymoron if there ever was one). Yet Berman's project itself may be thoroughly modernist in its expression of a sense of loss or of decline-and-fall that discovers a Great Zero at the heart of the (post)modern condition and yearns nostalgically backward to recover lost origins or "roots." But at the same moment this sensibility reveals itself to be out of sympathy, and also out of chronological alignment, with twentieth-century modernisms. In other words, it reveals itself to be postmodernist. Certainly literary and artistic modernisms are themselves marked by a sense of loss and of nostalgia as much as by any positive sense of the new, or of surpassing or supplanting past insufficiencies and lacks. They define themselves, as Meisel says, in terms of a fetishistic "structure of compensation" (3). So do postmodernisms.

Conrad is an exemplary modernist both because he calls nineteenth-century realism into question and because of his apparently nihilistic belief that what stands in the place of discredited religion and equally discredited scientific materialism (and also fictional realism) is just more illusion, just another fetishistic structure of compensation. But he is also exemplary in terms of his own compensatory exoticism and fetishizing of style or art, of adherence to duty, and of personal credit in the quite old-fashioned, nonmonetary, aristocratic sense of honor. Conrad's "'impressionistic' will to style," in Jameson's phrase, is at once a will to romance and a denial of romance (*Political Unconscious* 208). It is to maintain this set of would-be romantic illusions-as-values that Marlowe lies to Kurtz's Intended at the end of *Heart of Darkness*. Civilization itself, Conrad suggests, is based on just such a collection of illusions and nothing more. In Kurtz's case, the illusions have given way during his confrontation with the great, demoralizing reality of Africa, that sublime object of ideology (combining, according to Western stereotype, darkness, terror, and superstition). But this disillusioning process has really been a self-confrontation with the yawning, "hollow man" or "mass man" abyss that constitutes Kurtz's personal "heart of darkness." (Tautologically, Kurtz can discover the "horror" of being a hollow man because he was a hollow man to begin with, rather like Henry Morton Stanley's superficial, mirrorlike discovery of David Livingstone in central Africa in 1872: "Dr. Livingstone, I presume?").[16]

If from Conrad's perspective civilization is a bundle of illusions, so too are civilized nation-states. In *Nostromo*, Conrad describes the creation of the Republic of Sulaco on the basis of the illusions of all of its central characters, from the "idealistic" materialism of Charles Gould through the "incorruptible" vanity of Nostromo to the illusion of total disillusionment of Martin Decoud (the self-confrontation of the hollow man). Decoud represents, as numerous commentators have pointed out, the position closest to Conrad's own. Above all, Sulaco emerges as a nation-state on the phantasmal basis of the credit that it derives from its Great Zero: the San Tomé silver mine, including even the credit it ironically derives from the disappearance of the great treasure of silver entrusted to Nostromo and Decoud. Two men of credit (or honor) who seem to deserve the high trust that Charles Gould and the other supporters of law and order and the future of the San Tomé mine place in them, Nostromo and Decoud nevertheless fail. Nostromo falls prey to vanity and greed, and Decoud, to his own inner hollowness and nihilism. And their quite different forms of failure only underscore the illusory basis of all worldly regard or credit (including, in both cases, self-regard).

16. Eliot, of course, draws one of the epigraphs to "The Hollow Men" from *Heart of Darkness*.

In the "rascally crucible of revolutions" that Conrad sees as Latin America (*Nostromo* 85), it is almost as if rival fetishisms are contending for a meaningless hegemony over worthless territory and even more worthless people, although among those fetishisms Conrad seems most willing to grant credit to Charles Gould's particular fetish of "material interests." As Gould tells his wife, "'I pin my faith to material interests'" (100)—an oxymoronic notion that parallels fetishistic worship of material objects, or (to invoke again nineteenth-century novelistic realism) that parallels the fetishism involved in the "faithful" representation of material reality. Gould's "faith" is, of course, not just the belief that the abyss of the mine contains a wealth of silver (an "incorruptible metal," as Nostromo repeatedly says) but the belief that the credit the mine will generate will magically help to transform anarchy into culture, or Costaguana into civilization. "Charles Gould . . . [kept] the idea of wealth well to the fore; but he brought it forward as a means, not as an end. . . . It was his lever to move men who had capital. . . . His faith in the mine was contagious" (93).

Gould's "faith" in the mine and in the progressive effects of "material interests," as history progresses or unravels in Conrad's novel, produces both an even greater fetishism (or collection of fetishes) in the form of public credit and—greatest fetish of all—the new nation-state of the Republic of Sulaco. It is the fetishism of nationalism that Decoud finds especially repellent and yet, as a journalist and protopolitician, hypocritically supports out of his despairing love for Antonia. Decoud has no hope of seeing his love returned until "the endlessness of civil strife" has ended with the establishment of a secure, prosperous, modernizing nation-state. Yet he sees nothing like such a result emerging from any possible politics: "After one Montero there would be another, the lawlessness of a populace of all colours and races, barbarism, irremediable tyranny. As the great Liberator Bolívar had said in the bitterness of his spirit, 'America is ungovernable. Those who worked for her independence have ploughed the sea.'" Decoud thinks the word *patriot* is meaningless for "cultured minds, to whom the narrowness of every belief is odious." Further, given eternal civil strife and rascality, the idea of patriotism is "hopelessly besmirched; it had been the cry of dark barbarism, the cloak of lawlessness, of crimes, of rapacity, of simple thieving" (177).

Conrad/Decoud's critique of patriotism is similar in several ways to Hobson's of jingoism and the fraudulent financial interests that promoted it. Patriotism in the case of the nonexistent Republic of Sulaco (let alone the patent absurdity of Costaguana) can only be corrupt "rascality," except for the two illusions that, according to Conrad, *per-haps* produce something better, more progressive, than just more vio-lence and robbery. The first is, again, Nostromo's vanity, involving credit in the sense of honor, that causes him to seem, until he decides to appropriate the disappeared treasure for himself, "incorruptible": an almost epic hero and leader of the working-class masses who appar-ently make up most of the population of Sulaco. And the second, more important illusion is Gould's "faith" in the steadying, progressive, civil-izing effects of "material interests," based on financial credit, which for him and everyone else in Sulaco boils down to getting the silver out of the mine (or rather, to getting the credit for getting the silver out of the mine).

Decoud tells Mrs. Gould that the silver will "'go north'" to the finan-cier Holroyd in San Francisco "'and return to us in the shape of credit'" (204). Well and good, thinks Mrs. Gould; except that she has now seen through the veil of illusions to what lies behind:

> The fate of the San Tomé mine was lying heavy upon her heart. It was a long time now since she had begun to fear it. It had been an idea. She had watched it with misgivings turn into a fetish, and now the fetish had grown into a monstrous and crushing weight. It was as if the inspiration of their early years had left her heart to turn into a wall of silver-bricks, erected by the silent work of evil spirits, between her and her husband. He seemed to dwell alone within a circumvallation of precious metal, leaving her outside with her school, her hospital, the sick mothers, and the feeble old men, mere insignificant vestiges of the initial inspiration. (204–205)

As always in Conrad, ideals are positive, virtuous, innocent, and pro-ductive only when young, in the beginning. But then they are also mirages or treacherous illusions, at least as viewed by those wiser, older, more cynical observers like Conrad who think they are no longer af-flicted by them, or who give themselves the apparently negative credit (which is, however, identical to the honor of being honest) of having been cured of fetishism by disillusionment. But only then—in youth, when fully believed—can illusions be credited with having any material or political results that Conrad is willing to think of as positive, albeit not progressive.

Fictional honor or honesty (Conrad's impressionistic revision of Vic-torian realism), as the cultural antithesis and support of Charles Gould's "faith" in "material interests," demands that illusions be disillu-sioned, credit discredited. Repeatedly Conrad asks his readers to fore-cast the end: both the total emptying out of the dark abyss of the San

Tomé mine and the victory of "material interests" in the establishment of the Republic of Sulaco. The fictional nation-state founded on the extraction of the "incorruptible metal" of silver from the bowels of the earth is also, simultaneously, founded on the Great Zero that the mine is or will become when totally mined or when its seemingly limitless credit is finally exhausted. And even before: Conrad asks (the novel is the question) which is worse, both for individuals and for the would-be republic, the possession of the fetishized silver or its disappearance? For both Nostromo and Charles Gould, the answer is the same: they are heroes—nation builders—only in the early going, when they do not possess what they idealize. Once the burden/absence of the silver overwhelms them, they are less than heroic—materialists, egoists, fetishists, hollow men (terms perhaps interchangeable for Conrad). Like credit, fetishism imagines as real what is not there; what simultaneously annihilates and renews fetishistic illusions is the impossible, unrepresentable, and therefore sublime burden of the real.

Nostromo, helpless against his own secret corruption, is able at least to draw a partial moral from his downfall. He tells Dr. Monygham:

> "There is something in a treasure that fastens upon a man's mind. He will pray and blaspheme and still persevere, and will curse the day he ever heard of it, and will let his last hour come upon him unawares, still believing that he missed it only by a foot. He will see it every time he closes his eyes. He will never forget it till he is dead—and even then— Doctor, did you ever hear of the miserable *gringos* on Azuera, that cannot die? Ha! ha! Sailors like myself. There is no getting away from a treasure that once fastens upon your mind" (385).

Of course part of the irony of Nostromo's situation is that he is no different from the "miserable *gringos* on Azuera," the ghosts that supposedly haunt that island, fetishistically guarding a treasure they cannot possess, as Nostromo haunts the treasure he has secreted. The great, "incorruptible" Capataz, already the victim of the fetishism known as vanity or egoism, turns out to be easy prey to the same fetishism that afflicts Charles Gould but is also identical to the economic credit that is the main illusory energy creating the Republic of Sulaco out of the chaos of violence, poverty, and fraud that was Costaguana. As the thoroughly disillusioned Martin Decoud begins to fear (hollow man whispering to hollow man), before he anchors himself with bars of silver and slides into the sea to his death, perhaps there is nothing worth the trouble of crediting, even one's own identity. The narrator says that, in contrast to Nostromo, Decoud completely loses faith in himself as in every other possible belief. He ceases to believe "in the reality of his action past and to come," and he begins to entertain "a doubt of his own individuality" (413): the self as the ultimate fetish but also as all that, in Conrad's view, one can finally invest with faith, whether or not that self is honorable or creditworthy.[17]

6

ONE CHARACTERISTIC of modernist projects from the turn to Catholicism of British decadent poets such as Lionel Johnson and Ernest Dowson to the fascisms of Lawrence, Pound, and Wyndham Lewis, from Yeats's interest in Spiritualism and Theosophy to his *A Vision*, and perhaps also from Matthew Arnold's valorization of culture to F. R. Leavis's and *Scrutiny*'s faith in Literature with a capital *L*, is a belief in the necessity of belief. The abyss of Conrad/Decoud's nihilism must be filled in with some positive faith, even if it is only the aestheticist worship of beautiful paintings and artworks (Pater's solution and partially Conrad's), or the affirmation of punctual, efficient work (Veblen's solution and also partially Conrad's).

In forging the modern, secular nation-state, both culture (Terry Eagleton's "ideology of the aesthetic") and industriousness (Veblenesque efficiency; the Conradian illusions of duty and of making the world shipshape) may be necessary ideological ingredients. As *Nostromo* suggests, equally necessary is belief in the wealth or at least the credit of the nation-state. The San Tomé silver and Charles Gould's "material interests" are, Conrad recognizes, "fetishes" but nonetheless *indispensable* for the creation of the Republic of Sulaco. And the republic is itself an illusion, a belief or an institutionalization of a nexus of beliefs in the reality of the silver, of credit, of material interests, of progress, of individual identity and honor, and so forth. In a similar manner, the most influential British economist of the twentieth century, John Maynard Keynes, understood money as a matter of faith and also understood the gold standard as, at best, a prop to that faith. For Keynes, gold—or any metallic standard for money—was important in terms of *other* people's beliefs about the soundness of a nation-state's currency and credit. But in reality, it was an irrational substitute for true value, which he generally identified with art or culture. As with all elitist championing of high culture, true value for Keynes tended to equal what he himself enjoyed, or the high level of his own taste, education,

17. One of the best commentaries on *Nostromo* is not a literary critical work focused on that novel or even on Conrad but is instead Michael Taussig's *The Devil and Commodity Fetishism in South America*.

and intelligence as influenced by Cambridge and Bloomsbury. This is a standard, however, that in economistic terms is no more or less defensible than the utilitarian standard of individual desire (whatever *homo economicus* desires, just so long as it does not inflict pain on somebody else, is whatever *homo economicus* should produce to satisfy that desire). It is also a standard that Lawrence, especially after he had, on Bertrand Russell's invitation, visited Cambridge and met Keynes, thoroughly detested. Lawrence both feared and hated Russell's and Keynes's cultural elitism, their condescension, their rationalism, and no doubt also their homosexuality.[18]

Perhaps Lawrence's negative reaction to Keynes and Bloomsbury had most to do with their ironic, skeptical stance toward anything passionate and overwrought, including the passions aroused by patriotism and war. In these terms, during World War I, Wells had also reacted negatively to the pacifist aloofness of the Bloomsbury intellectuals. "Genteel Whiggism," as Wells put it, was the opposite of doing all that you could in support of your endangered father- or motherland (Bell 68). Keynes's most important early work, *The Economic Consequences of the Peace*, was a scathing attack on British and Allied policy toward defeated Germany, that some readers interpreted as the reverse of patriotic. Yet no economist has wielded more political and governmental power in British affairs than Keynes was to do between the world wars. Furthermore, Keynes is the one economic theorist since Marx who has had a major impact on global history. And no liberal economist after, perhaps, J. S. Mill better understood the destructive effects of bourgeois economism.

Keynes believed the gold standard was "an essential emblem and idol of those who sit on the top tier of the [economic] machine" (*Collected Writings* 9:223–224). That was largely because it was also a stabilizing illusion for the masses, whose belief in the soundness of the currency was essential for the legitimacy of any modern nation-state. Sounding like Henry Thornton, Keynes declared that even in the extreme inflationary conditions in Germany, Russia, and elsewhere after World War I, "a trust in the legal money of the state is so deeply implanted in the citizens of all countries that they cannot but believe that some day this money must recover a part at least of its former value. To their minds it appears that value is inherent in money as such, and they do not apprehend that the real wealth which this money might have

18. "Bloomsbuggery," as it was later called, may have been the main stimulus of Lawrence's nightmare about "a beetle that bites like a scorpion" (Herzinger 175–177).

stood for has been dissipated once and for all" (2:151). Under certain conditions, the mere illusion of wealth that wishful thinking projected onto even the most inflated paper money might have the positive effect of stimulating production and restoring public prosperity where none existed. At the same time, Keynes believed, such a restoration would be both impossible and meaningless without the support of the corollary illusions provided by the arts on the one hand and productive employment or labor on the other.

"The ancient world knew that the public needed circuses as well as bread" (28:341), Keynes writes at the start of "Art and the State." His 1936 essay was commissioned by J. R. Ackerley, editor of the BBC's *Listener*, for an issue surveying state policy toward the arts throughout western Europe, including accounts of the arts policies of Hitler's Germany, Mussolini's Italy, and Stalin's Soviet Union. Keynes believed that these modern dictatorships understood the societal role of the arts better than did their democratic rivals.[19] In his opening sentence, Keynes both hints at what he approves in the public arts policies of regimes more authoritarian than Britain's and distances himself from the utilitarian tradition of nineteenth-century economics. This distance measures cultural modernism's central, contradictory ideological project in regard to the supposed economic, political, and moral health (or legitimacy, or hegemony) both of modern nation-states and of the arts that Keynes understood as the expressions and, indeed, public "possessions" or even most valuable "treasures" of those states. Keynes was above all a liberal humanist who believed deeply in the Arnoldian doctrine of high culture as that which could develop the "best self" from its mediocre, ordinary, perhaps evil alternative selves *and* of the state as the one institution capable of converting such a transformation of ordinary selves into a general civilizing process, thereby overcoming both individual infantilism and social barbarism (cf. Arnold 96–97).

Already in his Cambridge days, under the influence of G. E. Moore's *Principia Ethica*, Keynes and his fellow "Apostles" had "escaped from the Benthamite tradition," which "I do now [in the 1930s] regard as the worm which has been gnawing at the insides of modern civilisation and is responsible for its moral decay" (10:445). J. S. Mill, Arnold, Ruskin, and many other nineteenth-century intellectuals back through Coleridge and the Romantics had perceived Benthamite economism as an insufficient basis on which to understand society and history, let alone

19. Fascism, as Walter Benjamin declared at the end of "The Work of Art in the Age of Mechanical Reproduction" (*Illuminations* 242), involved the aestheticization of politics, whereas Marxism involved the politicization of aesthetics.

on which to ground ideals of social interaction, reform, and community. As Williams demonstrates in *Culture and Society*, their most common solution involved turning to art and culture as repositories, at least, of values and meanings that economism and utilitarianism ignored or repressed. So, too, Keynes recognized the necessity for something more emotive and inspiriting than "the Treasury view" of public affairs: "This view was the utilitarian and economic—one might almost say financial—ideal, as the sole, respectable purpose of the community as a whole; the most dreadful heresy, perhaps, which has ever gained the ear of a civilised people. Bread and nothing but bread, and not even bread, and bread accumulating at compound interest until it has turned into a stone" (28:342). Inheriting this narrowly financial view of their responsibilities, the British governments of the modern era, Keynes believed, were in danger of losing the public's loyalty and thereby of undermining the legitimacy of the nation-state. In contrast, with their grand public rituals and nationalistic architecture and art, the authoritarian regimes in Germany, Italy, and the Soviet Union were fulfilling the basic "human craving for solidarity" (28:347).

"Solidarity" did not point Keynes toward Marx, whose theories he called "the final *reductio ad absurdum* of Benthamism" (10:446). He was not thinking of *class* "solidarity" but rather of the sort of unity inspired by the nation-state, although he was also aware of where such social fusion could lead: "The glory of the nation you love is a desirable end—but generally to be obtained at your neighbour's expense" (2:20). Keynes believed that the "craving for solidarity" could be dangerously crazy when it involved an "aggressive racial or national spirit" (28:347). But the failure of the "Treasury view" to acknowledge *any* "human craving" beyond supposedly rational self-interest and public thrift or stinginess was just dismal. Keynes argued that an enlightened cultural policy should rely on state funding and sponsorship for a broad range of the arts, from architecture to opera. For one thing, such sponsorship would help to cure unemployment (in his *General Theory* and elsewhere, Keynes advocated increased governmental expenditure on public works as an antidote to economic depression). And for another, state sponsorship of culture would go a long way toward fulfilling the "human craving for solidarity."

As G. E. Moore had done, Bloomsbury and Keynes stressed the anti-utilitarian ideals of the pleasure of human relations and the love of beauty (Mini 100). The aesthetic ethics or ethical aestheticism of Bloomsbury, which valorized the attainment of refined "states of mind" (Bell 37), reproduced Moore's philosophical impressionism in many forms, styles, behaviors, and theories, not least in Keynesian economics.[20] In the arts, Keynes, in common with Roger Fry, Virginia Woolf, E. M. Forster, and the other Bloomsburyites, perceived a form of public or national credit that transcended gold, the pound sterling, or even "bread" in the sense of the mere barebones, material welfare of the general population. Culture—in the Arnoldian sense of "the best which has been thought and said" (*Culture and Anarchy* 6; Keynes might have added, the best which has been acted, danced, or sung)—was the category that made history finally worth the candle. And for many of the high literary and artistic modernists, both in Britain and throughout western Europe and the United States, culture meant a refinement of taste and of illusions. It meant an intensification of those most intelligent, sensitive, aesthetic "impressions" or "states of mind" also valorized by Arnold and by Walter Pater in *The Renaissance*, stressed or intensified if not exactly refined by Oscar Wilde and the decadents including Yeats, and then stressed again by Conrad, Pound, T. S. Eliot, Virginia Woolf, and Bloomsbury as one of the chief defining characteristics of literary modernism.

Like George Eliot's Theophrastus Such, Keynes worried as much about "debasing the moral [and cultural] currency" as about strictly economic issues (Eliot, *Theophrastus Such* 84).[21] People were variously motivated by, among other factors, the emotional and sexual valences and values they carried over from infancy into adulthood. Though never an orthodox Freudian, Keynes granted psychoanalytic concepts a kind of provisional status within his economic and political theories (cf. Clark 417). "For Keynes," as Mini observes, "the subject-matter of economics, like matters of the heart, falls between algebra and the

20. Keynes always meant his economic theories to be broadly connected to his cultural theories. Such connections are ignored or overruled in positivist economism, even when it seems to be advocating Keynesianism. But that doctrine (if that is the appropriate name for it) was always an attempt to galvanize the corpse of scientistic economics— that is, to *aestheticize* that corpse—even if the results, theoretically speaking, were something like Dr. Frankenstein's.

21. According to Theophrastus Such, "debasing the moral currency" means "lowering the value of every inspiring fact and tradition so that it will command less and less of the spiritual products, the generous motives which sustain the charm and elevation of our social existence—the something besides bread by which man saves his soul alive. The bread-winner of the family may demand more and more coppery shillings, or assignats, or greenbacks for his day's work, and so get the needful quantum of food; but let that moral currency be emptied of its value—let a greedy buffoonery debase all historic beauty, majesty, and pathos, and the more you heap up the desecrated symbols the greater will be the lack of the ennobling emotions which subdue the tyranny of suffering, and make ambition one with social virtue" (84).

nightmares that Dr. Freud was called upon to interpret" (113). The old *homo economicus* of the classical, utilitarian economists was a reasoning machine who so thoroughly understood Bentham's "felicific calculus" of pleasure and pain in relation to his or her own supposedly enlightened self-interest that the equally rational economist could make no mistake as to the outcomes of profits, interest, progress, or pleasure. But in the post–World War I context of boom and bust, of skyrocketing inflation and the global depression of the 1930s, and perhaps also of modern sexual permissiveness (including Keynes's bisexuality), *homo economicus* seemed to Keynes, as also to Conrad, or Virginia Woolf, or D. H. Lawrence, more psychotic than rational.[22]

Keynes did not follow the trail of tears or of nihilist resignation all the way to Freud's *Beyond the Pleasure Principle*, with its Manichaean depiction of the "death instinct" gripped in mortal combat with the "pleasure principle." Nevertheless, at times he thought of civilization in Conradian or Freudian terms as a veneer of cultured illusions barely disguising if not actively containing destructive human passions. It was at best a mere holding operation, he believed, performed by the educated and ruling elites within all modern nation-states. Lawrence may have considered Keynes's (and Bloomsbury's) views to be no more than a "thin rationalism skipping on the crust of the lava, ignoring both the reality and the value of the vulgar passions," in Keynes's own words (10:450); but that was what Keynes thought the "Treasury view" amounted to.

Poised somewhere between the thin rationalism of Benthamism and the primitivist irrationalism of Lawrence, Keynes supported a liberal, cultured welfarism that, while it stopped short of socialism, nevertheless implicated the state in cultural policy in ways that Arnold might have approved and that Franklin Delano Roosevelt and the New Deal adopted.[23] Keynes's arguments for supporting "circuses" as well as "bread," or cultural rather than merely economic solutions to social problems, were influenced by fascism in one direction and, in another, involving state welfarism and state support of the arts, constitute *the* most influential social science alternative to the Marxist variations on

22. Keynes's biographers, more interested in economics than psychology, have both understated the Bloomsbury connection (irrelevant to economics) and Keynes's sexual proclivities (also irrelevant—supposedly—to economics).

23. Piero Mini remarks that Keynes was much more than just an economist; he was "a social philosopher" and "cultural leader interested in the cultural amelioration of society." For Mini, Keynes belongs in the tradition of Romantic and Victorian anti-utilitarian theory, "closer to Coleridge-Arnold" than to most nineteenth- and twentieth-century economists (102).

the themes of debt, fetishism, and empire in the modernist period from, roughly, 1900 to the 1960s. His ideas also offer an important contrast to Veblen's about "barbarism" and "conspicuous consumption" in relation to—as Veblen thought of them—the pretensions of cultured elites like the Bloomsbury artists and intellectuals including Keynes. Keynes always seemed to know better or to see beyond capitalism and also beyond the modern nation-state with its imperial aspirations; he looked toward a cultured, perhaps utopian internationalism. Yet he seemed also intent on being pragmatic, on doing the best he could with the tools at hand, which in theoretical terms included capitalism at work within the boundaries of nation-states. More radical challenges to the status quo by what Raymond Williams called "the Bloomsbury fraction" came in E. M. Forster's and Leonard Woolf's critiques of British racism and imperialism. More radically still, from her feminist perspective, Virginia Woolf drew highly original political and economic conclusions from the aestheticist tendencies of literary modernism and of her own fiction.

7

IT HAS sometimes been suggested how, through her poetic employment of stream-of-consciousness narration, Woolf reshaped the tradition of domestic realism from Jane Austen through Elizabeth Gaskell and George Eliot, in part by giving it an inwardness and intimacy which, however, removed that tradition farther from politics and the public sphere than was the case even with Austen. In *Mary Barton* and *Felix Holt*, Gaskell and Eliot wrote stories that belong to the subgenre of political novels. And Eliot's *Middlemarch*, though sometimes cited as a point of origin for the "psychological realism" that leads through literary impressionism to modernist inwardness, is centrally concerned with analyzing the small-scale public sphere for which it is titled as well as the larger public sphere—Britain in the 1830s—that lies beyond. In contrast, Woolf's fictional world has seemed to many readers to be constricted to a handful of upper-class characters in domestic or family situations, upon whose concerns external events like World War I act only as unwelcome intrusions. As Ian puts it, "The reflexive novel . . . fetishizes its own interiority" (125).

But like *Middlemarch*, Woolf's *To the Lighthouse* and *Mrs. Dalloway* are about much more than just the inward, private thoughts and feelings of her small collections of mostly well-to-do characters. They are, for one thing, very much about the quality of the lives those characters are empowered to lead. *Mrs. Dalloway* in particular deals centrally with the relationships between the characters and the larger public sphere to which they belong, a public sphere variously named London, England, India, the Empire. Though no doubt obliquely, *Mrs. Dalloway* is just as concerned with the condition of England as is *Tono Bungay*. Indeed, given Woolf's overtly public, political themes in *A Room of One's Own* and *Three Guineas*, it would be quite strange if her fiction did not also deal with those themes. Read in terms of how they at least implicitly construct public spheres for their characters' most private thoughts and actions, Woolf's novels appear to be intensely political rather than apolitical and merely privatistic. As Neil Nehring contends, for a variety of reasons, "the inwardness of modernist aestheticism" has come to seem "more exclusively conservative" or at least apolitical than it in fact is (41). In Woolf's case, literary impressionism challenged the positivist, reified conventions of bankrupt novelistic realism, and in this manner it offered a form of ideological critique; it also expressed a radical feminism that, albeit through irony and indirection, sought at every turn to subvert the words, deeds, and institutions of patriarchy.

Raymond Williams declared that the chief defining value of "the Bloomsbury fraction" was "the unobstructed free expression of the civilized individual" as the culmination of "bourgeois enlightenment." Bloomsbury

> was against cant, superstition, hypocrisy, pretension and public show. It was also against ignorance, poverty, sexual and racial discrimination, militarism and imperialism. But it was against all these things in a specific moment of the development of liberal thought. What it appealed to, against all these evils, was not any alternative idea of a whole society. Instead it appealed to the supreme value of the civilized *individual*, whose pluralization, as more and more civilized individuals, was itself the only acceptable social direction. ("Bloomsbury" 165)

Though this passage accurately describes Keynes's and perhaps E. M. Forster's, Roger Fry's, and Clive Bell's cultural ideas, Williams surely misses a beat in regard to Virginia Woolf. For her, "sexual . . . discrimination" was not one item among many that all "civilized individuals" should oppose; rather, it was *the* chief category to place at the head of any list of social injustices. It was *the* central mystery (in contrast to Lawrence's phallocentric mystery of sex) to be fathomed before "any alternative idea of a whole society" that was at all workable could arise. Williams does not recognize that, as latter-day feminists would declare, "the personal is political." Inwardness and intimacy are not separated by some Chinese wall from politics and the public sphere; they are, rather, where all politics begin and end. And if the first questions for any political philosophy concern the Hegelian master-slave dialectic (or who dominates whom, how, and why), the most basic of those questions is surely the one raised by feminists: the question of patriarchy, or of the domination of women by men through most of recorded history. It is just this question, of course, that Woolf raises in *A Room of One's Own* and *Three Guineas*.

What is it, Woolf asks in the latter essay, that separates women's from men's spheres—supposedly the private from the public, or the inward and intimate from the political? Is this separation natural, logical, fair, sane? And is the divisive power that causes it related to—perhaps even identical to—the power that drives men and nations to war? For she has been asked by a male friend to support a society for the prevention of war. But why should she or any woman do so, she replies, if in general women have been deprived of political influence by men, and if in general war is the result of a male—not female—"instinct" to competition, domination, and bloodshed? "For though many instincts are held more or less in common by both sexes, to fight has always been the man's habit, not the woman's. Law and practice have developed that difference, whether innate or accidental. Scarcely a human being in the course of history has fallen to a woman's rifle; the vast majority of birds and beasts have been killed by you, not us" (6).

"Law and practice," buttressed by the strange sentiment known as "patriotism," have erected a vast system of power and institutions—church and state, the schools and universities, the nation and its colonies—from the running of which women are virtually excluded. This vast apparatus of power and privilege, also buttressed by professions and disciplines from which women are generally excluded, constitutes the great war machine of the nation-state of Britain (or France, or Germany, etc.). It may be understandable that the war machine should elicit the state worship known as "patriotism" from the men whose own power and privilege are derived from it, but women, Woolf thinks, do not have similar motives for patriotism. Women have passions and interests, but they do not have these motives—at least not until the men they love, or try to love, go to war over their own quite distinct passions and interests. Rather than being a patriot, a reasonable woman will instead belong, says Woolf, to the ever expanding "Outsider's Society" and will, as an outsider, not automatically wax patriotic when asked to do so by a man:

> When he says, as history proves that he has said, and may say again, "I am fighting to protect our country" and thus seeks to rouse her patriotic

emotion, she will ask herself, "What does 'our country' mean to me an outsider?" To decide this she will analyse the meaning of patriotism in her own case. She will inform herself of the position of her sex and her class in the past. She will inform herself of the amount of land, wealth and property in the possession of her own sex and class in the present— how much of "England" in fact belongs to her. (107)

From her rational survey, Woolf says, the outsider will conclude "that her sex and class has very little to thank England for in the past; not much to thank England for in the present; while the security of her person in the future is highly dubious" (108) largely because the male insiders and power brokers who surround her, act like they own her, and seem to make all the decisions for her are very apt to go to war against the equally patriotic male insiders of other nation-states.

Woolf here suggests that the position of the members of the female Outsider's Society in England is parallel to the position of those nationalities and cultures dominated by Britain through its empire—"the Indians or the Irish, say" (108)—and she goes on to declare that, having treated woman "as a slave" throughout history, "our country" has no claim on her loyalty: "as a woman, I have no country. As a woman I want no country. As a woman my country is the whole world." Therefore the member of the Outsider's Society, she says, "will bind herself to take no share in patriotic demonstrations; to assent to no form of national self-praise; to make no part of any claque or audience that encourages war; to absent herself from military displays, tournaments, tattoos, prize-givings and all such ceremonies as encourage the desire to impose 'our' civilization or 'our' dominion upon other people" (109).

If "patriotic demonstrations" and the rest are public activities leading up to war, Woolf leaves no doubt that, in her estimation, the initial motives for war are planted in private, in childhood, in the inwardness and intimacy of family life. On the issue of admitting women to the priesthood of the Church of England, she cites a Freudian theologian, Professor Grensted of Oxford, who points out that, whatever the rational merits of the case, the issue raises a "strong emotion" governed by an "infantile fixation," a "non-rational sex taboo" (126). Woolf extrapolates from Grensted's testimony the suggestion that this same "infantile fixation" is the "egg" or "germ" from which other "strong feelings" of exclusion grow—indeed, from which the entire system of patriarchy grows: "Society it seems was a father, and afflicted with the infantile fixation too" (135).

Although Woolf does not use the word, *fetishism* is clearly a term that would cover many of the symptoms, at least, of this generalized "infantile fixation," above all, the male rituals of exclusion and domination she describes. (Lawrence's worship of Quetzlcoatl, were it not fictional and foreign, would fit easily among these rituals.) In an early passage listing the centers of power "crowded together" in London—"St. Paul's, the Bank of England, the Mansion House . . . the Law Courts . . . Westminster Abbey and the Houses of Parliament" (18)—Woolf goes on to enumerate the symbols of power its denizens wear: "every button, rosette and stripe seems to have some symbolical meaning" (19). Just as Veblen had scathingly dissected the atavistically barbaric costumes, adornments, and behaviors of the leisured class, so Woolf practices a similar iconoclasm: the "wearing pieces of metal, or ribbon, coloured hoods or gowns, is a barbarity which deserves the ridicule which we bestow upon the rites of savages. . . . Even stranger, however, than the symbolic splendour of your clothes are the ceremonies that take place when you wear them. Here you kneel; there you bow; here you advance in procession behind a man carrying a silver poker; here you mount a carved chair; here you appear to do homage to a piece of painted wood." (20).

Here once again is fetishism at work at the very heart of Britain's institutions of national and imperial power. This "barbaric," psychologically regressive behavior is, moreover, indistinguishable from the equally barbaric deployment of political symbols by the dictatorships in Germany and Italy. Woolf's critique could hardly be more at odds with Keynes's admiration of the arts policies of Nazism and Italian fascism. In insisting that no aspect of the Outsider's Society be bound by rules, rituals, and symbolic displays, and also that it involve no hierarchies of power or distinction, Woolf writes, "Here . . . the example of the Fascist States is at hand to instruct us—for if we have no example of what we wish to be, we have, what is perhaps equally valuable, a daily and illuminating example of what we do not wish to be. With the example then, that they give us of the power of medals, symbols, orders and even, it would seem, of decorated ink-pots to hypnotize the human mind it must be our aim not to submit ourselves to such hypnotism" (114).

Fetishistic rituals involving objects such as "decorated ink-pots" or "painted pieces of wood," flags or medals, are of course instances of patriotism, that is, of the general fetishizing of the nation-state. Rooted in an "infantile fixation" at least on the part of the male sex, patriotism is the product of neurotic, compensatory, dominative behaviors first within families and then beyond them, in the world at large, in the phenomena associated with the growth of nation-states, the acquisition of empires, and war. Woolf's recurrent image of history as "vicious circle, the dance round and round the mulberry tree," suggests that the same infantile fixation has governed human behavior for ages, producing patriarchy, slavery, rebellion, imperialism, genocide. It is a fixation whose familiar names are greed and egoism: "'Here we go round the mulberry tree, the mulberry tree, the mulberry tree. Give it all to me, give it all to me, all to me. Three hundred millions spent upon war'" (59). This is, no doubt, the same "mulberry tree" of infantilism, metamorphosed into a "prickly pear," round which T. S. Eliot's "Hollow Men" were dancing their way toward the end of the world, "not with a bang but a whimper" (Woolf heard both the whimper and the bang: they were the same sound). Her "mulberry tree" is also identical to "the poison tree of intellectual harlotry" or the prostitution of culture through advertising and warmongering journalism which Hobson had earlier charged with the destruction of "the credit of printed matter." The chief aim of any critical, emancipatory political practice, Woolf suggests, must be to break out of the vicious circle, to end the zombified dance that, because its participants are fetishistically spellbound by absurdities of power- and status-symbols like "decorated ink-pots," leads over and over again to war.[24]

Woolf's quasi-utopian Outsider's Society will take no part in the state-building, warmongering activities of ages-old politics. I say "quasi-utopian" not because her Society did not really exist but because to be fully utopian would involve imagining the reconstitution of society in general on the basis of different, positive premises or values. Here one might object that, because it refuses to imagine the reconstitution of society, the Outsider's Society must necessarily remain inside, and complicitous with, the given, flawed, patriarchal society it opposes. But direct opposition is not what Woolf advocates; she calls instead for a seemingly apolitical "indifference." And the objection that the Outsider's Society is not utopian is beside the point for another reason, because its membership is made up of all women throughout history,

24. Unless the dance round the mulberry tree can be disrupted, history is doomed to repeat itself, to be the nightmare from which Stephen Dedalus said he was trying to awake. In relation to infantile fixation and fetishism, compare Woolf's and Eliot's mulberry tree to the story Gabriel tells in "The Dead" (in Joyce's *Dubliners*) about old Patrick Morkan and his horse, Johnny. The horse has gone round and round most of its life, turning the old man's mill. So when Patrick Morkan hitches him to a wagon to drive out among "the quality" in Dublin, all goes well until they come upon the statue of "King Billy." The poor horse proceeds to go round and round the statue and the old man can get it to do nothing else—an instance, of course, of Joyce's theme of "paralysis."

that is, all women under patriarchy. Woolf remorselessly, ironically refuses to be political in the standard, common sense of the term because politics refuses to include women. Why redesign society, when society does not provide women with any tools for redesigning it? But this seemingly indifferent, apolitical stance is calculated, through irony, to be highly troublesome to Woolf's male lawyer friend, correspondent, and political animal (and perhaps just as troublesome to somewhat solemn male critics like Raymond Williams).

The unfixed or fluid, ruleless, apolitical aestheticism that Woolf associates with the Outsider's Society is also calculated to be antithetical in several ways to the fetishized worship of pieces of painted wood, ribbons, flags, and medals that male professionals such as lawyers practice. Instead of public display and "pageantry," writes Woolf, a key aim of the members of the Outsider's Society will be "to increase private beauty; the beauty of spring, summer, autumn; the beauty of flowers, silks, clothes . . . the scattered beauty which needs only to be combined by artists in order to become visible to all" (*Three Guineas* 114). It is just this sort of "private," "scattered beauty" that several of Woolf's most important women characters disseminate: Mrs. Ramsay in *To the Lighthouse*, for example, with Lily Briscoe as the somewhat more public and conventional artist trying to combine the beautiful impressions that Mrs. Ramsay "scatters" even after her death. And it is also "private," "scattered beauty" that Clarissa Dalloway disseminates, specifically through her nonprofessional, seemingly not very significant nor very dignified role as "hostess" to the party with which the novel ends, but more generally through her radiant, cheerful, generous character— through being just who she is.

8

THAT THERE is nothing overtly, traditionally political about either *To the Lighthouse* or *Mrs. Dalloway* is part of Woolf's point. Her women characters cannot participate directly in the politics that her male characters espouse, practice, and in some sense live every day of their fetishistic lives. Mr. Ramsay is a philosopher rather than a politician, but he is just as much an embodiment of the patriarchy as is Richard Dalloway, M.P. Indeed, Ramsay is more obviously patriarchal than Dalloway, because the latter, though a Conservative M.P. in close touch with the prime minister, is a good sort of fellow who apparently lacks strong opinions and feelings except for his love of family, friends, and country. At least he loves Clarissa, brings her roses, and does not overtly attempt to impose his will on her.[25] Marching around the garden spouting lines from "Charge of the Light Brigade," imagining himself a second Duke of Wellington or Admiral Nelson, Mr. Ramsay seems more like the infantile nineteenth-century patriarchs Woolf anatomizes in *Three Guineas* than does Clarissa's unobstrusive husband or, for that matter, Peter Walsh, Clarissa's old love and an imperial administrator in India.

The antithesis of values involved in the contrast between the luminous personality of Mrs. Ramsay and that of her egoistic, fetishistic husband is thus more evident than that involved in the contrast between Clarissa and Richard Dalloway. But *Mrs. Dalloway* is nevertheless a more explicitly political novel than *To the Lighthouse* (political, that is, in some of the ways *Coningsby* and *Phineas Finn*), if only because Richard is an M.P., Peter Walsh has been an Indian administrator, the prime minister comes to the party, and the story takes place in London, in the environs of Buckingham Palace and Parliament, the Bank of England and the Inns of Court. But just as *Three Guineas* is a sort of anarchistic, antipolitical political tract, so *Mrs. Dalloway* is an antipolitical political novel. And just as *Three Guineas* is also a pacifist tract (even while Woolf expresses her reluctance to support a male pacifist society), so *Mrs. Dalloway* is an antiwar novel. If Keynes in his *General Theory* was in some sense rewriting *The Wealth of Nations*, what Virginia Woolf offers in her novels is an account of the poverty of nations, and the bankruptcy of ordinary politics and economics in general—male, middle- and upper-class business as usual.

The ruinous effects of World War I are strewn throughout the pages of *Mrs. Dalloway*. As Maureen Howard puts it, along with death "the other terrible presence in the novel is war: *Mrs. Dalloway* is one of the great post-war novels. Septimus Smith, shell-shocked, broken, is a constant reminder of war's waste" (Introduction to *Mrs. Dalloway* xii). The account of Smith's depression and paranoia, leading up to his suicide, forms the major subplot of the novel, casting a pall over the otherwise successful, happy climax of the party: "Oh! thought Clarissa, in the middle of my party, here's death, she thought" (183). If Smith is one additional, belated casualty of the war, so too, of course, is his young Italian wife Rezia, without friends or family in London and, after his suicide, thoroughly bereft, miserable. But the party goes on—Smith

25. In his earlier appearance in *The Voyage Out*, Richard Dalloway is clearly much closer to the patriarchal Ramsay than he is in *Mrs. Dalloway*. He kisses Rachel Vinrace. He vociferously espouses a macho imperialism that, however, Clarissa and the other characters all seem to approve (Woolf, like Rachel, keeps her distance).

and his wife are not connected by either family or friendship to the Dalloways—and that, too, is part of the point.

Woolf is not saying just that life must go on, or that Clarissa is too brave and cheerful to let the news of a stranger's suicide disturb her for more than a moment. That the Dalloways do not know Smith—that he is therefore a seemingly gratuitous, incidental addition to the main plot—helps to underscore the alienation that is a major aspect of his victimization. He is not merely a belated casualty of the war; he is also a symbol or symptom of a society that produces both war and forms of domestic estrangement and insanity so severe that, for some at least, no help is possible. On the contrary, society also produces forms of patriarchal, professional expertise that themselves perpetuate rather than alleviate alienation. One of the most obvious embodiments of patriarchy in *Mrs. Dalloway* is the eminent psychiatrist Sir William Bradshaw, who has been treating Smith. As the professional man of expertise and himself a model of (patriarchal) sanity, Bradshaw is the counterpart both of the pacifist lawyer to whom Woolf addresses *Three Guineas* and of Mr. Ramsay in *To the Lighthouse*.

It is Lady Bradshaw who, in excusing their late arrival at the party, mentions Smith's suicide to Clarissa. Earlier, it is Sir William who elicits from the narrator the novel's only obvious narrative interpolation— almost a sermon. "Proportion, divine proportion, Sir William's goddess," says the narrator, is the chief idol of his seemingly rational, scientific worship (99). Faith in "proportion," that is, in his version of sanity and normality, is what Sir William tries to impose on his patients. But like Septimus Smith, Bradshaw's patients are not sane; they lack "proportion," the very thing Bradshaw exhorts them to go forth and have. In a tautological, vicious-circle manner, Bradshaw has made his professional fame and fortune by telling unreasonable people to be reasonable.

The narrator suggests that Bradshaw's is just the sort of hidden madness, disguised as sanity and even as professional expertise, that is involved when Britain and other western nation-states, having conquered nonwestern, nonchristian, supposedly barbaric societies, tell those societies to become civilized and Christian. Here Lawrence would undoubtedly have agreed with Woolf. For "Proportion has a sister, less smiling, more formidable, a Goddess even now engaged—in the heat and sands of India, the mud and swamp of Africa, the purlieus of London, wherever in short the climate or the devil tempts men to fall from the true belief which is her own—is even now engaged in dashing down shrines, smashing idols, and setting up in their place her own stern countenance. Conversion is her name, and she feasts on the wills of the weakly, loving to impress, to impose, adoring her own features stamped on the face of the populace" (100). Woolf thus approximates one of the themes of the later antipsychiatry movement of R. D. Laing, Thomas Szasz, Michel Foucault, and others: to impose a model of sanity or of rationality on the supposedly insane or irrational is imperialist, totalitarian, itself irrational.

Without realizing it, Sir William behaves like Hitler or Mussolini. As in *Three Guineas*, Woolf sees little difference between the patriarchal state and the fascist state: the latter is only an inflated version of the former. And Sir William is only one instance among many of the tragic conversion of "private" brothers and fathers into Creons, ready to put their Antigones to death in the name of the state. Patriarchal society converts "the private brother," respected and beloved of their private sisters, into "a monstrous male, loud of voice, hard of fist, childishly intent upon scoring the floor of the earth with chalk marks, within whose mystic [national, sexual, class] boundaries human beings are penned, rigidly, separately, artificially; where, daubed red and gold, decorated like a savage with feathers he goes through mystic rites and enjoys the dubious pleasures of power and dominion while we, 'his' women, are locked in the private house" (*Three Guineas* 105). Here Lawrence, with his fantasies of "plumed serpents," might well have disagreed with Woolf.

That Sir William Bradshaw worships Proportion and imposes it on his patients is not so much his personal weakness, perhaps, as it is a flaw intrinsic to his professional discipline, his scientific expertise, and more generally to British and European manhood or masculinity. The facts that women were by and large excluded from the discipline of psychiatry and that, from Woolf's perspective, psychiatry amounts to little more than an unconscious idolatry of "proportion" or of male rationality make the dicipline all the more insidious and dangerous. *What* Sir William worships, moreover—the two weird, cannibalistic sisters Proportion and Conversion—seems like a double, nightmare version of eighteenth-century caricatures of "Lady Credit," "Fortuna," "Luxuria," and other vaporish female phantasms. Why should a feminist writer indulge in such apparently antifeminist personifications? Precisely because those personifications are emanations of the patriarchal, albeit unconscious, fetishizing imagination of Sir William Bradshaw (or of psychiatry), and also precisely because these two weird sisters, Proportion and Conversion, have actually a third sister (or perhaps she is their mother). The name of this third monstrous female goddess or idol is "Britannia."

"Britannia" is certainly the name of the chief goddess worshiped by another interestingly symptomatic character in *Mrs. Dalloway*, and that is Lady Millicent Bruton, herself both something of an amazon and distinctly *not* a practicing member of Woolf's Outsider's Society. On the contrary, Lady Bruton is the incarnation of the purest, most conservative patriotism in the novel:

> For she never spoke of England, but this isle of men, this dear, dear land, was in her blood (without reading Shakespeare), and if ever a woman could have worn the helmet and shot the arrow, could have led troops to attack, ruled with indomitable justice barbarian hordes and lain under a shield noiseless in a church, or made a green grass mound on some primeval hillside, that woman was Millicent Bruton. Debarred by her sex and some truancy, too, of the logical faculty . . . she had the thought of Empire always at hand, and had acquired from her association with that armoured goddess her ramrod bearing, her robustness of demeanour, so that one could not figure her even in death parted from the earth or roaming territories over which, in some spiritual shape, the Union Jack had ceased to fly. To be not English even among the dead—no, no! Impossible! (180–181)

Lady Bruton might easily be dismissed as just a minor figure who provides comic relief. But she is evidently more than that to Woolf: she is instead everything that a good "soldier's daughter" may become. Though excluded from all the roles that the empire makes available to men, including soldiering, she nevertheless (here the "truancy" of her "logical faculty" comes into play) bends over backward to do everything in her (negligible) power to support the empire, the work of her fathers, and the monster (as Woolf almost calls it in *Three Guineas*) that is also the phallic mother known as Britannia. Lady Bruton is thus everything that a member of the Outsider's Society should avoid becoming. She is, nevertheless, a well-meaning person, the unwitting victim of the patriarchy, which is more than can be claimed for Sir William Bradshaw. Also, Lady Bruton's worship of the phallic mother Britannia is forthright; Bradshaw's worship of the cannibal sisters, Proportion and Conversion, is secretive, unconscious, insidious—not at all a worship in any fetishistic or irrational sense, of course, at least according to the scientific Bradshaw.

In her claim that the monstrous, fetishistic phallic mother is a recurrent, even defining figure in literary and artistic modernisms, Marcia Ian has an ally in Woolf. At least Woolf was aware of and attempted through irony and satire to deconstruct the figure of the phallic mother that, if Sir William Bradshaw is any example, lurks within psychiatric discourse. But if the argument of *Three Guineas* is correct, it is more than just psychiatry that suffers from a hidden fetishism: it is all male professions with their supposedly expert discourses and hierarchies of authority. For Woolf, these are structures of compensation rather than of genuine discipline and rationality. In the Name of the Father arise those patriarchal laws and boundaries and knowledges that culminate in the ultimate monster who has thus far been the main "subject" of the Enlightenment: the modern nation-state with its Repressive and Ideological State Apparatuses. Or so Virginia Woolf comes close to saying, without benefit of Jacques Lacan or Louis Althusser. And it is patriotism, politics, and empire building, too, that are products of that "infantile fixation," that "egg" or "germ" of human weakness and egoism, or in other words, that general fallibility that leads men toward domination rather than love. Meanwhile, all of (patriarchal) history has conspired to teach women—even when they know how to love—not to know how to cope with the weakness in men that cries out for pity and love and that leads, through worship of phallic mothers like Britannia, to patriarchy, war, and empire.

6

POSTINDUSTRIAL, POSTCOLONIAL, POSTMODERN: "ANARCHY IN THE U.K." (1945–1994)

"The jewel in the crown is made, these days, of paste."

—Salman Rushdie

"Believe in the ruins."

—The Sex Pistols

1

AT THE start of *The Enchanted Glass: Britain and Its Monarchy*, Tom Nairn writes that the British "are luckier but ultimately less fortunate than other peoples" in having a special "mirror," the monarchy, through which their national identity is consolidated as it is reflected back to them. They are "luckier," perhaps, only in the sense that the mirror of monarchy seems to present them with such a clear, traditional image of national identity. They are "less fortunate than other peoples" because, in Nairn's estimation, "this enchanted glass reflects only a decreasingly useful lie" (9) as "Ukania" continues to decline and fall through its post–World War II, postindustrial, postcolonial, postmodern senescence. Perhaps Nairn would agree, however, that other nation-states and national identities are also in some sense "decreasingly useful lies" and furthermore that in the postmodern era these "lies" are becoming exposed and unraveled. The collapse of the Soviet Union and the socialist regimes of eastern Europe is most dramatic, but also apparent is the general weakening of perhaps all modern nation-states in the era of multinational corporations and the world economic system (Amin, *Empire* 7–18; Miyoshi; Sklair 238–239). This weakening, it is often argued, is a key symptom of "the postmodern condition." "The great narratives are now barely credible," says Lyotard ("Universal History" 318), including the narratives that nation-states tell about themselves and their empires: their nationalist mythologies, histories, and literatures.

Perhaps the most credible aspect of much post–World War II British writing (including Nairn's) has been that it so clearly registers a sense of the mounting ruins, of "Ukania" in disarray if not yet in complete dissolution. By 1983, Britain had become, declared Raymond Williams, a "small and increasingly marginal society" with "a weak, second-grade capitalist economy" (*Resources* 165). It was a nation-state that, after over a century of world leadership, had since World War II "little chance of independent initiatives" in the emergent world system of internationalized, "nomad capitalism" (*Resources* 165, 124).

In the British as in other national contexts, one way that decline-and-fall is currently expressed is through the recognition of all versions of national identity as fetishistic. Thus Nairn understands the "lie" of national identity (British or otherwise) to be based on a fetishistic psychic structure that consistently misrecognizes symbols and images for realities. "If we aren't all mad, what are we?" he asks. Part of the answer is that "we" (the British) are all fetishists, after the definition of Charles de Brosses in his 1760 *Du culte des dieux fétiches*, which Nairn quotes early in *The Enchanted Glass*: "'Fetishism: a sort of lower idolatry in which the idol is rather the embodiment than the symbol of the associated spiritual power'"(25)—in other words, in which the idol is mistaken for the real thing. Nairn's further point is that British "popular" adoration of the monarchy is as thoroughly, perhaps unabashedly fetishistic as modern and postmodern nationalisms get. This is the case in part because the monarchy is so obviously anachronistic. The anachronism works (is effectively appropriate) both because it expresses a fetishistically compensatory nostalgia for an absent unity and because it arises from and symbolizes "Great Britain's unique version of capitalist development: the prolonged and baroquely gilded hegemony of 'early' or commercial capital over all subsequent phases" (241).

Nairn here expresses a version of the "exceptionalist" argument about British development which explains Britain's twentieth-century decline from imperial and industrial hegemony partly in terms of its having been first, and therefore in some sense premature, to develop a global empire and to industrialize (for an early statement of this case, see Hobsbawm, *Industry*). According to this interpretation, because Britain consolidated its global imperialist and capitalist power before the Industrial Revolution, which itself began first in Britain during the second half of the eighteenth century, British capitalism—particularly London commercial, banking, and money market interests—became allied with the aristocracy. Centered in "the City" (the Bank of England, the Treasury, the stock market) and represented by the great Whig families that wielded enormous political and economic power for two centuries and more, this alliance has outranked and outflanked the industrial bourgeoisie. Geoffrey Ingham contends that capitalism in Britain has been "divided" between commercial or financial and industrial interests, and the former have continued to thrive even as the latter eroded: "Not only has the City survived, it now prospers as much as it ever did in the late nineteenth and early twentieth centuries" (36). This situation has come about, he asserts, through the "increasing independence of Britain's non-productive forms of capital from domestic production" (8; Leys 131–135).

The British divorce between financial and industrial interests is mirrored, however, in the global situation of "late capitalism," in which financial markets in currencies and "futures" trading, together with the World Bank and the International Monetary Fund, seem from about 1970 forward to have taken precedence even over transnational corporations that produce actual commodities (Harvey 189–197; Rotman 87–97). Also, after the too-early Civil War of the 1640s, Britain never experienced a bourgeois revolution like the ones in France and the American colonies. The anachronistic alliance of aristocracy with commercial (as opposed to industrial) finance, both Nairn and Ingham argue, has persisted to this day and is the substance behind the "gilded" imagery of monarchy. That imagery partly compensates for and partly masks the harsh reality of the disintegration of Britain's former industrial, domestic prosperity and imperial power and glory.

Nairn's thesis agrees in most of its details with Perry Anderson's analyses of British exceptionalism in the pages of *New Left Review* (essays now anthologized in Anderson's *English Questions*). It emphasizes the ironic craziness of the British "popular" (or perhaps "authoritarian populist") tendency to cling all the more adoringly, fetishistically to its national identity, reflected in the "enchanted glass" of monarchy, as the very sources of prosperity and rational community crumble. A key symptom of this contemporary fetishism of monarchy was the Falkland Islands war in 1982, which solidified Margaret Thatcher's popularity as Britain's "Iron Lady" and which she herself claimed "put the Great back into Britain" (quoted in Barnett 83). In relation to the Ukanian victory over an inept Argentine military, history seemed to be repeating itself—as Anthony Barnett, paraphrasing Marx, contends in *Iron Britannia*—less as farce than as televised spectacle. "It was understood right from the outset that the honour of our people and our country was at stake," Thatcher farcically declared; victory in the Falklands "boosted Britain in the international world colossally" (quoted in Barnett 86). In other words, from the prime minister's standpoint, the Falklands War was a "colossal" (even sublime) affair that restored British national credit both at home and abroad—though only weak-kneed Liberals and Labourites sank so low as to believe that Britain's credit had ever declined. According to Thatcher, the war in the South Atlantic put to rest those "secret fears . . . that Britain was no longer the nation that had built an Empire and ruled a quarter of the world. . . . The lesson of the Falklands is that Britain has not changed" (quoted in Barnett 63). But the Falklands War should more probably be seen, Barnett suggests, as the last reactionary knee jerk of a world imperialist domination that by 1982 had already declined and fallen: Thatcherism in this view is the final twitchings of the corpse before rigor mortis sets in. Raymond Williams says much the same when he writes: "It is not because the British people are excessively nationalist and self-confident that you got the absurd jingoism of the Falklands episode. It is because the real national self-identification and self-confidence . . . have gone, that a certain artificial, frenetic, from-the-top, imagery of a nation can be injected" (*Resources* 164). But, *pace* Williams, a defensive chauvinism, racism, and xenophobia now radiate from other sectors of British society than just the government.

The British case is, of course, exceptional in several respects. The greatest of Western imperialist powers in the nineteenth century, Britain's divestment of its empire, its experience of decolonization, has been all the more dramatic in the twentieth century. The first modern nation-state to industrialize, Britain may perhaps become the first postmodern nation-state to "de-industrialise," or as Andrew Gamble puts it, "to return across the watershed of industrialisation" (37). The worst-case scenario of the theorists of de-industrialization (or Britain as the vanguard *postindustrial* society, perhaps) goes beyond even the thought that Britain will soon join the global economic and environmental slum of the so-called Third World it has played such a major role in creating. In his 1972 poem "Going, Going," Philip Larkin foresees the conversion of Britain into the "first slum of Europe" (190). This is the vision of the Ukanian present and future expressed also in many British films from the 1970s to the present (see Friedman, *Fires Were Started: British Cinema and Thatcherism*), including Derek Jarman's *Jubilee* (1978) with its punk rock motif as well as his *Last of England* (1987). "They say the ice age is coming," declares the narrative voice-over in the latter film; "the ice in your glass is radioactive, Johnny. . . . The household gods have departed. . . . On every green hill, the mourners stand and weep for the last of England." The narrator goes on to speak of how World War II demolished "one-hundred one years of middle-class assurance. The bombs dropped with regular monotony . . . all aspiration withered in the blood." Jarman's Britain has dissolved into ruins, fires, drugs, terrorism, and incoherence. And as if World War II were not enough of a cause for the chaos, later in the film a Margaret Thatcher-like mourner asks a masked terrorist, his assault rifle at the ready, "Did you enjoy the Falklands?" Terrorist: "Yes, mum." "Preparing for the next one?" "Yes, mum." "It's going to be a big one, isn't it?" "I hope so, mum." "Keep up the good work."

According to the extreme view, the decline and fall of the new Rome will bring on a thoroughgoing reversion to "barbarism" (cf. Gamble 37) perhaps not far removed from the depredations and violence of Jarman's punks and terrorists, or from Anthony Burgess's dystopian vision of the Ukanian future in *A Clockwork Orange* (1963), or from Ian MacEwan's similarly dismal guide through the near-future ruins in his "condition of England" novel *The Child in Time* (1987). Well before Thatcherism and the Falklands War, in Burgess's *The Wanting Seed* (1962), in Edward Bond's play *Early Morning* (1968), and in J. G. Ballard's apocalyptic novel *High-Rise* (1975), the supposedly civilized British degenerate, in Kurtz-like fashion, until they reach the ultimate nadir (beyond fetishism?) of cannibalism.

Besides industrialism, nationalism arose first in England, which with the possible exception of the Netherlands emerged as a modernizing nation-state nearly two centuries before France or any other comparable nation-states (Greenfeld 14). Ironically, "the break-up of Britain," according to Nairn, is now threatened, at least, by the resurgence of Scottish and Welsh neonationalisms starting in the 1970s (Irish nationalism has, of course, been a continuous thorn in Ukanian ribs). Paralleling the external decolonization marked most dramatically by Indian and Pakistani independence in 1947, there are increasing strains and cracks in Britain's internal multinational structure. Quite apart from Irish, Scottish, and Welsh nationalisms, from a neoconservative or National Front perspective, the rebarbarization of Britain has come about through the postwar influx of "blacks" from India, Pakistan, and the Caribbean. "The idea of the city as a jungle where bestial, predatory values prevailed preceded the large-scale settlement of Britain by blacks in the post-war period," writes Paul Gilroy; but that idea "has contributed significantly to contemporary definitions of 'race', particularly those which highlight the supposed primitivism and violence of black residents in inner-city areas. This is the context in which 'race' and racism come to connote the urban crisis as a whole" (Gilroy 228–229).

The internal colonialism that led to the eighteenth-century consolidation of England with its nearest neighbors into "Great Britain" was matched by its conquest and consolidation of what, from the end of the Napoleonic Wars in 1815 down to World War I, became by far the largest of modern empires; Britain was unrivaled as an imperialist power between 1815 and the 1880s, a period during which it was also preeminent as the first industrialized and economic power in the world. In the Victorian period, therefore, at the apogee of British imperial and industrial success, perhaps British celebrations of national glory as reflected in "the enchanted mirror" of the monarchy—Queen Victoria's diamond jubilee in 1887, for example—were in some sense more authentic or at least less obviously phantasmagoric than similar celebrations today. Insofar as Nairn bases his semisatirical analysis of postmodern celebrations of the monarchy on the discrepancy between the national unity expressed and the many visible symptoms of decay and disunity (including nonwhite immigrants in what racist-nationalists have considered the stronghold of Anglo-Saxon racial purity), then such celebrations are perhaps more obviously fetishistic now than a century ago. But Nairn also suggests (as did Virginia Woolf in *Three Guineas*) that any adoration of the symbols of national identity in any time and place is fetishistic, based on illusion rather than reality. From this latter perspective, the British case does not appear "exceptional"; it represents instead the quite standard model of nationalism and national identity as these make their trajectories through modern and now postmodern history.

In analyzing some of the many connections among debt, fetishism, and empire in British cultural history from the late seventeenth century down to the present, I have tried to keep arguments about British exceptionalism in balance with an alternative view (Marx's, for one) that modern Great Britain's historical path is the one all capitalistic, imperializing, industrializing nation-states must travel. In several obvious respects, the British experience is unique; but it may nevertheless be paradigmatic, the vanguard nation-state Marx took it to be. In its spectacular rise as well as in its dramatic decline, in other words, Britain may be both exceptional and paradigmatic. Also, though worship of the British monarchy may today seem excessive—like the Falklands War, both farcical and counterfeit in relation to Britain's declining prosperity and position in the world—the British experience is clearly not exceptional in relation to the fetishism that characterizes all nationalisms and, indeed, all versions of national identity formation.

Here the festishistic looniness that Nairn unmasks can, perhaps, be usefully compared with Žižek's analysis of "national identification" in *For They Know Not What They Do*, especially because one of Žižek's primary examples is "Englishness" during the Thatcher era. In Zizek's account, "Englishness" is only an obvious instance of the fetishism at work in national identity formation, which occurs through the internalization of external borders (and vice versa). The lines in the sand that demarcate different nations are reflected as internal limits, through which individuals define themselves as "English" (for instance) by marking the otherness of the Irish, the Scots, the Chinese, and so forth. But simultaneously there arises another stage or level of the process, involving the question of "who among the English are 'the real English', the paradigm of Englishness; who are the Englishmen [sic] who correspond in full to the notion of English?" Žižek continues:

> Are they the remaining landed gentry? Factory workers? Bankers? Actually, in the political imagery of Thatcher's government, a revolution has taken place, with a shift in the centre of gravity of "the real Englishness": it is no longer the landed gentry who preserve the old traditions, but self-made men from the lower strata who have "made themselves" English. However, the final answer is of course that *nobody* is fully English, that every empirical Englishman [sic] contains something "non-English"— Englishness thus becomes an "internal limit", an unattainable point which prevents empirical Englishmen from achieving full identity-with-themselves. (*For* 110)

It is precisely into this gap or lack, this sense of never quite being "English" enough or even, perhaps, "English" at all, that the fetishistic symbols of "English" national identity flow. But the process is just the same in the case of "British"—or Irish, or Scottish, or Canadian, or Indian, or Turkish—national identity. Nationalisms are forms of secular belief, celebration, and ritual in which the objects of worship may be variously the flag, the crown, the royal family, the constitution, the Founding Fathers, the Liberty Tree, a battleground, the birthplace or grave of Abraham Lincoln or Shakespeare, and so forth. The money authorized and issued by the nation-state functions to bind the diverse fetish objects (often commodities) of national identity together in "imagined community." As Keynes understood, the creditworthiness of a nation's money is perhaps the primary evidence to the faithful (the citizens) that the ultimate object of their faith, the nation-state, is real, powerful, and legitimate: it pays; it is the ultimate "guarantor of value"

(Giddens 24). Also, the more any symbol of national identity including money is shorn of its original authority or exchange value, the more it is likely to be insisted upon by diehard nationalists like Enoch Powell or Thatcher as sacrosanct.

But the monetary systems of modern nation-states are founded and funded on zeroes, on national debts and the financial institutions that underwrite them. Nationalist fetishizing of the nation-state is the psychic-cultural process through which its imaginary or ideological, foundationless structure of public credit and national debt is mystified. Nationalist history making is an obvious expression of this process, as the Thatcherite glorification of the Falklands victory suggests ("We have ceased to be a nation in retreat," etc.; see Barnett 149–153). Žižek points out that nationalism creates history as a "myth of Origins": "national identity constitutes itself through resistance to its oppression— the fight for national revival is therefore *a defence of something which comes to be only through being experienced as lost or endangered.* The nationalist ideology endeavours to elude this vicious circle by constructing a myth of Origins—of an epoch preceding oppression and exploitation when the Nation was *already there* (the Khmer kingdom in Cambodia, India before English colonialism, Ireland before the Protestant invasion, and so on)—the past is trans-coded as Nation that already existed and to which we are supposed to return through a liberation struggle" (*For* 213–224).

But the "liberation struggle" for the nostalgic politics of Thatcherism has not been just against the "oppression" of the Argentine dictatorship in the faraway Falkland Islands, with their tiny population of only about eighteen hundred. The major enemies have been internal: socialism, the trades unions, the IRA, the burgeoning ethnic minorities from the far reaches of the former empire, but also, above all, both "the fiscal crisis of the state" and the apparent lack of confidence or credit in British imperial and industrial power and glory, past, present, and future. In regard to the British state's financial dilemma, "state expenditure as a percentage of national income" has swollen dramatically since the turn of the century, until by 1975 it amounted to 57.9 percent, whereas total state revenue in that year amounted to only 46.6 percent, leaving a "borrowing requirement" of 11.3 percent (Leys 314–315). According to Colin Leys, like Reaganism in the United States, Thatcherism has been partly an "anti-tax, anti-state reaction" to this fiscal bind: cut state spending, especially in the welfare sector, and rely on "free" market forces (317). Thatcherism has also been a reaction against the apparent failure of nerve in contemporary British culture and society, a failure Thatcher and her adherents interpret as both cause and main symptom of "the British disease."

2

THE NATIONALIST construction of political and historical fictions of state parallels and partially masks the economic process through which national indebtedness is transubstantiated into the wealth of nations. Both processes are fetishistic because both misrecognize the imaginary, symbolic structures (history and money) they create out of nothing as always already something—as, indeed, the most substantial realities in most peoples' lives. But nationalist history making in the British context is now acutely problematic (except perhaps in Thatcherite rhetoric and in the tabloids). While Britain's overseas investments continue to generate wealth for the banking and financial elites connected to "the City," its industrial base, which together with empire was the main source of power and glory between 1815 and 1914, has weakened, albeit not fallen into complete shambles. As Andrew Gamble writes in his diagnosis of "the British disease":

> Britain has now been in decline for a hundred years. It has become the most observed and analysed decline in modern history, provoking a speculative literature of enormous dimensions. Few explanations have not been proferred, few causes not dissected, few remedies not canvassed at least twice. The decline has been the central fact about British politics for a century, a major preoccupation of its political intellectuals and intermittently, but increasingly, of its political leaders.

Gamble adds that there are two main, interconnected aspects to Britain's falling fortunes: "the absolute decline in the power and status of the British imperial state, and the relative decline of the British economy with its long-standing failure to match the rates of expansion of its rivals" (xiv).

It is not just that there is now a huge "speculative literature" diagnosing "the British disease," to which Gamble's own *Britain in Decline* is an important addition. British culture since World War II, or even since World War I, is pervaded by the theme of decline-and-fall. In literature, that theme was already a characteristic one in many of the novels now associated with high modernism (*Heart of Darkness, Dubliners, The Wasteland,* even *Mrs. Dalloway* and *Passage to India*). Premonitions of the demise of the empire go back at least as far as the vogue for "invasion scare" novels starting with Sir George Chesney's *The Battle of Dorking* in

1872 (for other examples, see my *Rule* 233–236). Closely related is the line of British spy fiction from Kipling's *Kim*, Conrad's *Secret Agent*, Erskine Childers's *Riddle of the Sands* (1903), and John Buchan's *Greenmantle* (1916) through Ian Fleming's James Bond stories and John Le Carré's *Perfect Spy* (1986) and *Russia House* (1989); such fiction expresses the embattled paranoia of imperial Britain in decline (Richards, *Imperial Archive* 114–145). Although a case for imperialism continued to be made through the "Manichaean aesthetic" of many novels from *Kim* through Joyce Cary's *Mr. Johnson* (1939) down to Anthony Burgess's *Devil of a State* (1961) and beyond, imperialism was also increasingly treated as both a dirty and a losing business, as in George Orwell's *Burmese Days* (1934) and Paul Scott's *Raj Quartet* (1966–1975). Meanwhile Irish independence in 1922 and the international success of such Irish writers as Yeats, Shaw, Synge, O'Casey, Joyce, and Beckett, coupled with the more general internationalism of British literary modernism (including the American factor, especially Pound and Eliot), made the moorings of the specifically *English* literary culture that I. A. Richards, F. R. Leavis, L. C. Knights, and others tried to shore up and defend look increasingly frayed (Sinfield 182–201).

The term *postcolonial* is associated with the post-1945 breakup of the British and other European empires, but the international dimension of modernist literature before World War II can be understood as the first stage of a general "decolonizing of imagination" that has taken place more rapidly since 1945 (see Pieterse and Parekh). At the same time, "postcolonial" does not exactly signify the independence or, in Kant's model of coming-to-Enlightenment, the "maturity" of new nations that have now gained their political (though not necessarily economic) autonomy from the metropolitan powers. So-called Third World nations may be "postcolonial," but they are now enmeshed in the global debt crisis caused by western war making, exploitation, and imperialism in the first place. In the mid-1970s, notes Gamble, the sudden inflation of the global oil price "created major imbalances in the world system, the most serious being the enormous debts incurred by so many Third World countries, often far exceeding their ability to repay through export earnings. The mountain of debt overhanging so many parts of the world economy threatens a major financial collapse . . . with all the dislocation that would bring" (185). But from the beginning of ostensible political independence, the indebtedness of newly decolonized nation-states has made them economically dependent on the metropolitan powers. As Sujit Bose, using Paul Scott's phrase, puts it, "What the British handed over to the Indians in 1947 was a 'ghastly mess'" (Bose 109). This is one way in which postcolonialism turns out to be, at least in economic terms, *neocolonialism*, a term first used by Kwame Nkrumah in 1965 to describe the plight of newly (politically) independent Ghana and other African nation-states.

At the same time, there are several ways in which the academic or theoretical emergence of the idea of "postcolonial" cultures also suggests a rather different international—and academic—situation that might more realistically be called "neocolonial" or "neoimperialist." In specifically literary terms, the new, postcolonial literatures written in English are, of course, written in the language of the first modern imperialist and industrialized nation-state, though they are also in many ways changing, reinventing, perhaps subverting English, as Colin MacCabe for one has argued: "If the members of the United Kingdom are all nominally British, it is instructive to recall that English as a language has been imposed, often by force, throughout the British Isles. And the peoples of those islands find that along with the imposed language they have acquired a literature to which their relationship is profoundly ambiguous—one need only think of Joyce or [Hugh] McDiarmid to realise exactly how ambiguous" (MacCabe 11). In his 1988 essay "Broken English," MacCabe offers an outline history of "a literature of decolonisation—from Joyce and Yeats to Rushdie and Lessing."[1] This would be a history of "a literature in broken English," though for MacCabe *breaking* is a positive rather than a negative term, akin to creativity: "The cultural monolith that was institutionalized in the study of English literature is now broken open as a contradictory set of cultural and historical moments—a past understood not as a tradition to be transmitted but a set of contradictions to be used" (12).

MacCabe presents *Finnegan's Wake* as a revolutionary work in "broken English," and Joyce himself as "the prototype of the postcolonial artist" (12; and cf. Said on Yeats, *Culture and Imperialism* 220–238). MacCabe's argument can be usefully supplemented by the theory of "minor literature" offered by Gilles Deleuze and Félix Guattari in *Kafka*; they point also to Joyce, Beckett, and other Irish writers as examples of the production of writing that "a minority constructs within a major language" (16), subverting and at the same time energizing that language from within. Their concept of "minor literature" corresponds, moreover, to their theory of "deterritorialization," especially under postmodern or late-capitalist conditions, whereby "nomadic" frictions

---

1. This is a history that Edward Said has now at least partly written in *Culture and Imperialism*.

and "flows" of transgressive populations—"desiring machines"—within and over artificial national boundaries wither away "state apparatuses." In regard to language, Deleuze and Guattari write:

> How many people today live in a language that is not their own? Or no longer, or not yet, even know their own and know poorly the major language that they are forced to serve? This is the problem of immigrants, and especially of their children, the problem of minorities, the problem of a minor literature, but also a problem for all of us: how to tear a minor literature away from its own language, allowing it to challenge the language and making it follow a sober revolutionary path? How to become a nomad and an immigrant and a gypsy in relation to one's own language? Kafka answers: steal the baby from its crib, walk the tightrope. (*Kafka* 19)

"English" literature has always been an ambiguous category. It is not just, as Michel Foucault and others have insisted, that *literature* is a modern concept, invented in the eighteenth century or perhaps even more recently, in the Romantic era (see Eagleton, *Literary Theory* 17–22). Nor is it just that the English language has been imposed on the Irish, the Scots, the Welsh, and—through the external empire—on many other populations and parts of the world. Does the phrase "English literature" refer to all literature written in the English language, or does it refer only to "canonical" literature written by "Englishmen" (and a few Englishwomen such as Jane Austen), the literature specifically of the nation called "England," with the possible addition of some of its major imperial satellites? To put the question in this way is already to suggest the illogical, anachronistic quality of the *national* concept of both the English language and English literature.

Although "postmodern" and "postcolonial" are not synonymous, they are closely related both as period designations (for western and global history since World War II) and as indicators of the dismantling of the empires the European "great powers" acquired from the Renaissance forward. The end of the formal European empires is an aspect of the weakening and in some cases collapse of at least some modern nation-states. "Postmodernism can best be defined," asserts Robert Young, "as European culture's awareness that it is no longer the unquestioned and dominant centre of the world" (19; and see Lyotard, "Universal History" 322).

In the British context, perhaps the terms *postmodern* and *postcolonial* most obviously coincide in the emergence of ethnic and immigrant "subcultures" and literatures within Ukania's borders. The postwar increase of West and East Indian immigration has produced new forms of domestic conflict, giving rise to a renewed racist-nationalist rhetoric and politics and to the Thatcherite emphases on law and order and also on the virtues of Englishness. "The empire strikes back" in many ways, however, not least in the emergence of forms of cultural expression that hardly seem "English" in any traditional sense, certainly not in any ethnic or racial sense (Centre, *Empire*). Dick Hebdige, Simon Frith, and others have pointed out the West Indian (Rastafarian and reggae) influence on postwar youth subcultures and rock music. Meanwhile, postwar writing in Britain, after the apparently antimodernist "Movement" and "Angry Young Men" decade of the 1950s, has grown increasingly *un*-English through the publications of such figures as Kazuo Ishiguro, Doris Lessing, Timothy Mo, V. S. Naipaul, Caryl Phillips, and Salman Rushdie.

In the works of these and many other postcolonial writers, the construction and deconstruction of both empires and nation-states is a major theme. Ishiguro's *An Artist of the Floating World* (1986) concerns the rise and fall of the modern Japanese empire. Mo's *An Insular Possession* (1986) deals with the creation of Hong Kong. Naipaul's *Guerillas* (1975) describes a liberation struggle in the Caribbean. Phillips's *Cambridge* (1991) analyzes the struggle against slavery, the slave trade, and racism of its black title character. And Rushdie's 1980 *Midnight's Children* depicts the births and parallel lives or histories of its narrator, Saleem Sinai, and of the new nation-state of India: "I was born in the city of Bombay . . . on August 15th, 1947 . . . at the precise instant of India's arrival at independence" (3). In particular, Rushdie takes on the theme of nationalisms and national identities as forms of collective hallucination or "mass fantasy." According to Saleem, India in 1947 was just "a new myth to celebrate," like the old religious ones:

> a nation which had never previously existed was about to win its freedom, catapulting us into a world which, although it had invented the game of chess and traded with Middle Kingdom Egypt, was nevertheless quite imaginary; into a mythical land, a country which would never exist except by the efforts of a phenomenal collective will—except in a dream we all agreed to dream; it was a mass fantasy shared in varying degrees by Bengali and Punjabi, Madrasi and Jat, and would periodically need the sanctification and renewal which can only be provided by rituals of blood. (129–130)

Saleem adds that "the new myth" of India is "a collective fiction in which anything was possible, a fable rivalled only by the two other mighty fantasies: money and God" (130).

Both in his novels and in several of the essays in *Imaginary Homelands*, Rushdie stresses the fictionality of national identity, a theme characteristic of postcolonial literatures and cultural theory. He and other postcolonial writers have no "enchanted glass" of monarchy or of unproblematic national identity to gaze into and see their own images reflected back; they have instead, as Rushdie puts it, only "broken mirrors, some of whose fragments have been irretrievably lost" (*Imaginary Homelands* 11). This is one reason why Saleem's memory in *Midnight's Children* is erratic. And in regard to his own experience, Rushdie writes:

> It may be that writers in my position, exiles or emigrants or expatriates, are haunted by some sense of loss, some urge to reclaim, to look back, even at the risk of being mutated into pillars of salt. But if we do look back, we must also do so in the knowledge—which gives rise to profound uncertainties—that our physical alienation from India almost inevitably means that we will not be capable of reclaiming precisely the thing that was lost; that we will, in short, create fictions, not actual cities or villages, but invisible ones, imaginary homelands, Indias of the mind. (*Imaginary Homelands* 10)

Rushdie approximates Partha Chatterjee's analysis of nationalism as "a derivative discourse" in colonial and postcolonial contexts. Nationalism, from Chatterjee's perspective, is a western, modernizing ideology related to "the bourgeois-rationalist conception of knowledge, established in the post-Enlightenment period of European intellectual history, as the moral and epistemic foundation for a supposedly universal framework of thought which perpetuates, in a real and not merely a metaphorical sense, a colonial domination." An imposed ideology at least in nonwestern contexts, nationalism is also inherently contradictory: "Nationalist thought, in agreeing to become 'modern,' accepts the claim to universality of this 'modern' framework of knowledge. Yet it also asserts the autonomous identity of a national culture. It thus simultaneously rejects and accepts the dominance, both epistemic and moral, of an alien culture" (Chatterjee 11).

The Enlightenment dream of universal emancipation, as Lyotard also notes, has thus far amounted to the "modern . . . project of conquest" ("Universal History" 316). When the dream has arisen in the non-European world as in India, it has bred new forms of "conquest" or of domination from within the supposedly independent framework of the new nation-states. This was one of the dangers that Frantz Fanon warned against in his analysis of "the pitfalls of national consciousness" and "national culture" in *The Wretched of the Earth* (148, 206–209). With the continuation of class conflict and the importation of the capitalist mode of production ("modernization"), Fanon believed, nationalism could provide little more than the illusion of unity, covering over an abyss like the fetish of silver or of the San Tomé mine in *Nostromo*: "National consciousness, instead of being the all-embracing crystallization of the innermost hopes of the whole people, instead of being the immediate and most obvious result of the mobilization of the people, will be . . . only an empty shell, a crude and fragile travesty of what it might have been" (148). Fanon might here be summarizing Naipaul's pessimistic accounts of liberation struggles and nationalism in Third World contexts—a Caribbean island in *Guerillas*, a new African nation-state in *A Bend in the River* (1979), the India of *A Wounded Civilization* (1976). (That Naipaul sees himself as echoing Conrad's themes of the related "lies" of imperialism and nationalism in *Heart of Darkness* and *Nostromo* is also evident in his essay "Conrad's Darkness," collected in *The Return of Eva Peron*.) According to Fanon, the newly independent or postcolonial nation-states of Africa and the rest of the world will be ruled by their small bourgeoisies, a "national middle class" that emulates western models of culture, politics, and commerce, pretending these are universal and emancipatory while they continue the exploitation of "the masses" under the fiction of nationalist liberation (149–152).

Echoing Nietzsche, Foucault declared that if "the concept of liberty" is only "an 'invention of the ruling classes'" (*Language* 142), then it would seem that the emancipatory gospel of the Enlightenment can only lead to the production of new nation-states with their internal and sometimes external forms of colonization. From the postmodern cul-de-sac of late capitalism with its increasing global hegemony of multinational corporations, perhaps history amounts only to "the endlessly repeated play of dominations": "Humanity does not gradually progress from combat to combat, until it arrives at universal reciprocity, where the rule of law finally replaces warfare; humanity installs each of its violences in a system of rules and thus proceeds from domination to domination" (150–151). If this is the dismal case, then perhaps it would also be just as well for history to do what one of Tom Crick's high school students, in Graham Swift's *Waterland*, says it is likely to do: "'The only important thing about history, I think, sir, is that it's got to the point where it's probably about to end'" (6).

3

OR so it would seem, unless there is some small emancipatory potential in the very recognition, pessimistic though it may be, that Foucault expresses. For Foucault, there was always a glimmer of hope implicit in his conception of resistance. Though Chatterjee could hardly be described as optimistic, let alone utopian, he more hopefully writes, "The critique of nationalist discourse must find for itself the ideological means to connect the popular strength of those struggles with the consciousness of a new universality, to subvert the ideological sway of a state which falsely claims to speak on behalf of the nation and to challenge the presumed sovereignty of a science which puts itself at the service of capital" (170).

There is much speculation among radical intellectuals of various persuasions and in many national contexts about forms of local activism and resistance that are developing or could develop global networks, trespassing across or transgressing national boundaries. These tendencies include postcolonial constructions of emergent transnational or postnational identities, both "hybrid" and "nomadic," individuals and groups, whose loyalties will no longer be solely or mainly determined by or perhaps even connected to nation-states and nationalities (among others, see Brecher, Childs, and Cutler; Miyoshi; Michael Smith; Bhabha, *Location*, esp. chaps. 8, 9, and 11). According to Eric Hobsbawm:

> It is not impossible that nationalism will decline with the decline of the nation-state, without which being English or Irish or Jewish, or a combination of all these, is only one way in which people describe their identity among the many others which they use for this purpose, as occasion demands. It would be absurd to claim that this day is already near. However, I hope it can at least be envisaged. After all, the very fact that historians are at least beginning to make some progress in the study and analysis of nations and nationalism suggests that, as so often, the phenomenon is past its peak. The owl of Minerva which brings wisdom, said Hegel, flies out at dusk. It is a good sign that it is now circling round nations and nationalism. (*Nations* 182–183)

Just how much hope should be invested in the postmodern weakening of nation-states and the emergence of trans- or postnational identities remains to be seen, however. Even as it weakens in the postmodern context of transnational capitalism, the nation-state remains the most powerful agency in contemporary global politics and perhaps also in current identity formation (especially if, following Althusser, the family is understood as an "ideological state apparatus").

Against the hopeful prospect of the "defaillancy" of nation-states must be weighed the terrifying possibility that, if there is nothing better to put in their place, into their lacks or Great Zeroes will flow more and more stateless, unpoliced, ultraviolent ethnic and national, racial and religious conflicts, as in former Yugoslavia. None of the terms in the title of this chapter—postindustrial, postcolonial, postmodern—can be construed optimistically without something positive, perhaps necessarily utopian, to insert into the minuses signified by the prefix *post.* As Chatterjee indicates, the vacuum of postcoloniality has already been filled by new nation-states. Poverty, slums, unemployment, "de-industrialisation" in Manchester, Sheffield, and Glasgow (not to mention Detroit, Boston, and Seattle) now occupy the "post" in "postindustrial." And the "hyperreal" emptiness of postmodernity continues to be flooded with nationalistic images—"simulations"—all more or less incredible because they are also, as Baudrillard says, commodified "fetish-objects."

In the Indian context, perhaps there always was, even in the nationalist movement, through Gandhism, a critical awareness of the dangers of importing or imposing western "modernization," including in that term both the economic and the political. But India's postcolonial situation, as Chatterjee suggests, has been dominated by the construction of a modern and modernizing nation-state headquartered in New Delhi. The centralization of the subcontinent, with its many diverse regions, religions, ethnic groups, and languages, into three nation-states (India, Bangladesh, and Pakistan) with legal codes and governmental institutions based on the British model, was the outcome of imperialism. So was the advent of industrialization. Perhaps both modernizing processes seemed from the outset more artificial, more "imaginary," than those same processes appeared to be in the context of modern European history. It may not be accidental, therefore, that the conception expressed by the first term in the title of this chapter—"postindustrial"—arose first in India.

According to Arthur J. Penty (a disciple of William Morris's, a "guild socialist," and an advocate of the arts and crafts movement), the person who coined "post-industrial" was the Sinhalese intellectual and art historian Ananda Coomaraswamy. In his 1922 book *Post-Industrialism,* Penty writes:

> From one point of view, Post Industrialism connotes Medievalism, from another it could be defined as "inverted Marxism." But in any case it means the state of society that will follow the break-up of Industrialism, and might therefore be used to cover the speculations of all who recognize Industrialism is doomed. The need of some such term sufficiently inclusive to cover the ideas of those who, while sympathizing with the . . . Socialists, yet differed with them in their attitude towards Industrialism has long been felt. (14)

Penty then adds that he owes the term "Post-Industrialism . . . to Dr. A. K. Coomaraswamy" (14). What Penty and Coomaraswamy both mean by "postindustrialism" and also by "inverted Marxism" echoes Morris in ways that should qualify the standard, rather dismissive reading of Morris's *News from Nowhere* as just another instance of Romantic/ Victorian nostalgia for the Middle Ages. The Anglo-Indian hybridity of the idea of postindustrialism also suggests the possibility that the anti-machinery attitudes shared by John Ruskin and Gandhi, Morris and Coomaraswamy affected not only what Martin Wiener has called the "decline of the industrial spirit" in Britain but also the decline of British imperialism in India and elsewhere. In *Hind Swaraj*, Gandhi declared, "It is machinery that has impoverished India" (93).

For Penty and Coomaraswamy, "postindustrialism" is not a pessimistic term expressing the collapse of the British (or any other) economic mode of production but instead a utopian one suggesting an alternative emancipatory ethics (rather than a politics leading to a new round of domination as in Virginia Woolf's "Here we go round the mulberry bush"). From this perspective, "inverted Marxism" would be one that no longer valorizes machine production nor insists that every society must be force marched through the needle's eye—the universalizing history or metanarrative—of capitalist "development" or "modernization." Sounding like Gandhi and Rabinandrath Tagore as much as like Marx, Coomaraswamy writes, "The manufacturer for profits must . . . create an ever-expanding world market for his surplus produced by those whom Dr. [Albert] Schweitzer calls 'over-occupied men'. It is . . . the incubus of world trade that makes of industrial 'civilisations' a 'curse to humanity', and from the industrial concept of progress . . . that modern wars have arisen and will arise; it is on the same impoverished soil that empires have grown" (7). Coomaraswamy concludes, as do Morris, Penty, Tagore, and Gandhi, that the chief product of industrialism has been the destruction rather than the progress of civilization, that is, the destruction of the very possibility of a social formation in which both justice and beauty prevail.

In the British context, however, most discourse about postindustrialism, or "de-industrialisation," has been anything but utopian or even hopeful (see Blackaby). Since the sharp rise in the price of oil and the economic crisis of the mid-1970s, and despite the discovery of North Sea oil, both mining and manufacturing have gone into a prolonged nose dive that the Keynesian economic policies enacted by postwar Labour governments were unable to halt. On the contrary, from a neo-conservative perspective those policies were the cause rather than the cure of "the British disease." Yet neither have the Tories been able to reverse the course of Britain's falling economic fortunes. From her 1979 election forward, Margaret Thatcher governed during the most severe economic decline since the Great Depression. Dozens of businesses went bankrupt. The unemployment rate soared, leaving more than three million jobless; manufacturing productivity plummeted 19 percent and new investment in industry dropped 36 percent (Gamble 194). At first, Thatcher was able to blame these dismal results on the past excesses of Labour governments with their Keynesian policies. Economic monetarism, coupled with the dismantling of the state-supported welfare system and the privatization of those industries that had been nationalized in the 1940s (the Bank of England was an exception; it has remained nationalized since 1946), became the panacea. Corresponding to Reaganomics in the United States, Thatcherite monetarist policy aimed to give free reign to the capitalist marketplace. According to the monetarists, unemployment was inevitable; the goal of full employment announced in the Beveridge Report of 1942 was only a Labourite-Liberal pipedream.

In *Beyond the Casino Economy*, Costello, Michie, and Milne observe that after a decade of Tory monetarism "aimed at rolling back the frontiers of the state, tax cutting and nursing the [private] enterprise culture," public spending was increasing in real terms and had "only declined fractionally as a percentage of national income" (92). Meanwhile industry did not rebound and unemployment remained high. "The government's response [was] to continue with its attempts to offload essential public services on to the private sector. . . . Tory policies during the 1980s helped to increase earnings for most of those in employment. But they did not solve any of the fundamental problems of the economy" (92). By the 1990s, it became possible to blame Britain's continuing economic woes on monetarism and Thatcherism instead of on Keynesianism and the welfare policies of pre-1979 governments. But a major part of the difficulty is that, among all its other symptoms of postcolonial and postindustrial decline, Britain is no longer so splendidly insular and independent as it was before 1914. Its economic destiny is inexorably tied to that of the European Union; and in the "late" or transnational capitalist "world system," even the control of national currencies is no longer national. In *The Rise and Fall of Monetarism*, David Smith points to the phenomenon of "stateless money" (158–160)—or the internationalization of the world's financial markets—that has eroded the power of any national government to control what happens in the economic sector, including its own production and regulation of the money supply. The world is hardly confronting the "death of money," as Joel Kurtzman announced in his 1993 Jeremiad; but he like Smith is correct in seeing in the computerization and internationalization of currencies and money flows both causes and symptoms of the postmodern weakening of nation-states. One of Kurtzman's section headlines reads "Nation States Lose Economic Clout" (18).

The hegemony of monetarism may be fading in Britain, as David Smith contends; but money is certainly not giving up the ghost, there or internationally. On the contrary, as Britain's industrial base has continued to erode and as successive governments have failed to cure "the British disease," money, partly through the continuing power and apparent success of the City of London's financial institutions, seems to have taken on a life of its own. "With the advent of postmodernism, the notion of the sublime has staged a spectacular comeback," writes Terry Eagleton. "For the sublime is concerned with that which defeats representation; and if for the eighteenth century this was a matter of star-studded skies and tumultuous oceans, the name of this infinity for us today is money" ("Vulgar," 7). Part of what now seems sublime about money, however, is not so much its infinite quantity as its potentially infinite absence—or at least the sense that money seems decreasingly tied to any material economic productivity.

4

NEVERTHELESS, IN the midst of the mounting ruins, and even as its exchange rate declines against the dollar, the deutsche mark, and the yen, the once almighty pound continues to lead a sort of spectral/spectacular existence. This is one of the messages of much British literature of the 1980s and 1990s, which in a variety of ways announces that a decrepit Ukania, a mere ghost of its former glory, is now postindustrial, postcolonial, and postmodern—but is also thoroughly monetarized. As Edward Bond writes in "After the Raid," the prefatory poem to his *War Plays*:

> The merchants built high towers but where the money came from
> even the bankers didn't know
> It was as if the heavy ledgers squeezed it from the rows of figures

In Malcolm Bradbury's novel *Rates of Exchange*, Professor Angus Petworth leaves his provincial university for London, on his way to a fictional eastern European nation and its capital city, Slaka, where there

are no less than five different "rates of exchange." This monetary craziness is not much worse, however, than what is going on in Britain,
where it is the summer of 1981 with London preparing for a royal
wedding (recall Nairn's "enchanted glass" of monarchy), a time of celebration perhaps but also of "pouring rain" and of "recession and unemployment, decay and deindustrialization":

> The age of Sado-Monetarism has begun; in the corridors of power, they
> are naming the money supply after motorways, M1 and M2 and M3, to
> try to map its mysteries better. The bombs explode in Ulster, the factories
> close, but it has been a ceremonial summer; the patriotic bunting has
> flown, the Royal couple whose images are everywhere have walked the
> aisle. The nuptials, it seems, have been celebrated much by foreigners,
> come for the season to enjoy the splendour and stability of British tradi-
> tions, and the collapse of the coin. Shards and fragments, chaos and
> Babel; so summer London has seemed to Petworth. (20)

While in London, Petworth observes that most of the shoppers are
Arabs; most of the crowd that gathers to watch the changing of the
guard are Japanese; the clerk at Petworth's hotel "speaks only Portuguese, and that not well"; the electric tea kettle in his room carries
directions in six languages, none of them English; and "in the street,
black whores in sunglasses and short tunics laugh in doorways." As if to
add insult to injury, Petworth dines "on an American-style hamburger"
(21). Thus Bradbury depicts a postcolonial London whose multi-
cultural chaos contains very little that is characteristically "English" except for the changing of the guard and perhaps Petworth himself.

   In Slaka, Petworth never learns "the rate of exchange," though he
discovers that there are five different ones (148); but he does learn a
great deal about "the British disease." From the Slakan perspective,
Britain does not seem especially important or powerful. His lover Katya
Princip tells him that he himself is "'really not a character in the world
historical sense. You come from a little island with water all around,'" a
place that does not amount to much; from her socialist point of view,
Britain's main claim to fame is that Karl Marx is buried in Highgate
Cemetery (139). Shortly after this, the slippery character Plitplov, who
shadows Petworth everywhere, offers his diagnosis of "the British disease": "'I think nobody in Britain wants to work now any more.'" In
response, the none too steady Steadiman, second secretary at the British Embassy, admits that Britain's "'industrial reputation isn't too high
here just now,'" and Plitplov continues, "'But doesn't your economy
collapse? Won't you one day be socialist economy like us?'" "'I don't

think so,'" says another Brit named Blenheim; "'not our cup of tea, really'" (167).

Later, when Petworth travels to the city of Glit to give a lecture on English linguistics, one Professor Vlic returns to this theme: "'I always please [sic] to see a visitor from Britain. And your British disease, you still have it? Or does it go away and everyone likes again to work? Your Iron Lady, how does she? Does she perform, does she make her miracle?'" (264). Instead of Britain's capitalist economy collapsing and its becoming a socialist regime, six years after *Rates of Exchange* appeared came the collapse of socialist regimes in eastern Europe and the Soviet Union. The triumphant rhetoric—the demise of the "evil empire," the supposed opening up of the entire world to the workings of "democracy" and "free markets"—with which these cataclysms were greeted by Prime Minister Thatcher, President George Bush, and other neoconservatives in the West has sounded particularly hollow, less than triumphant, in the British context. While some socialist nation-states like the fictional one in Bradbury's novel seem to have vanished overnight, revealing the fragility with which their "imagined communities" were held together to begin with, Britain, the original powerhouse of capitalist industrialism, has continued its century-long decline. No, the "Iron Lady" did not "make her miracle," and "Iron Britannia" today seems frailer than ever, but it still exists.

British culture since *Rates of Exchange* has often also seemed to be monetarized in the sense that it, too, reflects or depicts the hollowness of Thatcherism and "the age of Sado-Monetarism." In a variety of texts, money seems to float free from its moorings in industrial and commercial production, just as the financial side of British capitalism represented by the monetary institutions of the City and the national debt seems now almost to have parted company with the industrial, productive side. Money in these novels, plays, and films continues to have far-flung global ramifications, colonial and postcolonial, but is completely disjoined from the maintenance of a healthy society at home in Britain.

In Caryl Churchill's "City Comedy" *Serious Money*, for instance, the mad-hatter financiers, stockbrokers, and bankers who populate the play are all transnational in their focus—on Peruvian copper, Nigerian oil, the International Monetary Fund, and so forth—whereas the condition of British manufacturing concerns them only if it affects their profit margins. But this global focus is also strictly a focus on money; among these monetarist sharks, there is no more concern about ordinary living conditions in Peru or Nigeria than in Britain. Thus in regard to the "terrible situation in Nigeria" and the rest of Africa, Nigel Abjibala, who is himself African ("an importer from Ghana") says:

> The continent is such a frightful mess.
> One's based in London so one's operation
> Is on the right side of exploitation.
> One thing one learned from one's colonial masters,
> One makes money from other people's disasters. (69)

The Peruvian businesswoman Jacinta Condor says much the same when she considers whether she is willing to do Peru any good, economic or otherwise: "I do not want to help, I want to be rich" (63).

Like the forms of money in which they speculate, the characters in Churchill's play seem hyperactive but also hyperreal, sharing a zany fantasy of snowballing wealth and prosperity—for themselves, at least—which is ultimately based on nothing more substantial than commodity fetishism and greed. Life is reduced to money and also to a level of obscenity that again evokes prostitution, as in the "Futures Song" that the traders on the floor of the stockmarket burst out singing ("Out of furious trading emerges the song," says the stage direction):

> Money-making money-making money-making money-making
> Money-making money-making money-making caper
> Do the fucking business do the fucking business do the fucking
> business
> And bang it down on paper (62)

Among the traders on "the floor of LIFFE, the London International Financial Futures Exchange" (54) in Churchill's play, you're fucked if you don't but also fucked if you do make money, because money itself seems finally to be nothing solider than everyone's fantasy of screwing somebody else. Moreover, as Scilla Todd, one of the LIFFE "futures" traders, remarks, it is just as possible to profit from the absence of money as from its presence. In "futures" trading,

> of course you don't have to take delivery of anything at all.
> You can buy and sell futures contracts without any danger of end-
> ing up with ten tons of pork bellies in the hall.
> On the floor of LIFFE the commodity is money.
> You can buy and sell money, you can buy and sell absence of
> money, debt, which used to strike me as funny. (54)

This is commodity fetishism taken to such a hyperreal extreme that "futures"—or *the* future, even—are independent of all commodities except for the supercommodity, money. "Xenomoney, by making no promise to deliver anything," Rotman points out (95), is merely speculation on its own future increase; all other considerations such as productivity are secondary. And if money is lacking to invest in "futures," credit can still work its fetishistic alchemy magic: a successful futures trader is never lacking for something to invest, even if what she invests is debt—an investment of debt in future debt. The ultimate victims of this phantasmagoric realm of high finance, where the lack of money can function just as well as its possession, are the average citizens of Britain, Peru, Nigeria, and the rest of the world, who are simply trying to make ends meet, to get and to keep jobs, to feed their families, and to live decent, orderly, rational lives. If "futures" trading like that depicted in *Serious Money* is the only economic future Britain now has, Churchill suggests, then it will have no future other than the drastically curtailed and vacuous one that the characters call for in the Thatcherite reelection song that ends the play:

> . . . we're saved from the valley of tears for five more glorious years
> pissed and promiscuous, the money's ridiculous
> send her victorious for five fucking morious
> five more glorious years (112)

In a sense, this future—Thatcher's reelection, her nonexistent economic "miracle"—will be no different from the past, or perhaps only a farcical repetition of it. Thus Churchill's satire begins with the reproduction of a scene from Thomas Shadwell's 1693 play *The Volunteers, or The Stock-Jobbers*, with its foreshadowings of the crazy investment schemes and scams that led to the inflating and bursting of the South Sea Bubble in the 1720s.

Martin Amis's novel *Money: A Suicide Note* is another "Sado-Monetarist" text that hinges on the fetishistic production of money seemingly out of thin air. The plot involves the making and losing of large sums invested in a movie that itself turns out to be counterfeit, a scam. The protagonist-narrator John Self, who as a sleazeball, jack-of-no-trades, alcoholic pornographer and con artist is no better than the con artists who cheat him out of his money, declares at the start of the story: "Making lots of money—it's not that hard, you know. It's overestimated. Making lots of money is a breeze. You watch" (23). Self also declares, just as forthrightly as the money-mad characters in Churchill's *Serious Money*: "My dream in life—is to make lots of money. I would cheerfully go into the alchemy business, if it existed and made lots of money" (92). At first, fulfilling his life's dream appears easy, though by the end, bankrupt and as alcoholic as ever, he opines, "Money, money stinks. It really does" (364). In between these antipodes, Self shuttles between London and New York, trying to help finance a movie that will be called either "Bad Money" or "Good Money" (it is never decided; the movie is never produced). Besides the production of the fraudulent movie, which has the same function in Amis's narrative as does Augustus Melmotte's fake Mexican railway in Trollope's *The Way We Live Now* (a sort of black hole down which vast amounts of money disappear), much of the story concerns Self's struggles with alcohol, women, and—money, which seems to flow in and out of his possession as easily as air or booze.

"Money, now this has to be some *good* shit" (148), Self believes, because money is what turns the world. His shady, petty dealings in high finance mirror the supposedly legitimate, grand-scale monetary dealings of Thatcherite Britain, Reaganite America, and much of the rest of the world. Just as Churchill's LIFFE stockbrokers think transnationally (leaving, for all they are concerned, particular nation-states or even entire continents twisting in the wind), so as he treks back and forth between London and New York, John Self acquires a sort of transnational patina. This is, no doubt, Amis's version of "the global joke which keeps money cracking" (148). Meanwhile, according to Self,

> there are some pretty primitive creatures driving around with money in their Torpedoes and Boomerangs, or sitting down with money, in the shops, in the pubs, in the streets. They are all shapes and colours, innocent beneficiaries of the global joke which keeps money cracking. They don't do anything: it's their currencies that do things. Last year the pubs were full of incredulously [sic] spendthrift Irishmen: they didn't have money in their pockets any longer—they had Euromoney, which is much more powerful stuff. There's some bundle in the Middle East, and a new squad of fiscal space invaders starts plundering the West. Every time the quid gets gang-banged on the international exchange, all the Arab chicks get a new fur coat. There are white moneymen, too, English, native. They *must* be criminals, with their wads, the crap they talk, their cruel, roasted faces. I am one. I am one of them. (148)

At least John Self is honest about his dishonesty. As both this passage and the entire novel suggest, however, the world seems to be more and more populated by fiscal gangsters, con artists, and sleazeballs like John Self. His name alone suggests that Self is not exceptional; for Amis, he seems instead to represent a postindustrial, postcolonial, postmodern British (and American) norm.

"Money is very versatile," Self says; "You really have to give money credit for that" (57). But in *Money*, money also seems powerless to halt the moral, social, political, environmental, global rot that money causes. *Money* itself is a commodity, and Martin Amis has no compunction about writing himself into the story as a character, prepared to hobnob with sleazeballs like Self and, for a price, to revise the (fictional, nonexistent, not creditworthy) film script. (Bradbury, too, in his Author's Note says of *Rates of Exchange* that "like money, this book is a paper fiction, offered for exchange.") In both London and New York, though money flows freely in all directions through John Self's experience, and though everything and everyone can be bought and sold, nothing and no one are safe, no identity (even "Self") seems sane or stable, and nothing has any fixed, determinate value. From Amis's perspective, these two metropolitan centers of postcolonial, postindustrial "defaillancy," and yet of continuing financial power, are both has-been cities, slums of the alleged First World, in which the ruins are mounting fast. But as London and New York go, so goes the rest of the world . . . and who is paying the price? "We are all stomped and roughed up and peed on and slammed against the wall by money," says Self; "should the earth enter turnaround tomorrow, nuke out, commit suicide, then we'll already have our suicide notes, pain notes, dolour bills" (254). Or as Self's hoodlum pal Fat Paul puts it, no doubt with his own health ("elf") in mind, "Money . . . is not worf two bob, is it, without your fuckin elf" (142).

5

"WHAT SO many people in Britain find incomprehensible about Britain's present state," writes Andrew Gamble, "is how a nation that was on the winning side of two world wars could lose the peace and succumb to the commercial challenge of rivals defeated on the battlefield. How could a nation that showed such unity in the Second World War, and was so long renowned for its traditions of civility and consensus, appear so disunited and wracked by conflict, envy, and cynicism, in the 1960s and 1970s?" (xx). Two more decades can now be added to Gamble's statement.

From the 1960s on, Britain's most influential cultural product has probably been not the novel, or the drama, or even film and such BBC productions as "Masterpiece Theatre," but rock music (Nehring 166–174; Sinfield 171–178; Hebdige, *Subculture*). The spectacular global success (obviously including monetary success) of such groups as the Beatles and the Rolling Stones has, however, seemed to many intellectuals of various political persuasions to be just another symptom of decay, of the moral and cultural rot that, along with race riots and soccer hooliganism, appears to have become a permanent feature of Ukanian life since 1945. If the postmodern condition is marked by the blurring, reversal, or erasure of the modernist "great divide" (as Andreas Huyssen has called it) between high- and mass cultural forms, then contemporary Britain, like Baudrillard's America, is certainly postmodern. From the European standpoint, the increasing hegemony of what Adorno and Horkheimer called "the culture industry" has often been understood as an aspect of the postwar "Americanization" of everyday life. And in the land of Shakespeare, Matthew Arnold, and F. R. Leavis, the dominance of mass, commodified cultural forms such as rock music is experienced very directly as loss, regression, barbarism.

Theories of the postmodern that take commodity fetishism as their central category echo the countless ways in which, throughout the modern period from Veblen's 1890s to the 1960s, mass culture was condemned as ideology, as kitsch, and as source or cause of fascism and Nazism, whereas high culture in contrast was defined as a refuge from the "barbaric" depredations of the masses. But high culture has not lived up to its billing (it has not prevented the barbarisms of World War I, World War II, Vietnam, Bosnia . . .). As a variant on faith in Enlightenment reason, faith in high culture seems if anything rather to have contributed to barbarism. "There is no document of civilization," said Walter Benjamin, "which is not at the same time a document of barbarism" (*Illuminations* 256). An inadequate, subjective authority at best, high culture has today apparently also been co-opted, bought up or bought out, swamped by commercialized mass culture. The postmodern condition can thus be understood as one in which the resort to high culture (like the resort to the gold standard, or the referent, or the real) as a solution to the dilemmas and depredations of transnational capitalism is barred or rejected as a nonsolution.

From its advent in Britain during the apocalyptic summer of 1976, punk rock especially has both expressed and capitalized on Britain's decline and that of traditional cultural authority. The "nihilist aesthetic" of the Sex Pistols, the Clash, the Who, and other bands appeared to achieve new heights or depths of youthful rebellion (Hebdige, *Subculture* 28). Punk style and music, explains Dick Hebdige, "were *dramatizing* what had come to be called 'Britain's decline'" through such "symbolic acts of treason" as the Sex Pistol's song, "Anarchy in the U.K." (87, 64). Punk anarchism was a direct response to an economic and political situation that seemed itself increasingly anarchic because increasingly hopeless. Perhaps the most telling punk lyrics are those from the Sex Pistol's "God Save the Queen":

> NO FUTRE
> NO FUTURE
> NO FUTURE FOR YOU
> NO FUTURE
> NO FUTURE
> NO FUTURE
> NO FUTURE FOR ME.

There is "no future in England's dreaming." Quoting this "mordant chant" in *Lipstick Traces*, Greil Marcus adds that with "God Save the Queen," the Sex Pistols tried to break the spell of "England's dream of its glorious past, as represented by the Queen, the 'moron,' the nation's basic tourist attraction, linchpin of an economy based on nothing, salve on England's collective amputee's itch for Empire" (11). Or at least this is what Johnny Rotten and his band, screaming "*We're the future! Your future!*" gave the world to understand was their interpretation of the postmodern condition of (formerly "Great") Britain. This is the *non*future also as depicted in Jarman's *The Last of England*: "And tomorrow?" asks the narrator, "tomorrow's been canceled."

"Every youth movement presents itself as a loan to the future, and tries to call in its lien in advance," says Marcus; "but when there is no future all loans are canceled" (11). In regard to postmodern British culture, until there are clear, progressive alternatives to "Sado-Monetarism" and to a Ukanian nation-state that seems to grow increasingly decrepit, ruinous, and fetishistic (both incredible and uncreditworthy), Johnny Rotten's injunction "Believe in the ruins" may be as hopeful as anyone can reasonably get. It goes without saying, however, that Britain, though less "great" than it used to be, has not collapsed and is unlikely to do so, at least in the near future (but who can tell?). Like other European nation-states, it will probably gradually blend into the emerging European federation. At the same time, it is possible that, with new leadership, Britain's economy, if not its old industrial base (much less its old imperial power and glory), may be revitalized. In view especially of the internationalization of capital since World War II, Raymond Williams, just before his death in 1988, concluded that "the strategy" both for the British Left and for British renewal "is all still to be found, but what blocks it . . . is [the] old model of creating a relatively powerful, united Britain with a 'successful' sovereign economy. That, I think, is what history has ruled out" (*Resources* 315). Meanwhile class conflict, high unemployment, the state's seemingly insoluble fiscal crisis, the continuing "troubles" in Northern Ireland (despite the recent cease-fire), increasing demands for devolution on the part of Scots nationalists, and racism and racial tensions that are not about to disappear suggest that the dystopian visions of the future—or nonfuture—expressed by Orwell's *1984*, Larkin's "Going, Going," Burgess's *Clockwork Orange*, Jarman's *The Last of England*, Martin Amis's *Money*, and the Sex Pistol's "Anarchy in the U.K." may be features of British culture for some time to come.

WORKS CITED

Addison, Joseph. *The Spectator*, no. 3 (3 March 1711). Ed. Donald F. Bond, 1:14–17. Oxford: Clarendon, 1965.

——. *The Tatler*, no. 249 (11 November 1710). Ed. Donald F. Bond, 3:269–273. Oxford: Clarendon, 1987.

Adorno, Theodor. *Minima Moralia*. London: Verso, 1978.

——. "Veblen's Attack on Culture." In *Prisms*, 73–94. Cambridge, Mass.: MIT Press, 1983).

Adorno, Theodor, and Max Horkheimer. *Dialectic of Enlightenment*. New York: Herder and Herder, 1972.

Althusser, Louis. "Ideology and Ideological State Apparatuses." In *Lenin and Philosophy*, 127–186. New York: Monthly Review Press, 1971.

Altick, Richard. *The Presence of the Present: Topics of the Day in the Victorian Novel*. Columbus: Ohio State University Press, 1991.

Amin, Samir. *Empire of Chaos*. New York: Monthly Review Press, 1992.

——. *Eurocentrism*. New York: Monthly Review Press, 1989.

Amis, Martin. *Money: A Suicide Note*. London: Cape, 1984.

Anderson, Amanda. *Tainted Souls and Painted Faces: The Rhetoric of Fallenness in Victorian Culture*. Ithaca: Cornell University Press, 1993.

Anderson, Benedict. *Imagined Communites: Reflections on the Origin and Spread of Nationalism*. 1983. Rev. ed. London: Verso, 1991.

Anderson, Perry. *English Questions*. London: Verso, 1992.

Appleby, Joyce Oldham. *Economic Thought and Ideology in Seventeenth-Century England*. Princeton: Princeton University Press, 1978.

Apter, Emily, and William Pietz, eds. *Fetishism as Cultural Discourse*. Ithaca: Cornell University Press, 1993.

Arnold, Matthew. *Culture and Anarchy*. 1869. Ed. J. Dover Wilson. Cambridge: Cambridge University Press, 1963.

Atkins, John. *A Voyage to Guinea, Brasil, and the West Indies*. 1735. Northbrook, Ill.: Metro Books, 1972.

Avineri, Shlomo. *Hegel's Theory of the Modern State*. Cambridge: Cambridge University Press, 1972.

Backscheider, Paula. "Defoe's Lady Credit." *Huntington Library Quarterly* 80 (1981): 89–100.

Bagehot, Walter. *Lombard Street: A Description of the Money Market*. London: John Murray, 1927.

Bakhtin, Mikhail. *The Dialogic Imagination.* Austin: University of Texas Press, 1981.

Ballantyne, Robert M. *The Gorilla Hunters: A Tale of the Wilds of Africa.* 1861. Philadelphia: Henry T. Coates, 186–.

Balzac, Honoré de. *The Wild Ass's Skin.* 1831. Harmondsworth: Penguin, 1977.

Bantock, G. H. *Culture, Industrialisation, and Education.* London: Routledge and Kegan Paul, 1968.

Barnett, Anthony. *Iron Britannia.* London: Allison and Busby, 1982.

Barraclough, Geoffrey. *An Introduction to Contemporary History.* Harmondsworth: Penguin, 1967.

Barthes, Roland. *Mythologies.* 1957. New York: Hill and Wang, 1972.

Baudrillard, Jean. *America.* London: Verso, 1989.

——. *For a Critique of the Political Economy of the Sign.* St. Louis: Telos, 1981.

——. *In the Shadow of the Silent Majorities . . . or the End of the Social.* Brooklyn: Semiotext(e), 1983.

——. *Simulations.* Brooklyn: Semiotext(e), 1983.

Bauman, Zygmunt. *Modernity and the Holocaust.* Ithaca: Cornell University Press, 1989.

Beer, Gillian. *Darwin's Plots: Evolutionary Narrative in Darwin, George Eliot, and Nineteenth-Century Fiction.* London: Routledge and Kegan Paul, 1983.

Bell, Quentin. *Bloomsbury.* London: Weidenfeld and Nicolson, 1968.

Benjamin, Walter. "Central Park." *New German Critique* 34 (Winter 1985): 32–58.

——. *Charles Baudelaire: A Lyric Poet in the Era of High Capitalism.* London: New Left Books, 1973.

——. *Illuminations.* New York: Schocken, 1969.

Bentham, Jeremy. "A Plan for Saving all the Expense and Trouble in the Transfer of Stock." In *Works,* 3:105–153. New York: Russell and Russell, 1962.

Berkeley, George. *Works.* Vol. 6. London: Nelson, 1953.

Berman, Marshall. *All That Is Solid Melts into Air: The Experience of Modernity.* New York: Penguin, 1988.

Bhabha, Homi K. *The Location of Culture.* (New York: Routledge, 1994.

——. ed. *Nation and Narration.* New York: Routledge, 1990.

Binkley, Robert C. *Realism and Nationalism, 1852–1871.* (New York: Harper and Row, Torchbooks, 1963).

Binswanger, Hans. *Money and Magic: A Critique of the Modern Economy in the Light of Goethe's Faust.* Chicago: University of Chicago Press, 1994.

Birken, Lawrence. *Consuming Desire: Sexual Science and the Emergence of a Culture of Abundance, 1871–1914.* Ithaca: Cornell University Press, 1988.

Blackaby, Fred, ed. *De-Industrialisation.* London: Heinemann, 1978.

Blake, William. *Letters of William Blake.* Ed. Geoffrey Keynes. Oxford: Clarendon Press, 1980.

——. *Selected Poetry and Prose.* Ed. Northrop Frye. New York: Random House, Modern Library, 1953.

Bolingbroke, Lord (Henry St. John). *Works.* 4 vols. London: Henry G. Bohn, 1844.

Bonar, Harold. *Hungry Generations.* New York: King's Crown, 1955.

Bond, Edward. *The War Plays: A Trilogy.* London: Methuen, 1991.

Bongie, Chris. *Exotic Memories: Literature, Colonialism, and the Fin de Siècle.* Stanford: Stanford University Press, 1991.

Bose, Sujit. *Attitudes to Imperialism: Kipling, Forster, and Paul Scott.* Delhi: Amar, 1990.

Boucicault, Dion. *London Assurance.* 1841. Ed. James L. Smith. London: Black, 1984.

Bourne, H. R. Fox. *The Romance of Trade.* London: Cassell, Petter and Galpin, 1871.

Bowlby, Rachel. *Just Looking: Consumer Culture in Dreiser, Gissing, and Zola.* London: Methuen, 1985.

Bradbury, Malcolm. *Rates of Exchange.* London: Secker and Warburg, 1983.

Brantlinger, Patrick. *Bread and Circuses: Theories of Mass Culture as Social Decay.* Ithaca: Cornell University Press, 1983.

——. "'Dying Races': Rationalizing Genocide in the Nineteenth Century." In *Decolonization of the Imagination,* ed. Parekh and Pieterse, 431–56.

——. "*News from Nowhere:* William Morris's Socialist Anti-Novel." *Victorian Studies* 19 (September 1975): 35–49.

——. *Rule of Darkness: British Literature and Imperialism, 1830–1914.* Ithaca: Cornell University Press, 1988.

Brecher, Jeremy, John Brown Childs, and Jill Cutler, eds. *Global Visions: Beyond the New World Order.* Boston: South End Press, 1993.

Brennan, Timothy. "The National Longing for Form." In *Nation and Narration,* ed. Bhabha, 44–70.

Brewer, John. *The Sinews of Power: War, Money, and the English State, 1688–1783.* New York: Knopf, 1989.

Brown, Laura. *Alexander Pope.* Oxford: Blackwell, 1985.

Buck-Morss, Susan. *The Dialectics of Seeing: Walter Benjamin and the Arcades Project.* Cambridge, Mass.: MIT Press, 1989.

Bunn, James H. "The Aesthetics of British Mercantilism." *New Literary History* 11 (1980): 303–321.

Burke, Edmund. *Letters on a Regicide Peace.* 1795–1797. Vol. 9 of *Works.* Boston: Little, Brown, 1881.

——. *A Philosophical Enquiry into the Origin of Our Ideas of the Sublime and the Beautiful.* 1756. Menston, England: Scolar, 1970.

——. *Reflections on the Revolution in France.* 1790. Harmondsworth: Penguin, 1969.

——. "Speech on the Nabob of Arcot's Debts." 1785. In *The Speeches of the Right Honourable Edmund Burke,* 3:92–179. London: Longman, Hurst, Rees, Orme, and Brown, 1816.

Burn, Joseph. *Stock Exchange Investments in Theory and Practice, with Chapters on the Constitution and Operations of the Bank of England and the National and Local Debts of the United Kingdom.* London: Charles and Edwin Layton, 1909.

Caffentzis, Constantine George. *Clipped Coins, Abused Words, and Civil Government: John Locke's Philosophy of Money.* Brooklyn: Autonomedia, 1989.

Calhoun, Craig, ed. *Habermas and the Public Sphere*. Cambridge, Mass.: MIT Press, 1992.

Calleo, David P. *Coleridge and the Idea of the Modern State*. New Haven: Yale University Press, 1966.

Cameron, Keith Neill. "Shelley, Cobbett, and the National Debt." *JEGP* 42 (1943): 197–209.

Carey, John. *The Intellectuals and the Masses: Pride and Prejudice among the Literary Intelligentsia, 1880–1939*. London: Faber and Faber, 1992.

Carlyle, Thomas. *The French Revolution*. 1837. *Works*. London: Centenary Edition, 1896–1899. Vol. 4.

——. *Past and Present*. 1843. Boston: Houghton Mifflin, Riverside, 1965.

——. "Signs of the Times." 1829. In *Scottish and Other Miscellanies*, 223–245. London: Dent, Everyman's Library, 1964.

Carpenter, Mary Wilson. *George Eliot and the Landscape of Time: Narrative Form and Protestant Apocalyptic History*. Chapel Hill: University of North Carolina Press, 1986.

Carretta, Vincent. *The Snarling Muse: Verbal and Visual Political Satire from Pope to Churchill*. Philadelphia: University of Pennsylvania Press, 1983.

Carswell, John. *The South Sea Bubble*. London: Cresset, 1960.

Castle, Terry. *Masquerade and Civilization: The Carnivalesque in Eighteenth-Century English Culture and Fiction*. Stanford: Stanford University Press, 1986.

Centre for Contemporary Cultural Studies. *The Empire Strikes Back: Race and Racism in '70s Britain*. London: Hutchinson, 1982.

Chace, William M. *The Political Identities of Ezra Pound and T. S. Eliot*. Stanford: Stanford University Press, 1973.

Chartier, Roger. *The Cultural Origins of the French Revolution*. Durham: Duke University Press, 1991.

Chatterjee, Partha. *Nationalist Thought and the Colonial World: A Derivative Discourse*. 1986. (Minneapolis: University of Minnesota Press, 1991.

Checkland, S. G. *The Rise of Industrial Society in England, 1815–1885*. London: Longmans, Green, 1964.

Christensen, Jerome. *Practicing Enlightenment: Hume and the Formation of a Literary Career*. Madison: University of Wisconsin Press, 1987.

Churchill, Caryl. *Serious Money: A City Comedy*. London: Methuen, 1987.

Clapham, Sir John H. *The Bank of England: A History*. 2 vols. Cambridge: Cambridge University Press, 1944.

Clark, Ronald W. *Freud: The Man and the Cause*. New York: Random House, 1980.

Cobbett, William. *The Autobiography: The Progress of a Ploughboy to a Seat in Parliament*. Ed. William Reitzel. London: Faber and Faber, 1947.

——. *Paper against Gold and Glory against Prosperity*. 2 vols. London: J. McReery, 1815.

Coleridge, Samuel Taylor. *The Friend*, pts. 1 and 2. 1809, 1818. Vol. 4 of *The Collected Works*, ed. Barbara E. Rooke. Princeton: Princeton University Press, 1969.

——. *Lay Sermons.* Ed. R. J. White. Vol. 6 of *The Collected Works.* Princeton: Princeton University Press, 1972.

——. *Letters Hitherto Uncollected.* Ed. W. F. Prideaux. London: Printed for Private Circulation, 1913.

——. *On the Constitution of Church and State.* 1829. Ed. John Colmer. Vol. 10 of *The Collected Works.* Princeton: Princeton University Press, 1976.

Colley, Linda. *Britons: Forging the Nation, 1707–1837.* New Haven: Yale University Press, 1992.

Collins, Michael. *Money and Banking in the U.K.: A History.* London: Croom Helm, 1988.

Comte, Auguste. *Auguste Comte and Postivism: The Essential Writings.* Ed. Gertrud Lenzer. New York: Harper and Row, Torchbooks, 1975.

Connor, Steven. *Postmodernist Culture: An Introduction to Theories of the Contemporary.* Oxford: Blackwell, 1989.

Conrad, Joseph, *Heart of Darkness.* 1899. New York: Norton, 1963.

——. *Nostromo.* 1904. London: Penguin, 1990.

Coomaraswamy, Ananda K. *What Is Civilisation? and Other Essays.* New Delhi: Indira Gandhi National Centre for the Arts and Oxford University Press, 1989.

Costello, Nicholas, Jonathan Michie, and Seumas Milne. *Beyond the Casino Economy: Planning for the 1990s.* London: Verso, 1989.

Crouzet, François. *The Victorian Economy.* London: Methuen, 1982.

Danahay, Martin D. "State Power and the Victorian Subject." *Prose Studies* 15 (April 1992): 61–83.

Davenant, Charles. "The True Picture of a Modern Whig." In *Political and Commercial Works,* 4:127–266. 1702. Farnborough: Gregg, 1967.

Davidson, James Dale. *The Plague of the Black Debt: How to Survive the Coming Depression.* Baltimore: Strategic Investment Limited Partnership, 1993.

De Bolla, Peter. *The Discourse of the Sublime: Readings in History, Aesthetics, and the Subject.* Oxford: Blackwell, 1989.

Defoe, Daniel. *The Compleat English Tradesman.* 2 vols. London: Charles Rivington, 1727.

——. *The Life of Captain Singleton.* 1720. London: Dent, Everyman's Library, 1951.

——. *Review.* 22 vols. Ed. Arthur Wellesley Secord. New York: AMS Press, 1965.

——. *Roxana: The Fortunate Mistress.* 1724. Harmondsworth: Penguin, 1982.

Delamaide, Darrell. *Debt Shock: The Full Story of the World Credit Crisis.* New York: Doubleday, 1984.

Deleuze, Gilles. *Empiricism and Subjectivity: An Essay on Hume's Theory of Human Nature.* New York: Columbia University Press, 1991.

Deleuze, Gilles, and Félix Guattari. *Anti-Oedipus: Capitalism and Schizophrenia.* Minneapolis: University of Minnesota Press, 1983.

——. *Kafka: Toward a Minor Literature.* Minneapolis: University of Minnesota Press, 1986.

Derrida, Jacques. *Given Time I: Counterfeit Money.* Chicago: University of Chicago Press, 1992.

——. *Of Grammatology.* Baltimore: Johns Hopkins University Press, 1976.

——. *Specters of Marx: The State of the Debt, the Work of Mourning, and the New International.* New York: Routledge, 1994.

Dickens, Charles. *Dombey and Son.* 1848. Oxford: Oxford University Press, 1989.

——. *Hard Times.* 1854. Oxford: Oxford University Press, 1989.

——. *Little Dorrit.* 1855–1857. Oxford: Oxford University Press, 1989.

——. *Our Mutual Friend.* 1864–1865. Oxford: Oxford University Press, 1989.

——. *The Posthumous Papers of the Pickwick Club.* 1836. Oxford: Oxford University Press, 1989.

——. *A Tale of Two Cities.* 1859. Oxford: Oxford University Press, 1989.

Dickens, and W. H. Wills. "The Old Lady of Threadneedle Street." In *Charles Dickens' Uncollected Writings from Household Words, 1850–1859,* ed. Harry Stone, 1:123–135. Bloomington: Indiana University Press, 1968.

Dickson, P. G. M. *The Financial Revolution in England: A Study in the Development of Public Credit, 1688–1756.* London: Macmillan, 1967.

Dijkstra, Bram. *Defoe and Economics: The Fortunes of Roxana in the History of Interpretation.* New York: St. Martin's, 1987.

Disraeli, Benjamin. *Coningsby, or The New Generation.* 1844. Bradenham Edition, vol. 8. New York: Knopf, n.d.

——. *Sybil, or The Two Nations.* 1845. Harmondsworth: Penguin, 1987.

——. *Tancred; or The New Crusade.* 1847. Bradenham Edition, vol. 10. New York: Knopf, n.d.

Doody, Margaret Anne. *The Daring Muse: Augustan Poetry Reconsidered.* Cambridge: Cambridge University Press, 1985.

Doyle, Michael W. *Empires.* Ithaca: Cornell University Press, 1986.

Doyle, Sir Arthur Conan. *The Lost World.* New York: Review of Reviews Co., 1912.

Dumont, Louis. *From Mandeville to Marx: The Genesis and Triumph of Economic Ideology.* Chicago: University of Chicago Press, 1977.

Dutt, Romesh. *The Economic History of India under Early British Rule.* 1901. London: Routledge and Kegan Paul, 1956.

Dvorak, Will. "Dickens's Ambivalence as Social Critic in the 1860s: Attitudes to Money in *All the Year Round* and *The Uncommercial Traveller.*" *Dickensian* 80 (1984): 89–104.

Eagleton, Terry. *Literary Theory: An Introduction.* Minneapolis: University of Minnesota Press, 1983.

——. "Vulgar, Vain, and Venal." *Times Literary Supplement,* 28 May 1993, 7.

Eliot, George. *Daniel Deronda.* 1876. Oxford: Clarendon, 1984.

——. *Felix Holt, the Radical.* 1872. Oxford: Clarendon, 1980.

——. *The Impressions of Theophrastus Such.* 1879. Ed. Nancy Henry. London: William Pickering, 1994.

——. *The Mill on the Floss.* 1860. Oxford: Clarendon, 1980.

——. *Selections from George Eliot's Letters.* Ed. Gordon S. Haight. New Haven: Yale University Press, 1985.

Export, Valie. "The Real and Its Double: The Body." *Discourse* 11 (fall–winter, 1988–89): 3–27.

Fanon, Frantz. *The Wretched of the Earth.* New York: Grove Press, 1991.

Feltes, Norman. *Literary Capital and the Late Victorian Novel.* Madison: University of Wisconsin Press, 1993.

———. *Modes of Production of Victorian Novels.* Chicago: University of Chicago Press, 1986.

Fetter, Frank Whitson. *Development of British Monetary Orthodoxy, 1797–1875.* Cambridge: Harvard University Press, 1965.

Flynn, Carol Houlihan. *The Body in Swift and Defoe.* Cambridge: Cambridge University Press, 1990.

Foucault, Michel. *Discipline and Punish.* New York: Pantheon, 1977.

———. *Language, Counter-Memory, Practice.* Ithaca: Cornell University Press, 1977.

———. *The Order of Things: An Archaeology of the Human Sciences.* New York: Vintage Books, 1973.

Francis, John F. *History of the Bank of England.* 2 vols. London: Willoughby, 1846.

Fraser, W. Hamish. *The Coming of the Mass Market, 1850–1914.* Hamden, Conn.: Shoe String Press, Archon, 1981.

Freedman, Jonathan. *Professions of Taste: Henry James, British Aestheticism, and Commodity Culture.* Stanford: Stanford University Press, 1990.

Freud, Sigmund. *The Basic Writings of Sigmund Freud.* Ed. A. A. Brill. New York: Modern Library, 1938.

———. *Civilization and Its Discontents.* 1930. New York: Norton, 1961.

———. "Fetishism." 1927. In *Standard Edition,* ed. James E. Strachey, 21:149–57. London: Hogarth, n.d.

———. *Group Psychology and the Analysis of the Ego.* 1921. New York: Norton, 1959.

Friedman, Lester, ed. *Fires Were Started: British Cinema and Thatcherism.* Minneapolis: University of Minnesota Press, 1993.

Gagnier, Regenia. *Idylls of the Marketplace: Oscar Wilde and the Victorian Public.* (Stanford: Stanford University Press, 1986.

———. "On the Insatiability of Human Wants: Economic and Aesthetic Man." *Victorian Studies* 36 (winter 1993): 125–153.

Galbraith, John Kenneth. *The Age of Uncertainty.* Boston: Houghton Mifflin, 1977.

———. *Money, Whence It Came, Where It Went.* Boston: Houghton Mifflin, 1975.

Gallagher, Catherine. "The Bioeconomics of *Our Mutual Friend.*" In *Subject to History: Ideology, Class, Gender,* ed. David Simpson, 47–64. Ithaca: Cornell University Press, 1991.

———. *The Industrial Reformation of Fiction, 1832–1867.* Chicago: University of Chicago Press, 1985.

———. Response to "Medusa's Head." In *The End of the Line,* 194–196.

Gamble, Andrew. *Britain in Decline.* London: Macmillan, 1985.

Gandhi, Mohandas K. *Hind Swaraj.* 1909. Ahmedabad: Navajivan, 1958.

Gellner, Ernest. *Thought and Change.* London: Weidenfeld and Nicholson, 1964.

George, Susan. *A Fate Worse Than Debt.* New York: Grove Press, 1990.

Giddens, Anthony. *The Consequences of Modernity.* Stanford: Stanford University Press, 1990.

Gilroy, Paul. *There Ain't No Black in the Union Jack: The Cultural Politics of Race and Nation.* Chicago: University of Chicago Press, 1991.

Gissing, George. *New Grub Street.* 1891. Boston: Houghton Mifflin, Riverside, 1962.

Goethe, Johann Wolfgang von. *Faust.* Ed. Charles E. Passage. Indianapolis: Bobbs-Merrill, 1965.

Goux, Jean-Joseph. *The Coiners of Language.* Norman: University of Oklahoma Press, 1994.

——. *Symbolic Economies: After Marx and Freud.* Ithaca: Cornell University Press, 1990.

Gramsci, Antonio. *Selections from the Prison Notebooks.* New York: International Publishers, 1971.

Greenfeld, Liah. *Nationalism: Five Roads to Modernity.* Cambridge: Harvard University Press, 1992.

Gunn, J. A. W. "Public Spirit to Public Opinion." In *Beyond Liberty and Property: The Process of Self-Recognition in Eighteenth-Century Political Thought,* 260–315. Montreal: McGill-Queens University Press, 1983.

Habermas, Jürgen. *The Structural Transformation of the Public Sphere: An Inquiry into a Category of Bourgeois Society.* Cambridge, Mass.: MIT Press, 1989.

——. *The Theory of Communicative Action.* Vol. 2. Boston: Beacon, 1989.

Hall, Stuart, and Martin Jacques, eds. *The Politics of Thatcherism.* London: Lawrence and Wishart, 1983.

Hamilton, Alexander. *Papers on Public Credit, Commerce, and Finance.* New York: Columbia University Press, 1934.

Hargreaves, Eric L. *The National Debt.* London: Edward Arnold, 1930.

Harvey, David. *The Condition of Postmodernity.* Oxford: Basil Blackwell, 1989.

Harvie, Christopher. *The Centre of Things: Political Fiction in Britain from Disraeli to the Present.* Winchester, Mass.: Unwin Hyman, 1991.

Hayek, F. A. *Denationalisation of Money—the Argument Refined: An Analysis of the Theory and Practice of Concurrent Currencies.* London: Institute of Economic Affairs, 1990.

Hayes, Carlton J. *Nationalism: A Religion.* New York: Macmillan, 1960.

Hebdige, Dick. *Subculture: The Meaning of Style.* London: Methuen, 1979.

Hegel, G. W. F. *The Philosophy of History.* New York: Dover, 1956.

——. *The Philosophy of Right.* London: Oxford University Press, 1967.

Heilbroner, Robert, and Peter Bernstein. *The Debt and the Deficit: False Alarms/ Real Possibilities.* New York: Norton, 1989.

Heinzelman, Kurt. *The Economics of the Imagination.* Amherst: University of Massachusetts Press, 1980.

Hemmings, F. W. J., ed. *The Age of Realism.* Harmondsworth: Penguin, 1974.

Henwood, Doug. "Behind the Bankruptcy Boom." *Nation,* 5 October 1992, 345, 360–364.

Hertz, Neil. *The End of the Line: Essays on Psychoanalysis and the Sublime.* New York: Columbia University Press, 1985.

——. "Medusa's Head: Male Hysteria under Political Pressure." In *The End of the Line,* 161–193.

Herzinger, Kim A. *D. H. Lawrence in His Time, 1908–1915.* Lewisburg, Penn.: Bucknell University Press, 1982.

Hirschman, Albert O. *The Passions and the Interests: Political Arguments for Capitalism before Its Triumph.* Princeton: Princeton University Press, 1977.

Hirst, Francis W. *Gladstone as Financier and Economist.* London: Ernest Benn, 1931.

Hobbes, Thomas. *The Leviathan.* 1651. New York: Crowell Collier and Macmillan, Collier Books, 1962.

Hobsbawm, Eric. *Industry and Empire.* Harmondsworth: Penguin, 1969.

——. *Nations and Nationalism since 1780: Programme, Myth, Reality.* Cambridge: Cambridge University Press, 1990.

Hobsbawm, Eric, and Terence Ranger, eds. *The Invention of Tradition.* Cambridge: Cambridge University Press, 1983.

Hobson, John A. *Imperialism: A Study.* 1902. Ann Arbor: University of Michigan Press, 1965.

——. *The Psychology of Jingoism.* London: Grant Richards, 1901.

Hogan, W. P., and Ivor Pearce. *The Incredible Eurodollar: Or Why the World's Monetary System Is Collapsing.* London: Allen and Unwin, 1982.

Horsefield, J. Keith. *British Monetary Experiments, 1650–1710.* Cambridge: Harvard University Press, 1960.

Houghton, John. *Culture and Currency: Cultural Bias in Monetary Theory and Policy.* (Boulder, Col: Westview, 1991).

House, Humphry. *The Dickens World.* London: Oxford University Press, 1960.

Howe, Irving. *Politics and the Novel.* New York: Noonday, Meridian, 1957.

Hume, David. "Of Public Credit." In *Writings on Economics,* ed. Eugene Rotwein, 90–107. Madison: University of Wisconsin Press, 1970.

——. "Of the First Principles of Government." In *Political Essays,* ed. Charles W. Hendel, 24–27. New York: Liberal Arts Press, 1953.

——. *A Treatise of Human Nature.* 1739–40. London: Penguin, 1984.

Humphreys, A. R. *The Augustan World: Society, Thought, and Letters in Eighteenth-Century England.* 1954. New York: Harper and Row, 1963.

Huyssen, Andreas. *After the Great Divide: Modernism, Mass Culture, Postmodernism.* Bloomington: Indiana University Press, 1986.

Hymer, Stephen. "Robinson Crusoe and the Secret of Primitive Accumulation." In *Radical Political Economy,* ed. Samuel Bowles and Richard Edwards, 1:19–36. Aldershot: Elgar, 1990.

Ian, Marcia. *Remembering the Phallic Mother: Psychoanalysis, Modernism, and the Fetish.* Ithaca: Cornell University Press, 1993.

Ingham, Geoffrey. *Capitalism Divided? The City and Industry in British Social Development.* New York: Schocken, 1984.

Jameson, Fredric. *The Political Unconscious: Narrative as a Socially Symbolic Act.* Ithaca: Cornell University Press, 1981.

——. *Postmodernism, or The Cultural Logic of Late Capitalism.* Durham: Duke University Press, 1991.

Jevons, William Stanley. *The Theory of Political Economy.* 1871. New York: Kelley, 1957.

Johnson, Samuel. *Poems.* Oxford: Clarendon, 1941.

Johnstone, Charles. *Chrysal, or the Adventures of a Guinea.* 4 vols. 1760–1765. London: Becket and Hondt, 1768.

Judt, Tony. "The New Old Nationalism." *New York Review of Books,* 26 May 1994, 44–51.

Kennedy, Paul. *The Rise and Fall of the Great Powers.* New York: Random House, Vintage, 1989.

Kettle, Arnold. "The Early Victorian Social-Problem Novel." In *From Dickens to Hardy,* ed. Boris Ford, 169–187. Harmondsworth: Penguin, 1968.

Keynes, John Maynard. *The Collected Writings.* 30 vols. London: Macmillan; New York: St. Martin's, 1971–1989.

Kidd, Benjamin. *Social Evolution.* 1894. (New York: Macmillan. 1894.

Kierkegaard, Søren. *The Present Age.* 1846. New York: Harper and Row, 1962.

Kindleberger, Charles. *A Financial History of Western Europe.* 2d ed. New York: Oxford University Press, 1993.

——. *Manias, Panics, and Crashes: A History of Financial Crises.* New York: Basic Books, 1989.

Kingsley, Charles. *His Letters and Memories of His Life.* 2 vols. London: Macmillan, 1894.

Kramnick, Isaac. *Bolingbroke and His Circle: The Politics of Nostalgia in the Age of Walpole.* 1968. Ithaca: Cornell University Press, 1992.

Kurtzman, Joel. *The Death of Money: How the Electronic Economy Has Destabilized the World's Markets and Created Financial Chaos.* New York: Simon and Schuster, 1993.

Lacan, Jacques. *Ecrits: A Selection.* New York: Norton, 1977.

Langer, Gary F. *The Coming of Age of Political Economy, 1815–1825.* Westport, Conn.: Greenwood, 1987.

Larkin, Philip. *Collected Poems.* New York: Farrar, Straus and Giroux, 1989.

Lawrence, D. H. *Kangaroo.* 1923. New York: Viking, 1960.

——. *Movements in European History.* 1921. Cambridge: Cambridge University Press, 1989.

——. *The Plumed Serpent.* 1926. Harmondsworth: Penguin, 1955.

Lecky, W. E. H. *History of the Rise and Influence of the Spirit of Rationalism in Europe.* 2 vols. New York: Appleton, 1890.

Levin, Harry. *The Gates of Horn: A Study of Five French Realists.* London: Oxford University Press, 1966.

Leys, Colin. *Politics in Britain: From Labourism to Thatcherism.* London: Verso, 1989.

Lipietz, Alain. "The Debt Problem, European Integration and the New Phase of World Crisis." *New Left Review* 178 November/December 1989): 37–50.

——. *The Enchanted World: Inflation, Credit, and the World Crisis.* London: Verso, 1985.

Lippmann, Walter. *The Phantom Public.* New York: Harcourt, Brace, 1925.

Liu, Alan. *Wordsworth: The Sense of History.* Stanford: Stanford University Press, 1989.

Locke, John. *Locke on Money*. Ed. Patrick Hyde Kelly. 2 vols. Oxford: Clarendon Press, 1991.

Lyotard, Jean-François. *Libidinal Economy*. Bloomington: Indiana University Press, 1993.

———. *The Postmodern Condition: A Report on Knowledge*. Minneapolis: University of Minnesota Press, 1984.

———. "Universal History and Cultural Differences." In *The Lyotard Reader*, ed. Andrew Benjamin, 314–323. Oxford: Blackwell, 1989.

Macaulay, Thomas Babington. *The History of England*. Vols. 1 and 3. London: Dent, 1966.

———. "Lord Bacon." *Complete Writings*. Westminster Edition, 4:1–165. New York: Brampton Society, n.d.

MacCabe, Colin, ed. *Futures for English*. Manchester: Manchester University Press, 1988.

Maccoby, Simon, ed. *The English Radical Tradition, 1763–1914*. London: Black, 1952.

MacEwan, Arthur. *Debt and Disorder: International Economic Instability and U.S. Imperial Decline*. New York: Monthly Review Press, 1990.

Mackay, Charles. *Extraordinary Popular Delusions and the Madness of Crowds*. 1841, 1852. New York: L. C. Page, 1932.

MacKenzie, John M. *Propaganda and Empire: The Manipulation of British Public Opinion, 1880–1960*. Manchester: University of Manchester Press, 1984.

McKeon, Michael. *The Origins of the English Novel, 1600–1740*. Baltimore: Johns Hopkins University Press, 1988.

MacKinnon, William A. *On the Rise, Progress, and Present State of Public Opinion in Great Britain and the Rest of the World*. 1828. Shannon: Irish University Press, 1971.

McLuhan, Marshall. *The Gutenberg Galaxy*. Toronto: University of Toronto Press, 1962.

Macpherson, Crawford B. *The Political Theory of Possessive Individualism: Hobbes to Locke*. Oxford: Clarendon, 1962.

Malkin, Lawrence. *The National Debt: How America Crashed into a Black Hole and How We Can Crawl Out of It*. New York: New American Library, 1987.

Mandel, Ernest. *Late Capitalism*. London: New Left Books, 1975.

Mannoni, Octave. *Clefs pour l'imaginaire ou l'autre scéne*. Paris: Seuil, 1969.

Manuel, Frank E. *The Eighteenth Century Confronts the Gods*. Cambridge: Harvard University Press, 1959.

Marcus, Greil. *Lipstick Traces: A Secret History of the Twentieth Century*. Cambridge: Harvard University Press, 1989.

Marinetti, Filippo Tommaso. "The Futurist Manifesto." In *Italian Fascisms from Pareto to Gentile*, ed. Adrian Lyttelton, 209–221. London: Cape, 1973.

Martineau, Harriet. *Dawn Island: A Tale*. Manchester: J. Gadsby, 1845.

———. *The Farrers of Budge Row*. Vol. 9 of *Illustrations of Political Economy*. London: Charles Fox, 1834.

Marx, Karl. *Capital*. 3 vols. London: Penguin, 1976, 1978, 1981.

———. *Grundrisse*. London: Penguin Books, 1973.

Marx, Karl, and Friedrich Engels. "Manifesto of the Communist Party." In *The Marx-Engels Reader*, ed. Robert C. Tucker, 469–500. New York: Norton, 1978.

——. *On Colonialism*. New York: International Publishers, 1972.

——. *On Literature and Art*. Moscow: Progress, 1978.

Matthew, H. C. G. "Disraeli, Gladstone, and the Politics of Mid-Victorian Budgets." *Historical Journal* 22 (1979): 615–643.

Meisel, Perry. *The Myth of the Modern: A Study in British Literature and Criticism after 1850*. New Haven: Yale University Press, 1987.

Mestrović, Stjepan G. *The Barbarian Temperament: Toward a Postmodern Critical Theory*. London: Routledge, 1993.

Metz, Christian. *The Imaginary Signifier: Psychoanalysis and the Cinema*. Bloomington: Indiana University Press, 1982.

Michaels, Walter Benn. *The Gold Standard and the Logic of Naturalism: American Literature at the Turn of the Century*. Berkeley and Los Angeles: University of California Press, 1987.

Mill, James. *The History of British India*. 1817. Chicago: University of Chicago Press, 1975.

——. *Selected Economic Writings*. Ed. Donald Winch. Chicago: University of Chicago Press, 1966.

Mill, John Stuart. "Civilization." 1836. In *Mill's Essays on Literature and Society*. ed. J. B. Schneewind, 148–182. New York: Crowell Collier and Macmillan, 1965.

——. *Of Representative Government*. 1861. New York: Liberal Arts Press, 1958.

Miller, Andrew. "*Vanity Fair* through Plate Glass." *PMLA* 105 (1990): 1042–1054.

Miller, Michael. *The Bon Marché: Bourgeois Culture and the Department Store, 1869–1920*. Princeton: Princeton University Press, 1981.

Mini, Piero V. *Keynes, Bloomsbury and the General Theory*. New York: St. Martin's, 1991.

Misselden, Edward. *The Circle of Commerce, or the Balance of Trade*. 1623. New York: Augustus M. Kelley, 1971.

Mitchell, W. J. T. *Iconology: Image, Text, Ideology*. Chicago: University of Chicago Press, 1986.

Miyoshi, Masao. "A Borderless World? From Colonialism to Transnationalism and the Decline of the Nation-State." *Critical Inquiry* 19 (summer 1993): 726–751.

Montag, Warren. *The Unthinkable Swift: The Spontaneous Philosophy of a Church of England Man*. London: Verso, 1994.

Nairn, Tom. *The Break-up of Britain*. 1977. London: Verso, 1981.

——. *The Enchanted Glass: Britain and Its Monarchy*. London: Random Century, Hutchinson, 1988.

Nehring, Neil. *Flowers in the Dustbin: Culture, Anarchy, and Postwar England*. Ann Arbor: University of Michigan Press, 1993.

Nicholson, Colin. *Writing and the Rise of Finance: Capital Satires of the Early Eighteenth Century*. Cambridge: Cambridge University Press, 1994.

Nixon, Cornelia. *Lawrence's Leadership Politics and the Turn against Women*. Berkeley and Los Angeles: University of California Press, 1986.

Nokes, David. *Raillery and Rage: A Study of Eighteenth Century Satire*. New York: St. Martin's, 1987.

Nordau, Max. *Degeneration*. New York: Appleton, 1895.

Nunokawa, Jeff. *The Afterlife of Property: Domestic Security and the Victorian Novel*. Princeton: Princeton University Press, 1994.

Nussbaum, Felicity, and Laura Brown, eds. *The New Eighteenth Century: Theory, Politics, English Literature*. New York: Methuen, 1987.

O'Brien, Patrick. "The Imperial Component in the Decline of the British Economy before 1914." In *The Rise and Decline of the Nation State*, ed. Michael Mann, 12–46. Oxford: Blackwell, 1990.

Paine, Thomas. "The Decline and Fall of the English System of Finance." 1797. In *Writings*, ed. Moncure Daniel Conway, 3: 286–312. New York: AMS Press, 1967.

Palmer, Paul A. "The Concept of Public Opinion in Political Theory." In *Essays in History and Political Theory in Honor of Charles Howard McIlwain*, ed. Carl Wittke, 230–257. Cambridge: Harvard University Press, 1936.

Paxton, Nancy. *George Eliot and Herbert Spencer*. Princeton: Princeton University Press, 1991.

Payer, Cheryl. *The Debt Trap: The International Monetary Fund and the Third World*. New York: Monthly Review Press, 1974.

Peacock, Thomas Love. *Paper Money Lyrics*. In *Works*, Halliford Edition, 7:95–146. London: Constable, 1931.

Pêcheux, Michel. *Language, Semantics, and Ideology*. New York: St. Martin's, 1982.

Penty, Arthur J. *Post-Industrialism*. London: Allen and Unwin, 1922.

Perkin, Harold. *The Rise of Professional Society: England since 1880*. London: Routledge, 1989.

Pieterse, Jan Nederveen, and Bhikhu Parekh, eds. *Decolonization of Imagination*. London: Zed, 1995.

Pietz, William. "The Problem of the Fetish, I, II, and III." *Res* 9 (spring 1985); 5–17; 13 (spring 1987): 23–45; 16 (autumn 1988): 105–123.

Pitkin, Hannah Fenichel. *Fortune Is a Woman: Gender and Politics in the Thought of Niccolo Machiavelli*. Berkeley and Los Angeles: University of California Press, 1984.

Pitt, William. *Speeches*. 3 vols., 3d. ed. London: Longman, Hurst, Rees, Orme, and Brown, 1817.

Plumb, J. H. *The Growth of Political Stability in England, 1675–1725* Harmondsworth: Penguin, 1973.

Pocock, J. G. A. *The Machiavellian Moment: Florentine Political Thought and the Atlantic Republican Tradition*. Princeton: Princeton University Press, 1975.

——. "The Political Economy of Burke's Analysis of the French Revolution." *Historical Journal* 25 (1982): 331–349.

——. *Virtue, Commerce, and History: Essays on Political Thought and History, Chiefly in the Eighteenth Century*. Cambridge: Cambridge University Press, 1985.

Polanyi, Karl. *The Great Transformation.* New York: Farrar and Rinehart, 1944.

Pope, Alexander. *Poems.* ed. John Butt. New Haven: Yale University Press, 1963.

Powell, Ellis T. *The Evolution of the Money Market, 1385–1915.* London: Financial News, 1916.

Price, Martin. *To the Palace of Wisdom: Studies in Order and Energy from Dryden to Blake.* New York: Doubleday, 1964.)

Rasler, Karen A., and William R. Thompson. "The Innovation of Public Debt." In *War and State Making: The Shaping of the Global Powers,* 89–118. Winchester, Mass.: Unwin Hyman, 1989.

Rawson, Claude. *Order from Confusion Sprung: Studies in Eighteenth-Century Literature from Swift to Cowper.* London: Allen and Unwin, 1985.

Ray, Gordon. *Thackeray: The Uses of Adversity.* 2 vols. New York: McGraw-Hill, 1955–1958.

Reed, John R. "A Friend to Mammon: Speculation in Victorian Literature." *Victorian Studies* 27 (winter 1984): 179–202.

Rees, James Frederick. *A Short Fiscal and Financial History of England, 1815–1918* London: Methuen, 1921.

Ricardo, David. *The Principles of Political Economy and Taxation.* New York: Dutton, Everyman's Library, n.d.

Richards, Thomas. *The Commodity Culture of Victorian Britain: Advertising and Spectacle, 1851–1914.* Stanford: Stanford University Press, 1990.

———. *The Imperial Archive: Knowledge and the Fantasy of Empire.* London: Verso, 1993.

Rist, Charles. *History of Monetary Theory and Credit from John Law to the Present Day.* New York: Macmillan, 1940.

Rogers, Pat. *The Augustan Vision.* London: Weidenfeld and Nicolson, 1974.

Rose, Sir George Henry, ed. *Merchant Papers.* 3 vols. London: John Murray, 1831.

Rotman, Brian. *Signifying Nothing: The Semiotics of Zero.* New York: St. Martin's, 1987.

Rousseau, Jean Jacques. *The Social Contract and Discourses.* Ed. G. D. H. Cole. London: Dent, Everyman's Library, 1950.

Rushdie, Salman. *Imaginary Homelands: Essays and Criticism, 1981–1991* London: Granta Books, 1991.

———. *Midnight's Children.* 1980. New York: Penguin, 1991.

Ruskin, John. *Fors Clavigera.* Vols. 27, 28, and 29 of *Works.* Ed. E. T. Cook and Alexander Wedderburn. London: George Allen, 1903–1912.

———. *Munera Pulveris.* Vol. 17 of *Works.*

Russell, Norman. *The Novelist and Mammon: Literary Responses to the World of Commerce in the Nineteenth Century.* Oxford: Clarendon, 1986.

Saab, Ann Pottinger. "Disraeli, Judaism, and the Eastern Question." *International History Review* 10 (November 1988): 517–688.

Sadleir, Michael. Introduction to *Autobiography,* by Anthony Trollope.

Said, Edward. *Culture and Imperialism.* New York: Knopf, 1993.

———. *Orientalism.* New York: Random House, 1978.

——. *The World, the Text, and the Critic.* Cambridge: Harvard University Press, 1983.

Saintsbury, George. *The Peace of the Augustans: A Survey of Eighteenth-Century Literature as a Place of Rest and Refreshment.* New York: Russell and Russell, 1916.

Samuel, Raphael, ed. *Patriotism: The Making and Unmaking of British National Identity.* 3 vols. London: Routledge, 1989.

Schabas, Margaret. "The Worldly Philosophy of William Stanley Jevons." In *Energy and Entropy: Science and Culture in Victorian Britain,* ed. Patrick Brantlinger, 229–247. Bloomington: Indiana University Press, 1989.

Scott, Bonnie Kime, ed. *The Gender of Modernism: A Critical Anthology.* Bloomington: Indiana University Press, 1990.

Scott, Sir Walter. *Letters.* Ed. H. J. C. Grierson. 12 vols. London: Constable, 1932.

——. *The Prefaces to the Waverly Novels.* Ed. Mark A. Weinstein. Lincoln: University of Nebraska Press, 1978.

——. *Two Letters on Scottish Affairs, from Edward Bradwardine Waverley, Esq. to Malachi Malagrowther.* London: John Murray, 1826.

Sedgwick, Eve Kosofsky. *Between Men: English Literature and Male Homosocial Desire.* New York: Columbia University Press, 1985.

Sekora, John. *Luxury: The Concept in Western Thought, Eden to Smollett.* Baltimore: Johns Hopkins University Press, 1977.

Semmel, Bernard. *The Liberal Ideal and the Demons of Empire: Theories of Imperialism from Adam Smith to Lenin.* Baltimore: Johns Hopkins University Press, 1993.

Shell, Mark. *Money, Language, and Thought: Literary and Philosophical Economies from the Medieval to the Modern Era.* Berkeley and Los Angeles: University of California Press, 1982.

Shelley, Percy Bysshe. "A Philosophical View of Reform." In *Shelley's Prose, or The Trumpet of a Prophecy,* ed. David Lee Clark, 229–261. Albuquerque: University of New Mexico Press, 1954.

——. *Poetical Works.* Ed. Thomas Hutchinson. London: Oxford University Press, 1970.

Shoup, Carl S. *Ricardo on Taxation.* New York: Columbia University Press, 1960.

Silver, Harold. *The Concept of Popular Education.* London: MacGibbon and Kee, 1965.

Simmel, Georg. *The Philosophy of Money.* New York: Routledge, 1990.

——. *The Sociology of Georg Simmel.* Ed. Kurt H. Wolff. Glencoe, Ill.: Free Press, 1950.

Simpson, David. *Fetishism and Imagination: Dickens, Melville, Conrad.* Baltimore: Johns Hopkins University Press, 1982.

Sinclair, Keith. *A History of New Zealand.* Harmondsworth: Penguin, 1969.

Sinfield, Alan. *Literature, Politics, and Culture in Postwar Britain.* Berkeley and Los Angeles: University of California Press, 1989.

Sitter, John. *Arguments of Augustan Wit.* Cambridge: Cambridge University Press, 1991.

Sklair, Leslie. *Sociology of the Global System.* Baltimore: Johns Hopkins University Press, 1991.

Smith, Adam. *The Wealth of Nations.* 1776. New York: Random House, Modern Library, 1965.

Smith, David. *The Rise and Fall of Monetarism.* London: Penguin Books, 1987.

Smith, Grahame. *Dickens, Money, and Society.* Berkeley and Los Angeles: University of California Press, 1968.

Smith, Michael Peter. "Can You Imagine? Transnational Migration and the Globalization of Grassroots Politics." *Social Text* 39 (summer 1994): 15–33.

Snyder, Jack. *Myths of Empire: Domestic Politics and International Ambition.* Ithaca: Cornell University Press, 1991.

Speare, Morris. *The Political Novel.* New York: Oxford University Press, 1924.

Spence, William. *Tracts on Political Economy.* London: Hurst, Rees, Orme, and Brown, 1822.

Spencer, Herbert. *The Man versus the State, with Four Essays on Politics and Society,* 1884. Ed. Donald MacRae. (Harmondsworth: Penguin, 1969.

Stabile, Donald R., and Jeffrey A. Cantor. *The Public Debt of the United States: An Historical Perspective, 1775–1990.* New York: Praeger, 1991.

Stone, Lawrence, ed. *An Imperial State at War: Britain from 1689 to 1815.* New York: Routledge, 1994.

Sudrann, Jean. "*Daniel Deronda* and the Landscape of Exile." *ELH* 37 (1970): 433–455.

Suleri, Sara. *The Rhetoric of English India.* Chicago: University of Chicago Press, 1992.

Sutherland, C. H. V. *English Coinage, 600–1900.* London: Batsford, 1973.

Swift, Graham. *Waterland.* London: Heinemann, 1983.

Swift, Jonathan. *The Examiner, 1710–1711.* In *Prose Works,* ed. Herbert Davis, vol. 3. Oxford: Blackwell, 1966.

——. *Gulliver's Travels.* New York: Norton, 1970.

——. *The History of the Four Last Years of the Queen.* Ed. Herbert Davis. Oxford: Basil Blackwell, 1951.

——. *Poetical Works.* Ed. Herbert Davis. London: Oxford University Press, 1967.

Taussig, Michael. *The Devil and Commodity Fetishism in South America.* Chapel Hill: University of North Carolina Press, 1980.

——. *The Nervous System.* New York: Routledge, 1992.

Thackeray, William Makepeace. *The Newcomes.* 1853–55. 2 vols. London: Dent, Everyman's Library, 1962.

——. *Vanity Fair.* 1847–48. Boston: Houghton Mifflin, Riverside, 1963.

Thornton, Henry. *An Enquiry into the Nature and Effects of the Paper Credit of Great Britain.* 1802. Ed. F. A. von Hayek. New York: Farrar and Rinehart, 1939.

Tilden, Freeman. *A World in Debt.* New York: Funk and Wagnalls, 1936.

Tilly, Charles. *Coercion, Capital, and European States, A.D. 990–1990.* Oxford: Blackwell, 1990.

Torgovnick, Marianna. *Gone Primitive: Savage Intellects, Modern Lives.* Chicago: University of Chicago Press, 1990.

Torrens, Robert. *Essay on the Production of Wealth.* 1821. New York: Kelley, 1965.

[Trenchard, John, and Thomas Gordon]. *Cato's Letters.* Vol. 1. New York: Da Capo, 1971).

Trollope, Anthony. *Autobiography.* 1883. Oxford: Oxford University Press, World's Classics, 1953.

——. *Phineas Finn, the Irish Member.* 1869. 2 vols. in 1. New York: Oxford University Press, 1973.

——. *The Way We Live Now.* 1875. 2 vols. in 1. Oxford: Oxford University Press, World's Classics, 1951.

Vaughn, Karen I. "Invisible Hand." In *The New Palgrave: A Dictionary of Economics,* 2:997–998. London: Macmillan, 1987.

Veblen, Thorstein. *The Theory of the Leisure Class.* New York: Penguin, 1979.

Vernon, John. *Money and Fiction: Literary Realism in the Nineteenth and Early Twentieth Centuries.* Ithaca: Cornell University Press, 1984.

Veseth, Michael. *Mountains of Debt: Crisis and Change in Renaissance Florence, Victorian Britain, and Postwar America.* New York: Oxford University Press, 1990.

Vickers, Douglas. *Studies in the Theory of Money, 1690–1776.* Philadelphia: Chilton, 1959.

Vilar, Pierre. *A History of Gold and Money, 1450–1920.* London: New Left, 1976.

Vincent, John. *Disraeli.* Oxford: Oxford University Press, 1980.

Vološinov, V. N. *Marxism and the Philosophy of Language.* Cambridge: Harvard University Press, 1973.

Voltaire. *L'Ingénu—Micromegas.* 1767. Ed. Jacques Spica. Paris: Bordas, 1977.

Warren, Samuel. *Ten Thousand A-Year.* 1841. In *Works,* vols. 2, 3. Edinburgh: Blackwood, 1854.

Watt, Ian. *The Rise of the Novel.* Berkeley and Los Angeles: University of California Press, 1959.

Weiss, Barbara. *The Hell of the English: Bankruptcy and the Victorian Novel.* Lewisburg, Penn.: Bucknell University Press, 1986.

Wells, David. *Marxism and the Modern State: An Analysis of Fetishism in Capitalist Society.* Brighton, England: Harvester, 1981.

Wells, H. G. *Tono-Bungay.* 1909. Boston: Houghton Mifflin, 1966.

Wicke, Jennifer. "Modernity Must Advertise: Aura, Desire, and Decolonization in Joyce." *James Joyce Quarterly* 30/31 (summer/fall 1993): 593–613.

Wiener, Martin. *English Culture and the Decline of the Industrial Spirit, 1850–1980.* Cambridge: Cambridge University Press, 1980.

Williams, Glyndwr. "'The Inexhaustible Fountain of Gold': English Projects and Ventures in the South Seas, 1670–1750." In *Perspectives of Empire,* ed. John E. Flint and Glyndwr Williams, 27–53. New York: Harper and Row, 1973.

Williams, Raymond. "Base and Superstructure in Marxist Cultural Theory." In *Problems in Materialism and Culture,* 31–49. London: Verso, 1980.

——. "The Bloomsbury Fraction." In *Problems in Materialism and Culture,* 148–169.

——. *Culture and Society, 1780–1950.* New York: Columbia University Press, 1983.

——. *Resources of Hope.* London: Verso, 1989.

Williams, Rosalind. *Dream Worlds: Mass Consumption in Late Nineteenth-Century France.* Berkeley and Los Angeles: University of California Press, 1982.

Wills, W. H. "Review of a Popular Publication." *Household Words* 27 July 1850, 426–431.

Wilson, Arthur M. "Enlightenment Came First to England." In *England's Rise to Greatness, 1660–1763,* ed. Stephen Baxter, 1–28. Berkeley and Los Angeles: University of California Press, 1983.

Wilson, Charles. *England's Apprenticeship, 1603–1763.* (New York: St. Martin's, 1965.

Winch, Donald. *Classical Political Economy and Colonies.* London: Bell, 1965.

Wolin, Richard. *Walter Benjamin: An Aesthetic of Redemption.* New York: Columbia University Press, 1982.

Woolf, Virginia. *Mrs. Dalloway.* 1925. New York: Harcourt Brace Jovanovich, 1981.

——. *A Room of One's Own.* 1929. New York: Harcourt Brace Jovanovich, 1957.

——. *Three Guineas.* 1938. New York: Harcourt Brace Jovanovich, 1966.

——. *The Voyage Out.* 1915. New York: Harcourt Brace Jovanovich, 1948.

Young, Robert. *White Mythologies: Writing History and the West.* London: Routledge, 1990.

Žižek, Slavoj. *Enjoy Your Symptom!* New York: Routledge, 1992.

——. *For They Know Not What They Do: Enjoyment as a Political Factor.* London: Verso, 1991.

——. *The Sublime Object of Ideology.* London: Verso, 1989.

INDEX

accounting, 24, 76–77, 106, 150, 156, 158, 163–165
Adams, Henry, 190
Addison, Joseph, 55–57, 85–86, 144, 160
Adorno, Theodor, 23, 32, 65, 125, 126, 189, 194, 261
advertising, 5, 13, 79, 99, 147, 166, 167, 189, 190–191, 193, 194, 200, 203–205, 207–211, 228. *See also* commodity; consumerism
Africa, 5, 12, 17, 42, 43, 59–60, 74, 81–84, 124, 127, 185, 199, 208, 212, 231, 245, 249, 257. *See also* Rhodesia; South Africa
alchemy, 6, 25, 41, 46–47, 56, 58, 60, 64, 86, 149, 152, 206, 258
Algeria, 5, 81
Althusser, Louis, 6, 15, 173, 234, 250
America. *See* Canada; South America; United States; West Indies
American Revolution, 38, 51, 88, 89, 100, 103, 116, 140, 185, 237
Amis, Martin, 4, 7, 258–260, 263
Anderson, Benedict, 4, 11–13, 16, 40, 99, 142–143, 183
Anderson, Perry, 31, 237
Anne, Queen, 53, 54, 70, 72
Anti-Corn Law League, 140, 186
anti-Semitism, 115, 156, 167, 175, 179, 181, 182, 197, 202
Apollinaire, Guillaume, 212
Arabia, 175–178, 180, 182
Arbuthnot, Dr. John, 48
Arcot, Nabob of, 107–108, 119
Argentina, 237, 242
Arnold, Matthew, 22, 118, 129, 180, 190–191, 196, 204, 217, 219, 221, 222, 261
Asia, 12, 199. *See also specific nation-states*
Atkins, John, 42, 43
Augustan period. *See* Enlightenment

Augustan satire, 4, 41–42, 47, 48–75, 85–86, 94, 118, 133–134, 143, 144–145, 149, 160, 168, 171, 206, 210. *See also* Gay, John; Pope, Alexander; Swift, Jonathan
Austen, Jane, 151, 171, 223, 246
Australia, 12, 141, 185, 188

Bacon, Sir Francis, 31, 129, 137
Bagehot, Walter, 39
Ballantyne, John, 152
Ballantyne, R. M., 43
Ballard, J. G., 239
Balzac, Honoré, 23, 45, 78, 86, 87, 138, 147, 151–152, 154, 158
Bangladesh, 251
Bank of Amsterdam, 36
Bank of England, 3, 7, 18, 22, 31, 36, 39, 47, 54, 55, 57, 58, 63, 66, 73, 89, 102, 105, 110–115, 132–142, 144, 157, 159–162, 172, 227, 237, 253
bank reform acts (1826, 1833, 1844), 139–141, 162
Bantock, G. H., 204
Baring, Sir Francis, 160
Baudelaire, Charles, 79, 86, 146–148, 193, 204, 211, 212
Baudrillard, Jean, 5, 8–9, 24, 44, 64, 79, 99, 251, 261
Bayle, Pierre, 124
Beard, George, 196
Beardsley, Aubrey, 193
Beatles, the, 260
Beckett, Samuel, 244, 245
Bell, Clive, 224
Belloc, Hilaire, 192
Benjamin, Walter, 79, 146–148, 193, 204, 261
Bennett, Arnold, 205

Bentham, Jeremy, 104–105, 178, 185, 219–220

Berkeley, George, 33, 34, 36, 91–92, 94, 95, 97, 104, 105, 125, 137

Beveridge Report, 253

Blackmore, Sir Richard, 48, 64

Blackstone, Sir William, 142

Blake, William, 7, 62, 78, 80, 111–112, 114, 126, 137, 141, 153

Bloomsbury, 201, 217–234

Boer War, 13, 195, 199

Bolingbroke, Henry St. John, 6–7, 36, 39, 48–49, 60, 62, 68, 73–74, 85, 94, 95, 149, 195, 197

Bolívar, Simón, 214

Bond, Edward, 239, 254

bookkeeping. *See* accounting

Boucicault, Aristide, 146

Boucicault, Dion, 145–146

Boyle, Robert, 66

Bradbury, Malcolm, 254–256

Brazil, 2, 4, 81

Bright, John, 100

British Empire. *See* imperialism; *specific colonies*

Brontës (Anne, Charlotte, and Emily), 152

Brossis, Charles de, 124, 236

Buchan, John, 208, 244

bullionist controversy (1797–1821), 112–114

Bulwer-Lytton, Edward, 145

Burgess, Anthony, 239, 244, 263

Burke, Edmund, 31, 39, 51, 88, 94, 95, 97, 99, 104, 105–110, 118, 119, 126, 128, 133, 149

Bush, George, 3, 256

Cambodia, 242

Canada, 1, 81, 185, 241

capitalism, 3, 5–6, 9, 13, 16, 21, 22, 25–28, 31–47, 51, 53, 62, 64, 74–75, 77–87, 92, 96, 98, 99, 101–102, 125, 138–150, 152, 158–171, 174, 186–199, 204, 213–216, 235–243, 248–249, 250, 252–253, 256. *See also* commodity/commodification

Caribbean. *See* West Indies

Carlyle, Thomas, 33, 99, 118, 137–138, 176, 196

Carpenter, Edward, 195

Cary, Joyce, 244

Cavalcanti, Giovanni, 55

Ceylon (Sri Lanka), 81, 251–252

Chamberlain, Joseph, 16

Charcot, Jean-Martin, 199

Charles I, 42

Charles II, 53

Chartism, 134, 140, 176

Chatterjee, Partha, 17, 248, 250–251

Chesney, Sir George, 243–244

Childers, Erskine, 244

China, 188, 241

Christensen, Jerome, 34, 95, 98, 106, 129

Churchill, Caryl, 7, 42, 256–259

Churchill, Winston, 206

cinema, 7, 8, 190, 194, 238, 258–260

Civil War (American), 140, 190

Civil War (British), 31, 51, 66, 237

classicism, 41–42, 49–50, 53, 61, 109, 219. *See also* Augustan satire

Cobbett, William, 93, 104, 114–118, 126, 131–135, 136, 141, 195, 206

Cobden, Richard, 100

Coleridge, Samuel Taylor, 7, 78, 90–91, 114, 119, 126–135, 138, 196, 219, 222

Colley, Linda, 6, 18–19, 51, 88, 89

commodity/commodification, 5–6, 7, 8, 23, 25, 26, 28–29, 34–35, 36, 41, 48, 51, 53, 61–63, 64, 69, 76, 79, 82–83, 86–87, 98, 101–102, 106, 112, 123–124, 125, 144, 146–150, 152–154, 156, 157, 163–172, 183–184, 187, 189, 190, 193, 194, 199, 200, 204–205, 206, 207–211, 241, 251, 257–258, 260, 261. *See also* advertising; capitalism; fetishism; luxury; prostitution

community, 8, 13, 22, 40, 97, 142, 174, 184, 189, 220, 237, 241. *See also* Anderson, Benedict; mass communications

Comte, Auguste, 124–125, 138

Connolly, Cyril, 204

Conrad, Joseph, 7, 21, 43, 72, 81, 82, 195, 200–201, 203, 207, 208, 211, 212–217, 221, 222, 239, 243–244, 249

conservatism. *See* monetarism; Reagan, Ronald; Thatcher, Margaret; Tory Party

consumerism, 28, 29, 36, 79, 92, 139, 141, 146–150, 189–191, 193, 194, 196–197, 200, 203–205, 207–211. *See also* advertising; commodity/commodification; luxury

Coomaraswamy, Ananda, 251–252

counterfeit money, 24, 34, 41, 47, 48, 49, 86, 112, 142, 152, 158, 161, 167–169, 171, 198, 206–207, 209–210
Courbet, Gustave, 139
credit. *See* debt, private; public credit
credit and trade cycles, 130–131, 133, 161, 207–211. *See also* depression, economic
Crédit Mobilier, 138, 161
Crimean War, 190
Cruikshank, George, 147, 169
Cruikshank, Isaac, 147
culture. *See* high culture; mass communications; mass culture; national cultures
Czechoslovakia, 1

Darwin, Charles/Darwinism, 14, 23, 139, 154, 179–180, 187, 188, 191, 192, 195
Davenant, Charles, 54
debt, private, 26, 28, 76–77, 133, 139, 141–146, 151–162, 163, 166–168, 205. *See also* international debt crisis; national debt; public credit
decadent movement, 193, 217, 221
Defoe, Daniel, 1, 23, 47, 54–57, 59, 74–85, 87, 95, 143–144, 150, 156, 162, 164
democracy/democratization, 17–18, 22, 99, 106, 173, 178, 179, 190, 191–192, 194, 204, 219, 256. *See also* American Revolution; French Revolution; liberalism; public opinion
depression, economic, 25, 102, 140, 141, 190, 206, 220, 222, 253. *See also* credit and trade cycles
Derrida, Jacques, 9, 11, 24, 86–87, 147, 148, 206
Dickens, Charles, 4, 45, 55, 79, 87, 136, 142–146, 150–154, 157–165, 169–172, 173, 203, 207
Disraeli, Benjamin, 16, 135, 137, 141, 143, 152, 173–183
Dostoyevsky, Fyodor, 211
Douglas, Major C. H., 197
Dowson, Lionel, 217
Doyle, Sir Arthur Conan, 192
Drake, Sir Francis, 182
Dreiser, Theodore, 139

East India Company, 34, 74, 76, 107–108, 118
East Indies, 37, 76, 84

economics, 4, 7, 8, 14, 23, 28–29, 30–37, 46, 66–68, 75–85, 88–107, 111–119, 123–133, 136–142, 161, 169, 170, 185–192, 194, 195, 200, 217–223, 230, 253–254. *See also* accounting; capitalism; monetarism; utilitarianism
Education Act (1870), 196
Egypt, 247
Eliot, George, 143, 144, 145, 146, 165, 173–175, 178–183, 221, 223
Eliot, T. S., 42, 201, 203, 212, 213, 221, 228, 243
Ellis, Havelock, 199
empire. *See* imperialism
empiricism, 31, 32, 71, 78, 83, 91, 95, 129
Engels, Friedrich, 74, 150, 188, 204
English literature. *See* national cultures
Enlightenment, the, 4, 5, 9, 17, 20–23, 26, 31, 38, 41, 44, 45, 53, 65–66, 99, 102, 106, 109, 118, 123, 124–125, 185, 203, 224, 234, 244, 248, 249–250, 261
Eurocentrism, 5, 9, 42, 202
Euromoney, 24–25, 28, 259
European Union, 253

Falklands war, 237–238, 240, 242
Fanon, Frantz, 248–249
fascism, 2, 13, 19, 32, 176, 197, 202, 217, 219, 222, 227, 261. *See also* Futurism; Nazism
Federalist Papers, 103
feminism, 223–234
fetishism, 3, 4, 5–6, 8–9, 10, 20–21, 23, 25–26, 28–30, 36, 40–44, 46, 53, 58, 59–61, 64, 67–69, 73, 79, 82–83, 86–87, 90–91, 101–102, 107, 108–110, 113, 115, 118, 119, 123, 124–127, 133, 146–151, 154, 159, 168, 169–171, 187, 189, 192–195, 199–207, 210, 212–217, 226–229, 231–234, 236–243, 249, 251, 257–258, 261, 262. *See also* alchemy; phallocentrism
Fielding, Henry, 84, 150
Flaubert, Gustave, 87
Fleming, Ian, 244
Forster, E. M., 112, 221, 223, 224, 243
Foucault, Michel, 8, 10, 11, 21, 41, 212, 232, 246, 249–250
Fourierism, 194

France, 6, 10, 17, 18, 22, 26, 31, 32, 37, 38, 47, 51, 52, 57, 68, 70, 73, 82, 89, 101, 105–110, 112, 126, 138, 140, 146, 156, 161, 179, 193, 199, 204, 225, 237, 239
Francis, J. F., 162
Frazer, Sir James, 201
French Revolution (1789), 51, 88, 94, 97, 105–110, 138, 140, 237
Freud, Sigmund, 5, 6, 8, 43–44, 73, 108, 147, 170, 195, 199–204, 221–222, 226
Fry, Roger, 201, 221, 224
Futurism, 193–194

Gallagher, Catherine, 54, 138, 143, 161
Galsworthy, John, 205
Galt, John, 173
Gamble, Andrew, 238, 243, 244, 253, 260
Gandhi, Mohandas K., 251–252
Gaskell, Elizabeth, 140, 143, 145, 223
Gauguin, Paul, 200
Gay, John, 47, 48–51, 60
George I, 42, 56
George III, 53
George IV, 42
Germany, 1, 15, 26, 140, 190, 196, 218, 219, 220, 225, 227
Ghana, 245, 257
Gide, André, 41, 206, 207, 210
Gillray, James, 56, 118–121, 141, 147
Gissing, George, 139, 152, 153–154, 162, 164, 168–172, 173, 174, 191, 205, 207
Gladstone, William, 102, 137, 140
Glanvill, Joseph, 78
Glorious Revolution (1688), 38, 47, 49, 51, 62, 64, 70, 71, 105, 116, 133, 135, 176
Goethe, Johann Wolfgang von, 8, 26, 41, 46–47, 87, 108, 117, 119, 123, 151
gold standard, 23, 24, 25, 35–36, 40, 45, 55–56, 83, 86, 88, 92, 93, 109, 110–114, 117, 123, 141, 144, 158, 169, 205–207, 209, 217, 218, 221
Gordon, Thomas, 59
Gore, Catherine, 145
Goux, Jean-Joseph, 24, 123, 144, 205–207
Grandville, 147, 169
Great Exhibition (1851). See World Exhibitions
Greece, 41, 85, 106, 109
Gresham, Sir Thomas, 93

Haggard, H. Rider, 208
Hamilton, Alexander, 103–104
Hardy, Thomas, 86, 151
Harley, Edward (earl of Oxford), 49, 68
Hastings, Warren, 107–108
Hazlitt, William, 99
Hegel, G. W. F., 6, 10, 11, 126–130, 192, 225, 250
Henry VIII, 175, 176
Herder, Johann Gottfried, 10
high culture, 7, 123, 143–144, 152, 154, 164–166, 168, 192, 194, 198, 204, 209, 217–223, 261
Hilferding, Rudolf, 195
Hitler, Adolf, 219, 232
Hobbes, Thomas, 6, 32, 33, 79, 81–82, 186
Hobsbawm, Eric, 3, 12–13, 18, 102, 190, 236, 250
Hobson, John A., 13, 107, 134, 191, 192, 195–199, 203–204, 214, 228
Hogarth, William, 60–61, 64, 106, 147
Hoggart, Richard, 204
Holland. See Netherlands
Hong Kong, 247
Horkheimer, Max, 32, 65, 125, 126, 189, 261
Hume, David, 7, 11, 33, 34, 62–63, 91–99, 104, 105, 113, 124, 125, 129, 132, 137
Huysmans, Joris-Karl, 193
Hyndman, H. M., 191

Ian, Marcia, 54, 201–203, 223, 233–234
immigration/immigrants, 2, 19, 93, 239, 246–248
imperialism, 2, 3, 4, 5, 6–22, 26, 27, 29, 31–47, 49, 51, 57, 58, 61–63, 66, 67, 69–73, 74, 79, 81–84, 88, 89, 91, 93, 100–105, 107–108, 110, 114, 116, 117–118, 119, 125, 129, 132–135, 139–143, 145, 149–150, 162, 167, 171, 173, 174, 177–184, 185–192, 195–201, 203, 207–211, 212–214, 223–229, 236–252, 255–257, 262
impressionism, 10, 205, 213, 215, 220–221, 223–224, 229
India, 1, 2, 17, 19, 26, 34, 38, 45, 72, 100, 103, 104–105, 107–108, 128, 133, 149, 156–157, 180, 185, 187–188, 190, 205, 224, 226, 230, 231, 239, 241, 242, 244–252

individualism, 16–17, 18, 20, 32–33, 75, 123, 170, 174, 191–192, 200, 217, 224
industrialization/Industrial Revolution, 3, 5, 7, 13, 16, 18–19, 21, 26, 31, 38, 44–46, 75, 79, 88–90, 98, 101–103, 111, 114, 118, 128, 138–143, 152–153, 164, 170, 176, 190–192, 194, 196, 204, 208, 211, 236–243, 248, 251–253. *See also* postindustrialism
inflation, 25, 45, 218–219, 222
Ingham, Geoffrey, 237
international debt crisis, 5, 8, 26–28, 29, 100, 103, 184, 244
International Monetary Fund, 103, 237, 256
Iran, 17
Iraq, 1
Ireland, 2, 18, 19, 26, 49, 53, 66, 91, 100, 140, 183, 190, 226, 239, 241, 242, 244–246, 255, 259, 263
Ishiguro, Kazuo, 247
Israel, 2, 181
Italy, 26, 37, 156, 181, 219, 220, 227, 230

Jacobitism, 55, 89
James, G. P. R., 158
James, Henry, 139, 151, 191, 205
Jameson, Fredric, 5, 27, 143, 153, 194, 213
Japan, 15, 26, 247, 255
Jarman, Derek, 7, 238–239, 262, 263
Jevons, William Stanley, 191
Johnson, Lionel, 217
Johnson, Samuel, 52, 62, 76, 78
Johnstone, Charles, 85–86, 148, 150–151, 154, 162
journalism, 4, 13, 31, 73, 76, 99, 142–143, 154, 166, 184, 190, 193, 195–199, 211, 228, 243
Joyce, James, 194, 200, 201, 205, 228, 243, 244, 245

Kafka, Franz, 245–246
Kant, Immanuel, 65, 73, 185, 244
Keynes, John Maynard, 7, 105, 205, 207, 217–223, 227, 230, 241, 252–253
Kidd, Benjamin, 188
Kierkegaard, Søren, 98–99
Kingsley, Charles, 143, 175, 180, 182–183
Kipling, Rudyard, 14, 244
Knights, L. C., 244

Kramnick, Isaac, 36, 48–49, 53, 59, 73, 74

Labour Party, 19, 190, 238, 252–253
Lacan, Jacques, 8, 27, 29, 65, 234
Laing, R. D., 232
Larkin, Philip, 238, 263
Law, John, 46–47, 57, 139
Lawrence, D. H., 185, 201–205, 207, 217, 218, 222, 224, 227
Leavis, F. R., 204, 217, 244, 261
Le Bon, Gustave, 44, 195
Le Carré, John, 244
Lecky, W. E. H., 138–139
Lenin, V. I., 134, 199
Lessing, Doris, 245, 247
Lewis, Wyndham, 217
liberalism, 17, 18, 22, 31–33, 40, 53, 91, 99–100, 125, 133, 170, 180–181, 185, 191, 218–224, 238, 253. *See also* democracy/democratization; Whig Party/Whiggism
Lincoln, Abraham, 241
literature. *See* Augustan satire; high culture; impressionism; modernism; national cultures; novels
Lippmann, Walter, 99
Livingstone, David, 82, 213
Locke, John, 24, 25, 31, 33
Lowe, Robert, 196
Luxemburg, Rosa, 134
luxury, 52, 60–64, 72, 73, 76, 79, 86, 91–94, 190. *See also* commodity; commodification; consumerism
Lyotard, Jean-François, 9, 10, 24, 27, 28–29, 40, 235, 246, 248

Macaulay, Thomas Babington, 19, 51, 70, 129, 133–134, 137, 138, 162
MacEwan, Ian, 239
Machiavelli, Niccolò, 55
Mackay, Charles, 58
MacKinnon, William, 99
MacLeod, Henry Dunning, 205
McLuhan, Marshall, 11, 212
Major, John, 18
Mallarmé, Stéphane, 193
Malthus, Thomas, 33, 90, 126, 186
Mandeville, Bernard, 33
Martineau, Harriet, 135, 152, 186–187
Marx, Karl, 3, 6, 8, 22, 23–24, 25, 37–38, 41, 53, 72, 73, 74–75, 82, 101–102,

Marx, Karl (*cont.*)
    124–125, 138, 139, 140, 146, 147–
    150, 169, 186, 188, 189, 194, 195,
    199, 204, 211, 212, 218, 220, 237, 240,
    255
Marxism, 3, 4, 5, 6, 8, 19, 21, 35, 123,
    191, 206, 222–223, 251–252
mass communications, 4, 99, 190, 193–
    194, 196, 205, 211, 237–238, 260–261
mass culture, 7, 13, 32, 79, 99, 143, 190,
    191, 192–194, 196–199, 203–205,
    209, 211, 213, 228, 247, 260–263. *See
    also* advertising; cinema; journalism;
    mass communications
materialism, 23, 32, 71, 78, 87, 124–125,
    127, 138–143, 146, 148, 151, 153,
    156, 164, 165, 168, 169, 200, 201, 203,
    204, 210, 212–217, 221. *See also* Marx-
    ism; realism
Mazzini, Giuseppe, 181
McDiarmid, Hugh, 245
Meason, Malcolm Laing, 161
Menger, Carl, 191
mercantilism, 31, 37, 38, 61, 75, 84
Meredith, George, 152, 173
Mexico, 1, 26, 45, 126, 167, 201–203,
    207, 227, 259
Middle Ages, 2, 31, 37, 64, 88, 94, 95,
    131, 149, 251–252
Mill, James, 118, 137, 186, 187–188
Mill, John Stuart, 31, 99, 112–113, 118,
    137, 139, 185, 186, 187, 218, 219
Milton, John, 80, 109
Misselden, Edward, 34–35
Mo, Timothy, 247
Moderator, 54–56
modernism (literary, artistic), 5, 7, 143,
    146–147, 165, 185–234, 243–246
modernity/modernization, 10, 13, 16–17,
    18, 20, 22, 24, 26, 29–30, 34, 35, 38,
    41, 42, 44, 47, 48–51, 54, 65, 75, 79,
    103, 127, 146–147, 148, 184, 185–
    234, 236, 239, 240, 248–249, 251–
    252. *See also* Enlightenment; industrial-
    ization; modernism; postmodernity/
    postmodernism; progress
monetarism, 253–260
money. *See* counterfeit money; gold stan-
    dard; paper money
Montesquieu, Charles de Secondat, 106
Moore, G. E., 219–221

Morris, William, 7, 174, 182, 184, 192–
    193, 195, 196, 251–252
Mulock, Dinah, 145
multinational corporations. *See* transna-
    tional capital and corporations
Mun, Thomas, 34–35
Mussolini, Benito, 202, 219, 232

Naipaul, V. S., 247, 249
Nairn, Tom, 2, 7, 19, 27, 235–240, 255
Napoleon, 7, 177
Napoleon III, 138
Napoleonic Wars, 7, 38, 110, 116, 240
national cultures, 4, 10, 19, 22, 128–129,
    179, 219–220, 245–249
national debt, 1, 3, 6, 7, 8, 9, 20–22, 25,
    26, 29, 30, 35, 37–41, 44–47, 48, 51,
    52–58, 60, 65–75, 88–96, 100–135,
    136–143, 145, 149, 154, 155, 157,
    159–162, 175–176, 189, 195, 197,
    199, 205, 211, 213–216, 223, 242,
    243, 256. *See also* public credit
National Front, 2, 19, 239
national identity formation, 6, 7, 10–13,
    16, 18, 20, 27, 143, 171, 172–184,
    235–238, 241, 247–248, 250
nationalism, 1, 2, 3, 4, 6, 10–13, 15–22,
    29, 40, 71–72, 89, 90, 95, 97, 125,
    128, 129, 133, 135, 143, 149, 160, 171,
    172–184, 189, 190, 195–199, 214–215,
    220, 225–234, 235–243, 246–252
Nazism, 15, 227, 261
Netherlands, the, 16, 22, 26, 37, 77, 89,
    135, 175–176, 239
New Zealand, 103, 185
Newton, Sir Isaac, 31, 44, 66
Nicholson, Colin, 36–37, 49, 50, 53, 55,
    64, 66, 69
Nietzsche, Friedrich, 192, 194, 211, 249
Nigeria, 183, 256–258
Nkrumah, Kwame, 245
Norris, Frank, 139
novels, as genre, 4, 7, 10–11, 14, 23, 41,
    45, 75–87, 91, 136–184, 200, 205–
    207, 223, 260

O'Brien, Bronterre, 93
O'Casey, Sean, 244
orientalism, 174–183
Ortega y Gassett, José, 44, 58
Orwell, George, 117, 244, 263

Ottoman Empire, 177
Overend, Gurney, and Co., 141, 161
Owen, Robert, 7, 93, 136

Paine, Tom, 104, 115–116, 117, 131–132
Pakistan, 239, 251
Palestine, 1, 176
Palmerston, Henry Temple, 15
paper money, 7, 22, 23, 35–36, 40, 46–
    47, 55–56, 63–64, 83, 86–87, 89, 90,
    93, 104, 105, 109–121, 123–135, 136,
    138, 140, 144, 158, 161–162, 165,
    169, 205–207, 211, 219, 260
Pater, Walter, 217, 221
patriotism. *See* nationalism
Peacock, Thomas Love, 118–122, 134,
    141, 168
Penty, Arthur J., 251–252
Pereire, Isaac and Émile, 138
Persia, 116
Peru, 5, 256–258
Peterloo Massacre, 116
phallocentrism, 6, 8, 30, 46, 67–69, 71,
    73, 108, 110, 123, 128, 185, 201–204,
    206–207, 223–234. *See also* fetishism
Phillips, Caryl, 247
Phillips, John, 85
piracy, 71–73, 74, 79–85
Pitt, William, 56, 110, 120, 149
Pocock, J. G. A., 32, 33, 36, 40, 54, 55,
    95, 110
Pope, Alexander, 7, 36, 41, 42, 44, 47,
    48–52, 57, 60–6, 74, 79, 123, 149,
    168, 195, 197, 210
populism, 20, 197, 237
Portugal, 17, 37, 42, 76, 81, 255
positivism, 23, 29, 124–125, 175, 178,
    224
postcolonial era/postcolonialism, 9, 12,
    235, 238, 239, 243–252
postindustrialism, 2, 9, 235, 238, 252–
    263
postmodernity/postmodernism, 1, 5, 6, 7,
    8, 9, 10, 20, 21, 24–28, 29, 32, 34, 36,
    37, 40, 42, 44, 79, 92, 143, 148, 184,
    192, 194, 205, 212, 235–236, 240,
    246–263
postnational future, 9, 13, 250. *See also*
    transnational capital and corporations
poststructuralism, 4, 8, 10–12, 21, 32,
    194

Pound, Ezra, 197, 212, 217, 221, 244
Powell, Enoch, 2, 242
Price, Dr. Richard, 149
primitive accumulation, 3, 37–38, 75, 79,
    81, 84, 91
progress, 9, 10, 26, 30, 41, 45, 51, 72, 99,
    116, 118, 127, 132, 138, 178, 185–
    192, 209, 211–212, 214, 217, 222,
    252. *See also* modernity/modernization
prostitution, 62, 76–80, 108, 147, 166,
    172, 228, 257
Proudhon, Pierre-Joseph, 138
psychoanalysis, 4, 5, 8, 32, 43–44, 201–
    203, 221–222, 226. *See also* fetishism;
    Freud, Sigmund; Lacan, Jacques
public credit, 1, 3, 4, 7, 11, 20–22, 24–
    26, 29, 30, 34, 36, 37, 39–41, 46–47,
    48, 50, 52–59, 62–64, 65–75, 78, 83,
    86–87, 89–99, 101, 103–110, 112–
    135, 139–141, 143, 144–145, 149,
    153, 154, 155, 157, 160, 161–162,
    168, 171, 184, 197–199, 210–211,
    213–216, 217, 219–221, 228, 238, 242
public opinion, 11, 13, 22, 31, 32, 66, 91,
    95–100, 125, 126, 129–130, 133, 138–
    142, 143, 195–199

Quebec, 1

racism, 2, 3, 4, 6, 32, 156–157, 175, 176–
    183, 185–192, 220, 223, 224, 238,
    239–240, 246–247, 250–251, 261,
    263. *See also* anti-Semitism
Reade, Charles, 145
Reagan, Ronald, 3, 242, 253, 259
realism, novelistic, 7, 23, 44–45, 74–87,
    139–146, 150–184, 194, 200, 203,
    205–207, 212, 214, 215, 223, 224. *See
    also* empiricism; materialism; novels; *spe-
    cific novelists*
Reform Bill of 1832, 134
Reformation, the, 16–17, 175, 176
Renaissance, 1, 8, 44, 131, 188, 189, 203,
    221, 246
representation, 8–9, 10, 21, 27, 44, 123,
    127, 144, 205–207, 216, 254
Rhodes, Cecil, 197, 199
Rhodesia, 197
Ricardo, David, 24, 33, 90, 126, 137–138,
    186
Richard I, 182

Richards, I. A., 204, 244
Richards, Thomas, 13–15, 16, 147, 189, 191, 244
Robinson, Emma, 118
Rolling Stones, 260
Roman Empire, 2, 41, 116, 239
Romanticism, 7, 55, 86, 90–91, 97, 111–119, 123–134, 138, 153, 174, 178, 180, 182, 213, 219, 246, 252
Roosevelt, Franklin Delano, 222
Rotman, Brian, 24–25, 40, 90, 206, 237, 258
Rotten, Johnny, 262–263
Rousseau, Jean-Jacques, 9, 97, 106, 186
Rushdie, Salman, 235, 245, 247–248
Ruskin, John, 118, 137–138, 161, 196, 219, 252
Russell, Bertrand, 218
Russia, 1, 10, 26, 82, 140, 218
Russian Revolution, 140

Sadleir, John, 159
St. Simonianism, 138, 194
Saintsbury, George, 52
Schreiner, Olive, 195
Schweitzer, Albert, 252
Scotland, 2, 18, 19, 88, 182, 183, 205, 239, 241, 246, 263
Scott, Paul, 244–245
Scott, Sir Walter, 86, 151–153, 164, 171, 175, 182
Seven Years' War, 89, 108
sexology, 199–201, 204–205
Sex Pistols, 235, 260–263
Shadwell, Thomas, 57, 258
Shakespeare, William, 41, 71, 109, 233, 241, 261
Shaw, George Bernard, 193, 244
Shell, Mark, 24, 46, 85, 87
Shelley, Percy Bysshe, 7, 114–119, 123, 126, 141, 195
Simmel, Georg, 23–26, 174, 196, 205, 207
Simpson, David, 42, 82, 127, 170, 203
slavery, 5, 37, 42, 57, 72, 81, 82, 85, 93, 116–117, 163, 226, 228, 247
Smiles, Samuel, 164
Smith, Adam, 7, 26, 27, 30, 46, 57, 88, 90–91, 100–102, 106, 112–113, 125, 126, 127, 133, 134, 137, 170, 185, 186, 211, 230

socialism, 1, 7, 19, 93, 190, 191, 196, 222, 235, 251–252, 255–256. See also Marx, Karl; Marxism
South Africa, 188, 190, 195–199
South America, 12, 37, 57, 139, 213–217. See also specific nation-states
South Sea Bubble, 7, 44, 49, 52, 57–61, 63–64, 67, 74, 88, 91–92, 118, 134, 139, 211, 258
Soviet Union, 219, 220, 235, 256. See also Russia; Russian Revolution
Spain, 6, 17, 26, 37, 38, 52, 57, 76, 89, 139, 182
Speculation. See stock exchange/stock jobbing
Spence, William, 137
Spencer, Herbert, 179, 180, 191–192
Stalin, Josef, 219
Stanley, Henry Morton, 213
Stevenson, Robert Louis, 208
Strachey, James, 201
stock exchange/stock jobbing, 5, 22, 24, 28, 31, 32, 48, 51, 52, 53, 54, 57–60, 66, 74, 91–93, 102, 105, 115, 128, 131, 133, 142, 145–146, 149, 157, 159, 161, 167, 168, 171, 172, 237, 256–259
sublime, theories of the, 27–28, 108–110, 183, 216, 254
Sweden, 5
Swift, Graham, 249
Swift, Jonathan, 4, 7, 36, 39, 41, 44, 47, 48–53, 56, 57, 60, 62, 65–75, 79, 81, 85, 88, 91, 118, 121, 123, 133, 149, 160, 168, 195, 197, 210
Synge, John Millington, 244
Syria, 177–178
Szasz, Thomas, 232

Tagore, Rabinandrath, 252
Tasmania, 67, 187
taxation, 29, 37, 38, 39, 62, 65, 88, 89, 93, 94, 101, 102, 118, 132, 137, 242
Tennyson, Alfred Lord, 19, 51, 230
Thackeray, William Makepeace, 45, 141, 144, 152–157, 164, 169, 170, 172
Thailand, 4
Thatcher, Margaret, 2, 18, 19–20, 237–243, 247, 253, 256, 258, 259
Thatcherism. See monetarism; National Front; Thatcher, Margaret; Tory Party

Third World, 2, 5, 27, 30, 238, 244, 249. *See also* international debt crisis, *specific nation-states*

Thornton, Henry, 7, 46, 89–91, 110, 112–114, 133, 138, 218

Thornton, Samuel, 112

Tilden, Freeman, 1, 3, 25, 65, 100, 205

Tocqueville, Alexis de, 58

Tönnies, Ferdinand, 13

Torrens, Robert, 187

Tory Party/Toryism, 6–7, 48, 52–55, 65–75, 85, 94, 135, 175–178, 180, 253. *See also* Thatcher, Margaret

transnational capital and corporations, 5, 9, 17, 24, 235–237, 250, 253, 256–263

Treasury (British), 31, 54–55, 68–69, 142, 220, 237

Trenchard, John, 59–60

Trollope, Anthony, 45, 87, 141, 142, 144, 146, 159, 163–173, 207, 209–211, 259

Trollope, Frances, 152, 163

Trollope, Thomas Adolphus, 152, 163

Turgot, Anne Robert Jacques, 106

Turkey, 1, 4, 81, 241

unemployment, 2, 190, 219, 220, 251, 253, 255, 256, 263

United States, 1–2, 3, 4, 6, 16, 19, 21, 22, 26, 27, 38, 79, 89, 103–104, 140, 146, 163, 167, 190, 194, 196, 197, 205–206, 221, 242, 244, 253, 255, 259, 261

utilitarianism, 36, 71, 104–105, 169, 175, 187–188, 191, 218–220

Veblen, Thorstein, 194–195, 196–197, 209, 210, 217, 227, 261

Victoria, Queen, 18, 135, 240

Victorian period, 2, 7, 45, 100–103, 128, 133–135, 137–184, 185–200, 203, 205–207, 209, 211–212, 215, 240, 252

Vietnam, 261

Voltaire, François Marie Arouet de, 70, 106

Wakefield, Edward Gibbon, 185

Wales, 2, 18, 19, 239, 246

Walpole, Robert, 68

Walras, Leon, 191

war. *See* imperialism; *specific wars*

War of the League of Augsburg, 38, 70

Warren, Samuel, 142, 145

Weber, Max, 20, 174

Wells, H. G., 14, 139, 151, 207–211, 218, 224

West Indies, 2, 19, 57, 84, 100, 239, 246–247, 249

Whig Party/Whiggism, 7, 33, 39, 51, 52–56, 65–75, 105–110, 133–135, 162, 175–176, 182, 218, 237. *See also* liberalism

Whitman, Walt, 212

Wiener, Martin, 138, 252

Wilberforce, William, 112

Wilde, Oscar, 193, 196, 204, 221

William III, 38, 39, 70, 73–74, 116, 135

Williams, Raymond, 14, 22–23, 124, 129, 204, 205, 220, 223, 224, 229, 236, 238, 262

Williams, William Carlos, 212

Wills, W. H., 160, 162

Wood, William, 49

Woolf, Leonard, 223, 243

Woolf, Virginia, 7, 185, 203, 205, 221–234, 252

Wordsworth, William, 7, 99, 134

World Bank, 103, 237

World Exhibitions, 146–147

World War I, 2, 19, 25, 102, 103, 137, 141, 198, 201, 203, 208, 211, 218, 222, 223, 230, 240, 243, 260, 261

World War II, 2, 102, 103, 218, 235, 236, 239, 243, 244, 246, 260, 261, 262

Wright, Whittaker, 209

Yeats, William Butler, 196, 198, 201, 203, 207, 217, 221, 244, 245

Yugoslavia, 1, 182, 251, 261

Zionism, 174, 178–182

Žižek, Slavoj, 1, 4, 5, 6, 27, 29, 102, 147, 171, 241–242

Zola, Émile, 23, 79, 86, 139, 190